Time Out

Camping

Our favourite sites in Britain

Time Out Guides Ltd
Universal House
251 Tottenham Court Road
London W1T 7AB
United Kingdom
Tel: +44 (0)20 7813 3000
Fax: +44 (0)20 7813 6001
Email: guides@timeout.com
www.timeout.com

Published by Time Out Guides Ltd, a wholly owned subsidiary of Time Out Group Ltd.
Time Out and the Time Out logo are trademarks of Time Out Group Ltd.

© **Time Out Group Ltd 2012**
Previous edition 2010

10 9 8 7 6 5 4 3 2 1

This edition first published in Great Britain in 2012 by Ebury Publishing.
A Random House Group Company
20 Vauxhall Bridge Road, London SW1V 2SA

Random House Australia Pty Ltd 20 Alfred Street, Milsons Point, Sydney, New South Wales 2061, Australia

Random House New Zealand Ltd 18 Poland Road, Glenfield, Auckland 10, New Zealand

Random House South Africa (Pty) Ltd Isle of Houghton, Corner Boundary Road & Carse O'Gowrie, Houghton 2198, South Africa

Random House UK Limited Reg. No. 954009

Distributed in USA by Publishers Group West
1700 Fourth Street, Berkeley, California 94710

Distributed in Canada by Publishers Group Canada
250A Carlton Street, Toronto, Ontario M5A 2L1

For further distribution details, see www.timeout.com.

ISBN: 978-1-84670-205-1

A CIP catalogue record for this book is available from the British Library.

Printed and bound by Firmengruppe APPL, aprinta druck, Wemding, Germany.

The Random House Group Limited supports the Forest Stewardship Council® (FSC®), the leading international forest certification organisation. All our titles that are printed on Greenpeace approved FSC® certified paper carry the FSC® logo. Our paper procurement policy can be found at www.randomhouse.co.uk/environment.

Time Out carbon-offsets its flights with Trees for Cities (www.treesforcities.org).

While every effort has been made by the author(s) and the publisher to ensure that the information contained in this guide is accurate and up to date as at the date of publication, they accept no responsibility or liability in contract, tort, negligence, breach of statutory duty or otherwise for any inconvenience, loss, damage, costs or expenses of any nature whatsoever incurred or suffered by anyone as a result of any advice or information contained in this guide (except to the extent that such liability may not be excluded or limited as a matter of law). Before travelling, it is advisable to check all information locally, including without limitation, information on transport, accommodation, shopping and eating out. Anyone using this guide is entirely responsible for their own health, well-being and belongings and care should always be exercised while travelling.

Published by

Time Out Guides Limited
Universal House
251 Tottenham Court Road
London W1T 7AB
Tel +44 (0)20 7813 3000
Fax +44 (0)20 7813 6001
email guides@timeout.com
www.timeout.com

Editorial
Editor Cath Phillips
Researchers Emily Baker, William Crow,
Emily Sargent, Jamie Warburton

Editorial Director Sarah Guy
Series Editor Cath Phillips
Editorial Manager Holly Pick
Management Accountants Clare Turner, Margaret Wright

Design
Art Director Scott Moore
Art Editor Pinelope Kourmouzoglou
Senior Designer Kei Ishimaru
Group Commercial Designer Jodi Sher

Picture Desk
Picture Editor Jael Marschner
Picture Desk Assistant/Researcher Ben Rowe

Advertising
New Business & Commercial Director Mark Phillips
Magazine & UK Guides Commercial Director St John Betteridge
Magazine & UK Guides Account Managers Jessica Baldwin,
Michelle Daburn, Ben Holt

Marketing
Senior Publishing Brand Manager Luthfa Begum
Guides Marketing Manager Colette Whitehouse
Group Commercial Art Director Anthony Huggins

Production
Group Production Manager Brendan McKeown
Production Controller Katie Mulhern-Bhudia

Time Out Group
Chairman & Founder Tony Elliott
Chief Executive Officer David King
Chief Operating Officer Aksel Van der Wal
Group Financial Director Paul Rakkar
Group General Manager/Director Nichola Coulthard
Time Out Communications Ltd MD David Pepper
Time Out International Ltd MD Cathy Runciman
Time Out Cultural Development Director Mark Elliott
Chief Technical Officer Remo Gettini
Group Marketing Director Andrew Booth

Contributors Alf Alderson, Ismay Atkins, Karen Chung, William Crow, Simon Coppock, Keith Davidson, Andrew Eames, Peter Fiennes, Ronnie Haydon, Daniel Neilson, Anna Norman, John Oakey, Emma Perry, Jonathan Perugia, Chris Pierre, Cath Phillips, Damian Rafferty, Aleida Strowger, Emma Woodhouse, Yolanda Zappaterra.

Tent guide, Festival camping, Wild camping Daniel Neilson. **Essential equipment** Cath Phillips.

The Editors would like to thank Isles of Scilly Travel (www.islesofscilly-travel.co.uk), Virgin Trains (www.virgintrains.co.uk), Ismay Atkins, Sarah Guy, Mike Harrison, Rick, Jane, Bruce and Richard Jones, Daniel Neilson, Susie Williams. And, of course, all the campsites featured in the book.

Maps Kei Ishimaru.

Cover photography Andy Stothert.

Back cover photography Cath Phillips, Jonathan Perugia, Daniel Neilson and featured establishments.

Illustrations Nicola Wilson.

Photography pages 6 (bottom and middle top), 7 (top and middle bottom), 23 (top), 31, 66, 67, 69, 70, 72, 73, 74, 82, 83, 85, 86 Jonathan Perugia; pages 6 (middle bottom), 191 (top left), 197, 215 (top) Shutterstock.com; pages 7 (middle top), 24 (bottom), 36, 37, 39, 40, 44, 46, 48, 49, 54, 55, 58 Ismay Atkins; page 7 (bottom) Aleida Strowger; pages 8, 23 (bottom), 94 (middle and bottom), 95, 127 (bottom), 167, 169, 170, 177, 244, 245, 246, 247, 248, 249, 250, 259, 260, 261, 262 Cath Phillips; page 13 www.oconnerscampers.co.uk; page 19 Ashley Pickering/Shutterstock.com; pages 32 (bottom), 33 (top left and bottom) Simon Coppock; page 41 Britta Jaschinski; pages 42, 43 (top) Andrew Ray; page 43 (bottom) Ben Rowe; pages 57, 205, 291 Alamy; pages 91, 92, 97 (bottom left and right), 98, 108, 109, 100, 110, 224, 225, 226 Leon Murphey; page 97 David Pickering; pages 102, 103, 104 Susie Williams; pages 107 (top), 115 William Crow; pages 111, 112 (right), 113, 132, 133, 136, 137 (except bottom left), 146 Chris Pierre; pages 116, 117 (bottom) Anna Norman; page 120 (top) Pete Fiennes; page 125 Rachel Higgs; pages 127 (top), 128 Woodland Skills Ltd; pages 129, 130/131, 157, 158, 159, 161, 162, 171, 172, 173, 178, 180, 182, 183, 185, 186, 187, 188, 220, 221 (bottom), 222, 228, 229, 231, 232, 236, 237, 239, 240, 242, 243 Daniel Neilson; page 134 John Dominick; page 138 Marcus Jackson Baker; pages 148, 149, 150, 151 Damian Rafferty; page 190 Kevin Eaves/Shutterstock.com; pages 191 (right and bottom) John Oakey; page 196 Steve Harling/Alamy; page 201 Andy Stothert/Britain on View; pages 203, 213 Alan Bryant/Shutterstock.com; page 204 Thierry Maffeis/Shutterstock.com; page 206, 207 Andrew Kneath; page 209 (top) Matthew Gough/Shutterstock.com; page 209 (bottom left) Nick Reynolds Photography/Shutterstock.com; page 209 (bottom right) Brian A Jackson/Shutterstock.com; page 210 Will Iredale/Shutterstock.com; page 211 Photoseeker/Shutterstock.com; page 215 (bottom) Falk Kienas/Shutterstock.com; pages 233, 234, 235 Yolanda Zappatera; pages 251, 252, 253 (left and bottom), 255, 256, 257, 264, 265, 266, 267, 268, 269, 271, 273, 275 (except middle right), 276 Ronnie Haydon; page 263 John Wormald; pages 277, 287, 288 Stuart Walker; pages 278, 293, 294, 295 Karen Chung; pages 283, 303 (except top left), 304, 309, 311 Jackie Deacon; pages 285, 286, 292, 297, 298, 300/301, 315 Keith Davidson; pages 299, 300 (bottom) James A Gordon; page 307 (top) www.visitscotland.com; page 307 (bottom) MacLeod Estate 2009.

The following images were supplied by the featured establishments: pages 6 (top), 14, 15, 17, 24 (top), 32 (top), 33 (top right and middle), 34, 45, 46 (bottom right), 94 (top), 96, 97 (top middle), 100, 101, 106, 107 (bottom), 109 (bottom), 112 (top and left), 117 (top and right), 118, 119, 120 (bottom), 121, 123, 137 (bottom left), 147, 179, 182 (top middle and bottom right), 183 (middle), 216, 219, 221 (top), 223, 253 (top right), 275 (middle right), 281, 303 (top left), 306, 313, 315 (top), 316.

About the guide

Welcome to *Time Out Camping*. Here are 100 of our favourite campsites, from Land's End to the far north-west coast of Scotland. They vary enormously, from tiny tent-only retreats to large sites that also accept caravans, motorhomes and campervans – though the emphasis throughout the guide is most definitely on sleeping in a tent. Sites with pre-erected yurts and tipis are increasingly popular, but we've also got vintage caravans, streamlined American trailers, wooden wigwams and grass-covered artists' cubes. The locations vary: next to beaches, beneath mountains, atop moors, tucked away in woodland. Some are on Forestry Commission land or in National Parks. A few fall under the auspices of the Camping & Caravanning Club or the National Trust. The majority, though, in the time-honoured way, are on working farms. But all provide the kind of camping we love: simple, unfussy, lacking fancy facilities and irritating rules, and located in some of Britain's most beautiful countryside.

CAMPSITE INFORMATION

We've provided as much detail as possible about each campsite, from months of operation and booking procedure (if any) to the facilities offered and whether there any restrictions (group bookings or noise curfews, for example).

Crucial factors are, obviously, the size of the campsite and the kind of camping it allows, so we've specified the number of pitches, and whether they're just for tents, or if caravans and motorhomes are also allowed (if motorhomes are accepted, then it's a given that campervans are too). To be frank, we're not that keen on caravans, so we've said if they are specifically banned. For yurts, tipis and other pre-erected structures, we've said how many they sleep. As for costs, some campsites charge per person, some by tent size or by time of year; it can all get a bit complicated, so the prices-per-night we've given are typical but don't cover every possible permutation. Some sites require that you book for at least two nights at weekends, longer in high summer.

Barbecues are allowed on almost every campsite – as long as you keep them off the ground, and don't burn the grass. Campfires are another matter. They're not quite as rare as hens' teeth, but they're certainly not something you can take for granted. We love them and wish more campsites permitted them; we've said if that's the case, and if you can buy firewood on site.

We've also told you what else there is in the area, from the nearest food shops and places to get a hot meal or a drink, to attractions and activities, including things of particular appeal to children. Brief details of other campsites nearby are also listed, just in case the reviewed site is full.

GETTING THERE

We've provided directions, whether you're driving or taking public transport. The location of each campsite is pinpointed on our maps (starting on p25 – three covering England, one each for Wales and Scotland). The six-digit OS map reference indicates the grid on the Ordnance Survey's nationwide maps in which you'll find the campsite. Type the reference into the Get-a-map section of the OS website (www.getamap.ordnancesurveyleisure.co.uk) to find the exact location.

DISCLAIMER

While every effort has been made to ensure the accuracy of the information contained in this guide, the publisher cannot accept any responsibility for errors it may contain. Businesses can change their arrangements at any time. So before you go out of your way, we strongly advise you phone ahead to checking opening times, prices and other particulars. If a campsite recommends booking, then we suggest you do that, especially in peak season, rather than turn up on spec and be disappointed.

ADVERTISERS

The recommendations in *Camping* are based on the experience of Time Out's reviewers. No payment or PR invitation has secured inclusion or influenced content. The editors choose which places to feature. Advertisers have no influence over content; an advertiser may receive a bad review or no review at all.

LET US KNOW WHAT YOU THINK

We welcome suggestions for campsites you think we should include in future editions, and take note of your criticism of our choices. You can email us at guides@timeout.com.

Contents

The campsites

ENGLAND   **31**

Channel Islands
Seagull   32

Isles of Scilly
St Martin's   35

Cornwall
Treen Farm   38
Namparra   41
Gwithian Farm   44
Beacon Cottage Farm   47
Tregedna Farm   50
Treloan   53
Highertown Farm   56
Cornish Tipi   59
South Penquite Farm   62

South Devon
Runnage Farm   65
Yurtcamp   68
Coombe View Farm   71

North Devon
Cherry Tree Farm   75
North Morte Farm   78
Little Meadow   81

Somerset
Westermill Farm   84
Batcombe Vale   87
Buckland Bell   90

Dorset
Eweleaze Farm   93
Tom's Field   96
Burnbake   99

Wiltshire
Stowford Manor Farm   102

Gloucestershire
Abbey Home Farm   105

Herefordshire
Doward Park   108

Buckinghamshire
Home Farm Radnage   111

Oxfordshire
Britchcombe   114

Isle of Wight
Vintage Vacations   116

Hampshire
Manor Farm   119
Roundhill   122

West Sussex
Stubcroft Farm   124
Woodland Yurting   126

East Sussex
Wowo   129
Blackberry Wood   132

Kent
Welsummer   135

Essex
Debden House   138

Suffolk
Harbour Camping   141
The Orchard   145

Norfolk
Woodside Farm   148
Deer's Glade   150
High Sand Creek   152
Deepdale   154

Shropshire
Middle Woodbatch Farm   157

Nottinghamshire
New Hall Farm   160

Peak District
North Lees   163
Haddon Grove   166
Upper Booth Farm   168

Yorkshire Dales
Gordale Scar   171
Masons   174

West Yorkshire
Jerusalem Farm   176

North York Moors
Spiers House   178
La Rosa   181

Lancashire
Clitheroe   184
Gibraltar Farm   186

Lake District
Low Wray   189
Eskdale   192
Wasdale Head   195
Side Farm   198

WALES 201

Gower
Three Cliffs Bay   202
Hillend   205

Pembrokeshire
Trefalen Farm   208
Newgale   211
Caerfai Farm   213
Ty Parke   215
Rhydhowell Farm   218
Fforest   220

Brecon Beacons
Ynysfaen   224
Llanthony Priory   227
Hollybush Inn   230

Mid Wales
Rhandirmwyn   233
Fforest Fields   236
The Yurt Farm   238
Tyllwyd Farm   241
Gwerniago Farm   244

Snowdonia
Cae Du   247
Graig Wen   251
Shell Island   255
Cae Gwyn Farm   258
Hafod y Llan   261
Llyn Gwynant   264
Gwern Gof Uchaf   267
Tan-y-Bryn Farm   270

Llyn Peninsula
Nant-y-Big   272
Mynydd Mawr   274

SCOTLAND 277

Southern Scotland
Solway View   278

Argyll & the Islands
Seal Shore   280
Machrihanish   282
Cove Park   284
Cashel   287

Central Scotland
Mains Farm   290
Comrie Croft   293

The Highlands
Red Squirrel   296
Rothiemurchus   299
Lazy Duck   302

Isle of Skye
Glenbrittle   305

The North-West
Morvich   308
Applecross   310
Clachtoll Beach   312
Badrallach   314

Features
About the guide   5
How to buy a tent   8
Essential equipment   14
Festival camping   19
Wild camping   21
Where to camp...   23
The best sites for beaches, walking,
campfires, families and much more.

Maps
England: south-west   25
England: south-east   26
England: north   27
Wales   28
Scotland   29

Useful contacts   317
A-Z index of campsites   318

How to buy a tent

Look around any campsite and you'll see a bewildering array of tents, in all shapes, sizes and colours, from a mind-boggling number of manufacturers. From flower-patterned pop-ups to 'I'm-climbing-Everest-it-had-better-be-strong' stalwarts, the choice is overwhelming. So how do you decide what's best for you? **Daniel Neilson** explain the options.

Use Start by narrowing down exactly what you want a tent for. Will you be driving to the Peak District for a sunny summer weekend or two, or are you an all-year-round, backpack-toting sort of camper? The easiest approach is to break the options down into the following types of tent: family, weekend, backpacking, mountain and static.

Family tents are large (four-plus capacity) affairs, for use on campsites. They often have different areas: separate sleeping pods, for example, and a communal zone for cooking or playing games. They are heavy, can take a long time to set up and require a car to transport.

Weekend tents tend to be cheaper dome or tunnel tents, perhaps used by a couple camping a few times over the summer. They are also suitable for festivals.

Backpacking tents need to be very lightweight, and able to cope with greater extremes of temperature. They generally accomodate no more than three people, and could be used on a campsite, for wild camping on a long hike, or for cycling tours.

Mountain tents are for serious adventures, and often have a geodesic design that makes them very strong and stable. If you're going climbing, mountaineering or setting out on a high-altitude trek, or are likely to be facing bad weather, a good (and expensive) mountain tent is essential.

Finally, there are static tents: bell tents, tipis and yurts. Capacious and substantial, these are ideal for longer stays, for families or groups of (close) friends. More and more campsites now offer pre-erected static tents, kitted out with kitchen equipment, a wood-burning stove and often beds and furniture. Some are almost as luxurious as a boutique hotel.

Size How many sleeping compartments do you need: one shared space, or separate berths for the kids? Would you like an extra area that's not for sleeping: a vestibule for storing luggage or bicycles, a separate cooking area or somewhere to lounge around in if it rains? If so, does it need to be enclosed? Note that when manufacturers refer to a 'two-person' or 'six-person tent', they mean the number of sleeping bags that can fit inside. It's wise to get a tent with one more space than the number of people using it.

Weight An essential factor for backpacking, trekking or cycle-touring, when you – not a car – will be carrying all the gear, and an extra half-kilo can hurt after a couple of days. There is often a pay-off between season rating and weight, although as materials technology moves apace, tents are getting very light. Also consider if the packed tent will fit in your rucksack, or can be split between a couple of people – a pop-up tent in a large, unwieldy, disc-shaped bag is probably a no-no.

Climate Tents, like sleeping bags, are beginning to be rated in terms of seasons. Although there's no standard measurement, the ratings are a guide to a tent's suitability for different extremes of heat and weather. A one-season tent should be used only in summer; it will have some waterproofing, but the light materials will suffer in strong winds. A four-season tent should be suitable for cold, harsh conditions.

Colour Mountain and backpacking tents tend to be brightly coloured for safety reasons, while weekend and family models usually come in natural colours.

❶ Dome ▼

Probably the most common tent design, although it is becoming outdated. It usually has two curved poles that cross at the top, creating a dome shape, and sometimes another pole that creates a storage area by the door. It's a very stable design, and guy ropes are only needed in particularly windy situations – although the higher the tent, the less stable it becomes. The shape has its drawbacks: the sides bend inwards, so it can feel claustrophobic, and unless it's very large you won't be able to stand up. Two-pole domes also lack space for baggage.
✔ Can be cheaper than other options. Sturdy structure, especially the lower ones. Quick to pitch.
✘ Can feel small.
Best for Family, weekend.

❷ Tunnel ▼

Tunnel tents are increasingly popular because of the larger internal space they offer over a dome shape. They're favoured by touring cyclists, because there is often room for bikes inside. Sizes range from one person to ten-person, but the basic structure of parallel arches of flexible poles remains the same. The design is not as structurally strong as a dome, and guy ropes are needed in all conditions (which can be a problem on very hard, or very soft, surfaces). Some tunnel tents have separate sleeping compartments.
✔ More internal space than a dome then. Often have room for luggage or bikes.
✘ Not freestanding. Tricky to pitch in a wind.
Best for Family, weekend.

Other factors

Once you've decided on the type of tent that meets your needs, it is important to consider a few more factors – some of which will affect the price. Do ask for help: staff at good outdoors shops are knowledgeable, and should provide impartial advice. Always find out if they can erect the tent in the shop, or ensure there is a suitable returns policy whereby you can set it up immediately at home and then return it if it isn't suitable.

Flysheets Nowadays, not all tents have separate flysheets; instead, many designs use internal compartments that hang from a single skin outer. This cuts down on weight, but a double-skin design is better for reducing condensation (you don't have to worry about touching the tent wall) and increasing insulation and ventilation.

However, the most essential element is the level of waterproofing provided. Coatings differ: acrylic is the cheapest, while silicone is used on the most expensive mountain tents. Look for the Hydrostatic Head (HH) measurement; the higher the figure, the better the waterproofing. The scale goes up to around 6,000 HH; to be considered waterproof, the rating should be at least 1,500 HH. It's usually higher for a groundsheet.

Also, good tents should be made of fabric designed to limit rips. If a tree branch pokes through by accident, it shouldn't open up a large hole.

Seams The weakest part of a tent. Look for taped seams, which strengthen the join.

Poles Most tents these days use flexible hollow poles made of aluminium or fibreglass, threaded through the centre with elastic cord. Aluminium is lighter and tends to be the preferred option, although it's a less flexible material and can bend if trodden on or subjected to very strong winds. Fibreglass costs less but is heavier – and cheap poles can splinter nastily. High-end tents tend to use flexible, carbon-fibre poles.

Pegs All tents come with their own pegs; the more expensive the tent, the better the peg. It's worth having spares, though, as pegs are easily damaged. There are dozens of different kinds – plastic, aluminium alloy, titanium, even biodegradable ones – in varying shapes and sizes. Alloy versions are popular because they're light, but can bend easily. Titanium is lighter still (so popular with backpackers), but might not work in a strong wind. V-section pegs offer more security than round ones.

Do use a mallet: it might seem old-school, but you're much less likely to bend the pegs.

TENT GUIDE

The smart way of giving

Give the perfect getaway

Browse the full range of gift boxes from Time Out

timeout.com/smartbox

❸ A-frame ▾

Imagine a Boy Scout camp in 1953: this is the A-frame tent (aka ridge tent). Although there are a few modern, top-of-the-range A-frames, most tend to be old and made from poor materials (canvas or polyester), with heavy poles. The sloping walls and upright poles diminish the space inside, and the poles poke through the outer fabric, allowing water in. That said, if the tents are to be used solely for sleeping, they offer a secure and steadfast option. Some lightweight models are favoured by hikers, while large A-frames make good additional areas for family holidays.

✔ Sturdy. Easy to erect.
✗ Often heavy. The internal space is small.
Best for Family, backpacking.

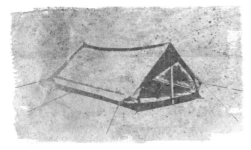

❹ Vis-à-vis ▾

Often tall enough to stand up in, 'face-to-face' tents are an evolution of both tunnel and dome tents, with two sleeping berths facing each other across a central communal area. The berths are often self contained, attached by hooks to the main outer tent, and can be removed. This can come in handy if you want to remove a berth to create space for bikes, say, but also means that the outer is only one layer thick and therefore not as waterproof as a tent with a separate flysheet. A variant is the pod-style tent, with multiple sleeping areas branching off from the middle.

✔ Big interior, providing separate sleeping areas and a communal hub.
✗ Complicated to put up. Heavy to transport. Not very stable, so guy ropes are needed.
Best for Weekend, family.

❺ Frame ▴

More like a house than a tent. Designed for families on long stays, frame tents use rigid poles that interlock at angles and provide a very large internal area (often divided into separate sections) and plenty of headroom. Many also have a big open porch for bikes, luggage, barbecues and seating; fridges, wardrobes and raised beds are common too, and you might even see the odd TV aerial attached to the top. Needless to say, they are strictly car-only touring tents.

✔ The most spacious design, with areas for seating, cooking, toys and luggage. Stable in windy weather.
✗ Unwieldy and slow to pitch. Needs a car to transport.
Best for Family.

❻ Pop-up ▴

Popular with festival-goers, pop-up tents consist of a coiled frame that bursts out of a disc-shaped bag to form a tent before your eyes. There are two kinds: cheap and expensive. The supermarket 'that'll-do-for-Glastonbury' version is lightweight but flimsy, and shouldn't be trusted in wet weather. It's strictly a summertime fun tent – so it doesn't matter if it gets destroyed by a drunken reveller stumbling across a guy rope. However, you can also buy superb pop-ups that are waterproof, spacious and as sturdy as tunnel tents. The major drawback is that the large bag they come in is cumbersome, and totally unsuitable for backpacking.

✔ Erected in seconds. Flexible in windy situations. The new pricier pop-ups are as good as mid-range tunnel tents.
✗ Unsuitable for trekking. Can be frustrating (or, for spectators, hilarious) to pack away.
Best for Weekend.

TENT GUIDE

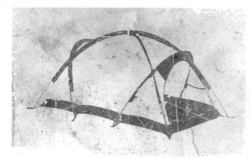

❼ Geodesic ▲

The mathematical term refers to the shortest possible line between two points on a curved surface. In tent terms, it tends to mean a criss-cross pattern of four or more poles that results in the most rigid type of tent available. Made from ultra-lightweight, weather-resistant materials, geodesics provide protection against high winds, snow and rain, and are aimed primarily at mountaineers. Climbing K2? You need one of these. The three-pole semi-geodesic version is smaller and not as sturdy, but perfect for long hiking trips in all but the most extreme of Britain's weather.
✔ The most stable design. Lightweight. Stands up against harsh conditions.
✗ Expensive. Not much internal space.
Best for Backpacking, mountain.

❽ Hybrid ▲

Usually a relatively high-tech affair that melds geodesic design elements with the size and space required for several people. Hybrid tents often resemble a large tunnel or dome tent, but the structure and strong poles offer excellent stability, especially for their size. They're also lighter. Many have two or more compartments, separating the extra-insulated sleeping area from a more open cooking or resting zone. Popular with discerning weekenders and groups of hikers.
✔ Larger tents designed for more difficult conditions. Good use of internal space.
✗ Costlier than more basic dome and tunnel tents. Can take a while to erect.
Best for Weekend, backpacking.

❾ Tipi ▼

The tipi (or tepee) is based on Native American nomadic shelters. Several long, rigid poles (usually made from wood), are arranged in a cone shape and then wrapped with canvas (animal skins or bark are traditional), leaving a small door. This creates a single internal space for sleeping, cooking and eating – though the sloping walls make it smaller than a yurt or bell tent. Modern tipis on campsites usually have a wood-burning stove and gas hob, but the originals had a small, contained fire in the middle, with the smoke rising through the gap where the poles meet. Tipis are particularly popular with families – kids love them. Many manufacturers now offer cheap, tipi-shaped tents made of polyester and with steel poles, aimed at festival-goers.
✔ Great fun. Dry and warm; fires can be built inside certain models.
✗ Cumbersome, and difficult to put up. Not as spacious as some other canvas tents.
Best for Family, static.

Canvas queens

Plenty of campsites now have pre-erected yurts, tipis, bell tents or wooden wigwams – some of which we've reviewed in this guide. Here are a few other options.

Yurts and tipis

http://ecoretreats.co.uk (Wales)
http://trellyn.co.uk (Wales)
http://yurt-holidays.co.uk (Devon)
www.long-valley-yurts.co.uk (Lake District)
www.yurtworks.co.uk (Cornwall)
www.yurt-holidays.com (links to various yurt campsites around the country)

Bell tents

http://belletentscamping.co.uk (Cornwall)
http://jollydaysluxurycamping.co.uk (Yorkshire)
www.billycancamping.co.uk (Sussex)
www.safaribritain.com (Sussex)

Wooden wigwams

www.wigwamholidays.com (mainly Scotland)

⑩ Bell tent ▲

These resemble Raj-era army tents: a large, one-room structure made from canvas, with a single entrance that can be closed with ties. They're supported by rigid, heavy poles (including one in the centre) and are high enough to stand up in. A bonus is that the sides can be rolled up for ventilation – they can get very hot inside. Bell tents that are permanently set up on campsites tend be well equipped and comfortable, with a wood-burning stove, cooking facilities and other little luxuries.

✔ A wonderful space in which to sleep. Can be used through the winter.

✘ Expensive. Large, heavy and bulky to pack. Takes hours to put up and tie down.

Best for Family, static.

⑪ Yurt ▲

Traditionally home to Mongolian and Central Asian nomads, yurts range from between nine to 21 feet in diameter. The walls are vertical for about five feet and then slant inwards, with a peak that is either open or covered in transparent plastic; the interior comprises one undivided space. To provide more light and ventilation, some yurts have small windows or roll-up sides. Fixed yurts on campsites usually come with a wood-burning stove (sometimes positioned to one side, unlike a true Mongolian yurt, which has the stove in the centre) and often a gas cooker. The floor, often made of wood, is raised off the ground for extra insulation. Yurts can be very luxurious (reindeer skin blankets, proper beds, table and chairs) and cost as much as a hotel room.

✔ Spacious, relaxing, comfortable. Warm and cosy, even in winter. Ideal for families and groups.

✘ Expensive. Very heavy and requires many people, and hours, to erect.

Best for Family, static.

Four wheels good

Of course, not everyone wants to camp in a tent. Standard caravans still have a distinctly fuddy-duddy image, but there are plenty of cooler options. Numerous outfits have joined the craze for all things retro, and hire out old-fashioned, brightly coloured VW campervans – either restored originals from the 1960s and '70s, or brand-new models imported from Brazil. They're increasingly popular at festivals. Alternatively, there are a few specialists in classic caravans or vintage Airstream trailers.

Airstream trailers
http://airstreamfacilities.com
www.americanretrocaravans.co.uk
www.vintageairstreams.co.uk

Campervans
www.camper4hire.co.uk
www.campinavdub.co.uk
www.classiccampervanhire.co.uk
www.cornwallcampers.co.uk
www.escapecampers.co.uk
www.nomadliving.co.uk
www.oconnorscampers.co.uk
www.outermotive.co.uk
www.slowlanecampers.co.uk
www.snailtrail.co.uk
www.summerlovinvwcamperhire.com
www.vwcamperco.com
www.vweekender.co.uk

Vintage caravans
http://whitehorsegypsycaravans.co.uk
www.hazydayscaravanhire.co.uk
www.lovelanecaravans.com

TENT GUIDE

Essential equipment

You don't need much to go camping, but some bits of kit can enhance rather than overload the whole outdoor experience. Here are a few of our favourite things.

And don't forget to take...

● A sturdy clear plastic storage box with a secure lid. It keeps food or kitchen equipment waterproof, and doubles as a table or seat. The Really Useful ones (available from Staples) are excellent and come in many sizes.

● A big builder's bucket. It has multiple uses, from carrying/doing the washing-up to storage, and works a treat as an ice-bucket too.

● Flip-flops or crocs. They're quick to slip on for a loo dash in the middle of the night. Wear them inside the tent to keep it free of mud.

● Wellies. Because it's Britain.

● Antiseptic wipes and a flannel. Sometimes it's too much effort to have a proper wash.

● Tea lights in old jam-jars and garden incense sticks. Together, they create a charming, fragrant glow around the tent or campfire.

● Self-gripping washing line. For drying towels and swimming costumes, or just keeping coats off the wet ground.

● 35mm film canisters. Ideal for storing spices, salt and 20ps for the shower.

❶ CamelBak Better Bottle
This 750ml water bottle from hydration supremo CamelBak marries expert design with good looks. The bite-valve mechanism means you can drink one-handed while on the move (perfect for bikers and walkers), the big handle is easy to carry or attach to a rucksack, it's dishwashable and, for the health-conscious, it's made from non-leaching, BPA-free plastic. And it comes in a rainbow of lovely colours. **£9, www.camelbak.com**

❷ Turboflame Original lighter
Sick of trying to light your stove in a gale? You need one of Turboflame's windproof lighters. The bulbous Original (available in assorted shiny bright colours, plus matt green for military types) resembles a mini blowtorch, with a 1,300°C jet that works in any direction and can be locked-on for up to ten minutes. The plastic-cap-on-a-chain is a bit fiddly, though. **£9.50, www.turboflame.co.uk**

❸ RAB silk sleeping bag liner
Add a touch of luxury to your camping with a silk sleeping bag liner. It keeps you toasty and your bag clean, and is much more comfortable on the skin than nylon. And if it's boiling hot, you can use it on its own. RAB does rectangular and mummy shapes in various lengths, as well as cheaper cotton ones. **£40 for standard size, www.rab.uk.com**

❹ MSR Quick 2 System cookware

True, you can take the saucepans and crockery from home, but it's hard to resist this nifty nesting cooking and eating set from Seattle-based MSR. It contains two anodized aluminium pans, two insulated stainless steel mugs with lids (admittedly, a rather awkward shape) and two polypropylene dishes – the whole lot fitting into the biggest pan and weighing less than a bag of sugar. Other campers will be sick with envy.
£59.99, http://cascadedesigns.com/MSR

❺ Petzl Tikka Plus 2 head torch

Head torches are invaluable: for midnight trips to the loo, reading in bed, cooking outdoors in the evening or searching for items in a messy tent. And kids love them. Petzl makes the best, and its new-generation Tikka Plus 2 has all the functions you could need: a white LED that works in three modes (bright, not so bright, flashing) and a red LED – very handy at night – with a continuous or strobe setting. The battery charge indicator is helpful too.
£37.50, http://petzl.com/en

❻ Lifeventure Trek Towel

Invaluable for backpackers, but also useful on general camping trips, travel towels are made of lightweight, quick-drying fabric and usually impregnated with an anti-bacterial treatment to avoid odours. And they pack down really small. Lifeventure's version is

particularly good, and comes in a wide range of sizes, from face towel to giant bath towel. A shame the only colours available are blue or pink.
£8-£20, www.lifeventure.co.uk

❼ Alpkit Airlok XTra dry bags

Waterproof bags keep your sleeping bag/undies/stuff clean, dry and easy to find. Lots of outfits make them, but we're fond of Alpkit's roll-top version because they're durable, come in plenty of sizes (from three to 65 litres) and have a carrying strap. The rubber loops on the bottom and one side are handy for attaching carabiners. Nice bright colours too. Alpkit's products are only available online from the company – one reason why its prices are so reasonable.
£5-£14, www.alpkit.com

❽ Kelly Kettle

As used by Irish fishermen, the kelly kettle works on an ingenious 'chimney' system that boils water using twigs, leaves, grass or paper. It comes in stainless steel or aluminium, in one- to three-pint sizes, and with lots of accessories to turn it into a full-blown cooker.
£39.95 2.5pint, www.kellykettle.com

❾ MSR Pocket Rocket stove

As the name suggests, this tiny stove from MSR literally fits in your pocket: it's only 10cm x 5cm x 5cm when folded up, and weighs just 85g. It's very

THE WORLD CAN BE AN UNJUST AND TREACHEROUS PLACE, BUT THERE ARE THOSE WHO STRIVE TO MAKE IT SAFE FOR EVERYONE.

Operating in some of the world's most dangerous and oppressed countries, **Human Rights Watch** conducts rigorous investigations to bring those who have been targets of abuse to the world's attention. We use strategic advocacy to push people in power to end their repressive practices. And we work for as long as it takes to see that oppressors are held accountable for their crimes.

KNOWLEDGE IS POWER. LEARN ABOUT LIFE-CHANGING EVENTS IN YOUR WORLD THAT DON'T ALWAYS MAKE THE HEADLINES AND HOW YOU CAN HELP EFFECT POSITIVE CHANGE.

Stay informed, visit HRW.org

HUMAN RIGHTS WATCH

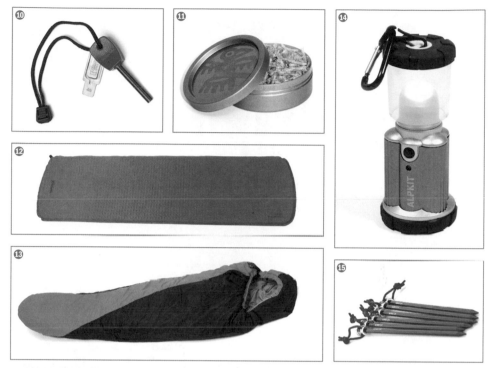

powerful, easy to adjust (even when wearing gloves) and can be used with most screw-top butane canisters. In short, the perfect trekking stove.
£25, http://cascadedesigns.com/MSR

⑩ ⑪ Light My Fire
FireSteel Scout & Maya Dust

Throw away the firelighters and matches, and start a fire the Swedish way. No Boy Scout experience is required – all you do is strike the metal plate against the firesteel to produce super-hot sparks. The compact Scout version is good for 3,000 strikes – enough to keep you in campfires for years. Maya Dust wood shavings are the perfect accompanying tinder. These are not just any old shavings, but ultra-flammable, resin-rich wood from Mexican pines.
£7.95, £2.99, www.lightmyfire.com

⑫ Multimat Adventure 25 self-inflating mat

Assuming you're not in the market for a big, ugly airbed, self-inflating mats are the best thing for providing insulation and a (relatively) good night's sleep. Therm-a-Rest is still the market leader, but you pay for its expertise, and there are alternatives that work just fine. Multimat's Adventure 25 mat provides a happy compromise between length (183cm, long enough for all but the most elongated camper), weight (680g) and bulk (26cm x 16cm when packed).
£55, www.multimat.uk.com

⑬ Snugpak Softie Technik 4 sleeping bag

This West Yorkshire-based company is rare in that it still manufactures its products – rucksacks, sleeping bags, lightweight tents and travel accessories – in the UK. This four-season bag (with synthetic insulation) is easily cosy enough for most camping in Britain, and should be comfortable at temperatures down to -10°C. There's a two-way zip and a neck baffle to keep your head warm. It is quite heavy (2.2kg), but packs down to a manageable 28cm x 23cm.
£160, www.snugpak.com

⑭ Alpkit BULB lantern

This is the cutest camping lantern we've seen. It's tiny (just 13cm high) but ultra-bright, and works in high, low or flashing mode. It comes with a mini carabiner attachment, so that you can hang it up from either end. Remove the top and you've got a floodlight.
£15, www.alpkit.com

⑮ Alpkit Spikes tent pegs

Our favourite tent pegs. It's partly the shiny red aluminium that appeals, but they also work really well. They're longer than usual (22cm), so are very secure; the flat top makes banging them in with a mallet a cinch (and means they're very unlikely to bend); and it's easy to pull them out with the cord handle. And they're not expensive.
£8 for pack of 6, www.alpkit.com

Get the local experience

Over 50 of the world's top destinations available.

Festival camping

Music, mud and tents don't mix. Proper preparation is the answer, says **Daniel Neilson**.

It was a classic headline. In bold letters, the front page of the free daily newspaper at Glastonbury read 'CHEERS GOD'. Underneath it, a photograph, which was reproduced in papers around the world, depicted the tops of two dozen tents, poking out of the floodwater. It had rained. A lot. The headline summed up the misery of 160,000 partygoers at Glastonbury 2004 – particularly those who didn't plan properly.

In the right weather, festivals are the greatest places on earth. Swaying to your favourite band, wrapped in a fug of perry, is a delight – but only when the sun shines. And Britain being Britain, that isn't terribly common. Despite the line about 'bringing people together' that Michael Eavis, Glastonbury's founding father, propounds at every mud-spattered event, wet festivals can be a drag.

And pivotal to festival happiness is your tent. It is a place of refuge from the surreal madness, a shelter when it rains, a place to relax and regroup. It needs to be equipped for the job. Nifty pop-up supermarket tents for a tenner may seem a bargain, but after three nights of torrential rain you may think otherwise. Then again, no one wants a £400 geodesic mountain tent ruined by someone else's inability to walk in a straight line after 18 lagers. Large hybrid or family tents are our recommendation. Even if there are only a couple of you, you'll be grateful for the space; besides, festivals are social experiences, and you might be cooking bacon for extra guests the next morning.

Travelling light isn't always the best mantra. You can eat from festival food stalls, of course, but that's notoriously expensive – so take a coolbox of bacon, sausages and beer, some couscous (a camping stalwart, thanks to its ease of cooking) and a stash of muesli bars. Campfires are rarely allowed, so a small stove is crucial for a morning cuppa. Otherwise, look at a festival as you would any other camping weekend, taking a torch, knife, matches, plates, cutlery and other such essentials. And wellies. Never forget wellies. Campgrounds are often a long trek from the car park, so a sturdy trolley will help – any large hardware store should have one.

Some objects can be particularly useful. Two address the horror that are festival toilets. For men, there's the Travel John (www.traveljohn.com) – basically a bag that solidifies waste. Women, meanwhile, have the Shewee; an ingenious funnel that allows them to pee standing up. Glastonbury provides special female urinals for this, with disposable Shewees. They're great for avoiding revolting loos, although perfecting the manoeuvre requires practice.

Other key items include wet wipes, earplugs, alcohol gel, condoms and, for the hygiene-conscious, dry shampoo and toilet seat covers. Avoid festival camping 'kits', though; any company offering a tent, airbed, sleeping bag and folding chair for less than £70 probably isn't giving away the highest-quality gear. And if all this sounds a little too much like hard work, take the soft option and book into one of the yurts, tipis and campervans offered by canny festival organisers across the land. For our favourite festivals for camping, *see p317.*

Top tips

Do some research Check the festival website for camping advice, and decide where you'd like to pitch in advance. Read the rules about bottles, alcohol, cooking gear and campfires.

Arrive early By 4pm on Wednesday at Glastonbury 2009, 75 per cent of the camping areas were already full.

Head for high ground Unless you want to lose all your belongings in a biblical deluge, camp on a slope. But avoid areas that could turn into a channel of water.

Choose your spot Don't pitch near toilets, burger vans, stages, walkways or any stall selling 'legal highs'.

Camp with your mates That way, there's more chance of someone keeping an eye on all the possessions. Don't padlock your tent; even if you haven't left your iPod in there, someone will think you have.

Take a flag Hoisting a banner to mark the whereabouts of your tent amid a sea of similar-looking shelters is very useful.

Take everything home Your tent will go into a landfill if it stays there – and every year, a handful of cows die at Glastonbury after ingesting tent pegs.

Offset your flight with **Trees for Cities** and make your trip mean something for years to come

www.treesforcities.org/offset

Trees for Cities
Charity registration number 1032154

Wild camping

Want to *really* get away from it all? **Daniel Neilson** explains the basics.

Even the best, most spacious campsites still remain social affairs, with only a piece of nylon between you and the sound of your neighbour's snoring. For true seclusion, you need to head to places like Snowdonia, Dartmoor and the Scottish Highlands – astonishingly vast swathes of land that can feel as distant as Patagonia or Newfoundland. By hiking off the beaten track, deep into a National Park or up into inhospitable hills, with only a tent and survival gear, you can awake to the sound of nothing more than skittish wildlife and a bubbling kettle.

For centuries, though, the British countryside has been carved up and redistributed among serfs, aristocracy, farmers, government bodies, trusts and landowners. Someone or something owns every part of the UK. So where *can* you camp?

In Scotland, things are clear-cut. Thanks to the forward-thinking Land Reform (Scotland) Act of 2003, wild camping is legal everywhere so long as it is responsible; away from homes and roads, for example. The Scottish Outoor Access Code is available at www.outdooraccess-scotland.com, and the Mountaineering Council of Scotland has information at www.mcofs.org.uk.

In England and Wales, there is no legal right to wild camp, and permission is, in theory, required everywhere. On farmland, it is, of course, only polite to ask the owner, who is unlikely to object to a discreetly pitched tent for a night or two. On very large holdings, it is often impractical to seek permission – and it is rare you'll ever meet the owner, if you pitch with care. If you're out of view and tidy up after yourself (and unless you inadvertently set fire to the hay barn), it's unlikely you'll run into problems. At worst you'll be asked to move – whether this is politely or not depends on the temperament of the farmer.

Officially, the National Trust does not allow wild camping on its land, although in reality, if you're sensibly pitched, rangers are unlikely to move you on just before nightfall. The Trust is, however, happy to let you stay for one night in the Lake District, if there are only two campers and your tent is over 450 metres from the nearest road. Britain's largest landowner, the Forestry Commission, does not allow wild camping anywhere. Certain areas of England and Wales are more accepting than others. The Peak District is not a welcoming place, largely because of the risk of accidental summer fires on the moors, but the Lake District is excellent. Dartmoor National Park is the only park that encourages wild camping – albeit within 'suggested areas'; see www.dartmoor.co.uk/site/what-to-do/wild-dartmoor.

Other choice spots include the Yorkshire Dales, the North York Moors, the Pennines, the North Downs and Northumbria. Wales too has some wonderfully wild and remote stretches of countryside, where you're unlikely to encounter any hassle; the Brecon Beacons and Snowdonia are particularly lovely.

Wild camping means escaping from civilisation – and as such, can be fraught with danger, if you don't prepare properly. It may feel like cheating to take a mobile phone, but it can be invaluable in an emergency; even very distant places can usally get some reception. But keep it turned off. Packing is a delicate balance between travelling light and being comfortable. Wild camping can be approached like any substantial camping trip (knife, torch, cooking equipment, map, compass, toilet paper and so on), but a trowel (for burying human waste) and a good first-aid kit are also essential.

Out of view is a useful mantra when it comes to choosing where to pitch, but there are other factors to consider. The ideal spot is sheltered from the wind and close to a stream or other source of water – though not so close that your tent will be in the path of a torrent if it rains heavily.

Top tips

● Stay on the move. Pitch your tent in the evening and leave the next morning. Don't stay more than two nights in the same place.

● Stay out of sight.

● Leave no trace: remove all rubbish, including food scraps, and bury waste (but not tampons or sanitary towels – take them with you).

● Be extremely careful when lighting (and extinguishing) fires.

● Use ecologically sensitive toiletries.

● If feasible, ask permission.

Where to camp...

Campfires allowed

England

Abbey Home Farm, Gloucestershire p105
Blackberry Wood, East Sussex p132
Britchcombe, Oxfordshire p114
Buckland Bell, Somerset p90
Burnbake, Dorset p99
Coombe View Farm, South Devon p71
Cornish Tipi, Cornwall p59
Debden House, Essex p138
Deer's Glade, Norfolk p150
Eweleaze Farm, Dorset p93
Manor Farm, Hampshire p119
Middle Woodbatch Farm, Shropshire p157
Namparra, Cornwall p41
The Orchard, Suffolk p145
La Rosa, North York Moors p180
Runnage Farm, South Devon p65
South Penquite Farm, Cornwall p62
Stubcroft Farm, West Sussex p124
Treen Farm, Cornwall p38
Treloan, Cornwall p53
Welsummer, Kent p135
Westermill Farm, Somerset p84
Woodland Yurting, West Sussex p126
Wowo, East Sussex p129
Yurtcamp, South Devon p68

Wales

Cae Du, Snowdonia p247
Fforest, Pembrokeshire p220
Fforest Fields, Mid Wales p236
Graig Wen, Snowdonia p251
Gwern Gof Uchaf, Snowdonia p267
Gwerniago Farm, Mid Wales p244
Hafod y Llan, Snowdonia p261
Hollybush Inn, Brecon Beacons p230
Llyn Gwynant, Snowdonia p264
Mynydd Mawr, Llyn Peninsula p274
Rhydhowell Farm, Pembrokeshire p218
Shell Island, Snowdonia p255
Tan-y-Bryn Farm, Snowdonia p270
Ty Parke, Pembrokeshire p215
Tyllwyd Farm, Mid Wales p241
Ynysfaen, Brecon Beacons p224
The Yurt Farm, Mid Wales p238

Scotland

Badrallach, The North-West p314
Comrie Croft, Central Scotland p293
Mains Farm, Central Scotland p290
Red Squirrel, The Highlands p296
Solway View, Southern Scotland p278

Fantastic for families

England

Abbey Home Farm, Gloucestershire p105
Batcombe Vale, Somerset p87
Beacon Cottage Farm p47
Burnbake, Dorset p99
Cornish Tipi, Cornwall p59
Debden House, Essex p138
Eskdale, Lake District p192
Eweleaze Farm, Dorset p93
Gwithian Bay, Cornwall p44
Harbour Camping, Southwold p141
Manor Farm, Hampshire p119
Masons, Yorkshire Dales p174
North Morte Farm, North Devon p78
The Orchard, Suffolk p145
Roundhill, Hampshire p122
South Penquite Farm, Cornwall p62
Spiers House, North York Moors p178
Stowford Manor Farm, Wiltshire p102
Stubcroft Farm, West Sussex p124
Tregedna Farm p50
Treloan, Cornwall p53
Yurtcamp, South Devon p68
Wowo, East Sussex p129

Wales

Fforest, Pembrokeshire p220
Llyn Gwynant, Snowdonia p264
Rhydhowell Farm, Pembrokeshire p218
Shell Island, Snowdonia p255
Three Cliffs Bay, Gower p202
Ty Parke, Pembrokeshire p215
Ynysfaen, Brecon Beacons p224
The Yurt Farm, Mid Wales p238

Scotland

Applecross, The North-West p310
Cashel, Argyll & the Islands p287
Comrie Croft, Central Scotland p293
Lazy Duck, The Highlands p302
Machrihanish, Argyll & the Islands p282
Rothiemurchus, The Highlands p299
Seal Shore, Argyll & the Islands p280

Made for walking

England

Blackberry Wood, East Sussex p132
Britchcombe, Oxfordshire p114
Clitheroe, Lancashire p184
Eskdale, Lake District p192
Gordale Scar, Yorkshire Dales p171
Haddon Grove, Peak District p166
High Sand Creek, Norfolk p152
Home Farm Radnage, Buckinghamshire p111
Jerusalem Farm, West Yorkshire p176
Low Wray, Lake District p189
Masons, Yorkshire Dales p174
Middle Woodbatch Farm see p157
North Lees, Peak District p163
La Rosa, North York Moors p181
Runnage Farm, South Devon p65
Side Farm, Lake District p198
South Penquite Farm, Cornwall p62
Spiers House, North York Moors p178
Upper Booth Farm, Peak District p168
Wasdale Head, Lake District p195
Westermill Farm, Somerset p84

Wales

Cae Du, Snowdonia p247
Cae Gwyn Farm, Snowdonia p258
Caerfai Farm, Pembrokeshire p213
Graig Wen, Snowdonia p251
Gwern Gof Uchaf, Snowdonia p267

Hafod y Llan, Snowdonia p261
Hillend, Gower p205
Hollybush Inn, Brecon Beacons p230
Llanthony Priory, Brecon Beacons p227
Llyn Gwynant, Snowdonia p264
Three Cliffs Bay, Gower p202
Trefalen Farm, Pembrokeshire p208
Tyllwyd Farm, Mid Wales p241
Newgale, Pembrokeshire p211
Ynysfaen, Brecon Beacons p224

Scotland
Badrallach, The North-West p314
Cashel, Argyll & the Islands p287
Clachtoll Beach, The North-West p312
Comrie Croft, Central Scotland p293
Glenbrittle, Isle of Skye p305
Morvich, The North-West p308
Red Squirrel, The Highlands p296
Rothiemurchus, The Highlands p299

Best for beaches
England
Beacon Cottage Farm, Cornwall p47
Cherry Tree Farm, North Devon p75
Deepdale, Norfolk p154
Eweleaze Farm, Dorset p93
Gwithian Bay, Cornwall p44
Harbour Camping, Southwold p141
High Sand Creek, Norfolk p152
Highertown Farm, Cornwall p56
North Morte Farm, North Devon p78
Namparra, Cornwall p41
St Martin's, Isles of Scilly p35
Seagull, Channel Islands p32
Stubcroft Farm, West Sussex p124
Treen Farm, Cornwall p38
Treloan, Cornwall p53

Wales
Cae Du, Snowdonia p247
Caerfai Farm, Pembrokeshire p213
Hillend, Gower p205
Nant-y-Big, Llyn Peninsula p272
Newgale, Pembrokeshire p211
Shell Island, Snowdonia p255
Three Cliffs Bay, Gower p202
Trefalen Farm, Pembrokeshire p208

Scotland
Clachtoll Beach, The North-West p312
Glenbrittle, Isle of Skye p305
Machrihanish, Argyll & the Islands p282
Seal Shore, Argyll & the Islands p280

Yurts, tipis, caravans, pods
England
Abbey Home Farm, Gloucestershire p105
Blackberry Wood, East Sussex p132
Britchcombe, Oxfordshire p114
Cornish Tipi, Cornwall p59
Deepdale, Norfolk p154
Deer's Glade, Norfolk p150
Eskdale, Lake District p192
Low Wray, Lake District p189
Manor Farm, Hampshire p119
The Orchard, Suffolk p145
La Rosa, North York Moors p181
South Penquite Farm, Cornwall p62
Treloan, Cornwall p53
Vintage Vacations, Isle of Wight p116
Wasdale Head, Lake District p195
Welsummer, Kent p135
Woodland Yurting, West Sussex p126
Wowo, East Sussex p129
Yurtcamp, South Devon p68

Wales
Fforest, Pembrokeshire p220
Graig Wen, Snowdonia p251
Hollybush Inn, Brecon Beacons p230
Ty Parke, Pembrokeshire p215
The Yurt Farm, Mid Wales p238

Scotland
Applecross, The North-West p310
Comrie Croft, Central Scotland p293

Cove Park, Argyll & the Islands p284
Lazy Duck, The Highlands, p302
Machrihanish, Argyll & the Islands p282
Mains Farm, Central Scotland p290
Solway View, Southern Scotland p278

Tents only
England
Blackberry Wood, East Sussex p132
Eweleaze Farm, Dorset p93
Jerusalem Farm, West Yorkshire p176
Masons, North York Moors p174
Middle Woodbatch Farm, Shropshire p157
North Lees, Peak District p163
St Martin's, Isles of Scilly p35
Welsummer, Kent p135
Wowo, East Sussex p129

Wales
Hafod y Llan, Snowdonia p261
Ynysfaen, Brecon Beacons p224

Scotland
Comrie Croft, Central Scotland p293
Lazy Duck, The Highlands p302

Year-round camping
England
Blackberry Wood, East Sussex p132
Britchcombe, Oxfordshire p114
Buckland Bell, Somerset p90
Deepdale, Norfolk p154
Deer's Glade, Norfolk p150
Home Farm Radnage, Buckinghamshire p111
North Lees, Peak District p163
The Orchard, Suffolk p145
Runnage Farm, South Devon p65
Spiers House, North York Moors p178
Stubcroft Farm, West Sussex p124
Wasdale Head, Lake District p195
Westermill Farm, Somerset p84
Woodside Farm, Norfolk p148
Wowo, East Sussex p129

Wales
Cae Gwyn Farm, Snowdonia p258
Gwern Gof Uchaf, Snowdonia p267
Hollybush Inn, Brecon Beacons p230
Llanthony Priory, Brecon Beacons p227
Rhydhowell Farm, Pembrokeshire p218
Tan-y-Bryn Farm, Snowdonia p270
Trefalen Farm, Pembrokeshire p208
Tyllwyd Farm, Mid Wales p241
Ynysfaen, Brecon Beacons p224

Scotland
Applecross, The North-West p310
Badrallach, The North-West p314
Comrie Croft, Central Scotland p293
Red Squirrel, The Highlands p296
Solway View, Southern Scotland p278

England south-west

KEY TO CAMPSITES

Channel Islands
① Seagull, p78

Isles of Scilly
② St Martin's, p35

Cornwall
③ Treen Farm, p38
④ Namparra, p41
⑤ Gwithian Farm, p44
⑥ Beacon Cottage Farm, p47
⑦ Tregedna Farm, p50
⑧ Treloan, p53
⑨ Highertown Farm, p56
⑩ Cornish Tipi, p59
⑪ South Penquite Farm, p62

Devon
⑫ Runnage Farm, p65
⑬ Yurtcamp, p68
⑭ Coombe View Farm, p71
⑮ Cherry Tree Farm, p75

⑯ North Morte Farm, p78
⑰ Little Meadow, p81

Somerset
⑱ Westermill Farm, p84
⑲ Batcombe Vale, p87
⑳ Buckland Bell, p90

Dorset
㉑ Eweleaze Farm, p93
㉒ Tom's Field, p96
㉓ Burnbake, p99

Wiltshire
㉔ Stowford Manor Farm, p102

Gloucestershire
㉕ Abbey Home Farm, p105

Herefordshire
㉖ Doward Park, p108

WALES

Ross-on-Wye ○

GLOUCESTERSHIRE

○ Cheltenham

Cirencester ○ ㉕

Swindon ○

WILTSHIRE

Salisbury Plain

Salisbury ○

㉔

Bristol ○

Glastonbury ○

SOMERSET

⑳

⑲

Yeovil ○

DORSET

Bournemouth ○

Bournemouth ○

㉓ ㉒ ○ Swanage

㉑

Weymouth ○

Lyme Regis ○

Taunton ○

Exmoor National Park

⑱

Lynton ○

⑯ ⑰ ○
Ilfracombe

⑮

Barnstaple ○

DEVON

Exeter ○

○ Torquay

Okehampton ○

⑬

Dartmoor National Park

⑫

Plymouth ○

Camelford ○

Bodmin Moor

⑪

⑩

Wadebridge ○

CORNWALL

St Austell ○

Falmouth ○ ⑧
⑦

⑥

⑤

Penzance ○

③

② *Isles of Scilly*

① *Channel Islands* ↗

KEY TO CAMPSITES

Buckinghamshire
㉗ Home Farm Radnage, p111

Oxfordshire
㉘ Britchcombe, p114

Isle of Wight
㉙ Vintage Vacations, p116

Hampshire
㉚ Manor Farm, p119
㉛ Roundhill, p122

Sussex
㉜ Stubcroft Farm, p124
㉝ Woodland Yurting, p126
㉞ Wowo, p129
㉟ Blackberry Wood, p132

Kent
㊱ Welsummer, p135

Essex
㊲ Debden House, p138

Suffolk
㊳ Harbour Camping, p141
㊴ The Orchard, p145

Norfolk
㊵ Woodside Farm, p148
㊶ Deer's Glade, p150
㊷ High Sand Creek, p152
㊸ Deepdale, p154

Hunstanton

◦ ㊸ ◦ ㊷ ◦ Cromer

Wells-Next-the-Sea ㊶

◦ King's Lynn ㊵

The Broads Great ◦

NORFOLK Norwich Yarmouth

Southwold

◦ Cambridge ㊳ ◦

SUFFOLK Aldeburgh
◦

㊴

BEDS ◦ Ipswich

Oxford BUCKS HERTFORDSHIRE ESSEX
◦

OXFORDSHIRE ㉗ ◦ Chelmsford

◦High
Wycombe ㊲

㉘ GREATER
LONDON

BERKSHIRE

Maidstone
◦ ◦
SURREY ㊱ Canterbury

Alton ◦ ㉚ ◦ Guildford KENT

HAMPSHIRE

㉝

Haywards Heath◦ ㉞ EAST SUSSEX

Southampton WEST SUSSEX ㉟
◦
㉛ ◦ Brighton ◦ Eastbourne

New Forest ◦ ㉜
ational Park Portsmouth

㉙
*Isle of
Wight*

England south-east

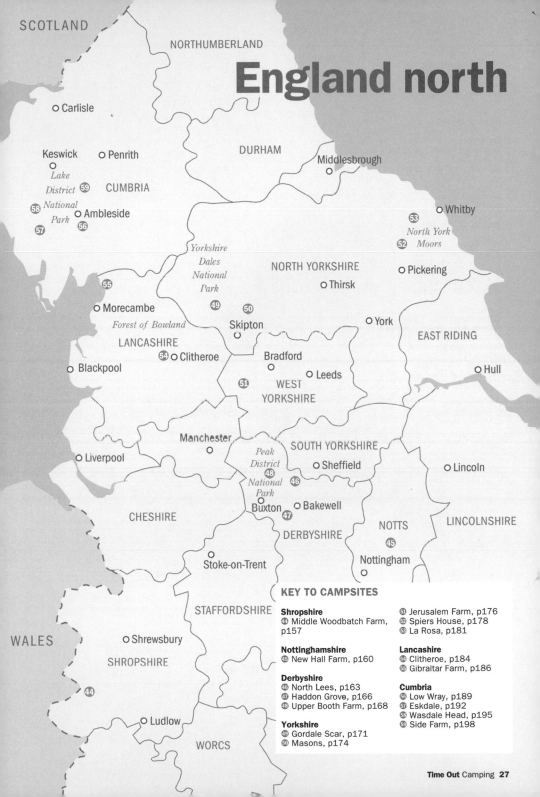

SCOTLAND

NORTHUMBERLAND

England north

Carlisle

Keswick Penrith

Lake District ㊾ CUMBRIA

㊽ *National Park* Ambleside

㊼ ㊻

DURHAM

Middlesbrough

㊳ Whitby

North York ㊲ *Moors*

Yorkshire Dales National Park

NORTH YORKSHIRE

Thirsk

Pickering

㊺

Morecambe

Forest of Bowland

LANCASHIRE

㊶ Clitheroe

㊾ ㊿ Skipton

York

EAST RIDING

Blackpool

Bradford

Leeds

㊿

WEST YORKSHIRE

Hull

Manchester

Peak District ㊽ *National Park*

Buxton ㊸ Bakewell

SOUTH YORKSHIRE

Sheffield

㊻

Lincoln

Liverpool

CHESHIRE

DERBYSHIRE

NOTTS

LINCOLNSHIRE

㊺

Stoke-on-Trent

Nottingham

STAFFORDSHIRE

WALES

Shrewsbury

SHROPSHIRE

㊹

Ludlow

WORCS

KEY TO CAMPSITES

Shropshire
㊹ Middle Woodbatch Farm, p157

Nottinghamshire
㊺ New Hall Farm, p160

Derbyshire
㊻ North Lees, p163
㊼ Haddon Grove, p166
㊽ Upper Booth Farm, p168

Yorkshire
㊾ Gordale Scar, p171
㊿ Masons, p174

㊿ Jerusalem Farm, p176
㊿ Spiers House, p178
㊿ La Rosa, p181

Lancashire
㊿ Clitheroe, p184
㊿ Gibraltar Farm, p186

Cumbria
㊿ Low Wray, p189
㊿ Eskdale, p192
㊿ Wasdale Head, p195
㊿ Side Farm, p198

KEY TO CAMPSITES

Gower
❶ Three Cliffs Bay, p202
❷ Hillend, p205

Pembrokeshire
❸ Trefalen Farm, p208
❹ Newgale, p211
❺ Caerfai Farm, p213
❻ Ty Parke, p215
❼ Rhydhowell Farm, p218
❽ Fforest, p220

Brecon Beacons
❾ Ynysfaen, p224
❿ Llanthony Priory, p227
⓫ Hollybush Inn, p230

Mid Wales
⓬ Rhandirmwyn, p233
⓭ Fforest Fields, p236
⓮ The Yurt Farm, p238
⓯ Tyllwyd Farm, p241
⓰ Gwerniago Farm, p244

Snowdonia
⓱ Cae Du, p247
⓲ Graig Wen, p251
⓳ Shell Island, p255
⓴ Cae Gwyn Farm, p258
㉑ Hafod y Llan, p261
㉒ Llyn Gwynant, p264
㉓ Gwern Gof Uchaf, p267
㉔ Tan-y-Bryn Farm, p270

Llyn Peninsula
㉕ Nant-y-Big, p272
㉖ Mynydd Mawr, p274

ISLE OF ANGLESEY

Llandudno
㉔

Bangor
㉓
㉒
㉑

CONWY

Betws-y-coed

Porthmadog

Snowdonia

⓴
GWYNEDD

⓳
National

㉖   ㉕

Barmouth ⓲ Park
○ Dolgellau

Welshpool ○

⓱

㉓ ... ⓰
Machynlleth

Aberystwyth

POWYS

⓯

Aberaeron ⓮

CEREDIGION

Builth Wells
⓭
Hay-on-Wye
⓫

○ Cardigan
❽
❼

⓬

Brecon
❾ Brecon Beacons
National Park

St Davids ❻
❺ ❹
PEMBROKE-
SHIRE

CARMARTHENSHIRE

Carmarthen

Abergavenny
⓾
MONMOUTH
SHIRE

○ Haverfordwest

❸

Swansea
❷ SWANSEA
❶

Cardiff

Wales

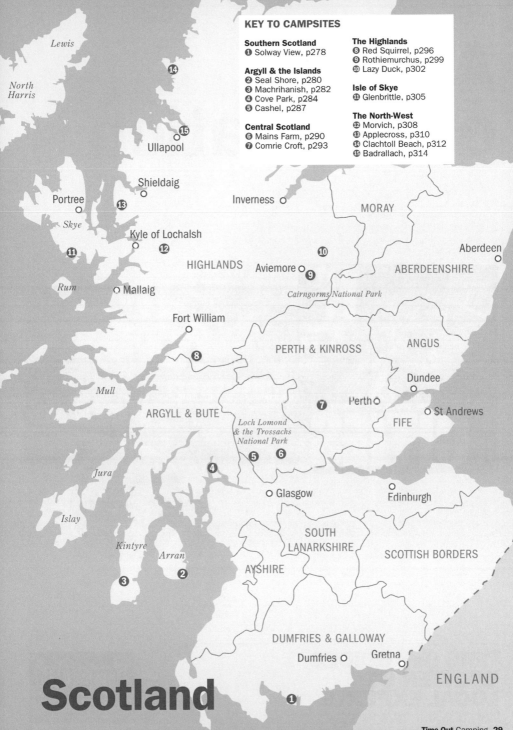

KEY TO CAMPSITES

Southern Scotland
❶ Solway View, p278

Argyll & the Islands
❷ Seal Shore, p280
❸ Machrihanish, p282
❹ Cove Park, p284
❺ Cashel, p287

Central Scotland
❻ Mains Farm, p290
❼ Comrie Croft, p293

The Highlands
❽ Red Squirrel, p296
❾ Rothiemurchus, p299
❿ Lazy Duck, p302

Isle of Skye
⓫ Glenbrittle, p305

The North-West
⓬ Morvich, p308
⓭ Applecross, p310
⓮ Clachtoll Beach, p312
⓯ Badrallach, p314

Lewis

North
Harris

⓮

⓯
Ullapool

Shieldaig

Portree ⓭
Skye

Inverness ○   MORAY

Kyle of Lochalsh
⓫   ⓬   ❿
HIGHLANDS   Aberdeen ○
Aviemore ○ ❾   ABERDEENSHIRE
Rum   Mallaig ○   Cairngorms National Park

Fort William ○
❽   PERTH & KINROSS   ANGUS

Mull   Dundee ○
ARGYLL & BUTE   ❼   Perth ○   ○ St Andrews
Loch Lomond   FIFE
& the Trossachs
National Park
Jura   ❺   ❻
❹

Islay   ○ Glasgow   ○ Edinburgh

Kintyre   SOUTH
Arran   LANARKSHIRE   SCOTTISH BORDERS
AYSHIRE
❸   ❷

DUMFRIES & GALLOWAY

Dumfries ○   Gretna
○
❶   ENGLAND

Scotland

A world of inspiration

England

North Morte Farm, North Devon, p78.

Seagull

Herm island; (below) the ferry from Guernsey.

Seagull Campsite
Herm Island, Guernsey GY1 3HR
01481 722377
camping@herm-island.com
www.herm-island.com/camping
Map p25 ❶

Number of pitches 36 tents. 28 hire tents.
Open End May-early Sept.
Booking By phone, online. Essential.
Minimum stay hire tent 3 nights.
Typical cost Tent £7 adult, £3.50 child.
Site fee £7.50. Hire tent £40-£62 per night.
Facilities Laundry facilities; showers (£1);
toilets; washing-up area.
Campfires Not allowed.
Dogs Not allowed.
Restrictions No unsupervised under-21s.
No noise after 10.30pm.
Getting there First, get to St Peter Port
on Guernsey – the website has details of
options by air or sea. Travel Trident ferry
(01481 721379) sails regularly to Herm;
the journey takes 20 mins. It's a 15-mins
walk from the pier to the campsite; a tractor-
trailer transports the luggage.

Three miles off the east coast of Guernsey, the tiny island of Herm is an unusual mix of old-fashioned bucket-and-spade resort and entrancing natural escape. The Seagull campsite is perfectly situated at the highest point of the island, and a cliff path haunted by seabirds and punctuated with wild flowers runs along the edge of one field.

Yet those who want to knot a hanky on their heads and have a paddle are within walking distance of both Belvoir Bay, a sheltered beach snuggled into dark cliffs, and the almost tropical arc of Shell Beach (so-called because of the myriad little shells that make up its three-quarters of a mile of sand). On Herm – just a mile and a half long and half a mile wide, with a permanent population of just 60 – nothing is more than half an hour away on foot.

The Seagull caters for people with their own tents, but also has pre-erected tents for hire: spacious, three-compartment constructions, with enough room for four adults and two kids. These come with a two-ring gas cooker/grill and saucepans in one corner, a trestle table out front and air mattresses in each 'bedroom'. If you pay extra for a cool box equipped with cutlery and crockery, all you need is a sleeping bag.

Wooded areas screen off different sections of the site, giving a pleasing amount of privacy even when the place is full, and grassy terraces mean that many areas have a sea view. Pitches are allocated in advance; request one of the clifftop pitches (66, 67, 68, 70, 87, 89 and 90) for terrific views across the Big Russell channel to Sark, another tiny inhabited island.

Facilities are serviceable: the coin-op showers in the concrete-floored block are hot (and there are enough of them), and the washing-up area is roofed against the weather. Free, lockable recharging points for phones and cameras are a thoughtful touch.

Although there's no direct transport to Herm from the mainland, some 65,000 visitors make it here each year, many of them day-trippers. Every one comes to relax. Perhaps because of the slow pace of an island where no cars are allowed, maybe because so many overnight visitors take the same self-catering lets year after year, the island has a uniquely calming and friendly community feel.

There's no nightlife beyond a pint in the Mermaid pub of an evening, but you don't exactly experience wild isolation either: 15 minutes' walk downhill from the campsite, the Harbour Village is an old-fashioned cluster of three gift shops, a post office, a hotel and a pub. Things may feel a little matronly to city types (signs on the beach prohibit the playing of radios, while the campsite doesn't take unaccompanied under-21s). Still, if that's the price of keeping things so peaceful, we're more than happy to pay it.

CHANNEL ISLANDS

Site specific

✔ With no cars allowed on the island – after all, there are no roads to drive on – the tranquillity and pace of Herm are magical.

✘ Groceries can be pre-ordered from the campsite, but you're pretty much dependent on one small shop in Harbour Village for basics. If you need supermarket prices and choice, stock up before you leave Guernsey (or hop over on the ferry).

Cauchie de Robert cove, and Caquorobert rock, one of many sheltered spots on the east coast.

EATING & DRINKING

At Shell Beach and Belvoir Bay, there are old-style beach cafés – the kind of places where you can hire a deck chair and buy a cuppa, cake and emergency cricket set for the kids – but the proper drinking and dining happens in Harbour Village.

Campers tend to make most use of the spacious and usually busy Mermaid Tavern (01481 710170), which serves a nice pint of Guernsey-made Les Rocquettes cider and good-quality pub grub (fresh-caught sea bream, for example). This is the affable social hub of the island: long-stay self-caterers who have visited Herm every summer for the past 20 years mix with residents, seasonal staff and day-trippers. Snacks and proper food appear at lunch and dinner in the large courtyard; in the evening the Black Rock Grill serves dishes you cook yourself on 'volcanic hot rocks'.

For something a bit more formal, the conservatory restaurant at the island's only hotel, the White House (01481 722159), serves dinner and impressive seafood lunches. The hotel's other restaurant, the Ship, offers breakfasts and brasserie-style lunches (local seafood is again a speciality), as well as hot drinks, cakes and ice-cream all day.

ATTRACTIONS & ACTIVITIES

Despite a tenth-century chapel and little dolmen (Neolithic burial chamber), the real attraction on Herm is the island itself. The cliff paths along the south coast are stunning, and the beaches cover every preference from secluded cove to sandy crescent. Puffin and tern regularly nest on the island, and you can rent rod and tackle to fish straight off Shell Beach or, cut off by the tide, from the Putrainez outcrop.

At Shell Beach, Outdoor Guernsey (www.outdoor guernsey.co.uk/herm-island.html) rents out kayaks

by the hour; alternatively, take one of the weekly two-hour horticultural tours led by the island's head gardener, Brett Moore.

If it rains, options are limited, so hop on the ferry to Guernsey and explore the capital, St Peter Port. Castle Cornet (01481 726518, www.museums.gov.gg, closed Nov-Mar), the harbour fortress that guarded the island from invaders for centuries, has a couple of good museums. A guided tour of Hauteville House (01481 723552, www.victorhugo.gg, closed Sun and Oct-Apr), home in exile to *Les Misérables* author Victor Hugo, is a must-visit – all surprising objects, secret doors and strategically located memento mori.

In fine weather, take a 45-minute boat trip from Guernsey to green and tranquil Sark (01481 832345, www.sark.info), for a bounce around the unpaved roads on a rented bike or a tour in a horse-drawn cart.

AMUSING THE KIDS

Herm could have been made for children. With no traffic, they're free to roam, and the beaches are an endless source of fun. At high tide, there's paddling or building castles on the fine sand; at low tide, crabs, shrimps and tiny fish are exposed in rock pools.

CAMPING NEARBY

There are good campsites on all the major Channel Islands. On Guernsey, try Fauxquets Valley (01481 255460/236951, www.fauxquets.co.uk, £10.50 adult, £3.20-£4.20 child), located in a country parish and equipped with a swimming pool should the mile-and-a-half walk to the nearest beach seem too much. On Sark, Pomme de Chien (01481 832316, £7.50 adult, £5 child) is based on a farm. Both campsites are open year-round and have pre-erected tents for hire.

St Martin's

St Martin's Campsite
Oaklands Farm, Middletown,
St Martin's, Isles of Scilly TR25 0QN
01720 422888
info@stmartinscampsite.co.uk
www.stmartinscampsite.co.uk
Map p25 ②
OS map SV920161

Number of pitches 50 tents. No caravans.
Open Mar-Oct.
Booking By phone. Essential end May,
end June-Aug.
Typical cost £9.50-£10.50 adult.
Facilities Camping supplies; freezers;
laundry facilities; showers (£1); toilets;
washing-up area; Wi-Fi.
Campfires Not allowed.
Dogs Not allowed.
Restrictions Single-sex groups and
unsupervised under-18s by arrangement.
No noise after 10.30pm.
Getting there You have three options: ferry,
small plane or helicopter, though the free
baggage allowance by air is only 15kg. The
Scillonian III ferry leaves Penzance in the
morning (no service Sun) and takes 2 hours
40 mins. SkyBus leaves from Land's End,
Newquay, Exeter, Bristol and Southampton;
flight times vary from 15 to 90 mins. The
helicopter from Penzance takes 15 mins.
All three arrive at St Mary's island, from
where it's a short boat ride to St Martin's
and then a walk to the campsite (a tractor
brings the luggage). For information on ferry
and plane travel, phone 0845 710 5555 or
see www.islesofscilly-travel.co.uk. Details
of the helicopter service are on 01736
363871, www.islesofscillyhelicopter.com.

There can be few more effective ways of
switching off from everyday life than pitching your
tent on a tiny off-island of the Isles of Scilly – a
small archipelago strung out in the Atlantic, some
30 miles off the tip of Cornwall. Trimmed with
deserted silver-sand beaches, shaped in perfect
half-moons and splashed by gin-clear waters, the
island of St Martin's could, on a sunny day, be
a miniature St Kitts – an illusion that tends to be
shattered the moment you venture into the sea,
which is rarely anything other than glacial.

Just two miles long and less than a mile wide,
St Martin's is a blissfully simple place: one pub,
one shop, one road and one boat out in the
morning. Happily stranded, visitors find
themselves slowing down and entertaining
themselves with nothing more complicated than
shell-collecting (the cowrie is particularly prized),
bird-watching, reading, walking or chatting over
a pint of Ales of Scilly.

One of Scilly's more sheltered campsites,
St Martin's also has the best facilities. Although
you can never be completely insulated from
the battering the islands regularly receive from
the Atlantic winds, the site is protected by the
dunes and the hedges that portion it up into
cosy strips.

Built with a grant from the English Tourist
Board, the toilet and shower block is modern
and invariably gleaming from its twice-daily
clean. The two showers per gender (£1 for seven
minutes) are reliably hot, with a comfortable
changing area and hairdryers. The laundry area,
with sinks for clothes washing, two washing
machines, a tumble-dryer and a spin-dryer, is
handy for families.

No electric hook-ups on the campsite means
minimal light and noise pollution, and the lack
of cars, caravans or motorhomes is a rare treat
– this is all about camping in its purest form.
You barely hear a zip opening after 10.30pm as
campers invariably fall in with the slower island
pace. There's a mobile-phone charging point in the
nearby barn, where ice packs can also be refrozen,

Site specific

✔ This is the chance to live out your
island paradise fantasies – you're a few
yards through the dunes from a deserted,
totally undeveloped white-sand beach.

✘ Thanks to a combination of a remote
location and a cornered market, transport
costs stack up. The ferry from Penzance,
or the quicker SkyBus plane, cost more
than £100 return (and you are likely to face
a surcharge for chunky camping luggage);
the boat from St Mary's to St Martin's is
another £8 return, plus £10 for luggage,
and the tractor for the short stretch from
the quay to the campsite is £7 return.
And due to water shortages on the islands,
the showers are £1 a pop. All of which,
of course, is a small price to pay for your
own little slice of paradise.

and a small money-in-the-tin stall selling camping gas, eggs, home-grown tomatoes and salad.

When you make it back to the mainland, you're sure to feel that you've returned from somewhere much further away.

EATING & DRINKING

A small shop on the island sells all the basics for campsite cooking, many packaged in usefully small sizes, but note that there is no fresh meat (consider stocking up at the Co-op supermarket on St Mary's). But best of all, St Martin's has its own bakery and a sprinkling of home-grown veg stalls along the road, selling organic courgettes, baby carrots and squash at reasonable prices – and you can buy juicy tomatoes and salad bags from the campsite barn.

For such a small island, St Martin's has a surprising number of eating options, most of them small but sensitive operations. The classy Polreath Tea Room in Higher Town (01720 422046, www.polreath.com, closed Sat) serves cream teas and café fare, with a curry night on Mondays from May to September. Nearby, Adam's Fish & Chips (01720 423637) offers a sterling rendition of the dish, with fish line-caught by Adam himself, and chips hand-cut from his own potatoes. The island also has its own vineyard (01720 423418, www.stmartinsvineyard.co.uk).

The Sevenstones Inn in Lower Town (01720 423560, www.sevenstonesinn.co.uk) is the friendly island pub, serving Ales of Scilly beer and a range of comfort food, including a seafood hotpot. Prices at all the island eateries tend to be high.

ATTRACTIONS & ACTIVITIES

Don't expect theme parks, nightlife or a cutting edge on anything except a fisherman's knife, just the unflashy excitement of outstanding natural beauty and the sound of silence. St Martin's is fringed at almost every turn with silver-flecked beaches and,

with the exception of the rather grey hotel on the westerly beach, entirely free from human construction. This makes a fantastic canvas for a holiday – footpaths criss-cross the island, over the purple-flecked moor, around the headlands and to Great Bay, a strong contender for Britain's finest stretch of beach. And as the island has just 100 residents, with a few hundred more visitors during the summer, it's incredibly easy to find a beach all to yourself. There is also a tennis court on the island.

If you want to to get into the water, Scilly Diving (01720 422848, www.scillydiving.com) offers various snorkelling and diving trips, as well as diving courses for beginners. Or you can hire kayaks, sailing dinghies and glass-bottom rowing boats from Bennett Boatyard (www.bennettboatyard.com); the boatyard is based on Bryher, but operates from the campsite from May to September.

AMUSING THE KIDS

The island is a dream for families; a place where there are scarcely any cars, crime is non-existent, beaches are a few metres away and older kids can be granted more independence than on the mainland. There are no purpose-built attractions or dedicated playgrounds, but you're unlikely to miss them.

CAMPING NEARBY

Troytown Campsite (01720 422360, www.troytown. co.uk, open all year, £7-£8 per person) on St Agnes is Britain's most south-westerly campsite, with a much wilder feel, thanks to a spectacular perch directly facing the Atlantic.

Other campsites on the islands include Bryher (01720 422559, www.bryhercampsite.co.uk, open Apr-Sept, £9.50) and St Mary's (01720 422670, www.garrisonholidays.com, open all year, £7.75-£10.50), which also has some self-catering cottages.

ISLES OF SCILLY

Treen Farm

Treen Farm Campsite
Treen Farm, St Levan,
Penzance, Cornwall TR19 6LF
01736 810273
www.treenfarmcampsite.co.uk
Map p25 ❸
OS map SW394230

Number of pitches Up to 100 tents/
campervans. No caravans/motorhomes.
Open Easter-Oct
Booking No bookings.
Typical cost Tent £2.50-£4. Campervan
£3-£4. Car £1. Adult £4.50, child £2.
Facilities Disabled facilities (toilet);
laundry facilities; shop; showers (25p);
toilets; washing-up area.
Campfires Not allowed.
Dogs Allowed.
Restrictions No noise after 10pm.
Getting there By road Take the A30
towards Land's End, then either the B3283
or the B3315 to Treen. At the bottom of
Treen Hill, turn left, then right at the car
park. The campsite is clearly signed.
By public transport Train to Penzance.
Bus 1A (0871 200 2233, www.firstgroup.
com) runs regularly, taking 35 mins to
the bottom of Treen Hill, from where it's
a short walk uphill to the campsite.

On a sunny day, the sand and sea at Pednvounder Beach – a steep clamber down the cliff path from Treen Farm Campsite – seems to have landed by some trickery from considerably more tropical climes. The sea is an unreal shade of turquoise, the sand pearly white and the flowers clinging to the cliffs a vivid shade of pink. On less clement days, it sometimes seems you've pitched your tent on a wind-battered precipice in the Andes. But then the type of people who choose to camp on top of a cliff a few miles from Land's End generally don't come looking for shelter – spending quality time with the elements is all part of the fun.

Treen is a friendly, intimate site consisting of two treeless fields perched just a few hundred yards from the cliffs. As a result, big sea views fill your line of sight (and, with a spot of thoughtful pitching, your porch window) – and the site has a wonderfully open, edge-of-the-ocean feel.

The facilities don't come with bells or whistles, and nor would you expect them to at these prices (note: payment is by cash or cheque only). Nonetheless, they are perfectly adequate and clean. The showers are operated by a 25p token, giving you a five-minute burst of water, and the two washing-up sinks, although exposed to the elements, have very hot water. There are no electric hook-ups, but visitors are welcome to charge electrical items briefly in the shop. It's simple, scenic and unspoilt: exactly how the crowd of walkers, families and locals that camp here – many returning season after season (it's been a campsite for over 50 years) – would like it to stay.

Given the site's relative isolation, the superb shop is a real bonus, trumping many larger 'luxury' campsites. It's stuffed with useful items such as buckets and spades, windbreaks, postcards, own-made pasties and cakes, tins, fresh local burgers, mud-spattered veg and eggs from the farm. There's even a box of old paperbacks, the proceeds of which go to charity.

Last but not least, the pitches are level and very well drained. If this sounds like faint praise, it's not meant to be – drainage swiftly becomes vitally important if a storm comes in off the ocean and the site is deluged with rain.

On our last visit, the sound of *La Traviata* at the open-air Minack Theatre at nearby Porthcurno was wafting dreamily across the cliffs as the sun sank behind the fields, and we sank a jug of Tribute ale (available to take away from the local pub) at the picnic table. Of course, we can't guarantee you such a prized set of conditions – but we heartily recommend you enter the draw.

EATING & DRINKING

The campsite's excellent shop is housed in a small wooden cabin, crammed with all manner of tins and basics, as well as fresh produce, baked goods and local

Site specific

✔ The location is fabulous: right on the coast, just a few miles shy of Land's End, yet only a short walk from a pretty village with a good pub and a small café.

✘ The campsite's no-booking policy makes it impossible to guarantee a space. In high season, you'll need to arrive at 8am in the hopes of nabbing one (though the owners can give you an idea of how full it's looking by phone). Less of a problem in low season.

CORNWALL

Penberth (left), one of many fishing villages along the coast path; and Porthcurno.

dairy products. There is a wider selection of comestibles at the small shop in St Buryan a couple of miles away, but for big supermarkets you'll need to drive the seven or so miles to Penzance.

A small café in Treen serves sandwiches and cream teas, and, as luck would have it, the nearest pub is a winner. A few minutes' walk away, the Logan Rock Inn (01736 810495) is full of character (and locals). There is a beer garden at the rear and real ales; the food is basic pub fare.

This remote corner of the country isn't about fine dining or wild nightlife, but that's not to say you can't get some great food and a nice pint of Cornish ale. Seven miles along the coast in Mousehole, 2 Fore Street (01736 731164, www.2forestreet.co.uk, closed mid Jan-mid Feb) serves bistro food and a lot of fresh fish in chic surrounds right on the harbour. Further afield, near Zennor on the north coast, the Gurnard's Head (01736 796928, www.gurnardshead.co.uk) is a superb inn that makes exciting use of local ingredients in a memorable setting between the moors and the crashing sea. Booking is essential at both places in high season.

ATTRACTIONS & ACTIVITIES

There are walks galore along this gorgeous stretch of coast, and two particularly fantastic beaches. The nearest to the campsite is Pednvounder, accessible, if not that easily, via steep steps (wear proper shoes). Note too that Pednvounder is a popular naturist spot. West along the coast, Porthcurno is bigger and more easily approached – either by car, or on foot along the coastal footpath. Dotted along the coast in a easterly direction are the pretty fishing villages of Penberth, Lamorna and Mousehole, all on the coast path.

Penzance houses the celebrated Penlee House Gallery & Museum (01736 363625, www.penlee house.org.uk, closed Sun), best known for its works by the 19th-century Newlyn School, and the newer, contemporary Exchange (01736 363715, www.newlyn artgallery.co.uk, closed Sun, and Mon Nov-Mar), with its undulating glass façade. The impossibly sweet fishing village of Mousehole is another arty enclave, with numerous galleries, a scattering of good restaurants and a picture-perfect harbour.

Avoid the Land's End theme park like the plague – this brash development on the county's most remote headland can only ever seem lame when compared to the drama of the real end-of-the-world scenery, just yards away outside.

AMUSING THE KIDS

There can be few more memorable theatre trips for children (or adults, for that matter) than a performance at the open-air Minack Theatre (01736 810181, www.minack.com), carved out of a granite cliff above Porthcurno Beach, with the ocean as its backdrop. Performances take place from May to September, but even if you don't make it to a show you can visit the museum and tour the theatre during the day (although not during matinées).

CAMPING NEARBY

Treverven Touring Caravan & Camping Site (01736 810200, www.chycor.co.uk/camping/treverven, open Mar-Oct, £14 2 adults), a mile to the east, is another great site set just back from the coast path.

Namparra

Namparra Campsite
Kuggar, Helston, Cornwall TR12 7LY
01326 290040
bookings@namparracampsite.co.uk
www.namparracampsite.co.uk
Map p25 ❹
OS map SW724165

Number of pitches 48 tents, 8 caravans,
8 motorhomes.
Open Easter-Oct.
Booking By phone, email. Advisable;
essential July, Aug.
Typical cost £12-£15 2 adults & 3 children,
£2 extra adult, £1 extra child.
Facilities Chimeneas; electric hook-ups (9);
laundry facilities; shop; showers (free);
toilets; washing-up area.
Campfires Allowed.
Firewood available (£4.50).
Dogs Allowed.
Getting there By road Take the A3083
out of Helston, then turn on to the B3293
towards St Keverne. Take the right turn
signposted to Kennack Sands; the campsite
is on the left as you come into the village
of Kuggar. **By public transport** Train to
Redruth. Bus 34 runs every couple of hrs
to Kuggar (request stop) and takes about
1 hr 10 mins. More details on www.cornwall
publictransport.info.

Kynance Cove

CORNWALL

In the rush for posh fish and chips in Padstow, surf shacks in Newquay and gallery-hopping in St Ives, many visitors overlook Cornwall's most secluded corner. The Lizard Peninsula, the bulge of land south of Helford River (in fact, south of everywhere in Britain) is on the way to nowhere. It's miles from the nearest large town, barely served by public transport, almost completely surrounded by water and – for all these reasons – it is heaven for peace-seeking campers.

Set well back off an already sleepy road, this six-acre family-run campsite in the tiny village of Kuggar is an ideal base for exploring the exceptional beauty of the Lizard, whose coast is dotted with secret coves, deserted sandy stretches and melodramatic outcrops. A 20-minute saunter through fields and woodland from the campsite leads you to Blue Flag-awarded Kennack Sands, a splendid band of sand (cut in half at high tide) that is perfect for rock-pooling, family bathing and beginner waves. This is also where you can connect to a particularly soul-stirring portion of the South West Coast Path (bring walking boots).

Only a few years old, Namparra has the traditional campsite formula in place: one large lush field with sea views, a basic shower block, a small shop in a wooden hut (open till 6pm) and as much peace and quiet as you can handle.

Kuggar is a tiny community with a phone box, a pub and one little shop (on a holiday park) – and is located some 14 miles from Helston, the nearest large town. There is virtually no mobile phone reception, no supermarket or 24-hour petrol station and not a whole lot of people. Calm weather-permitting, you will doze off to the sound of the sea swell and wake to the sound of birds in the trees.

The site might be basic by some measures, but it scores highly on simple luxuries. The wide, numbered pitches are laid out on the edge of a large field (sea views from the top, more solitude

Helford River

at the bottom), with a huge area in the middle for games and campfires, and also granting rare privacy when you emerge blinking and mat-haired from your porch in the morning. The small toilet and shower cabin is kept scrupulously free of puddles, and it's hard to overstate the joy of a covered washing-up area with piping hot water in foul weather. Accommodating owners Andrew Winn and mother-and-daughter Jo and Laura Morris seem to manage to be there when you want them, and not when you don't.

On-site entertainment comes in the shape of Toggles and Cinnamon, the affectionate pygmy goats that roam the adjacent field, also home to a family of ducks who pose cutely for photos on an old surfboard floating in a pond.

EATING & DRINKING

The on-site shop is strictly essentials only – but it does serve hot drinks for under £1. The only pub within easy walking distance is the unpicturesque

Site specific

✔ You can rent Mexican-style clay chimeneas for £1 a night. These small, freestanding 'chimneys' give off a wonderful natural glow while chucking out plenty of heat. Campfires are allowed away from the pitches – speak to the owners about borrowing some bricks.

✘ There is only one shower per sex – though it is hot, powerful, clean and free.

Potter's Bar in Kuggar, which features occasional live music. Down the road at Kennack Sands, a tiny basic café overlooks the beach.

More characterful eating and drinking can be had a short drive away at the 300-year-old Cadgwith Cove Inn (01326 290513, www.cadgwithcoveinn.com), a wonderfully atmospheric traditional pub just off the beach serving good cask ales and locally hauled fish and seafood.

Esteemed ice-cream maker Roskilly's (01326 280479, www.roskillys.co.uk) runs a lovely café/restaurant on its 200-acre, organic Tregellast Barton Farm, five miles away in the pretty village of St Keverne. It's open every day until dusk in the summer (weekends only in winter) and, given the pedigree of the cows, it's hard to imagine a creamier cream tea.

For a more upmarket outing, consider the New Yard restaurant at Trelowarren (01326 221595, www.trelowarren.co.uk, closed Sun dinner), around five miles away on the Helston/St Keverne road. This contemporary-styled restaurant in an 18th-century carriage house is one of Cornwall's best, serving a seasonal modern menu with plenty of local fish from the Helford River and platters of Cornish cheeses.

ATTRACTIONS & ACTIVITIES

Within perfect reach for a light walking day trip is Cadgwith, a pretty fishing village that was once a smugglers' hideaway. You may be able to get your hands on some sparkling fresh fish when the boats come in (usually late afternoon). A longer hike will take you to blustery Lizard Point, where you can thrill at being the most southerly person in Britain.

But the undoubted jewel in the Lizard's crown is idyllic Kynance Cove on the eastern side of the headland. In the right light, its sea-green serpentine

Near Helford Point

cliffs, crags and stacks, turquoise waters and sugary sands bring to mind Bermuda or any number of treasure islands. The beach is only accessible via steep steps from the car park. A word of warning: if there is mild to moderate swell, and the tide is high, swimmers – particularly children – should beware. There is a small café here, but nothing else.

In the unlikely event that you tire of the sea, venture inland to Trevarno (01326 574274, www.trevarno.co.uk), about ten miles away just beyond Helston. This 13th-century estate has dreamy gardens and an incredibly diverse plant life. It also houses the National Museum of Gardening, a café and a shop selling Trevarno's organic skincare range.

AMUSING THE KIDS

Half an hour's drive away, north of Helston, Poldark Mine (01326 563166, www.poldark-mine.co.uk, closed Sat mid Apr-mid July, Sept, Oct, all Nov-mid Apr) offers one-hour guided tours, as well as activities for children such as candle dipping, ceramic painting and gold panning. Candle-lit ghost tours are also run on Tuesday and Thursday evenings.

East of Helston, by the Helford estuary, Gweek's Seal Sanctuary (0871 423 2110, www.sealsanctuary.co.uk, open all year) has rescued seals to coo over, as well as penguins, sea lions, otters and other creatures – check the website for daily feeding times.

CAMPING NEARBY

Neighbouring Chy Carne Holiday Park (01326 290200, www.camping-cornwall.com, open Apr-Sept, camping £4-£10.50 per pitch), also located in Kuggar village, is an altogether more modern set-up, with mobile homes and chalets available for hire, as well as a large field for camping and hook-ups.

Endearingly eccentric Henry's (01326 290596, www.henryscampsite.co.uk, open all year, £7-£9.60 per adult), the most southerly campsite in Britain, set in nearby Lizard village, has panoramic sea views, cider served by the jug, and pigs, ducks and guinea pigs roaming at will.

Little Treginges Caravan & Campsite (01326 280580, www.stkevernevillagecampsite.com, open all year, £10-£16 for two adults) in St Keverne has stunning views across to Falmouth Bay – and several decent pubs within easy reach.

Trevarno

CORNWALL

Gwithian Farm

Gwithian Farm Campsite
1 Church Town Road, Gwithian,
Hayle, Cornwall TR27 5BX
01736 753127
camping@gwithianfarm.co.uk
www.gwithianfarm.co.uk
Map p25 ❺
OS map SW586412

Number of pitches 60 tents,
40 caravans, 20 motorhomes.
Open Apr-Oct.
Booking By phone, email. Advisable;
essential July, Aug. Minimum stay
5 nights school holidays.
Typical cost £14-£27 2 people,
£5 extra adult, £2 extra child.
Facilities Disabled facilities (toilet and
shower); electric hook-ups (70); laundry
facilities; shop; showers (free); toilets;
washing-up area; Wi-Fi.
Campfires Not allowed.
Dogs Allowed, on lead (£1).
Restrictions No noise after 10.30pm.
Getting there By road Leave the A30 at
Hayle roundabout; take the exit towards
Hayle. At the next mini-roundabout, turn
right on to the B3301, signposted Portreath.
It's 2 miles to Gwithian; the campsite is
in the village on the left, opposite the Red
River Inn. **By public transport** The nearest
train station is 3 miles away in Hayle, on the
main line between Plymouth and Penzance.
Bus 501 (May-Oct) runs four times a day
and bus 515 three times a day, and take
20 mins to Gwithian. Details on 01637
871871, www.westerngreyhound.com.

Gently curving round the eastern reaches of
St Ives Bay, Gwithian Beach is an impressive
three-mile stretch of sand. It reaches from the
mouth of the Hayle estuary all the way around
the bay to Godrevy Head – an epic spot guarded
by the Godrevy Lighthouse, thought to have been
the inspiration for Virginia Woolf's novel *To the
Lighthouse*. A world away from the cuteness
and crowds of St Ives, it's an altogether more
elemental spot, with big open skies and sunsets,
and is pounded by some of Cornwall's most
consistent surf. Local families flock for
guaranteed sandcastle-building space.

Located in the middle of Gwithian village,
about half a mile across the grassy duneland
known as the Towans, the campsite itself paints
a bucolic picture. A thatched farmhouse, home
to friendly owners Clair and Mike Hancock and
family, greets guests at the entrance and the site
has views of the village church and the gentle
slopes of the surrounding countryside.

Despite boasting the kind of coastal setting
that leads many a campground to nonchalance,
Gwithian Farm shows extraordinary committment
to high standards – providing the sort of cut-
above facilities that usually involve braving a
large, expensive holiday park. Tent-side luxuries
include a state-of-the-art shower block with long
lines of powerful showers, toilets and sinks; free,
help-yourself ice-packs from the freezer room;
free phone-charging points; a plethora of child-
friendly features (kids' bathroom, pet guinea pigs
and goats, and picnic area); and extremely large
pitches with careful planting to optimise privacy.

The greatest luxury for light sleepers
may well be the owners' low tolerance for
disruptive campers – no noise is allowed after
10.30pm and no vehicular movement after 11pm

(late arrivals are asked to use the car park) –
making it an unusually restful spot.

With a reliable pub just across the road and
the beach a 15-minute walk away, this is the sort
of campsite that gives you very little reason to
leave the immediate vicinity. Planned daytrips
have been known to go out of the tent window
in another round of cards, an extended table
tennis session or a fresh fish barbie at sunset.

Understated in Gwithian Farm's literature,
the contents of the shop is the stuff of campers'
dreams: miniature bottles of Filippo Berio
olive oil, fresh local fish from the visiting
fishmonger's van; kids' wetsuits, cricket bats
and Frisbees, OS maps, a selection of national

newspapers... and just about anything else (within reason) your camping heart desires.

EATING & DRINKING

The campsite shop is well supplied with essentials, plus local strawberries and disposable barbecues. Hayle offers a couple of supermarkets and plenty of smaller shops. For high-quality local meat and veg, and artisan bread, visit Trevaskis Farm Shop (01209 713931, www.trevaskisfarm.co.uk), a couple of miles away on the other side of the A30.

Gwithian's pub, the Red River Inn (01736 753223, www.red-river-inn.com), is all of 40 yards from the site, and serves real ales and good renditions of pub classics. The village's hip hangout, the Sandsifter (01736 757809, www.sandsiftercornwall.com), is nestled in the sand dunes at the Godrevy end of the beach. It attracts locals year-round for tasty food (own-made burgers, ciabatta, pizza), a well-stocked bar, late licence, and DJs and music events in the summer.

The Sunset Surf Shop & Café (01736 752575, www.sunsetsurfshop.co.uk, closed Tue, Wed Nov-Easter), perched on the cliffs at Gwithian, lives up to its name, with views out to sea and to the Godrevy Lighthouse. A popular post-surf refill station (with

surf school attached), it's usually packed with wet-haired youngsters wolfing chunky burgers, spicy wedges and monster breakfasts.

For a last-day-of-the-holiday blow-out, book a table at St Ives' hottest eaterie, the Porthminster Café (01736 795352, www.porthminstercafe.co.uk), a gorgeous old white deco house bang on the sands at Porthminster Beach. The sun-kissed menu, slick service and lovely views make it one of Cornwall's best restaurants.

ATTRACTIONS & ACTIVITIES

Holidaying in Penwith, Cornwall's 'first and last' peninsula, is all about the coast. There's no shortage of spectacular clifftop walks within striking distance of the site; as throughout Cornwall, the South West Coast Path (www.southwestcoastpath.com) means you can pick up a walk at any point along the coast. Two routes are particularly recommended: from the campsite past Godrevy Lighthouse and around the headland to a series of dramatic coves (where a colony of grey seals is often visible); and the stunning three-hour stretch from St Ives to Zennor.

Novice surfers can learn the basics at the Gwithian Academy of Surfing (01736 757579, www.surf academy.co.uk), located next to the Sandsifter, and at the Sunset Surf Shop.

CORNWALL

Godrevy Lighthouse and the coast path.

At least one day should be reserved for a trip to Britain's most perfect seaside town, St Ives. Long a magnet for artists thanks to the bay's extraordinary light, the town still has a wonderfully exotic feel. With its boutique hotels, classy restaurants and Tate gallery offshoot (01736 796226, www.tate.org.uk/stives, closed Mon Nov-Feb), it is every inch the embodiment of Cornish chic. The Barbara Hepworth Museum & Sculpture Garden (where she lived and worked, and also owned by the Tate) is a particular delight. Note that in high season you'll be jostling

for space with hundreds of other enchanted holidaymakers. Ten miles away on the south coast is the magical castle of St Michael's Mount (01736 710507, www.stmichaelsmount.co.uk, closed Sat), located on a tidal island spectacularly placed at the edge of Mount's Bay across from Penzance.

AMUSING THE KIDS

With three miles of sand on your doorstep, and play areas, ping-pong tables and goats on the campsite, you have every chance of enjoying a whine-free holiday. But for a change of scene, try Paradise Park (01736 753365, www.paradisepark.org.uk), a tropical bird park in Hayle with parrots galore, plus the Jungle Barn indoor play area. Tate St Ives (01736 796226, www.tate.org.uk, closed Mon Nov-Feb) has a good, year-round programme of activities for children.

CAMPING NEARBY

Churchtown Farm Caravan & Camping Site (01736 753219, www.churchtownfarm.org.uk, open Apr-Oct, from £14 for 2 adults, 2 children) is a few hundred yards from Gwithian Beach. It has 100 pitches for tents, caravans and motorhomes, disabled facilities and a big shop, but is a bit soulless.

Site specific

✔ It's an easy 15-minute stroll across the dunes to Gwithian Beach, Cornwall's longest stretch of sand. Surfers of all types (board, kite, wind) congregate here, thanks to consistent, year-round breaks.

✘ The campsite is hugely popular: advance booking is essential in the height of summer, and recommended at all times.

Beacon Cottage Farm

Beacon Cottage Farm
Beacon Drive, St Agnes, Cornwall TR5 0NU
01872 552347
beaconcottagefarm@lineone.net
www.beaconcottagefarmholidays.co.uk
Map p25 **G**
OS map SW704503

Number of pitches 70 tents/caravans/motorhomes. 2 cottages (sleeping 4).
Open Camping Easter-Sept.
Cottages all year.
Booking By phone, email, post.
Typical cost Camping £15-£22 2 people, £4.50 extra adult. Cottage £300-£780 per week.
Facilities Electric hook-ups (42); laundry facilities; play area; showers (free); toilets; washing-up area.
Campfires Not allowed.
Dogs Allowed, on lead (£2).
Restrictions No single-sex groups.
Getting there By road From the A30 take the B3277 to St Agnes. At the mini-roundabout in the middle of the village, turn left (signposted Chapel Porth) and follow the brown tourism signs to Beacon Cottage Farm. **By public transport** Train to Truro, from where buses 85 and 85A (0871 200 2233, www.firstgroup.com) run once or twice an hour to St Agnes. It's about a mile on foot to the campsite. The bus ride takes about half an hour.

Cornwall is hardly short of campsites offering sea views, but this one takes the promise of panoramic vistas to the extreme. Perched on the lower slopes of the St Agnes Beacon (one of the highest points in west Cornwall) just yards from the cliffs, Beacon Cottage Farm has uninterrupted views across miles of dramatic Cornish coastline. Beyond the steep cliffs of Porthtowan and Portreath, you can make out the dark lump of Godrevy Head and as far south as St Ives, 22 miles away.

The fact that it happens to be a superbly run and blissfully uncommercialised site makes for an embarrassment of camping riches. This is a working beef and arable farm with around 80 cows and some 300 acres, and the cluster of the pretty farmhouse and outhouses form the hub of the campsite. Making a pleasant change from the usual modern blocks and Portakabins, the toilets, showers and laundry have been tastefully converted from the old stables.

Owner Jane Sawle oversees things with friendly efficiency, and Beacon Cottage Farm should satisfy the needs of the fussiest of campers. The toilets, showers and washing-up areas (all fully enclosed) are kept in excellent condition: spotless and with an endless supply of hot water, hand soap and toilet rolls. The nappy-changing facilities, private family bathroom (ask for the key) and play area attract families, and there's a well-equipped laundry room with coin-operated washing machines, an iron and ironing board.

The elevated position has its drawbacks. Mild winds can be thoroughly invigorating in a commune-with-nature sort of way. But in a storm or westerly winds you may find nature comes rather too close for comfort; then a sturdy tent and expert pegging are essential. The landscaped paddocks at the back of the site (book ahead) are more sheltered and also more intimate thanks to surrounding trees and hedges – perfect for a group of friends.

We've seen more spacious pitches, but given the respectful campers the site seems to attract, noise is unlikely to be a problem. Come the evening, most people choose to read, cook or even paint, leaving just the sound of the wind racing across the moor to sing you to sleep and the birds to wake you up.

EATING & DRINKING

The campsite shop – basically, reception – offers the bare necessities: newspapers, milk, eggs (some from the chickens pecking outside), camping gas and a freezer block service (20p each).

Chapel Porth, the nearest beach – 15 minutes on foot via the coastal footpath – has a tiny National Trust café serving tea, coffee, snacks (including a fine onion soup) and, most importantly, its famed hedgehog ice-cream cone. This is a fantastically calorific affair: Cornish vanilla ice-cream covered in a thick layer of clotted cream and then dipped in chopped roasted hazelnuts.

The large village of St Agnes, a mile and a half away, has plenty of restaurants and watering holes. The 17th-century Driftwood Spars (01872 552428, www.driftwoodspars.co.uk), a perennially popular inn next to Trevaunce Cove, is frequented by a lively mix of locals, surfers and holidaymakers. It is divided into the old pub, dispensing beers from its own micro-brewery, and a modern restaurant, serving cheerful sea-inspired dishes. There are two beer gardens, and bands on summer weekends. Right on the beach is bright and breezy Schooners

CORNWALL

Bistro (01872 553149), also majoring in fish. Grab a seat on the outdoor balcony for the best views.

Better still, make the short drive to bar/restaurant Blue (01209 890329, www.blue-bar.co.uk) in Porthtowan. Nestled in the dunes, it's that rare beast, a locals' hangout that is popular year round. Expect post-surf comfort food par excellence, in the shape of burgers, stone-baked pizzas, and fish goujons with chips. There are regular comedy and music nights too.

ATTRACTIONS & ACTIVITIES

The short scramble to the top of the 629-foot high Beacon at sunset is an essential outing; from its rocky summit, you get spectacular 360-degree views of the surrounding hills and coast, including the cliffside engine houses of the old Wheal Coates tin mine. Look back to the campsite and try to spot the dot your tent makes on the vast landscape.

When it comes to beaches, you are spoiled for choice along this stretch of the north coast, where a series of classics – Porthtowan, Chapel Porth, Perranporth and, further north, Newquay – are pounded by Atlantic swells and backed by towering cliffs. Chapel Porth is something of a hidden gem, completely undeveloped save for the tiny NT café. Low water opens up huge swathes of sand to the east and west, but be careful not to get cut off as the tide rises.

Unusually for Cornwall, there are no major gardens or country mansions within immediate striking distance, but a half-hour drive will take you to two National Trust properties. Head north to Kestle Mill, near Newquay, for the Elizabethan manor house of Trerice (01637 875404, closed Fri), or to the opposite coast, beyond Truro, to the wonderful estuary views of Trelissick Gardens (01872 862090). Details of both on www.nationaltrust.org.uk.

For boutique shopping, smart bars and cafés, Truro is well worth a wander, but for the thrills and spills of holiday culture, many bomb up the A30 to Newquay, 30 minutes away.

AMUSING THE KIDS

The combination of farm animals – cows, chickens and, if you're lucky, chicks – and a good play area with swings and a climbing frame provide on-site entertainment. Newquay specialises in rainy-day, boredom-busting options, including the Blue Reef Aquarium (01637 878134, www.bluereefaquarium.

Chapel Porth, the nearest beach.

co.uk), Newquay Zoo (01637 873342, www.newquay zoo.org.uk) and Dairyland Farm World (01872 510246, www.dairylandfarmworld.com). The latter, a working dairy farm, offers demonstrations in a new space-age milking parlour, an indoor fun centre called the Bull Pen, a soft-play area, playgrounds and climbing nets.

CAMPING NEARBY

There are two choices near St Agnes, both clean and scenic. Based on an organic farm, Presingoll Farm Caravan & Camping Park (Penwinnick Road, 01872 552333, www.presingollfarm.co.uk, open Mar-Sept) is a good family option; adults pay £6.50, kids £1.50. Blue Hills Touring Park (01872 552999, www.bluehills camping.co.uk, £4-£5 per pitch, £3-£4 adult, £1-£1.50 child), has just 30 pitches and is open all year.

Site specific

✔ Experience one of the best views in Cornwall. With the right pitch, more than 20 miles of coast stretches out in front of your tent porch.

✘ As with so many campsites with epic views, you will receive the full force of any blusterous weather thrown at you.

CORNWALL

Tregedna Farm

Tregedna Farm Campsite
Tregedna Farm, Maenporth,
Falmouth, Cornwall TR11 5HL
01326 250529
tregednafarm@btinternet.com
www.tregednafarmholidays.co.uk
Map p25 ❼
OS map SW786303

Number of pitches 40 tents/caravans/
motorhomes. Lodge (3 dorms sleeping
2, 6, 8; 2 rooms sleeping 4).
Open Camping Easter-end Sept.
Lodge all year.
Booking By phone, email.
Essential school holidays.
Typical cost Camping £7.50 adult,
£3.50 3-13s. Lodge £18-£20 per person
dorm, £45-£50 family room.
Facilities Electric hook-ups (12); laundry
facilities; play area; shop; showers (free);
toilets; washing-up area.
Campfires Not allowed.
Dogs Allowed, on lead.
Restrictions Groups by arrangement.
No noise after 11pm.
Getting there By road Take the A39 to
Falmouth. As you approach the town centre,
you find yourself on a dual carriageway
heading uphill; at Hillhead roundabout,
turn right. Go straight across the next two
mini-roundabouts and continue for about
2 miles. This is the Maenporth Beach
road and Tregedna Farm is signposted
on the right before you reach the beach.
By public transport From Falmouth Town
rail station, walk down to Cliff Road and
catch the 400 bus (0871 200 2233,
www.firstgroup.com). It runs every 2 hrs
daily to Maenporth Beach (journey 25 mins),
which is a short walk from the campsite.

Those sick of cramped pitches – pre-chosen for
you by the owners at the click of a mouse – will
rejoice on arrival at Tregedna, a farm campsite
in possession of a huge unmarked field and a
relaxed pitching policy. Although many campsites
boast of their luxury facilities, the thing that
campers really want is space. That's to say,
a healthy distance between your airbed and
next door's chairs; and out of earshot of the
screaming baby two pitches down and the guy
across the way barking into his BlackBerry.

Stripped bare, camping is about getting
away from it all, and in that area Tregedna Farm
excels. Though the site is just a 15-minute amble
along the farm's own pretty woodland path to
Maenporth Beach, and a few miles outside the
lively seaside town of Falmouth, it manages
to feel like the depths of the countryside,
surrounded by rolling hills, cornfields and thick
woodland. Run by the friendly Harris family, it's in
a tranquil setting that tends to attract a peaceful
crowd of campers, plus the odd campervan and
caravan in search of a hook-up. Dorm and family
rooms are available in the converted barn too.

Clustered around the pretty, flower-strewn
farmhouse, the facilities aren't particularly posh,
but they are clean, dry and fully functioning.
There's always plenty of toilet paper, hand soap
and hot water, and the showers are hot and
free. Sitting in the top corner of the large field,
the loos are a fair trot uphill for those on the
further-flung pitches – so it's a case of weighing
up the benefits of seclusion and the bane of a
midnight toilet trek.

With its hand-painted signs, untrimmed grass
(bring wellies) and old red phone box, there is
something endearingly old-school about Tregedna.
That it has old-school prices to match makes it
all the more of a camping catch.

EATING & DRINKING

The on-site shop (open only in the morning and
early evening) is small and limited to the essentials:
tea bags, milk, bread, eggs and a few tins. But there's
a village shop less than a mile away at Mawnan
Smith, and you're only a few miles from Falmouth,
a busy port town with all manner of shopping options,
including several supermarkets.

The campsite is a 15-minute walk from the Cove
bar/restaurant (01326 251136, www.thecove
maenporth.co.uk) at Maenporth, which, despite its
rather drab exterior, is a smart seafood restaurant

Site specific

✔ The amount of room is a bonus. The
camping field is huge, and you can all
but guarantee not just a space but loads
of space.

✘ It's a struggle to find a completely flat
pitch as the field slopes gently throughout.
Still, the gradient is perfectly workable
except in the upper reaches.

CORNWALL

The campsite (centre and top); Trebah Beach (top right); Maenporth Beach (bottom).

Trebah Garden

with sea views and terrace seating. There is also a friendly little café (01326 251209) next to the beach.

The Three Mackerel (01326 311886, www.thethree mackerel.com), with a dreamy location above the clear blue waters of Swanpool – the next beach along from Maenporth – and well-executed Mediterranean and Modern British cuisine, is one of the stars of the local dining scene. Head one more beach along towards Falmouth, to Gyllyngvase and the Gylly Café (01326 312884, www.gyllybeach.com), a hip bar/restaurant with a wraparound seaside terrace and good, fairly priced food for breakfast, lunch and dinner.

ATTRACTIONS & ACTIVITIES

Aside from messing about on the lovely beaches on its doorstep, or walking on the South West Coast Path (www.southwestcoastpath.com), Tregedna is well placed for more organised attractions.

The National Maritime Museum Cornwall (01326 313388, www.nmmc.co.uk) in Falmouth is a strong contender for the title of the county's best museum. Housed in a polished harbourside building, it's packed with interactive exhibits, historical displays and a collection of impeccably restored boats suspended from the ceiling in the main hall.

Two fine fortresses built by Henry VIII – Pendennis Castle (01326 316594) and St Mawes Castle (01326 270526, closed Sat Apr-Oct, Mon-Fri Nov-Mar) – guard the mouth of the Fal estuary. More information is available from www.english-heritage.org.uk. It's a 20-minute ferry ride to St Mawes from Falmouth.

A short drive south through a string of pretty villages brings you to the charming neighbouring gardens of Glendurgan (01326 250906, www.national trust.org.uk, closed Mon except Aug, and Sun, closed Nov-mid Feb) and Trebah (01326 252200, www. trebah-garden.co.uk), located on the north bank of the idyllic Helford River. These two lush gardens both have a distinctly exotic feel, Glendurgan with its tall swaying palms, tree ferns and confusing laurel maze, and Trebah with its bamboo walk and giant, canopy-forming *Gunnera tinctoria* (aka giant rhubarb). Paths wind down the steep valley all the way to the river at the bottom; both have little sandy beaches.

AMUSING THE KIDS

There are two swings and a see-saw by the farmhouse, and buckets of room in the field to play ball games or tear around. In addition, the two beaches within immediate striking distance – Maenporth and Swanpool – have to be some of Cornwall's most child-friendly. Here, the sea is usually calm, shallow and swimmable, unlike at many beaches on the north coast. There are also lively rock pools, so bring some fishing nets. Both beaches have public toilets and car parks.

CAMPING NEARBY

Less than a mile away, Pennance Mill Farm Chalet & Camping Park (01326 317431, www.pennancemill. co.uk, open Mar-Oct, £6-£7 adult, £3-£3.50 child) has 70 pitches, a shop, and a meadow with swings.

Treloan

Treloan Coastal Holidays
Treloan Lane, Gerrans, near Portscatho,
Roseland Peninsula, Cornwall TR2 5EF
01872 580989
enquiries@coastalfarmholidays.co.uk
www.coastalfarmholidays.co.uk
Map p25 ❽
OS map SW873336

Number of pitches 65 tents/caravans.
1 snug (sleeps 2). 1 yurt (sleeps 3).
Open All year. Yurt Apr-Sept.
Booking By phone, email, online, post.
Advisable.
Typical cost Camping £13.50-£21.50
2 people. £4.50 extra adult, £3.50 extra
child. Snug £35-£50. Yurt £45-£55.
Facilities Electric hook-ups (65);
laundry facilities; showers (free);
toilets; washing-up area.
Campfires Allowed, in rented braziers
(£5, including firewood).
Dogs Allowed, on lead (£1).
Getting there By road Take the A3078
toward St Mawes. At Trewithian, turn off
towards Portscatho and Gerrans (there's a
large brown sign for Treloan Coastal Farm).
At Gerrans church and the Royal Standard
Inn, take Treloan Lane; the campsite is 300
yds down the lane, on the left. **By public
transport** Train to Truro. Bus 50 (www.first
group.com) runs every couple of hours and
takes 40 mins to Gerrans church, from
where the campsite is a few minutes' walk.
Details on www.cornwallpublictransport.info.

The surf lessons, blustery cliffs and stag-do
image of holidays in Cornwall may dominate the
headlines, but the area around the Roseland
Peninsula is another world – quietly beautiful,
wildly romantic and largely untouched. The
merging of river estuaries, protected from the
relentless Atlantic swell by the vast granite bulk
of the Lizard Peninsula, has created a magical
landscape: silent wooded creeks, secluded
beaches and rolling hills that drop gently into
the sea. At their very brink is Treloan's campsite
– just a field's breadth away from the open sea.

It's hard to put your finger on exactly what
makes this such a special site. It could be the
verdant, springy grass, the quiet, untroubled
atmosphere or, most probably, the 180-degree
sea views from your tent door. The pitches are

generous and there are no real duds: the whole
field slopes ever so slightly seawards, but not
enough to cause any significant rolling issues. All
the pitches have sea views, save perhaps those
up against the hedge at the bottom. Visitors
preferring protection from something firmer than
canvas can rent one of the mobile homes at the
top of the field, which have the best views of all.

Alternatively, there are two new accommodation
options: a cosy 12-foot yurt, equipped with
futon and pot-bellied stove, and the 'honeycomb
snug' – a tiny wooden house (also with its own
stove) that will make adults feel like kids again.

Owners Debbie and Peter Walker, who took
over Treloan in 2008, don't believe in erecting
signs all over the site telling people what they
can and can't do. Their trusting approach seems
to have paid off, with the site attracting a very
considerate bunch; campers seem more
interested in taking walks, strolling to the beach,
and enjoying a quiet beer than having raucous
late nights. You can hire braziers, and campfires
are allowed in the communal fire pit.

The toilet and shower cabin is built in a rustic
style – hardly state-of-the-art, but adequate
enough. Hot water is plentiful in all the sinks,
including those in the covered (but not enclosed)
washing-up area, which gently encourages
recycling with Yeats' famous line calling for
us to 'tread softly…' inscribed on the floor.

In the end, though, such practicalities tend to
pale into insignificance when measured against
the outstanding beauty of the area. Not only
are the raw materials exquisite – clear-watered
coves, soft sandy beaches and undulating fields
– but even the man-made additions are beautiful.
The nearby village of Portscatho paints an idyllic
scene, with its white cottages, miniature harbour
and traditional pubs – all amounting to a powerful
natural tranquiliser for stressed souls.

EATING & DRINKING

Although there is no shop on the campsite, it's an
easy ten-minute walk along an exquisite stretch of

Site specific

✔ The warm welcome – Debbie and Peter
run the site with unfailing friendliness.

✘ The Roseland Peninsula is remote and
not well placed as a base for a whistle-stop
tour of Cornwall.

CORNWALL

the coast path to Ralph's (01872 580702) in Portscatho. An excellent general store and deli, it sells a wide range of groceries, fruit and veg, newspapers, pastries, bread, freshly caught fish and local ale, and opens 7am to 10pm seven days a week July-Sept; it also has a cash machine.

Portscatho's best pub, the popular Plume of Feathers (01872 580321), is a fine, traditional affair – whitewashed on the outside and cosy on the inside, with Cornish ale on tap. Good, low-key food (burgers, sarnies, ham, eggs and chips) is served at lunch and dinner. Opposite the pub, the Boathouse (01872 580326, www.theboathouserestaurant.co.uk, closed Mon, all Nov-Easter) is a charming restaurant that serves cream teas, crab sandwiches, scampi and café classics during the day, and more substantial but

equally unpretentious fare in the evening. For fine dining, the best restaurant on the peninsula, and indeed one of the best in Cornwall, is at the Hotel Tresanton (01326 270055, www.tresanton.com) in St Mawes, some six miles away – a supremely elegant affair that is perfect for a blow-out.

ATTRACTIONS & ACTIVITIES

Treloan is superbly placed for basking on the beach and for walking; the many nearby beaches are quiet and undeveloped, and the South West Coast Path (www.southwestcoastpath.com), just yards from the site, is perfect for gentle rambles.

One of the delights of the Roseland is that it's easier, and quicker, to get around by boat than by road. Ferries ply the Carrick Roads waterway between

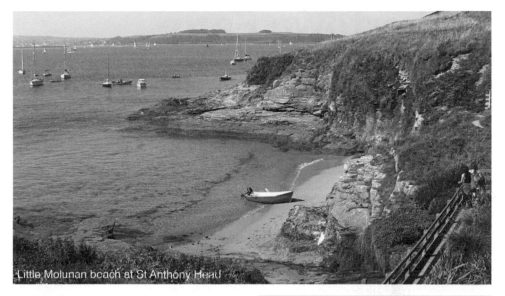
Little Molunan beach at St Anthony Head

the peninsula, Falmouth and Truro: it's ten minutes from Place Creek (on the opposite side of the peninsula to Treloan) to St Mawes (service Easter-Oct) and 20 minutes from St Mawes to Falmouth (service year-round). In Falmouth, you can visit the National Maritime Museum Cornwall, explore the 16th-century keep, secret tunnels and World War I guardhouse at Pendennis Castle (for both, *see p52*) or simply browse the shops.

For a fine example of a grand Cornish garden, hop on the King Harry Ferry from St Mawes to Trelissick Garden (01872 862090, www.nationaltrust.org.uk), across the river in Feock, planted with magnificent azaleas, rhododendrons, magnolias and palms.

Towan beach

AMUSING THE KIDS

Families are welcomed wholeheartedly at Treloan, and the bottom field (with the firepit) provides entertainment by way of chickens, rabbits and two handsome pigs, as well as a huge open space to let off steam away from the tents. If you're lucky, the owner Debbie will be running one of her games or campfires for little ones – and she often rounds up the kids to help her feed the animals.

The nearby beaches and coves tend to be much gentler and more manageable for children than those on Cornwall's north coast. The area is fairly undeveloped, so you won't find any theme parks, amusement arcades or water parks within easy reach.

CAMPING NEARBY

Trethem Mill (01872 580504, www.trethem.com, open Apr-early Oct, £17-£25 for two people) in St-Just-in-Roseland, a mile or so away, is an upmarket touring park with plenty of space and posh landscaping between the pitches.

Highertown Farm

Highertown Farm Campsite
Lansallos, Looe, Cornwall PL13 2PX
01208 265211
highertownfarmcampsite@nationaltrust.org.uk
www.nationaltrust.org.uk
Map p25 ❾
OS map SX173517

Number of pitches 16 tents, 3 caravans/
motorhomes (size restrictions apply).
Open Easter-late Oct.
Booking By phone, email. Advisable;
essential school holidays.
Typical cost £4-£5 adult, £2-£2.50 2-12s.
Facilities Disabled facilities (toilet and
shower); laundry facilities; showers (40p);
toilets (flush and composting); washing-up
area (hot water 20p).
Campfires Not allowed.
Dogs Allowed, on lead.
Restrictions No unsupervised under-21s,
no organised groups July-Sept. No noise
after 11pm.
Getting there By road From the A390
(Liskeard to St Austell road), take the
B3359 near East Taphouse. After about
5 miles, turn right for Lansallos. Continue
for about 3 miles; the campsite is in the
village immediately above the church.
By public transport Train to Looe, then
Polruan bus 281 to Lansallos church
(Mon-Fri, 08712 002233, journey 30 mins).

Camping is already a low-impact form of tourism,
provided you leave no trace, but at Highertown
Farm – a working farm in the tiny hamlet of
Lansallos, half a mile from the romantic south-
east coast of Cornwall – you could easily
reduce your footprint to a mere toeprint. By not
providing energy-guzzling luxuries (hairdryers,
tumble-dryers, endless hot water), the aim is
to keep the site simple, green and quiet, and
to minimise its environmental impact. As a result,
the facilities are basic, but by design rather than
neglect. As you might expect of a National Trust-
run site, the grounds are impeccably maintained,
the signage attractive and the facilities housed
in a smart, pine-panelled extension to the
handsome granite barn.

Posters on water consumption and solar power
hint at the site's gently green agenda, but visitors
suffer no great hardship. Solar-heated water is
available in the showers and washing-up tap at
20p a go (bring some coins – there is no source
of change in the village), and although you're
encouraged to use the two compost toilets
(surprisingly smart and unsmelly), the fully
flushing variety is available for doubters.
Organic food waste is welcomed in the
communal compost pot, recycling is made
easy and there are no electrical hook-ups.
Payment for extras such as freezer blocks
and the washing machine is left in the honesty
box at the entrance.

The campsite comprises just one lush field,
in the shadow of an old granite church tower,
with views across peaceful fields full of grazing
cattle. Those prone to lamenting blemishes
on this green and pleasant land will be in their
element in this untouched and quintessentially
English country setting.

A 15-minute walk across tranquil woodland
(uphill on the way back), and through an opening
in the rock – part of a track cut long ago, to haul
produce and smuggled goods into the village
by cart – leads to Lansallos Cove, a secluded
sand and shingle beach. It isn't the sort of beach
you'll find in seaside guides; the nick in the cliff
doesn't look like much on the OS map, and you'd
barely know it was there unless you glimpsed
its clear waters from the coastal footpath. On
a still, sunny day, the scene seems too serene
to be true: sheltered on both sides by stacks
of rocks, the sparkling waters resemble a huge
natural swimming pool. There are no facilities
whatsoever, and the only approach is on foot –
two facts that will hopefully ensure a quiet future
for this idyllic corner of Cornwall.

EATING & DRINKING

Part of Highertown Farm's charm lies in its out-of-
the-way feel and the tranquillity of the hamlet in
which it is located – but this does mean there is no
shop in the vicinity, and no food supplies of any sort
for several miles. The nearest grocer is in Pelynt,
three miles away, and you'll need to travel east to

Site specific

✔ The setting in a tiny hamlet, next to a
grand old country church – and the feeling
of having stepped back into simpler times.

✘ The nearest shops, pubs and restaurants
are several miles away, and the village of
Lansallos itself is spectacularly quiet.

CORNWALL

Polruan

CORNWALL

Looe, west to Fowey or north to Lostwithiel for a choice of shops. In terms of pubs, none is within easy walking distance. Bodinnick has the riverside Old Ferry Inn (01726 870237, www.oldferryinn.co.uk), Polperro the quayside Blue Peter Inn (01503 272743, www.thebluepeter.co.uk), and Polruan the cosy Russell Inn (01726 870292, www.russellinn.co.uk); all three are appealingly traditional affairs.

There is no nearby restaurant, so think about packing a decent camping kitchen and taking packed lunches for walks. By car, though, you can cross the estuary to Fowey, one of Cornwall's dining hubs, without too much ado (there's a car ferry from Bodinnick and foot ferries from Polruan). Restaurant Nathan Outlaw (01208 862737, www.nathan-outlaw. com, open dinner Tue-Sat), run by the Michelin-starred chef of the same name, is on the waterfront, The menu is seasonal, and might include the satisfying likes of lobster and porthilly sauce or wreckfish with saffron, mussels, peppers and olives.

Alternatively, the Old Quay House (01726 833302, www.theoldquayhouse.com, closed lunch mid Oct-mid Mar) has an uninterrupted view across the estuary. Book a table on the terrace and feast on Fowey River oysters and local pollock.

ATTRACTIONS & ACTIVITIES

The site is half a mile from a particularly unspoilt portion of the South West Coast Path (www.south westcoastpath.com). Just under an hour's walk away is Lantic Bay, with its exotic-looking beaches and yachts bobbing on the clear waters; pack some food, as there is nothing en route. Further west along the coast is the fishing village of Polruan,

which has perfect views of the pastel-painted townhouses of Fowey across the estuary.

Close to the small estuary town of Lostwithiel, a half-hour drive away, Restormel Castle (01208 872687, www.english-heritage.org.uk, closed Nov-Easter) and Lanhydrock (01208 265950, www.nationaltrust.org.uk, closed Mon Nov-mid Mar) are two of Cornwall's most impressive historic sights. The former is a circular Norman keep – probably the best-preserved in the country – and the latter a preposterously good-looking Victorian pile, which opens 50 of its rooms to visitors and is surrounded by glorious formal gardens.

AMUSING THE KIDS

There is no dedicated kids' playground at the campsite, just good old-fashioned green space. Note that access to Lansallos Cove – and Little and Great Lantic Beaches, further west – is via a footpath that is unsuitable for prams.

Older children will enjoy Restormel Castle: the shop sells toy swords and chain mail vests for re-enactment fun – and the commanding views and lawns make it perfect for a picnic. Fail-safe animal magic is provided by the Monkey Sanctuary (01503 262532, www. monkeysanctuary.org, closed Fri, Sat, closed Oct-Easter) in Looe, whose residents include woolly monkeys, capuchins and Barbary macaques.

CAMPING NEARBY

Polruan Holiday Centre (01726 870263, www.polruan holidays.co.uk, open Easter-Oct) is a well-kept camping and caravanning site a few miles west along the coast in Polruan. A tent pitch (all have sea views) costs from £7, adults from £3, children from £1.50.

Cornish Tipi

Cornish Tipi Holidays
Tregeare, Pendoggett,
St Kew, Cornwall PL30 3LW
01208 880781
info@cornishtipiholidays.co.uk
www.cornishtipiholidays.co.uk
Map p25 ⑩
OS map SX037799

Number of pitches 40 tipis.
Open Apr-Oct.
Booking By phone, email, post. Essential. Minimum stay 1 night; longer mid July-mid Aug.
Typical cost 3 nights medium tipi £275-£375, large tipi £325-£425, extra-large tipi £375-£475. 1 week medium tipi £375-£495, large tipi £435-£555, extra-large tipi £625-£745. Plus headage £50 per person (over-4s). Private site premium £20-£70.
Facilities Showers (free); toilets; washing-up area.
Campfires Allowed.
Firewood available (free).
Dogs Not allowed.
Restrictions Single-sex groups and unsupervised under-18s by arrangement.
Getting there By road Take the A39 towards Camelford. Just north of Camelford, turn on to the B3314 and go through the village of Delabole. After a couple of miles, turn left at the Port Gaverne crossroads towards St Teath and follow the main road around to the right, over an old railway bridge. Take the first right just before Normansland Cottage and follow the grassy track to the site. For sat-nav users, the site's postcode is PL30 3HZ. **By public transport** There's no direct public transport. The nearest train station is Bodmin Parkway, 16 miles away. From there, a taxi will cost about £33 (Parnells Taxis, 01208 78788, www.parnellstaxis.co.uk).

With 40 tipis set discreetly amid 16 acres of wooded valley surrounding a lake in what was once Treglldrans Quarry, Cornish Tipi offers a different kind of camping experience. Winding tracks lead through a natural environment of diverse micro-habitats: there's marsh, meadow, woodland, rocky outcrop, scrub and the long, narrow, crystal-clear lake, where you can swim, fish or go boating (kayaks and lifejackets are provided). Oak, ash, sycamore, elder, hazel, willow and hawthorn trees thrive alongside an array of flowering plants, including bluebells, orchids and foxgloves; 57 species of bird, among them barn owls and peregrine falcons, have been spotted; rabbits, dragonflies and frogs are among the wildlife that make the valley their home.

Combine this with the physical pleasures of chopping your own logs and cooking fresh local ingredients on an open fire – you can catch trout in the lake or buy the day's catch in nearby Port Isaac – and you may feel you're having a Ray Mears moment, albeit one where flushing toilets and hot showers are never more than a short stroll away.

The valley is a few minutes' drive inland from some of north Cornwall's most beautiful coastline and charming villages such as Port Isaac and Port Gaverne. Wadebridge, ten miles away, is the nearest town.

The site is cleverly laid out to offer the perfect pitch for everyone. Paths lead off into secluded areas with single or double tipis for couples,

however, not a hotel under canvas: you'll need to bring your own mattresses and bedding. Include a torch too as there's no on-site electricity.

Cooking on a fire with logs you've chopped yourself is a big part of the experience. A stout pair of shoes are handy when you're wielding the axe – if you value your toes. For those times when you don't want to get the fire going, gas cookers are provided inside the tipis.

Note that in addition to the tipi fee, you pay £50 'headage' per person on week-long bookings, so costs can mount up. Short breaks aren't usually allowed in high season, but it's worth checking in case of cancellations.

EATING & DRINKING

In St Kew, a couple of miles from the campsite, great Cornish pasties are available from local maker Aunt Avice (01208 841895). The St Kew Inn (01208 841259, www.stkewinn.co.uk), run by acclaimed chef Paul Ripley, has a lovely garden and serves St Austell Brewery's beers straight from wooden barrels behind the bar.

Dennis Knight Fish Merchant in Port Isaac (Fore Street, 01208 880498, closed Sun) stocks an excellent range of fresh fish. The village has several good restaurants and pubs: the Old School Hotel & Restaurant, also in Fore Street, (01208 880721, www.theoldschoolhotel.co.uk) offers simple, stylish food (crab salad, fish pie, risotto), while the Blue Tomato café (01208 880090) on New Road has great clifftop sea views and is handy for a pint and casual snacking. There's also a small Co-op, but you'll need to head to Wadebridge for a big supermarket.

Further north, the Mill House Inn (01840 770200, www.themillhouseinn.co.uk) in Trebarwith serves imaginative dishes using locally sourced ingredients.

It's a 13-mile drive south to Padstow (aka 'Padstein'), home of Rick Stein's empire, including his popular Seafood Restaurant (01841 532700, www.rickstein.co/the-seafood-restaurant.html) and cheaper Stein's Fish & Chips (takeaways available).

families or small groups, all spaced for adequate privacy; noise levels are not intrusive. (You do pay a premium for these outside the low season.) Communal 'village fields' provide groups of tipis of varying sizes for larger parties. There are toilets and showers at either end of the site, plus more showers near the warden's cottage. New in 2011 is 'wild' camping for tents and small campervans (£35 for two people).

The Native American-style tipis come in three sizes: medium (sleeps two, or three if one is a young child), large (up to six) and extra-large (nine, or up to 12 if some are young children). Inside, there's plenty of space and each is equipped with almost everything you'll need, including groundsheet and rugs, gas lamps, matches, a cool box, kettle, coffee pot, saucepans, cutlery and crockery. It is camping,

Site specific

✔ You can really get back to nature here with foraging, fishing and fire. Forget the supermarket and find your supper on site: several edible plants grow wild, including peppermint, garlic, sorrel and carrots – bring a book on foraging to avoid poisoning yourself – and the lake is stocked with rainbow trout (the owners leave a fishing rod beside the lake).

✘ Considering the cost, it wouldn't be unreasonable to expect a few sheepskins or even inflatable mattresses to save the hassle of providing your own beds.

For restaurant eating, you'll need to a reservation – most places get very busy in peak season and renowned restaurants are booked weeks in advance.

ATTRACTIONS & ACTIVITIES

The picture-perfect fishing villages of Port Isaac and Port Gaverne, with their whitewashed 18th and 19th-century cottages, have been the setting for various TV programmes – *Poldark* in the 1970s and, more recently, *Doc Martin*. Port Gaverne has the nearest (safe) swimming beach to the site. A few miles further west, Polzeath beach is a favourite with surfers and body boarders, while Daymer Bay is a windsurfing, sailing and water-skiing destination, with a superb flat sandy beach for sunbathers.

Rock (nicknamed Chelsea-by-the-Sea for its popularity with wealthy London visitors) faces Padstow across the Camel Estuary; a foot ferry links the two. Both places are quieter and more charming out of high season.

If you're interested in Cornwall's past (real or fictional), there's no more iconic a place to visit than Tintagel (01840 770328, www.english-heritage. org.uk/tintagel, check website for opeing times), about nine miles away. The 13th-century castle, now in ruins, was supposedly once the stronghold of King Arthur. There is no disputing that the location is awe-inspiring, with dramatic rocky cliffs, smugglers' caves and breathtaking views over the Atlantic.

Head to almost any nearby section of the coast for a walk to remember (visit www.southwest coastalpath.co.uk for information).

AMUSING THE KIDS

At Wadebridge you can join the 17-mile Camel Trail, a flat and easy bike route along an old railway line; the five-mile stretch to Padstow, running next to the Camel Estuary, is particularly scenic. There are plenty of places to hire bikes.

The Eden Project (01726 811911, www.eden project.com) is a 23-mile drive south, at St Austell. The world-famous 'bubble-wrap' domes of the Rainforest and Mediterranean biomes house a world of natural wonders, while the Core is home to Eden's inspirational Educational Centre.

CAMPING NEARBY

The nearest alternative tipi site is Mill Valley Tipis & Yurts near Wadebridge (01208 841163, www.millvalley.co.uk, open all year). Yurts and tipis (the latter available May-Sept only) cost from £25 per person.

CORNWALL

Port Isaac; and (bottom left) Merlin's Cave at Tintagel.

South Penquite Farm

South Penquite Farm
Blisland, Bodmin, Cornwall PL30 4LH
01208 850491
thefarm@bodminmoor.co.uk
www.southpenquite.co.uk
Map p25 ①
OS map SX104752

Number of pitches 40 tents/motorhomes.
No caravans. 4 yurts (sleeping 2, 4, 6).
Open May-Oct.
Booking By post, online. Advisable;
essential school holidays, and for yurts.
Minimum stay in yurt 3 nights weekend,
1 week school holidays.
Typical cost Camping £14 2 people,
£7 extra adult, £3.50 extra child.
Yurt 1 week small £220-£290, medium
£270-£340, family £290-£360. Half-price
for 3-night stays.
Facilities Disabled facilities (toilet and
shower); laundry facilities; play area;
showers (free); toilets; washing-up area.
Campfires Allowed.
Firewood available (£4.50).
Dogs Not allowed.
Getting there By road Take the A30
(Launceston to Bodmin road). About 14
miles south of Launceston, take the first
right signed to St Breward. Continue for
about 3 miles until you see the signpost
for South Penquite on your right. **By public
transport** The nearest train station is
Bodmin Parkway, 9 miles away. No buses
go nearby, so you'll have to get a taxi
(Parnells Taxis, 01208 78788,
www.parnellstaxis.co.uk, about £20).

On this busy island, we are rather short on
places where you can truly get away from it all –
'it' being buildings, people, noise, traffic, mown
lawns and other such trappings of modern life.
But Bodmin Moor, in Cornwall's eastern reaches,
is one such wilderness. It might not be as big
or as awesome as Dartmoor, but it has ample
drama in its relatively small scope to stir even
the most jaded of travellers: surreal granite tors,
wild moorland and rugged pastures.

There is no better way to experience the
primitive beauty of the moor than under canvas
– waking up to birdsong, hiking during the day
and building a campfire in the evening to fend
off the fast-falling temperatures.

South Penquite is a Soil Association-certified
organic farm, set amid open moorland, whose
friendly owners have set aside two grassy fields
for camping. In keeping with the untamed setting,
the pitching policy is unregimented, with no
landscaped partitions, numbered pitches or
tarmac. Book ahead in high season; to those
turned away in summer months, the campsite
might look half empty, or at the very least big
enough for 'just one more', but the owners
have worked out a comfortable maximum and,
admirably, they stick to it.

In contrast to the unruly surrounding scenery,
South Penquite's facilities are the height of
camping chic. The verandah-wrapped pine
shower block is heated by solar power, and the
enormous shower cubicles are in a league of their
own. Not only does each cubicle have a dry area
in which to get dressed (no more hopping on one
foot to avoid dipping your socks in puddles), but
there is also a chair, hooks and even phosphate-
free shower gel, provided free of charge. The
toilets are equally resplendent, with gleaming
white circular sinks and pine-clad walls and
floors. In both blocks, multicoloured sheets of
compressed plastic bottles and yoghurt pots have
been used instead of tiling, to striking effect.

Once out of your smart shower, though,
you'll need wellies and/or a good eye for turkey
droppings. One of the great pleasures of South
Penquite is the opportunity to stay on a working
farm, with real-life mud and a variety of poultry
pottering about the grounds, including chickens,
turkeys, geese and ducks.

There are no electric hook-ups, but you can
rent a locker with a power point in the utility room.
Those wanting more head room and some basic
home comforts can hire one of the four cosy
Mongolian yurts in the bottom field, furnished
with wood-burning stoves, lamps, sofas, cookers,
and with a table and chairs outside.

As if South Penquite didn't already have enough
unique selling points – wilderness setting, super-

Site specific

✔ The dramatic moor location and away-
from-it-all feel (though it's just a short drive
off the A30 trunk road).

✗ This superb site is hard to fault. Splitting
hairs, we wish the toilets were a bit closer
to the showers.

spacious camping, fantastic facilities, organic farm status – it is also one of the few sites that allows its guests to build campfires. Gathering around a flickering fire, under a vast, open sky, is the perfect end to a day on Bodmin Moor.

EATING & DRINKING

South Penquite sells its own-produced lamb burgers and sausages, and there is a well-stocked village shop (01208 851730) in nearby Blisland, which has strong links to local producers. The nearest supermarkets are in Bodmin, 15 minutes by car.

Self-evidently, Bodmin Moor isn't about wining or dining, but, thanks to the much-loved Blisland Inn (01208 850739), real ale lovers should be deliriously happy. This pretty, old-time pub on Blisland's village green is lauded by CAMRA and draws real ale buffs from miles around for its choice of draught beers. Pub food is served, with mains such as steak in a bap and the 'beast' burger all keeping close to the £5 mark. Also within a few miles is the cosy Old Inn (01208 850711, www.theoldinnandrestaurant.co.uk) at St Breward, whose restaurant is renowned for its vast specials board.

ATTRACTIONS & ACTIVITIES

Bodmin Moor isn't as big as it feels, but offers plenty of space for hiking, biking and generally getting away from vehicles. There is a surprisingly extensive farm trail within South Penquite's farmland, which wends along a river valley and past a large standing stone and Bronze Age hut circle. For a day's walk, consider tackling the twin peaks of Bodmin Moor: Rough Tor and Brown Willy. From the top of Brown Willy, Cornwall's highest point at 1,378 feet, you can see for miles around. The intriguingly named Cheesewring is a bizarre pile of weather-warped granite slabs, set high on a hill a mile from the campsite.

Given Bodmin Moor's remote feel, high on the granite spine of Cornwall, one would expect to be more isolated. In fact, it is deceptively well connected to the west thanks to the A30, which runs through the middle of the moor. As a result, you'll find numerous attractions within a 45-minute drive. Just south of Bodmin, National Trust-run Lanhydrock (*see p57*) is a vast Victorian house and estate with lovely gardens. The ruins of Tintagel Castle (01840 770328, www.english-heritage.org.uk), King Arthur's mythical birthplace, are spectacularly sited on the cliffs of the north coast, while Padstow is famed for its restaurants. On the other side of the peninsula, the mighty space-age domes of the (very popular) Eden Project (01726 811911, www.edenproject.com) are a riot of exotic greenery.

AMUSING THE KIDS

With a menagerie of wild poultry pecking around the grounds, not to mention the 200 ewes and 20 cows in the nearby fields, and the sweet working collies, South Penquite is much more exciting than a zoo – there are no closing times, and a lot more space. Signs ask parents not to allow their offspring to chase the poultry, but otherwise there are countless opportunities to get close to the animals – often right outside your tent. In addition, there is a playing field with goalposts and two swings, made from reclaimed telegraph poles. Older kids may be more interested in the table football and pool table in the small lounge.

CAMPING NEARBY

Bodmin Moor is a carefully protected Area of Outstanding Natural Beauty, so campsites are few and far between. On the northern edge of the moor, Belle Tents (01840 261556, www.belletentscamping.co.uk, open end Apr-end Sept) offers a handful of fully furnished, candy-striped bell tents. Rates start at £75 a night for two people, minimum stay two nights.

Ruthern Valley (01208 831395, www.self-catering-ruthern.co.uk, open Apr-Oct, tent/caravan pitch from £12.50 for two people), on the other side of Bodmin, is a small and pretty site, set in a valley. It also has wooden wigwams and huts, available all year round.

Runnage Farm

Runnage Farm
Postbridge, Dartmoor,
South Devon PL20 6TN
01822 880222
runnagecampingbarns@tiscali.co.uk
www.runnagecampingbarns.co.uk
Map p25 ⑫
OS map SX668784

Number of pitches Approx 40 tents/
motorhomes. No caravans. 2 camping
barns (sleeping 15). Bunk barn (sleeps 12).
Open All year (weather permitting in winter
for camping).
Booking By email, phone, post.
Minimum stay 2 nights weekends.
Typical cost Tent/motorhome £5 adult,
£3.50 children. Camping barn £85-£95.
Bunk barn £130.
Facilities Showers (free); toilets;
washing-up area.
Campfires Allowed, in firepits.
Firewood available (£4).
Dogs Allowed, on lead (£2).
Restrictions Single-sex groups by
arrangement. No unsupervised under-18s.
Getting there By road Take the B3212 from
Moretonhampstead towards Postbridge.
After about 7 miles, you'll pass the Warren
House Inn; continue for another 1.5 miles,
then take a sharp left turn (signposted
Widecombe). It's about a mile to the farm,
which is on the left. **By public transport**
Train to Exeter or Plymouth. Transmoor
Link bus 82 runs between the two cities
on Sun (June-mid Sept) and takes 65-85
mins to reach Postbridge. On Sat (June-Oct),
you'll have to catch a connecting bus
to Moretonhampstead (from Exeter) or
Yelverton (from Plymouth) to pick up the 82.
No service in the week. See www.dartmoor-
npa.gov.uk for details.

Driving at dusk into the heart of Dartmoor
National Park, to the one-horse village of
Postbridge, beware sheep snoozing in the
road and foals skittering out of the shadows.
Just outside the village, facing pine forests
and surrounded by lichen-encrusted dry-stone
walls, Runnage Farm spreads over 220 acres,
and has been farmed by the same family for
five generations. Philip and Christine Coaker
are tenants of the Duchy of Cornwall and the

conversion of the old horse stables and granary
into camping barns enables the family to
preserve their farming heritage.

Camping is in two meadows, separated by a
large patch of rushes. The far meadow, perfectly
manicured by Dartmoor ponies, is reserved for
families and small groups, while larger groups of
Scouts and Duke of Edinburgh Awarders get to
hare around in the near meadow, which is split by
a small stream and a boggy pond at the bottom
end. Tents are always well spaced, and rules
are few – the whole atmosphere is refreshingly
friendly and laid-back. There are overspill fields
for especially large gatherings, a nursery field for
hand-reared calves and lambs, sheep roaming
the meadows and round-bellied cows looking over
fences into the main farmyard. Bleary campers
criss-crossing the yard in the morning to and
from the basic communal showers should keep
an eye out for tractors and muddy quad-bikes:
this is a working farm (and children must be
accompanied by an adult at all times).

The raised pitches away from the river are a
good choice in case of rain (bring wellies), and
the area by the barn can be midgey when the sun
shines on moist ground. Have a windbreak handy
for those days when the wind tears up the valley.

The two camping barns are simple, strip-lit,
centrally heated and have kitchens and meeting
tables for planning the next day's hiking. The
granary, with ensuite showers and bunk beds, is
often commandeered by exhausted team leaders
grateful for a break from their hectic charges.

Farm-reared lamb, beef and burgers can be
purchased at the kitchen door, and cooked
over firepits. Three generations of farm dogs –
supposedly aloof working hounds – sneak up to
friendly campers for illicit cuddles. In the lambing
season, children are welcome to peek into the
lambing shed, and many newborns are given
names by enchanted young guests.

Paths lead into the pinewoods, and up to the
moor. A quite steep but particularly rewarding
hike ends at the Warren House Inn, with its
famous log fire, which has been burning, it's
claimed, since 1845. Grab a pint of Otter bitter
and sit on a bench overlooking miles of
undulating moorland.

EATING & DRINKING

It's a mile and a half to Postbridge for basic
provisions – and a memorable cream tea – in the
local shop/post office. The one pub, the East Dart
Inn (01822 880213, www.eastdart.co.uk), under new
ownership since summer 2010, serves steaks and

Christine and Paul Coaker

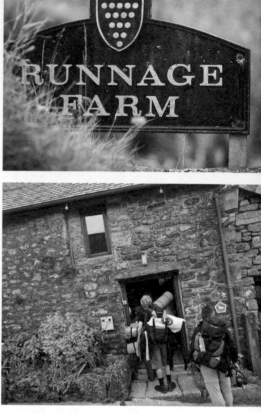

hearty pub grub (sausages with mash or ham, egg and chips) and real ales in the horse-brassy Huntsman's Bar. Look out for the village's historic clapper bridge – a Dartmoor speciality – made from four large granite slabs.

For an alfresco lunch with stunning views, wonky beams and a roaring fire, the best dining option is the atmospheric Warren House Inn (01822 880208, www.warrenhouseinn.co.uk) on the main road across the moor. Own-made rabbit pie, Dartmoor beef and lamb, and vegetarian options are generously piled on big plates. The ales are real, the cider is scrumpy and in winter the wine is mulled.

Princetown, five or so miles to the south, has a few pubs and a couple of cafés. Six miles in the opposite direction, Chagford has several daytime eating options, including the Courtyard wholefood café and shop (01647 432571, closed Sun); Blacks Deli (01647 433545, www.blacks-deli.co.uk, closed Sun) for sandwiches, quiches and salads; and Whiddons (01647 433406, closed Wed) for cream teas in a 16th-century thatched building.

ATTRACTIONS & ACTIVITIES

Runnage Farm is an ideal base for walkers, climbers, cavers, bikers and canoeists. Information on all these activities, including walks through nearby Bellever Forest and to East Dart waterfall, are available from the National Park tourist centre (01822 880272, www.dartmoor-npa.gov.uk, closed Nov-Easter) in Postbridge. You'll also find helpful staff and racks of leaflets on local attractions. The more substantial High Moorland Visitor Centre (01822 890414) in

Site specific

✔ The campsite is in the heart of wild and lovely Dartmoor National Park, with all the outdoor fun and adventure that offers.

✗ Runnage gets muddy after heavy rain, to the point that cars get can stuck. More showers are needed for busy times.

Princetown has a permanent exhibition with interactive displays and films about Dartmoor.

'Letterboxing', a combination of orienteering and treasure-hunting, which originated on Dartmoor in the 1850s, is a great way to enliven a hike. Clues are used to find boxes on the moor containing rubber stamps, which are collected in a personal book. Details at www.letterboxingondartmoor.co.uk.

Beside the grey granite wall of Dartmoor Prison in Princetown, the Dartmoor Prison Museum (01822 322130, www.dartmoor-prison.co.uk) tells the dark story of this infamous institution, and includes a collection of objects made by prisoners to aid escape, use as weapons or take drugs. For more peaceful cells and gardens, stained glass and the Benedictine monks' famous tonic wine – visit Buckfast Abbey (01364 645560, www.buckfast.org.uk, closed Sat), located about ten miles south-east on the A38.

If you're camping in September, you can join Old Uncle Tom Cobley and all at Widecombe Fair (www.widecombefair.com), at Widecombe-in-the-Moor, five miles east of Runnage.

AMUSING THE KIDS

Children can pet more numerous animals, including Shetland ponies, miniature horses, rabbits and guinea pigs, at the Miniature Pony Centre (01647 432400, www.miniatureponycentre.com, closed Nov-Mar), about six miles to the north. It also has an adventure playground and assault course. There's an even greater range of attractions at Pennywell Farm Activity Park (01364 645500, www.pennywellfarm.co.uk, closed Nov-mid Feb) near Buckfast Abbey.

CAMPING NEARBY

At the Plume of Feathers Inn (01822 890240) in Princetown, there is supposedly space for 75 tents and 10 campervans on a slightly sloping site, but that would be a squeeze. Adults pay £6.95 each.

A more intrepid option would be wild camping (*see p21*) on the open moor – Dartmoor is one of the few places where it's allowed. Visit www.dartmoor.co.uk/site/what-to-do/wild-dartmoor for more information.

Yurtcamp

Yurtcamp
Gorse Blossom Farm, Staplehill Road,
Liverton, Devon TQ12 6JD
01626 824666, 07768 665544
enquiries@yurtcamp.co.uk
www.yurtcamp.co.uk
Map p25 ⑬
OS map SX816739

Number of pitches 18 yurts (sleeping 5).
4 yurts (sleeping 2).
Open New Year, Feb-Dec.
Booking By phone, email. Essential.
Minimum stay 3 nights high season.
Typical cost Weekend (3 nights) small
yurt £235-£425, large yurt £275-£475.
Midweek (4 nights) small yurt £225-£465,
large yurt £275-£545. 1 week small yurt
£375-£665, large yurt £445-£795.
Bedding £5 per person.
Facilities Café/bar; disabled facilities
(toilet and shower); laundry facilities; play
area; showers (free); toilets; washing-up
facilities; Wi-Fi (reception and café).
Campfires Allowed, in firepits.
Firewood available (free).
Dogs Not allowed.
Restrictions Groups by arrangement.
Getting there By road Take the A38,
Exeter to Plymouth road. Leave at the
Drumbridges exit, about 12 miles outside
Exeter, and take the third exit at the
roundabout towards Liverton. Continue
straight for a mile, over a large bridge, then
turn immediately left on to Staplehill Road.
The campsite entrance is on the right,
after 150 yds. **By public transport** Train to
Newton Abbot. From the town centre catch
the free 76 bus to Trago Mills shopping
centre (takes 15 mins, Mon-Sat), which
is a 10-min walk from the campsite.
Buses 178 and 193 also run to Liverton,
a 20-mins walk away (01626 833664,
www.countrybusdevon.co.uk). Alternatively,
a taxi from Exeter costs about £35 (Capital
Taxis, 01392 433433, www.exeter.tc).

Devon's premier spot for luxury glamping is set
in 40 acres of oak woodland, on the eastern edge
of Dartmoor. Forget leaky tents and battles with
wayward guy ropes: here you sleep in a spacious
modern yurt, equipped with proper beds, duvets
and a table and chairs, and heated by a crackling
wood-burning stove. In the centre of the roof, a
clear dome reveals the starry night sky. And the
setting is glorious: from the car park below, a
gravel path leads up to a sun-dappled clearing,
surrounded by protected ancient woodland, with
a couple of large oak trees at its centre. Around
the clearing stand the café/bar, shower block
and playground, along with a pen occupied by
four adorable pygmy goats. There's a stack of
free firewood, and a covered play area with table
tennis and table football.

Left of the clearing, through a gap in the trees,
is the yurt village; a little bridge leads deeper into
the woodland, where about half the yurts are
situated, for visitors looking for more seclusion.
Each yurt comes with all the kitchen equipment
you'll need, plus a two-ring camping gas stove
and a coolbox (renew ice packs at the café). You
can cook on the log-burning stove too, while the
firepit outside the yurt is perfect for frying bacon
and eggs or toasting marshmallows. Duvets and
pillows are provided (bring towels) and lighting is
in the form of candles and paraffin lamps. The
large yurts have roll-down canvas partitions to
create separate sleeping areas.

Sharp-eyed campers might spot a red deer,
framed by the trees, or a buzzard flying overhead.
At dusk, lesser horseshoe bats and pipistrelles
flit around. (The site was once home to the Gorse
Blossom miniature railway, and an old railway
tunnel has been converted into a bat hibernation
cave.) Wellies or hiking boots are essential; the
ground becomes muddy after rain, especially
around the more remote yurts.

Yurtcamp allows its guests to experience the
great outdoors without compromising on creature
comforts – camping's answer to the boutique
hotel, if you will.

EATING & DRINKING

The licensed on-site café serves a vast breakfast
menu, including croissants and full English and
vegetarian breakfasts, along with cakes, organic
juices, teas and coffees. A blackboard sets out the
daily-changing lunch and dinner options.

A few miles away in Haytor, the 18th-century
Rock Inn (01364 661305, www.rock-inn.co.uk),
sources its ingredients from local suppliers and
delivers dependable gastropub fare.

It's four miles down the A38 to the foodie haven
of Ashburton, with its delis, specialist food shops,
several butchers and a greengrocer, including the
excellent Fish Deli (01364 654833, www.thefishdeli.
co.uk, closed Sun). For inventive and exceptionally
good food (roast Devon lamb with asparagus,

SOUTH DEVON

Cornish yarg gnocchi and rosemary gravy, say), book a table at Agaric (01364 654478, www.agaric restaurant.co.uk, closed Mon, Tue, Sun and lunch Sat) on North Street. Everything is made on the premises, from cheese and smoked fish to fruit vinegars and sorbets; the set lunch menu is an inexpensive way to sample the chef's talents.

The area's best family pub is the Rising Sun (01364 652544, www.therisingsunwoodland.co.uk) in Woodland, just outside Ashburton. It's an appealingly cosy old place, with real ales, fresh fish from the boats at Brixham and a varied menu for children.

ATTRACTIONS & ACTIVITIES

Dartmoor National Park (www.dartmoor-npa.gov.uk) is on the doorstep, offering miles of great walking and awe-inspiring scenery. The nearest visitor centre is at Haytor, beneath the dramatic granite outcrop of

Haytor Rocks, from where there are stunning views across the moorland and down to the coast.

For a complete change of scene, rummage around the boutiques and craft shops in Totnes, 13 miles to the south. Perched on a steep hill, with a Norman castle at the top and the River Dart at its foot, it's a lovely place for a stroll. There are markets selling local goodies on Fridays and Saturdays, and a relaxed, arty vibe; the town is famed for its bohemian leanings. For antique shops, head to Ashburton; the highest concentration is along North Street.

Twenty minutes' drive away, the seaside town of Teignmouth has elegant Georgian townhouses, a Victorian pier, and a sand and shingle beach, along with a play park and crazy golf course. Closer to home, the heated outdoor swimming pool in Bovey Tracey (01626 832828, www.boveyswimmingpool. co.uk) is open from April until mid September.

Becky Falls Woodland Park (01647 221259, www.beckyfalls.com, closed Nov-mid Feb) is ideal for families, with walking trails through the valley, a theatre, a craft centre and a petting zoo. It's in Manaton, half an hour's drive from the camp.

Site specific

✔ Yurtcamp is a blissfully easy alternative to camping – perfect for families with young babies, or more elderly visitors.

✘ The proximity to the A38 means there is a faint but persistent whirr of traffic.

AMUSING THE KIDS

Children can roam safely around the car-free site, exploring the woods, visiting the goats and chickens or playing on the see-saw and swings. There's also a grassy pitch for kickarounds, a tennis court, a zip-wire and even a woodland assault course.

Pennywell Farm (01364 642023, www.pennywellfarm.co.uk, closed Nov-mid Feb) in Buckfastleigh, a 15-minute drive, is a vast farm attraction with trampolines, tractors, go-karts, play areas and half-hourly activities and demonstrations, along with the resident ferrets, Shire horses, Dartmoor ponies and miniature pigs. From Buckfastleigh you can also ride a steam train to Totnes with the South Devon Railway (0845 345 1420, www.south devonrailway.co.uk). Alternatively, head to the River Dart Country Park (01364 652511, www.riverdart. co.uk, closed weekdays Oct-mid Mar) in Ashburton, with its nature trails, adventure playground, canoes and high ropes.

For a rainy day, the House of Marbles (01626 835358, www.houseofmarbles.com) in Bovey Tracey has a historic collection of marbles and games, along with ingenious – and enormous – marble runs, which you can watch in action, and a games garden.

CAMPING NEARBY

Twelve Oaks Farm Caravan Park (01626 335015, www.twelveoaksfarm.co.uk, open all year) in Teigngrace – about four miles down the A38 – has pitches for tents, caravans and motorhomes (£9-£15). There's also self-catering cottages, a swimming pool, shop and free fishing in the lake. Runnage Farm (*see* p65) is half an hour away, in the centre of Dartmoor.

Coombe View Farm

Coombe View Farm
Branscombe, Seaton,
South Devon EX12 3BT
01297 680218
glaspersltd@farmersweekly.net
www.branscombecamping.co.uk
Map p25 ⑭
OS map SY203903

Number of pitches 40 tents,
12 caravans/motorhomes.
Open Easter-Oct.
Booking By phone, email, post. Advisable.
Typical cost £10-£18 2 people,
£6 extra adult, £3 extra child.
Facilities Electric hook-ups (20);
showers (free); toilets; washing up area.
Campfires Allowed, in designated areas.
Dogs Allowed, on lead.
Restrictions Unsupervised under-18s
by arrangement.
Getting there By road Take the A3052,
which runs parallel to the coast from Lyme
Regis to Exeter. The turn-off to Branscombe
is 2 miles west of Seaton, 5 miles east of
Sidmouth; it's about half a mile to Coombe
View Farm. Sat-nav users, beware: the last
mile is inaccurate. **By public transport**
Train to Exeter. Stagecoach bus 52A/B
(0871 200 2233, www.stagecoachbus.com)
leaves twice an hour and takes 40 mins
to Sidmouth. From there, Coasthopper
bus 899 (0871 200 2233, www.jurassic
coast.com) takes 20 mins to Branscombe.
There's no service on Sun.

Set along a hilly lane in an undervisited part of
south-east Devon, about 15 miles east of Exeter,
Coombe View Farm is a deliberately simple affair.
Ducks, chickens and Exmoor ponies welcome
campers in the paddocks by the entrance, while
three camping fields slope gently towards the
trees and a hedgerow alive with birdsong. On the
other side of the hedge, the flinty ground banks
steeply down into the coombe (wooded valley)
where a stream flows towards the sea – visible
in the distance from the site's higher reaches.

Run by Sue Glasper and her husband Trevor,
it's a low-key place, without neat paths or defined
pitches. Instead, tents and caravans cluster
at the edges of the first field, leaving the centre
free for impromptu games of cricket, rounders
and football; larger groups are accommodated

in the furthest field, to avoid disturbing other
campers. There are also two static caravans
with sea views. Wooden picnic tables are dotted
around the site, and firepits punctuate the
middle field. The toilets and showers, housed
in a wooden block near the entrance, are basic,
but include a freezer.

As wind rustles the trees, and cloud shadows
race across distant meadows, it's a supremely
relaxing place to camp. For children, there are
plenty of adventures to be had in the thickets
of the coombe: exploring, collecting wood for
roasting marshmallows, or fishing for tiddlers
in the stream.

Footpath maps, available on site, detail the
abundance of walks in the surrounding
countryside, and the village of Branscombe is
a couple of miles down the (steep) hill. Once
a hotbed of smugglers, it hit the headlines in
2007 when the *MSC Napoli* cargo ship ran
aground just offshore, triggering frenzied looting;
today, the only reminder is the ship's enormous
anchor, displayed on a plinth by the seafront.

Aside from such maritime dramas, though,
Branscombe is idyllic. Said to be the 'longest
village in Britain', it straggles along a valley,
its picture-perfect thatched cottages festooned
with blooms, with a stone church and a long,
precipitous shingle beach, where a little crab
boat lands its daily catch.

EATING & DRINKING

Apart from fresh milk, there is no food or drink
available on site, so pack accordingly. The nearest
shop is at a petrol station around a mile and a half
away; it's located on a busy main road, so you'll
need to take the car.

In Branscombe, the Masons Arms (01297 680300,
www.masonsarms.co.uk) was named in honour of
the stonemasons who worked in the nearby quarries
and drank here centuries ago. It is a low-ceilinged,

Site specific

✔ The area has much lower rainfall than
North Devon, Exmoor and Dartmoor, so
dry and breezy summer days are likely.

✘ The wind can whistle up the valley from
the sea. Pitching behind the hedgerows
provides some protection, but this poses
a difficult choice between enjoying the best
views and keeping out of the wind.

cosy spot for a pint of local cider or real ale, with an above-average pub menu. The restaurant's smart set menu is also brimming with local meats and freshly caught fish. Book ahead, and note that the kitchen closes at 9pm. At the other end of the village, the 14th-century, flagstone-floored Fountain Head (01297 680359, www.fountainheadinn.com) serves hearty, home-made pub grub and Branoc ale from the Branscombe Vale Brewery. There are spit roasts on summer Sundays, and the odd musical performance.

The daytime-only Sea Shanty Shop & Beach Café (01297 680577, www.theseashanty.co.uk) offers cream teas and local fish and chips under a thatched roof – though beware the vigilant traffic warden in the beach car park. Alternatively, try the tea room at the Old Bakery.

ATTRACTIONS & ACTIVITIES

In Branscombe, the National Trust now runs the Old Bakery, Manor Mill & Forge (01752 346585, www.nationaltrust.org.uk, closed Nov-Mar). The 200-year-old blacksmith's forge (open all year) still produces and sells ironwork, while the Old Bakery houses a delightful tea room; you can also watch the water-powered mill in action.

A couple of miles along the coast, the Beer Quarry Caves (01297 680282, www.beerquarry caves.fsnet.co.uk, closed Nov-Mar) were worked from Roman times until the early 20th century, and provided stone for many of England's cathedrals. The vaulted caverns and imposing pillars are an awe-inspiring sight, with guided tours running throughout the year.

Forde Abbey (01460 220231, www.fordeabbey. co.uk, house closed Mon, Sat and Nov-Mar) in Chard, 15 miles from the farm, is a Cistercian monastery turned opulent private house. The gardens are magnificent, with a flourishing Victorian kitchen garden, a series of cascades and a fine arboretum.

For more sedentary sightseeing, the Seaton Tramway (01297 20375, www.tram.co.uk) runs narrow-gauge heritage trams through the Axe Valley, passing alongside the estuary and through

SOUTH DEVON

Branscombe

Trevor and Sue Glasper

two nature reserves. The trams depart from Seaton, and operate all year (there are three enclosed saloons, as well as colourfully painted open-tops).

AMUSING THE KIDS

The pebbly beach at Branscombe has plenty of rock pools to poke around in; for bathing, head for nearby Seaton or Sidmouth. Some ten miles around the coast, Lyme Regis is a lovely little seaside town, with sand and shingle beaches, crazy golf, the famous harbour wall known as the Cobb, and fossils galore.

When youngsters tire of the beaches, or searching for butterflies, glow-worms, stoats, badgers and rabbits around the site, take them to Pecorama (01297 21542, www.pecorama.info, in Beer. Run by the model train manufacturers Peco, it has an

exhibition hall full of gleaming, small-scale tracks and trains, and a miniature railway (though that doesn't operate in winter).

Around ten minutes' drive away in Sidmouth, the Donkey Sanctuary (01395 578222, www.the donkeysanctuary.org.uk) provides a home to retired and rescued donkeys, who adore being fussed over.

CAMPING NEARBY

In nearby Weston, Oakdown Touring & Holiday Caravan Park (01297 680387, www.oakdown.co.uk, open Mar-Nov, pitches £13.50-£27.50) accommodates tents and caravans on level, neatly mown pitches, and has plenty of facilities. The friendly feel, attention to detail and well-spaced pitches belie the campsite's large size; families, in particular, rate it highly.

Cherry Tree Farm

Cherry Tree Farm Campsite
Cherry Tree Farm, Jones Hill,
Croyde, North Devon EX33 1NH
01271 890495
camping@cherrytreecroyde.co.uk
www.cherrytreecroyde.co.uk
Map p25 ⑮
OS map SS443397

Number of pitches Approx 600 tents/
motorhomes. No caravans.
Open Spring bank holiday, July, Aug.
Booking By phone, email, post.
Minimum stay 3 nights.
Typical cost £13 adult; £6.50 child.
Facilities Showers (free); surf equipment;
toilets; washing-up area.
Campfires Not allowed.
Dogs Not allowed.
Restrictions Single-sex groups and
unsupervised under-18s by arrangement.
Getting there By road Take the A361 to
Braunton, then turn off on the B3231
towards Croyde and Georgeham. In
Croyde, cross the bridge and turn into
Jones Hill. Carry on up the hill; the
campsite is signposted on the left, just
before the road bends sharply to the right.
By public transport Train to Barnstaple,
from where bus 308 (0871 200 2233,
www.stagecoachbus.com) provides a
frequent service to Croyde; journey takes
40 mins. A taxi from Barnstaple to the
campsite will cost £25-£30 with Barnstaple
& District Value Taxis (01271 327777,
www.valuetaxis.co.uk).

The thatched cottages and clotted cream teas
of Croyde village and the golden sands of Croyde
Bay draw streams of holidaymakers to this idyllic
stretch of the north Devon coast, ten miles north
of Barnstaple. It's the perfect beach destination,
catering to surfers, sunbathers and children,
who hunt for crabs in its limpid rock pools. The
bay is bookended by two hills – head up either
to walk the coast path, with its spectacular sea
views and seal-spotting opportunities.

Set midway between the village and beach,
and a five-minute stroll from each, Cherry Tree
Farm is superbly located. The campsite has a
relaxed, low-key vibe, and is generally occupied
by a mix of surfers in old-style campervans,
couples and families. A carefully co-ordinated
pitch plan promotes camper harmony, dividing
families, couples and larger groups into different
areas. The campsite is open only in the school
holidays and although more fields get opened
to accommodate newcomers, you'll still need to
book early for summer.

Two shower blocks at either side of the eight-
field site supply constant hot water, and there are
enough toilet cubicles to avoid a queue. Workers
patrol regularly, emptying bins and checking fire
equipment, although the camp avoids being overly
manicured and is still pleasantly rough around
the edges (and hedges). Helpful young staff at the
office are happy to answer questions about the
site, and the local area. Note that the entrance
barrier is only manned until 10pm, so if you fancy
a midnight drive, you'll need to park outside.

Surfing equipment (new and second-hand)
can be hired or bought from the campsite
office, and there are several other surf shops
in Croyde; we like the Little Pink Shop (01271
890453, www.littlepinkshop.com) in Moor Lane
for its friendly and attentive staff. Pick up a free
copy of *EX33 Visitor* magazine in the office for
details of tide and bus times, and local amenities
and attractions.

If you tire of Croyde Bay's charms, head for
Putsborough Sands, Woolacombe Sands (winner
of the Blue Flag Beach 2009 award) or Saunton
Sands. Stretching for three miles, Saunton is
part of the North Devon Biosphere Reserve. Its
crescent of sand borders the magnificent dunes
of Braunton Burrows, a UNESCO World Heritage
Site that contains around 500 species of
flowering plants, including rare orchids.

EATING & DRINKING

Croyde has enough eating and drinking options if
you're not after anything too fancy. The two main
drinking dens, the Thatch (01271 890349, www.the
thatchcroyde.com) and Billy Budds (01271 890606) are
pleasant spots for a pint in the sunshine – the latter
has two terraced beer gardens. Both serve reasonable
pub food, including locally sourced fish at the Thatch.
For pudding, head to Croyde's Ice Cream Parlour
(01271 891003, open summer only) for delicious clotted
cream, vanilla or rhubarb and custard ices.

Away from the village – follow the coast path signs
to Baggy Point – Baggy's Surf Lodge & Cafe (01271
890078, www.baggys.co.uk) has sandwiches, pasties
and cream teas, and great views over the beach.

Squires Fish Restaurant & Takeaway (01271
815533, closed Sun Oct-May) in Braunton, about
four miles from Croyde, is considered by many locals
to serve the best fish and chips in Devon.

The post office in Croyde sells milk, bacon and other basic foodstuffs, as does the Costcutter at Ruda Holiday Park, but for a supermarket you'll need to head to Braunton.

ATTRACTIONS & ACTIVITIES

Outdoor types will be in heaven here. You can learn to surf, paddle ski or coaststeer (that's exploring hidden sea caves and jumping off rocks) with several local outfits: try extreme sport specialist

Point Breaks (07776 148679, www.pointbreaks.com) or Surfing Croyde Bay (01271 891200, www.surfing croydebay.co.uk). Horse riding is also popular; Roylands Riding Stables (01271 890898, www. roylands-stables.co.uk) is BHS-approved, and offers hacks along secluded forest paths, or on Putsborough Beach.

Then, of course, there's the cycling and walking, with coastal paths in either direction from Croyde Bay. Head one way to Putsborough, or for a short circular walk via Baggy Point; the other direction takes you to Saunton. You can also explore the Tarka Trail (www.devon.gov.uk/tarkatrail.htm), a 30-mile cycle route that follows the old railway lines between Braunton and Meeth; Henry Williamson wrote *Tarka the Otter* in 1927, while living in the nearby village of Georgeham.

Film lovers can pull up a pew (or, rather, a deckchair) at Croyde village hall for the Deckchair Cinema (01271 890804, www.croydedeckchair cinema.co.uk), whose eclectic programme ranges from hip surf flicks to golden oldies such as *Grease*.

It's ten miles to the resort town of Ilfracombe, from where you can board the Ilfracombe Princess (*see p83*) and sail through a marine conservation zone, with opportunities to spot seal, porpoise and dolphin along the way. Trips runs from Easter to the end of October.

AMUSING THE KIDS

Equipped with a fishing net and bucket and spade, kids will love roaming the beach and delving into rock pools. If that pales, a 40-minute drive will take you to the Big Sheep (01237 472366, www.thebig sheep.co.uk, closed Mon-Fri Nov-Easter) in Abbotsham. Bring a picnic, then watch the horse-whispering demonstrations, sheep races and 'duck trials' – during which ever-patient collies round up a gaggle of recalcitrant ducks. A little further away, the Milky Way Adventure Park (01237 431255, www.themilkyway.co.uk) boasts the biggest rollercoaster in Devon.

Don't imagine a little rain or chilly weather means that swimming is off the agenda. At Croyde's Ruda Holiday Park (01271 890671, www.ruda.co.uk) you'll find a public indoor swimming pool with rapids, a water slide and a toddlers' pool. (There's a camping field here too, among the static caravans.)

CAMPING NEARBY

Mitchams Campsites (07875 406473, 07891 892897, www.croydebay.co.uk, runs two nearby sites, one close to the village, the other backing on to the beach. The village site (open end June-Aug bank holiday) is set next to a road and is small, crowded and mainly occupied by groups of young people. The beach site (open late July-early Sept) has wonderful views, but often gets booked out.

Site specific

✔ The beachside location is glorious, and most pitches have uninterrupted sea views.

✘ Most pitches are on a slope, so tactical tent positioning is required; make sure you're facing feet down to avoid rolling sideways during the night. The three-night minimum stay might not appeal to all.

Croyde Bay; and (top) Baggy Point.

NORTH DEVON

North Morte Farm

North Morte Farm Caravan & Camping Park
Mortehoe, Woolacombe,
North Devon EX34 7EG
01271 870381
info@northmortefarm.co.uk
www.northmortefarm.co.uk
Map p25 ⑯
OS map SS461455

Number of pitches 150 tents,
30 caravans/motorhomes.
Open Easter-Oct.
Booking No booking for tents. By phone,
email for caravans/motorhomes.
Essential high season.
Typical cost Tent £12-£20.50 2 adults.
Caravan/motorhome £12-£20.50 2 adults.
Facilities Disabled facilities (toilet);
electric hook-ups (30); laundry facilities;
play area; shop; showers (free); toilets;
washing-up area.
Campfires Not allowed.
Dogs Allowed, on lead (£1.50-£2).
Restrictions No groups of more than
six adults, no single-sex groups.
Getting there By road Take the A361
(Barnstaple to Ilfracombe road). At
Mullacott Cross roundabout, take the
B3343 to Mortehoe/Woolacombe; after
2 miles turn right to Mortehoe. In Mortehoe
village, turn right at the post office – there's
a brown sign for North Morte Farm. The
site is 500 yards on the left. **By public
transport** From Barnstaple, bus 3 (daily)
takes about 45 mins to Ilfracombe. Here,
catch bus 31, which stops at Morthoe
post office, a short walk from the campsite.
The journey takes 20 mins, and the service
runs Mon-Sat. Details on 0871 200 2233,
www.firstgroup.com.

On the west tip of North Devon, less than two
miles by car from Woolacombe, the camping
fields of North Morte Farm slope down towards
a cliff overlooking Rockham Beach, and the
craggy coastline beyond. Divided by stone walls
and gorse hedges, the lush green fields are
punctuated by patches of meadow grass waving
in the breeze, while the silence is broken by the
occasional yell of a child charging down the hill.

Run by Judith Gilbert and her two daughters,
North Morte has been in the family for three
generations; people have been camping here
since the 1940s. Despite the campsite's size –
there's space for 150 tents, 30 caravans and
permanent caravans too – the friendly welcome
creates an intimate, family feel that sets it apart
from other large-scale sites.

A tarmac track leads through the regimented
rows of statics, curving past the children's play
area and immaculately clean, spacious shower
block. The camping fields are well drained and
maintained, with no marked pitches; guests
simply choose a likely-looking spot on arrival.
You can't book ahead, so arrive early to nab a
good spot. Wherever you decide to pitch, it's
wise to seek the shelter of the hedges and
walls, in case the wind picks up off the sea.

A stony path leads down to the beach, where
gulls wheel on the wind and oystercatchers
congregate in small groups on more secluded
coves; the sharp-eyed might glimpse a group of
seals, close to the rocks. The rocks and currents
offshore have wrecked countless ships, but
paddling in the pools and shallows is pretty safe.

Five minutes' walk from the site entrance is
Mortehoe, with its 13th-century church, heritage
centre, three pubs and handy village bakery.

A winding ten-minute drive along the coast,
or a three-mile walk along the South West Coast
Path (www.southwestcoastpath.com) around
Morte Point, brings you to Woolacombe's
expanse of golden sand, dotted with surfers
and rippled by the tide. Woolacombe is also
the place for more lively night-time entertainment
– although a stroll to the pub and a sky full of
stars suits most campers just fine.

EATING & DRINKING

The farm shop has all the basics, plus vegetables and
barbecue meat, and a hot drinks machine.

The village shop in Mortehoe has a small bakery
and sells general groceries. There are also three pubs.

Site specific

✔ Spectacular views out to sea and over
the Bristol Channel, the sun setting behind
Lundy Island, and the pure fresh air bring
people back here year after year.

✘ The site is exposed and sloping; it can
get very windy, and at busy times you may
not find a flat spot. Although there are water
taps in each field, it can be a long, uphill
walk to the toilets.

The three-mile sweep of sand at Woolacombe, just along the coast from the farm.

Head to the Chichester Arms (01271 870411) for local ales (from Barnstaple's Barum brewery), a garden, a kids' room and a skittle alley. It serves good-quality pub grub, using locally reared meat and fresh fish. The Ship Aground (01271 870856) has low, beamed ceilings and a sweetly old-fashioned feel; you can tuck into ploughman's, steak and kidney pie or fish and chips. Also on the Square, the Rockleigh (01271 870704, www.rockleighhouse.com) is a thoroughly British eaterie that champions local suppliers.

Alternatively, honour the ocean at the no-frills Mortehoe Shellfish (01271 870633, www.mortehoe shellfish.co.uk), a family-run seafood shack (booking recommended). Lobster, crab and fish caught on the family's boat are simply cooked and served with crusty bread, own-made potato salad and a jug of local scrumpy. The company's seafood van also visits the campsite, selling cockles, mussels, prawns and whelks, along with foil-wrapped fish for the barbecue.

For something more unusual, try the Barricaine Beach Café (no phone) just before Woolacombe. Open on clement summer evenings, it serves cheap, fragrant Sri Lankan curries and is set on a beach dotted with exotic shells, carried from the Caribbean by the Gulf Stream.

ATTRACTIONS & ACTIVITIES

The main attraction is, of course, the sea. The three-mile beach at Woolacombe is within easy reach of the site; for a change of scene, head to the Victorian seaside town of Ilfracombe, around 20 minutes' drive away. At one end of the High Street, tunnels dug by Welsh miners in the 1820s lead through the cliffs to a Blue Flag beach, tidal swimming pool and lovely café (www.tunnels beaches.co.uk). The town is also home to the newly refurbished Embassy Cinema (01271 862323,

www.cromer-movieplex.com). Catamarans set off from the harbour on wildlife-watching trips, and there is a ferry to Lundy Island (*see p83*).

For surfing lessons, contact Surf South West (01271 890400, www.surfsouthwest.com), whose outlets at Saunton Beach and Croyde are both within 15 minutes' drive of the campsite. In Woolacombe, the Nick Thorn Surf School (01271 871337, www.nickthorn.com) runs surfing courses and hires out equipment.

You can also kayak, abseil, mountain bike, quad bike, ride horses and go on nature and walking tours, organised by H2 Outdoor (07789 807424, www.h2outdoor.co.uk) in Woolacombe.

AMUSING THE KIDS

There's plenty of space on the camping fields for kickabouts, and the fenced-off playground has swings and a big wooden climbing frame.

Children can go rockpooling on Rockham Beach, and find exotic shells at Barricaine. Mortehoe's Heritage Centre (01271 870028, www.devon museums.net, closed Fri, Sat, all Nov-Easter) has hands-on games and puzzles, along with displays on local shipwrecks. In summer, tractor and trailer rides head to Morte Point for seal-spotting.

In Croyde Bay, Cascades Tropical Adventure Pool (01271 890671, www.parkdeanholidays.co.uk, closed Nov-Mar) has flumes and rides for rainy days.

CAMPING NEARBY

A couple of miles away, Warcombe Farm (01271 870690, www.warcombefarm.co.uk, open Mar-Oct, £12.50-£28 two adults) has 260 camping and caravan pitches, spread over 19 acres. The site has a fishing lake and wildflower zones, along with good facilities; barbecues and dogs are allowed.

Little Meadow

Little Meadow Caravan & Camping Site
Watermouth, Ilfracombe,
North Devon EX34 9SJ
01271 866862
info@littlemeadow.co.uk
www.littlemeadow.co.uk
Map p25 ⑰
OS map SS551481

Number of pitches 50 tents/caravans/
motorhomes.
Open Apr-end Sept.
Booking By post only. Essential.
Typical cost Tent/caravan £10-£22
2 people.
Facilities Disabled facilities (toilet and
shower); electric hook-ups (10, £2); laundry
facilities; play area; shop; showers (free);
toilets; washing-up area.
Campfires Allowed, off ground.
Dogs Allowed, on lead (£1-£2).
Restrictions No groups.
No arrivals after 9pm.
Getting there By road Little Meadow is on
the A399, about 2 miles east of Ilfracombe
and 3 miles west of Combe Martin. If you're
coming from the direction of Combe Martin,
the site is approximately 500 yds after
Watermouth Castle, on the left. **By public
transport** Train to Barnstaple. Catch the
30C bus going to Combe Martin and ask
the driver to let you off at Watermouth
Castle, then walk to the campsite from
there. The bus takes about 1 hr, but only
runs on North Devon College days; on other
days you may have to change at Ilfracombe
(0871 200 2233, www.firstgroup.com).

You needn't worry about where to pitch your
tent in order to get a good view at Little Meadow.
Perched on the very edge of the North Devon
coast, a few miles east of the faded Victorian
seaside resort of Ilfracombe, this hillside site's
flower-bordered terraces offer stunning views
over the Bristol Channel and north-west to the
Hangman Hills of Exmoor. Set on a 100-acre
organic farm, it's a delightfully low-key spot –
and a far remove from the Notting Hillbilly
boltholes of South Devon.

A little track leads to the farm shop, washing-
up facilities and well-maintained toilet block,
equipped with piping hot showers and – a rare
luxury, this – hairdryers. Outside, a large
sycamore tree with a handily low-hanging branch
provides a natural perch from which to watch
the changing seascape. Up a gentle slope to the
right, children whoop it up on the swings and rope
gym, or convene in the little willow-branch house.

From here, generously proportioned pitches
ascend the hillside on eight level, grassy
terraces, maximising the spectacular sea views.
(Indeed, nothing lies between you and the sea,
so bring a windbreak or park your car tactically
to get extra protection against the elements.)
Pitches are allotted according to tent size by
the site's charming owners, Nick and Sian
Barten; it was Nick's grandfather who founded
the campsite.

Above the top terrace is a grassy camping
field with numbered pitches, generally occupied
by larger groups, plus two sloping meadows –
perfect for lopsided ball games or a spot of
Frisbee-throwing. Organically reared cattle and
sheep roam the adjacent fields, along with a
group of friendly llamas.

Aside from the site's considerable charms,
the main attraction for campers is the proximity
to the North Devon coast, with its smugglers'
tunnels, craggy coves and limpid rock pools.
A private path meanders to Watermouth Harbour
and the South West Coast Path, which leads to
some splendid – if shingly – beaches.

EATING & DRINKING

The camp shop provides milk, bacon, eggs, cheese,
ham and ice-creams, plus local meat, crisps, soft
drinks and own-made cakes. You can also buy eggs,
meat and other fresh-from-the-fields bounty from
local farms. There's a Tesco in Ilfracombe.

Ilfracombe's quayside has two of the area's fanciest
eating establishments. Housed in an old police station,
La Gendarmerie (01271 865984, closed Mon all year,
and Tue, Wed, dinner Sun in low season) serves
brasserie-style dishes made from local produce; Lundy
lobster and chips is a standout. Artist Damien Hirst,
a local resident, owns neighbouring restaurant the
Quay (01271 868090, www.11thequay.co.uk – call for
opening times); there are plenty of Hirst's pieces to
contemplate, along with sumptuous sea views, as you
sample fresh crab claws, Cornish oysters or chicken
stuffed with sage and apricots. It's wise to book.

The best family fare is found at Hele-Billy's (01271
866488, www.helebillys.com), located on the main
road just before Ilfracombe. The vast menu includes
burgers, steaks and local seafood; standards are
high and prices modest. A ten-minute walk from
the campsite, the riverside Sawmill Inn (01271 882259,
www.thesawmillinn.co.uk) deals in real ales and
no-nonsense pub grub.

NORTH DEVON

Site specific

✔ Despite its covetable views and immense popularity, Little Meadow retains a relaxed, intimate atmosphere.

✘ Part of the site is a working farm and family residence. Parents need to keep a watchful eye on their offspring, and noise must be kept to a minimum after 10pm.

ATTRACTIONS & ACTIVITIES

The South West Coast Path (www.southwestcoast path.com) runs for 630 miles from Minehead in Somerset all the way around Devon and Cornwall to Poole in Dorset. Follow it east for just over three miles and you'll reach pretty Combe Martin – itself the starting point for numerous rambles and circular walks. Set in a fertile valley on the western edge of Exmoor National Park (www.exmoor nationalpark. gov.uk), it's a gloriously photogenic place, with a small, sheltered harbour and excellent rockpooling bays. The carnival in August brings a colourful parade, fireworks and wheelbarrow races.

To the west of Combe Martin, Berrynarbor is a trim, chocolate box-pretty village with a shop, a 16th-century pub, an art gallery and a tea room, all dominated by the tower of St Peter's Church.

A few miles' drive west is the seaside resort of Ilfracombe (*see pxx*). From the harbour, you can take to the waves aboard the Ilfracombe Princess (01271 879727, www.ilfracombeprincess.co.uk) in search of seals, porpoises and birds.

Or catch the ferry to Lundy Island, which is less than two hours away. Barely three and a half miles long, it's home to an astounding variety of flora and fauna, including puffins, wild goats and Lundy ponies; offshore, you might spot grey seals or basking sharks. Guided walks and snorkelling are available (01271 863636, www.lundyisland.co.uk).

Just over half an hour's drive away are the towns of Lynton and Lynmouth. Collectively nicknamed 'Little Switzerland', they are connected by a 19th-century funicular railway.

AMUSING THE KIDS

Ten minutes on foot, Watermouth Castle (01271 867474, www.watermouthcastle.com, closed Sat, all Nov-Mar) combines theme-park attractions for youngsters (a merry-go-round, dungeon labyrinth and gnome village) with Victorian beach resort throwbacks for adults (a tilting house, camera obscura and old-fashioned arcade machines). Tacky, but fun.

Assorted wildlife, both native and imported, is on show at Combe Martin Wildlife & Dinosaur Park (01271 882486, www.dinosaur-park.com), a sprawling set-up with picnic-friendly gardens. You can see lions, wolves, meerkats, sea lions and assorted monkeys, plus a couple of life-size animatronic dinosaurs.

CAMPING NEARBY

North Morte Farm (*see p78*) is nine miles away, on the other side of Ilfracombe.

Watermouth Harbour and (right) Castle

Westermill Farm

Westermill Farm
Exford, Exmoor, near Minehead,
Somerset TA24 7NJ
01643 831238/07970 594808
info@westermill.com
www.westermill.com
Map p25 ⑬
OS map SS824399

SOMERSET

Number of pitches 60 tents/caravans.
6 cottages (sleeping 1-8).
Open All year.
Booking By phone, email, post. Advisable
summer and bank holidays. Minimum stay
2 nights cottages.
Typical cost Tent £6.50 adult, £3.50 child.
Car £2.50. Cottage from £25 per person.
Facilities Laundry facilities; shop; showers
(free); toilets; washing-up area.
Campfires Allowed, in designated area.
Firewood available (£5).
Dogs Allowed, on lead (£2.50).
Restrictions No noise after 11pm.
Getting there By road From the A396
running between Minehead and Tiverton,
take the B3224 west towards Exford. Take
the Porlock road out of Exford village, with
the village green on the left and the post
office on the right. The road forks after
quarter of a mile; bear left on to a single
track. Continue for 2 miles until you see a
sign on a tree for the campsite. **By public
transport** Tricky. Buses do run from
Minehead and Tiverton to Exford (0871 200
2233, www.firstgroup.com), but it's still a
2.5-mile walk to the site. From Easter to
Sept, the Moor Rover bus (01643 709701,
www.atwest.org.uk) can pick up and drop
off anywhere within Exmoor National Park,
but you'll need to book well ahead.

Site specific

✔ Exmoor has something for everyone,
from the tranquillity of the campsite itself
to moorland walks, country pubs, fishing
villages and steam trains.

✘ In humid weather, midges swarm the
riverside fields. Bring insect repellent.

Camping at Westermill Farm is like discovering your own little riverside hideaway, tucked into the heart of Exmoor National Park. Fifteen acres of this leafy, 500-acre hill farm are divided into lush camping fields, stretched along the banks of the River Exe.

Collies in a kennel guard the entrance to the farmyard, which is occupied by plump hens and flanked by the owners' squat stone farmhouse, and the former milking parlour that now houses the farm shop. Past a rusty tractor and an old barn, the valley opens out in all its green glory. A narrow track leads to four camping fields, set along the bottom of the valley with the river at their foot. The first field, nearest the farmhouse, is the only one fenced off from the river, so stay here if you're camping with children. The fourth is the most secluded, and ideal for larger groups.

The site's solar- and gas-powered showers, sinks and washing-up facilities are handily situated, divided into two blocks in the first and third fields. The shop and farmhouse are also easily reached, while numerous hedges and trees lend the pitches an air of privacy.

Cheviot sheep and glossy-coated Aberdeen Angus cattle graze the surrounding hills, and thick hedgerows snake up the hillside on the other side of the river. Visitors are welcome to explore the farmland on waymarked trails, and the river is a lovely spot for bathing, or fly-fishing for trout.

The surrounding moorland is dotted with small hamlets and villages, which generally centre around a weathered parish church and a country inn or two. The closest village, a couple of miles away, is Exford, with its post office, general store, two pubs and attractive green.

For a change of scenery, the coast is less than half an hour's drive away at Porlock Weir: a shipshape little harbour with a shingle beach and lovely coastal walks, a mile or two west of the village of Porlock. And, for a proper day out at the beach, Woolacombe and Putsborough are within driving distance, across the border in Devon.

EATING & DRINKING

At Westermill's shop, you can stock up on farm-reared lamb steaks, beef, bacon and sausages – for sizzling over off-ground barbecues or fires in the far field – as well as groceries, wine, cider, own-made ice-cream and thoughtful extras such as toothbrushes. The shop in Exford has fruit and veg and other basics; for a supermarket, Minehead is 13 miles away.

Traditional fare using quality local ingredients prevails in the pubs nearby. In Exford, the Crown

01643 831554, www.crownhotelexmoor.co.uk) is a smart and traditional establishment, where tweedy types discuss the day's shoot over roast beef, sea bass and Cornish scallops. Less atmospheric, but with a wider range of dishes, the White Horse Inn (01643 831229, www.exmoor-whitehorse.co.uk) offers a carvery menu most evenings and a five-course feast with pheasant and venison alongside the carte.

There is more variety in Porlock, including a number of family-friendly pubs and eateries. The best is Piggy in the Middle (01643 862647, usually closed Mon, Sun Nov-Apr) on the High Street, whose focus is on local seafood, with a few meat and game options.

Overlooking Porlock Weir, the Cafe (01643 863300, www.thecafeporlockweir.co.uk) has been recently revamped. Pop in for smart sandwiches or a full-blown meal: Lynmouth Bay lobster with asparagus, say, or Devon crab, ginger and saffron tart, with herby new potatoes and chargrilled peppers.

ATTRACTIONS & ACTIVITIES

The area surrounding the campsite is packed with interest. There are spectacular walks across the moors (maps are available at the site), arresting views of the rugged coastline, and charming villages, accessed by winding lanes. Exmoor Safari (01643 831229) takes guests from Exford on a two-and-a-half-hour Land Rover expedition through the wilds of Exmoor, spotting red deer, stags and Exmoor ponies.

Around ten minutes from Westermill by car, Withypool is home to a medieval church and the excellent Royal Oak Inn (01643 831506, www.royaloakwithypool.co.uk). From here, a glorious walk leads through a mossy, wooded valley to Tarr Steps, an ancient clapper bridge formed of huge slabs of stone.

Ten miles to the south, Dulverton is dotted with boutiques and craft shops. The Exmoor Pony Centre (01398 323093, www.exmoorponycentre.org.uk)

offers half-day pony experiences for £40 per person, including a two-hour ride over Winsford Hill to Tarr Steps. There is also an angling and watersports centre at Wimbleball Lake (01398 371460, www.swlakestrust.org.uk), a 15-minute drive from Dulverton, along with a rainbow trout fishery.

For day trips to the coast, head for Porlock and Porlock Weir, or further west to the fishing village of Lynmouth, with its 19th-century water-balanced funicular railway, traditional tea rooms and steep, narrow streets.

AMUSING THE KIDS

Children adore exploring the farm – especially in lambing season at the end of March/early April.

At the opposite end of the spectrum, Butlins (01643 703331, www.butlins.com) is a spaceship-shaped beacon on the edge of the seaside town of Minehead. Day tickets are available, with access to the resort's swimming pool and waterslides, funfair, climbing wall and entertainment programme.

Perhaps the perfect compromise between the giddy thrills of Butlins and the sedate pleasures of moorland hikes is the West Somerset Railway (01643 704996, www.west-somerset-railway.co.uk), whose steam trains traverse a 20-mile scenic route from Minehead south to Bishops Lydeard.

For seaside fun, head to Devon. Woolacombe offers a thriving surfing scene and gently shelving, sandy beach, while Putsborough Sands is quieter and much less developed: paradise for younger children, content with an ice-cream and a poke around the rock pools. Both are about an hour's drive by car.

CAMPING NEARBY

Halse Farm (01643 851259, www.halsefarm.co.uk, open Mar-Oct), halfway between Westermill Farm and Dulverton, is a similarly intimate campsite on a working beef and sheep farm. Pitches (£14-£17) are set on flat ground, with glorious vistas across the hills. Facilities include a heated shower block, laundrette and playground, as well as good disabled facilities.

The scenic hills surrounding Westermill Farm

Batcombe Vale

Batcombe Vale Campsite
Batcombe Vale, Shepton Mallet,
Somerset BA4 6BW
01749 831207
gary.butler1@virgin.net
www.batcombevale.co.uk
Map p25 ⑲
OS map ST682377

Number of pitches 30 tents/caravans/ motorhomes.
Open Apr-Sept.
Booking By phone, email. Essential. Minimum stay 2 nights.
Typical cost £11.50 1 adult, £16,50 2 adults, £5 extra adult, £3 extra under-16.
Facilities Boating (free); electric hook-ups (17); fishing (£5); laundry facilities; showers (free); toilets; washing-up area.
Campfires Not allowed.
Dogs Allowed, on lead (£1). Certain breeds not permitted.
Restrictions No arrivals after dark.
Getting there By road The campsite is best approached via Evercreech or Bruton, not through the winding village of Batcombe, where large vehicles can easily get stuck. From Shepton Mallet take the A371 south, and then the left fork just past Prestleigh on to the B3081. After Evercreech, follow the brown and white campsite signs. There are also signs from Bruton. **By public transport** Castle Cary train station is 6 miles away; some trains also stop in nearer-still Bruton. Buses are next to non-existent in these parts, but a taxi will cost about £8 (Dovecot Taxis, 01749 812098).

Little disturbs the calm at Batcombe Vale, deep in the English countryside; even the tiny but charming village of Batcombe is a good 30-minute walk away. A steep, single lane drops you down into the campsite, set at the bottom of a tranquil, cow-lined vale.

With just 30 pitches, there's no chance of the quiet, sheltered site being overrun with campers. (It also means getting a place can be tricky, so do book.) A looped gravel road connects the pitches, which are all pretty level; most are provided with electric hook-ups. Campervans and the odd caravan give way to tents at the far end, pitched just a few feet from nonchalantly grazing cows. Adding to the enchantment is a completely hollow tree that children can climb inside to play games with their new-found friends.

The facilities are simple but just right. Cleaned twice a day and decorated with cut flowers, the toilet and shower block has hot water when you need it and, thanks to the open design, a refreshing breeze blowing through. There's no shop, but ice packs can be refrozen.

Best of all, there are four lakes on site – one for boating, three for fishing. The rudd and carp seem to bite for all but the unluckiest of anglers; get a tin of sweetcorn for bait and a starter kit from Tight Lines Angling (01373 455001) in Frome. You'll need a licence.

This is camping at its old-fashioned best, whether you want to take the kids on expeditions along little streams or wander the countryside and finish the day in a lovely old pub. A few miles away, the striking medieval town of Bruton is worth a wander for its historic church, museum and stepping stones across the river.

On site, sit back and take in the glowing sunsets after a day spent rowing around the boating lake or fishing. As evening falls, swallows, swifts and buzzards give up the night sky to the bats that inspired the area's name.

EATING & DRINKING

There's no shop on site, although the office sometimes sells scrumpy, alongside charcoal and firelighters.

It's a pleasant half-hour stroll to the Three Horseshoes Inn (01749 850359, www.thethree horseshoesinn.co.uk) in Batcombe. Notable for its sterling use of locally sourced produce and its hand-pumped ales and ciders, this 17th-century coaching inn is a welcoming, if pricey, gastro treat.

Bruton, a five-minute drive away, has several small supermarkets. The Olive Bowl (01749 812782, closed Sun) is a sweet little deli and café, next to the local museum, while the High Street Organics Community Co-Operative (01749 813191, closed Sat afternoon, Sun) sells everything from fresh veg to green nappies and Ecover products. The newest foodie addition to the area is the wonderful At The Chapel (01749 814070, www.atthechapel.co.uk, closed dinner Sun). A converted chapel is the setting for superb coffee and first-class contemporary food (such as devilled whitebait, slow-cooked lamb shank with horseradish mash, and wood-fired pizzas). It also has an excellent bakery and a wine shop.

Take a detour on your way back to the campsite to stock up on organic meat and veg – all of a very high standard, from local farmers – at Gilcombe Farm (01749 813710, www.somersetorganics.co.uk, closed Sat afternoon, Sun) on the A359.

SOMERSET

ATTRACTIONS & ACTIVITIES

There's plenty to do around the campsite. Paths meander around the lakes, there are free rowing boats, and the coarse fishing is excellent.

For rambles in the Mendips, come armed with an OS map, or visit the tourist information centre in Shepton Mallet (01749 345258). Leaflets for sale include suggestions for a four-mile and a six-mile walk through the countryside around Batcombe. Alternatively, walk or cycle along the Colliers Way (www.colliersway.co.uk), which runs from Bath to Frome via aqueducts, quiet lanes and disused railway lines, following the route of the old Somersetshire Coal Canal. Join it at Frome, around half an hour's drive from the site.

It's less than ten miles to the romantic lakeside temples, wooded walks and rhododendron dells of 18th-century Stourhead (01747 841152, www.national trust.org.uk, house closed Wed, Thur, all Nov-early Mar), as seen on the big screen in *Pride and Prejudice*.

In the opposite direction is the diminutive city of Wells and its splendid cathedral (01749 674483, www.wellscathedral.org.uk), where for centuries swans have rung a bell in the moat to request food. Those with alternative spiritual leanings can drive to Glastonbury, about 14 miles from Batcombe, to clamber up its famous Tor and quaff herbal tea in the hippyish cafés below.

Annual events include the Easter duck race in Nunney (www.nunney.org), when a flotilla of plastic ducks race down the stream that runs past the village's tiny 14th-century castle and moat. Towards the end of May, the two-week Bruton Festival of Arts (www.brutonfestival.co.uk) offers all kinds of cultural events, from acoustic nights and art exhibitions to storytelling sessions.

Visiting food-lovers will relish Frome's Cheese Show (01373 463600, www.fromecheeseshow.co.uk). Founded in 1861, it takes place each September and is now combined with an agricultural show.

AMUSING THE KIDS

Children love Batcombe Vale, but there's also a lot on offer outside the campsite. Mini troglodytes can head down Wookey Hole (01749 672243, www.wookey.co.uk), just beyond Wells. Parents might baulk at some of the attractions (life-size plastic dinosaurs, mini golf, an amusement arcade, circus shows), but the caverns are wonderfully atmospheric – beware the witch.

The East Somerset Railway puffs along a five-mile round trip between Cranmore and Mendip Vale stations. The other star attraction is Longleat, with its safari park, maze, historic house and grounds, just a 25-minute drive away. For more on both, *see p92*.

CAMPING NEARBY

It's ten miles to Greenacres Family Campsite (01749 890497, www.greenacres-camping.co.uk, open Easter-Oct, £8 adult, £3 child) in North Wootton, a family-centric site with masses of on-site activities. Tents and campervans only.

Alternatively, the adults-only Old Oaks Touring Park (01458 831437, www.theoldoaks.co.uk, open mid Feb-mid Nov, from £14 for two people) offers fine fishing and views of Glastonbury Tor.

Site specific

✔ A clutch of beautiful lakes provides endless entertainment, whether you're rowing a boat or relaxing with a rod and reel. Alternatively, follow the stream and roam the countryside.

✗ The naturally ventilated facilities might add an unwelcome nip to your ablutions on a chilly day. If your visit coincides with the Glastonbury Festival, beware traffic delays.

SOMERSET

Buckland Bell

Buckland Bell Campsite
Bell Inn, High Street, Buckland Dinham,
Somerset BA11 2QT
01373 462956
bellatbuckland@aol.com
www.bellatbuckland.co.uk
Map p25 ⑳
OS map ST752512

Number of pitches 40 tents/caravans/
motorhomes. Man shed (sleeps 1).
Open All year.
Booking By phone, email. Advisable.
Typical cost Tent £8 per pitch, £2 per
person. Man shed £50.
Facilities Restaurant (in pub); bush shower
(cold water); toilets; washing-up area.
Campfires Allowed, in designated areas.
Dogs Allowed.
Restrictions No amplified music after
midnight.
Getting there By road Buckland Dinham
is on the A362 between Radstock and
Frome, about 12 miles south of Bath.
By public transport Train to Frome, from
where Buckland is 10 mins by bus 414
(Frome Minibuses, 01373 471 474).
The service runs every couple of hours
and stops outside the pub.

For people who truly want to get back to nature,
nothing beats pitching a tent in a farmer's field
with few, if any, facilities. For others, close
proximity to a pub is a prerequisite for any
camping trip. Sometimes the two desires coincide
– in which case, the Buckland Bell must surely
be the best campsite in Somerset.

Enterprising landlords Jeremy and Lucy
Westcott have turned the field behind their
lovely 16th-century village inn into a campsite,
where you're woken by an indomitable cockerel,
allowed campfires, and can play a leisurely game
of boules before bedtime on a purpose-built
court. Chickens wander between the tents,
and ducks waddle around a fenced-off pond.

But the simplicity of the Bell's facilities belies
its delightfulness, and Heath Robinson-meets-
Robinson Crusoe touches. A cold water pipe
connected to a lampshade and colander create
an open-air bush shower, a large belfast sink
and cold tap comprise the washing facilities,
and the toilets are either in the pub (accessible
from 8.30am until closing time) or a Portaloo

when it's closed. There are a couple of large
firepits dotted around the site, or you can borrow
a modified metal beer barrel and make your own
small firepit or barbecue.

There's no shop, but Jeremy is happy to help
children find the chicken's newly laid eggs in the
morning, and sort out fresh milk. You can also
order takeaway pub meals and supplies from
Lucy, who delights in making campers' stays
as pleasurable and memorable as possible.

The duo are also cooking up new ways to
make the site more interestin. The latest
scheme is the man shed (men only!) – a garden
shed complete with a bed, chair and radio, as
well as a two-course meal from the restaurant
and the makings of a breakfast to cook on your
stove or barbecue.

Just under three miles away, Frome is a pretty
market town with a lively arts scene and a taste
for the bohemian. In July, the annual festival is
a spirited mix of film, comedy, theatre, music
and visual arts, fuelled by artisan food stalls
and cream teas. The small and enchanting village
of Mells is also within ten minutes' drive of the
campsite. Siegfried Sassoon is buried in the
graveyard of the 15th-century church, whose
stately avenue of clipped yews was designed
by Edwin Lutyens; after paying your respects,
stop by the splendid coaching inn for a pint.

EATING & DRINKING

The Bell Inn is, of course, the obvious food choice.
The menu is wide-ranging and the cooking basic
but good, with ingredients sourced from local
producers wherever possible (try Margaret's treacle
tarts, made in Frome). Typical dishes include hearty
sausages and mash, steak and ale casserole, fish and
chips, mixed grills, and steaks of various dimensions.
A fine selection of local brews, and even a local
brandy, are on hand to wash it all down.

Nearby Frome is an excellent place to pick up
provisions, as it has greengrocers, delis, bakeries
and a butcher's shop, along with an abundance of
cafés, takeaways and restaurants. The Garden Café
(01373 454178, www.gardencafefrome.co.uk) is open
for breakfast, lunch and early dinner, and until late
on Friday and Saturday. Its menu, served in an
elegant indoor space and lovely courtyard garden,
runs from big breakfasts to meze platters, toasted
sandwiches, curry and own-made cakes, with a focus
on organic ingredients. Pizzas and tapas are now
available on the evenings it opens late.

If you prefer pubs, but want to venture a little
further afield, try the Talbot Inn (01373 812254,
www.talbotinn.com) in Mells. Within easy walking

SOMERSET

distance of the Bell, it does excellent traditional pub grub in a stunning setting, whether you choose the restaurant, beer garden or cobbled courtyard.

ATTRACTIONS & ACTIVITIES

You're spoiled for choice when it comes to finding things to do around the Bell, beginning with terrific walks from the campsite. It is adjacent to Macmillan Way West (www.macmillanway.org), and a wide range of walking paths – one of which leads to the Westbury White Horse, visible in the distance.

It's just over a mile and a half to the Colliers Way (www.colliersway.co.uk), shared by cyclists and walkers, which passes through the Frome, Great Elm, Kilmersdon and Radstock. Follow it some nine miles to the imposing Dundas Aqueduct, or go for a shorter spin along the river and through quiet country lanes.

Frome and Mells are delightful for lunch and a leisurely potter; for a proper day out, Bath's honey-coloured Georgian terraces, museums and Roman baths are half an hour's drive away.

Back on the site, the Bell hosts a Ladies' Film Night in its 16th-century barn on the first Thursday of the month. These are convivial, small-scale affairs, with free screenings of rom-coms and melodramatic oldies (donations are requested for Cancer Research), and much wine-drinking.

AMUSING THE KIDS

Steam through the Mendip Hills on the East Somerset Railway (01749 880417, www.eastsomersetrailway. com, timetable varies) from Cranmore, then walk back on the wildlife trail that runs beside the tracks. With an engine shed, workshops, special holiday events such as Thomas the Tank Engine days, a museum and a café at Cranmore station, it's an absorbing day out.

A trip to Longleat House & Safari Park (01985 844400, www.longleat.co.uk, closed Nov-Feb), less than eight miles away, easily whiles away the best part of a rainy day – though if it's raining cats and dogs, you're not likely to see many monkeys.

CAMPING NEARBY

Seven Acres Camping Site (01373 464222, open Mar-Oct) in West Woodlands, just outside Frome, is friendly, and well placed for a Sainsbury's and plenty of activities. A wooden bridge over a stream leads to the decent-sized tent field (about £10 per night for two people), which is dotted with picnic tables.

Lower Grange Farm (01373 452938, www.lowergrangefarm.webs.com, open all year, from £12 two people) in Feltham, near Frome, overlooks Longleat Forest. It has two resident collie dogs, a field of alpacas, a pub within walking distance and good facilities; the owners will rustle up packed lunches (for an extra charge) if given 24 hours' notice.

Site specific

✔ The site is within 100 yards of the lovely Bell Inn, with its roaring log fires, good food, takeaway beer and cider, a gorgeous garden, and two of the friendliest hosts you're ever likely to meet.

✘ The proximity to the pub can mean tipsy fellow-campers. Also, the facilities are very basic.

Eweleaze Farm

Eweleaze Farm
Osmington Hill, Osmington, Dorset DT3 6ED
01305 833690
peter@eweleaze.co.uk
www.eweleaze.co.uk
Map p25 ㉑
OS map SY716831

Number of pitches Approx 160 tents. No caravans/motorhomes. Cottage (sleeps 6).
Open Eweleaze Aug. Northdown July.
Booking Online. Essential.
Typical cost Eweleze £7-£14 adult, £3.50-£7 child. Northdown £5-£10 adult, £2.50-£5 child. Booking fee £10 (£2 without motor vehicle). £10 extra motor vehicle. Cottage from £350-£820.
Facilities Food stalls; shop; showers (free); straw bales (£3); toilets (flush and composting); washing-up areas.
Campfires Allowed. Firewood available (£3).
Dogs Allowed.
Restrictions No amplified music except Sat before 11pm.
Getting there By road From the A35, take the B3390 and then the A353 to Osmington. Drive through the village and turn left at the 30mph speed limit sign (there's a sign for Eweleaze but it's easily missed – it's more obvious if you're coming from the other direction). Follow the bumpy stone track for half a mile over the hill and down to the farm. **By public transport** Train to Weymouth, then bus CoastLinX53 (0870 608 2608, www.jurassiccoast.com) towards Exeter. It takes 10 mins to the Spice Ship pub in Preston; from there, walk along Church Lane to the end, then follow the campsite signs through the pony paddocks. The bus runs every couple of hrs, end Apr-Oct.

At twilight, Eweleaze Farm resembles a medieval encampment, with hundreds of tents – all shapes, sizes and colours – strewn across the headland. Campfires twinkle in the distance and the smell of barbecues fills the air. Out to sea, across Weymouth Bay, the lights of Portland glimmer. Sky-lanterns are let off, drifting slowly into the darkening sky. It's a magical sight.

This state of affairs is only temporary, lasting for most of August, when Eweleaze Farm turns seven of its fields into a tent-only campsite. The two fields nearest the private shingle beach have the best views, but slope more (the flattest sections are at the top and bottom). You can't park next to your tent here; instead, there's a parking area near the entrance. The other fields, further inland, are flatter and permit cars.

The South West Coast Path runs along the bottom of the site, heading west to Weymouth and east to Osmington and a string of beaches, including Lulworth Cove. The market town of Dorchester is about eight miles inland.

Dotted in the corners of each field are mini wooden sheds – the surprisingly sweet-smelling compost toilets, erected newly each year – washing-up sinks and water taps. There are a few flush toilets (not so sweet-smelling) and three sets of showers, also in neat wooden cabins.

The central courtyard near reception is where campers come to stock up at the excellent shop (all the food and drink you could need, plus sky-lanterns), grab a wood-fired pizza, pie or ice-cream from two stalls, and buy logs. You can also help yourself to the huge pile of brushwood; fires are an essential part of the Eweleaze experience. In a stroke of genius, straw bales are also on sale, functioning as seats, tables, windbreaks, and building blocks for kids.

Piles of straw everywhere add to the laid-back, slightly hippyish vibe. The lack of rules and festival-like atmosphere are what's so appealing, but this is a highly organised operation. Every camper reports to reception on arrival, is logged on to the computer booking system, then given a map of the farm and a notice to affix to their car window. Families love the place – there's plenty of space to run and cycle around, plus the beach – as do groups of friends, who pitch in clusters, flying pennants to mark their spot. It may be the biggest campsite you'll ever see, but it manages to remain uncrowded and relaxed.

Eweleaze's nearby sister site opened for the first time in 2011. Northdown Farm operates throughout July, and shares use of the excellent shop and other amenities. It's not beside the coast, though the sea can still be seen from the site; prices are marginally lower, perhaps for this reason.

EATING & DRINKING

There's really no need to leave camp, thanks to the food stalls and fabulous shop. The latter's produce is mainly organic and local, including beef and lamb (from the farm), milk, top-quality bread, eggs, fresh veg, bottled beers (from the Isle of Purbeck) and wine. Forgot the marshmallows? Get them here.

DORSET

If you do venture out, there's a smattering of pubs within walking distance. Osmington village has the capacious Sunray (01305 832148, www.the-sunray.co.uk), where you can eat in the restaurant (steaks and meaty grills a speciality), bar or – most popular – the front and back gardens.

To work up an appetite, it's a two-mile walk along the coast path to the Smugglers Inn (01305 833125) at Osmington Mills. Heaving with hikers and families at weekends, it's an atmospheric, multi-roomed establishment with rows of outdoor tables, serving Dorset beers and huge platefuls of superior pub grub (think gammon steak, chilli roast salmon, sticky toffee pudding and Purbeck ice-creams). Take a torch if you're stumbling back along the path after dark.

Preston village has couple of pubs, including the friendly Spice Shop (01305 834651), fish and chip shops, a Spar and Co-op, and an off-licence. For a wider range of shops and supermarkets and a monthly farmers' market, head to Dorchester.

It's 15 minutes by car to the lovely Moreton Tea Rooms (01929 463647), housed in Moreton village's former schoolhouse. Café by day, restaurant by night (on Fri and Sat), it makes inventive use of seasonal local ingredients in first-rate salads, sandwiches and light dishes (try the Dorset Down mushrooms in blue vinny sauce with toast and salad), and serves knockout ice-cream sundaes. At the rear is a flowery terrace with seating in wooden gazebos.

ATTRACTIONS & ACTIVITIES

There's good walking to be had; a network of paths, including the South West Coast Path (www.southwest coastpath.com), radiates out from the campsite. The pebble beach at Ringstead Bay – a ten-minute drive or a trek eastwards along the coast path – has a warm, shallow lagoon at high tide (perfect for children) and a wooden shack selling beach clobber, hot drinks and snacks. Further east, about 20 minutes

Site specific

✔ Only tents are allowed – one reason why the atmosphere is so magical. The shingle beach below the site is a bonus too.

✘ It's big, busy and full of children. If you're looking for a small secluded campsite, this is not the place.

Moreton

by car, lie two of Dorset's most popular seaside spots, Durdle Door and Lulworth Cove.

Lawrence of Arabia fans can make a pilgrimage to various sites nearby. He died in a motorbike accident while living at Clouds Hill (01929 405616, www.nationaltrust.org.uk, closed Mon, Tue, all Nov-mid Mar), an isolated cottage ten miles from Eweleaze. The tiny, austere building, furnished as it was when Lawrence lived there, is remarkably atmospheric. From there it's not far to Moreton to visit St Nicholas Church, where his funeral was held. After admiring the stunning engraved-glass windows, designed by Laurence Whistler and fitted after the originals were bombed in the war, walk along the road to Lawrence's eloquently simple grave. The shallow ford, with overhanging vegetation and a footbridge, is a popular bathing spot. The Moreton Tea Rooms can provide an excellent lunch; photos of Lawrence's funeral line the walls, and the bier on which his coffin was carried now serves as a cake stand.

Continue the military theme at Bovington Tank Museum (01929 405096, www.tankmuseum.org),

with its fearsome armoured vehicles, recreation of a World War I trench and 'tank action' arena.

AMUSING THE KIDS

Messing about on the beach below the campsite – swimming, kayaking, kite-flying – will occupy many a happy hour. You can't fail with a visit to Monkey World (01929 462537, www.monkeyworld.co.uk), 11 miles away near Wool. Alongside 60 chimpanzees (the largest collection outside Africa) are orangutans, squirrel monkeys, macaques, marmosets and ring-tailed lemurs – many of them rescued from labs, circuses or the illegal wild animal trade – housed in spacious wooden enclosures in landscaped grounds.

CAMPING NEARBY

Above Osmington Mills, near the Smugglers Inn, Rosewall Camping (01305 832248, www.weymouth camping.com, open Mar-Oct) has space for 225 tents on a grassy but sloping site. There are also riding stables and a well-stocked fishing lake. Two people plus a tent and car pay £15-£20.

DORSET

Tom's Field

Tom's Field Campsite & Shop
Tom's Field Road, Langton Matravers,
Swanage, Dorset BH19 3HN
01929 427110
tomsfield@hotmail.com
www.tomsfieldcamping.co.uk
Map p25 ㉒
OS map SY995784

Wandering around Tom's Field on a bright and sunny morning, it's easy to understand why people become evangelical about this deservedly popular campsite. From the pretty shop area, with its collection of rusty barbecues and flower-filled terrace outside, to the gloriously unspoilt setting, this is a nearly perfect campsite. The four-and-a-half-acre campground is divided into different areas, including a family field and a more secluded ridge, from which some pitches offer views of Swanage Bay.

The ethos fostered by mother-and-daughter owners Sarah and Jo Wootton is one of sustainability and environmentally responsible camping – so out go the carrier bags and branded bread, and in come cotton shoppers and local produce, including fresh bread, bacon and free-range eggs. Admirable recycling facilities (including a fierce-looking can crusher), minimal light pollution, a compost heap, careful rotation of the fields so that the grass is allowed to flourish, and lots of information about car-free activities

Number of pitches 100 tents/motorhomes. No caravans. Stone room (sleeps 2). Bunkhouse (sleeps 9).
Open Mid Mar-Oct.
Booking By phone, email (school holidays only). Minimum stay 5 nights if booking; 2 nights bank holidays.
Typical cost Camping £12-£18 2 people. Extra adult £5-£6, extra 5-16s £2. Stone room £30. Bunkhouse £10 per person.
Facilities Disabled facilities (toilet and shower); electric hook-ups (14); laundry facilities; shop; showers (25p); toilets; washing-up area.
Campfires Not allowed.
Dogs Allowed, on lead.
Restrictions No unsupervised under-18s.
Getting there By road Take the A351 from Wareham towards Swanage. Go through Corfe Castle village and turn right on to the B3069. After about 1.5 miles, just before Langton Matravers, turn right on Tom's Field Road. The campsite is not far, at the end of the road. **By public transport** Train to Wareham, from where bus 40 (01983 827005, www.wdbus.co.uk) runs hourly to Langton Matravers. Journey takes about 25 mins.

add to the sense of careful consideration, which spills over into the way people behave on the site. This is one of the quietest, calmest and prettiest campgrounds you're ever likely to stay on – though you're not likely to be on it much. The coastal Purbeck Hills location is spectacular, and you can strike off in any direction for a terrific walk.

Don't rush around too much, though; once everyone's scooted off on foot, on bikes, in crusty campervans and in gleaming people carriers, you can have this perfectly formed campsite all to yourself. Here, the grass is impossibly green, and the silence is broken only by the chorus of birds tweeting in the sheltering trees and sheep baa-ing in the surrounding fields.

And when one of the resident rabbits pops out for a hop down the path, you'll get the eerie feeling that you've wandered on to the cover of a Jehovah's Witness brochure. Evangelical, indeed.

EATING & DRINKING

You could spend an enjoyable few days at Tom's Field without having to venture outside for meals, if you hire a barbecue (£1 for two nights) and stock up on fresh produce from the excellent shop. Just over two miles away, Swanage has two supermarkets, several bakeries and a butcher's shop, along with a market on Tuesdays (Easter-Oct, 8am-3pm).

It's a short walk to the village of Langton Matravers, where you'll find everything from a breakfast fry-up to a pile of scones for tea at the Poppy Tearooms, at Putlake Adventure Park (01929 422917, www.putlakeadventurefarm.com/tea.htm), open from 9am daily. The village has a good range of dinner or lunch venues; the Kings Arms (01929 422979) and the Ship (01929 423855, www.theship-swanage.co.uk), both located on the High Street, serve pub grub until 9pm. The latter wins out on views and atmosphere, so it's best to book.

And if you like your pubs with great views, eclectic live music and even a fossil museum, don't miss the wonderful Square & Compass in Worth Matravers (01929 439229, www.squareandcompasspub.co.uk), a couple of miles away, which can be reached via an ancient coastal track near the campsite, called the Priest's Way. There's no food to speak of, but a

Site specific

✔ The site's location, on the coast near Swanage, is its main draw – although once you've pitched your tent, the peace and quiet make it hard to leave camp.

✘ This is a popular spot. Reservations are only taken for Whitsun week and for a minimum of five nights during the summer holidays, so arrive very early on a Friday if you're planning a weekend stay in summer.

Following the South West Coast Path towards Dancing Ledge.

hot pasty goes down very well with the award-winning beer and cider, all delivered through a quirky little serving hatch.

ATTRACTIONS & ACTIVITIES

Tom's Field is mere minutes from a coastline that is England's only natural World Heritage Site – bring your walking boots. A footpath adjacent to the site leads to the magnificent rocks of Dancing Ledge, and Swanage is an easy walk along the South West Coast Path, or a few minutes by road.

Spellbinding, Jurassic-era wonders such as the fossil forest, Stair Hole, Durdle Door and Lulworth Cove lie around 20 miles west along the coast path – half an hour's drive away. If it's raining, Lulworth Castle (0845 4501054, www.lulworth.com, closed Sat) is a great place at which to stay warm and dry. Small fry can look for secret passages and imagine tales of gruesome goings-on, or play with the animals outside (weather permitting), while older children can pretend to be dashing knights or ladies at court. Woodland walks, impressive interiors and an adventure play area mean you can spend hours here. Regular events in the holidays include historical re-enactments, jousting displays, car rallies and concerts.

Lone adults might prefer a serene afternoon at the Blue Pool & Teahouse (01929 551408, www.bluepooluk.com, closed Nov-Mar) in Furzebrook, 15 minutes by car. The gorgeous pool changes colour as light is diffracted through fine clay suspended in the water. A suitably pretty tea room and 25 acres of heath woodland, bisected by sandy paths and walking trails dotted with benches, make for a tranquil afternoon.

AMUSING THE KIDS

Putlake Adventure Farm (01929 422917, www.putlakeadventurefarm.com) in Langton Matravers is a godsend for parents. A soft play zone and trampolines burn off any excess energy, while Shire horses, rabbits, alpacas and chipmunks should get everyone cooing happily before ice-creams in the Poppy Tearooms.

CAMPING NEARBY

This being Purbeck, there are plenty of options. The nearest alternative is Acton Field Campsite (01929 424184, www.actonfieldcampsite.co.uk, open spring bank holiday week, last week July-Aug, £6-£12 per tent), a family-friendly site half a mile outside Langton Matravers. You can pitch your tent where you please and look forward to the arrival of the mobile grocery van. Slightly further afield is Downshay Farm (01929 480316, www.downshayfarm.co.uk, open spring bank holiday week, mid July-Aug and during Swanage Folk Festival). With great views across the Purbeck Hills, this working dairy farm is good value too: £2-£4 tent pitch, £5 adult, £1-£2 child.

Burnbake Campsite (*see right*), on the north side of Purbeck, isn't far either.

Burnbake

Burnbake Campsite
Rempstone, Corfe Castle,
Wareham, Dorset BH20 5JH
01929 480570
info@burnbake.com
www.burnbake.com
Map p25 ㉓
OS map SY995832

Number of pitches 130 tents/motorhomes. No caravans.
Open Easter-Oct.
Booking By post, for spring and summer bank holidays only.
Typical cost Tent £8-£10 adult, £2-£4.50 extra adult, £1-£2 3-16s.
Facilities Freezer; laundry facilities; play area; shop; showers (30p); toilets; washing-up area.
Campfires Allowed, off ground.
Dogs Allowed, on lead.
Restrictions Single-sex groups and unsupervised under-18s by arrangement. No noise after 11pm.
Getting there By road Burnbake is on the Isle of Purbeck, halfway between Corfe Castle (3 miles away) and Studland (4 miles). From Wareham, take the A351 to Corfe Castle and turn left on to the B3351 towards Studland. Take the third turning on the left, signposted Rempstone. If you're coming from the other direction, from the Sandbanks Ferry, follow the road through Studland then fork right towards Corfe. The turning to Rempstone is the first on the right. It's a mile to the campsite, which is signed. **By public transport** The closest train station is Wareham, from where bus 40 runs hourly to Corfe Castle (15 mins); it's then a £7 taxi ride. Alternatively, from Bournemouth station take bus 50 to Studland. Buses run every 30-60 mins May-Sept and the journey, including the ferry trip across Poole Harbour, takes 1 hr. A cab from Studland is £12. Taxis: 01929 480507, www.valleytaxis.biz. Buses: 01983 827005, www.wdbus.co.uk.

There's something for everyone in Burnbake's 12 unspoiled acres, set in the heart of Dorset's Purbeck Hills and just minutes away from the stunning Jurassic coastline. You want a secluded, leafy woodland copse in which to pitch your tent? No problem; this intimate but surprisingly spacious site has a great range of large, level woodland pitches (on our visit, one nearby pitch was accommodating five tents of varying sizes, along with a gazebo, a range of cars and even a minibus – but more on that later). Moreover, most of them are within hearing range of the site's pretty little stream. Prefer to camp on soft, springy grass, sheltered by trees, with an attractive wooden play area for the children? The central parkland area should meet your needs.

Either way, you're never too far from the shower block or the log cabin loos, marked by a bright red telephone box. For families, there's also a baby room with changing and bathing facilities. Drinking water taps are dotted around the site, and it's a short hop to the shop for basics and bread.

So which pitch to choose? In our experience, the woodland pitches are where the party crowds head; despite requests from staff and fellow campers, the group next to us were partying until the rain arrived in the small hours, and a midnight stroll to the loos revealed plenty of other smaller parties taking place in the woods. On the grass pitches, all was quiet after 11pm, with both children and grown-ups happily worn out – the former thanks to a day on the beach and an evening on the rope swings; the latter thanks to their offspring and, judging by the overflowing recycling bins, a pleasant evening of wine and barbecues.

There's an endearingly sociable vibe on the ferry over from Poole, as returning visitors recognise old friends: this feels like the sort of campsite where people come with their parents when they're little, with friends when they are single, and with their own children when they become parents.

Site specific

✔ The varied mix of pitches and people is a real plus point; it's rare to find such wild woodland pitches alongside neatly manicured patches of green.

✘ The downside is choosing the perfect woodland pitch, not knowing whether your neighbours will be a peaceful party of four, or 24 raucous revellers. Bring earplugs, just in case.

DORSET

Burnbake campsite (centre and above); New Inn at Church Knowle (below).

DORSET

Swanage Railway, with Corfe Castle in the background.

EATING & DRINKING

The camp shop's 9am delivery of fresh bread, milk and cakes makes for a good start to the day – but there are lots of beguiling alternatives to tinned tuna for dinner, which is the best you're likely to get from a basic selection of packaged food. For a more varied choice of groceries, head for Swanage, a ten-minute drive away: the town has supermarkets, bakeries and a butcher's shop, along with a farmers' market on Tuesdays, held in the main beach car park.

In nearby Kingston, the Scott Arms pub (01929 480270, www.thescottarms.com) has stunning views across the valley to Corfe Castle, and wittily hosts a weekly Jamaican barbecue that impresses with its authenticity – sorrel punch, anyone? The wide-ranging menu also offers more traditional dishes, such as ham, eggs, chips and mushy peas. The 16th-century stone and thatched New Inn (01929 480357, www.thenewinn-churchknowle.co.uk) at Church Knowle, four miles from Burnbake, is equally enticing, specialising in locally caught, simply cooked fish.

For more seafood, visit the Shell Bay Restaurant (01929 450363, www.shellbay.net), located 200 yards from the ferry pier in Studland. It may look like a beach shack, but it serves some of the best fish you'll eat in the area, in one of the prettiest settings. Prices are significantly lower at lunchtime.

ATTRACTIONS & ACTIVITIES

This is arguably the choicest stretch of Dorset's coastline, and the area has plenty of attractions. Close to the campsite entrance is Rempstone Stables (01929 480490), which offers horse and pony rides and lessons. The terrain is enjoyably varied, whether you fancy an amble through the forest or a canter along the beach.

The dramatic ruins of Corfe Castle (01929 481294, www.nationaltrust.co.uk), looming above the pretty, Portland-stone cottages of the village of Corfe, are terrific, and an easy, enjoyable walk from Burnbake.

If it's overcast, a six-mile trip through glorious countryside on the Swanage Railway steam train (01929 425800, www.swanagerailway.co.uk, closed Jan, Feb and Mon-Fri Nov, Dec, Mar) from Norden's Park & Ride, just off the A351, is a lot of fun – and who knows, by the time you reach the seaside town of Swanage, the sun might have come out. If not, set off on the South West Coast Path for an exhilarating walk to the headland opposite Old Harry Rocks, whose majestic, 80-million-year-old chalk stacks might make you forget the small and fleeting matter of the weather.

AMUSING THE KIDS

From Sandbanks, hop on a ferry (01929 462383, www.brownseaislandferries.com, closed Nov-Easter) to discover the thriving populations of red squirrels and avocets on the enchanting 500-acre Brownsea Island; it's a ten-minute crossing. The island is owned by the National Trust, but is also home to the Dorset Wildlife Trust Reserve (01202 709445, www.dorset wildlife.co.uk, closed Nov-Mar), which offers a number of self-guided nature trails.

CAMPING NEARBY

The Camping & Caravanning Club's Corfe Castle site (01929 480280, www.campingandcaravanning club.co.uk, open Mar-Oct) has 80 pitches in a charming parkland setting, and is just ten minutes' walk from Corfe Castle. Prices start at £7.66 per adult, plus a £7.15 pitch fee for non-members.

Also, Tom's Field (*see p96*) isn't far away.

DORSET

Stowford Manor Farm

Stowford Manor Farm
Wingfield, Trowbridge, Wiltshire BA14 9LH
01225 752253
stowford1@supanet.com
www.stowfordmanorfarm.co.uk
Map p25 ㉔
OS map ST811576

Number of pitches 30 tents/caravans/
motorhomes. B&B 3 rooms (01225
781318).
Open Camping Easter-Oct. B&B all year.
Booking By phone, email. Essential.
Typical cost Tent £8 1-person tent,
£12 2-person tent, £14 family tent.
Caravan/motorhome £14. B&B £75
double room.
Facilities Café (3-6pm daily Easter-Sept);
electric hook-ups (16); showers (50p);
toilets; washing-up area.
Campfires Not allowed.
Dogs Allowed, on lead.
Restrictions No unsupervised under-18s.
Getting there By road From the A36
(Bath to Warminster road), turn on to the
A366 towards Trowbridge. The entrance is
on the right after Farleigh Hungerford; if
you've reach the crossroads with the B3109
you've gone too far. **By public transport**
Train to Bradford on Avon or Trowbridge,
both 3 miles away. A taxi will cost about
£7 (A&D Taxis, 01225 865620).

On the Wiltshire/Somerset border, a 15-minute
drive from Bath, sits this compact, laid-back
campsite. At the entrance is an attractive cluster
of old stone buildings – the 15th-century
farmhouse and stables, a former watermill and
assorted outbuildings (many of which are now
used as workshops by local artisans). Next
comes the wedge-shaped camping field, adjacent
to the River Frome and divided by trees from
the overflow field (which is next to the road,
so a bit noisier). Most people pitch along the
edges of the river field – beware midges if
you're beside the water – leaving space in
the centre for youngsters to run about. It's flat
and sheltered, but can get muddy after rain.

Hand basins, a couple of coin-operated
showers and washing-up sinks are in the ex-
stable block; just opposite are three toilets.
Meander over to the farmhouse in the afternoon
for a luscious cream tea, served on old-fashioned

crockery and with cream made from the farm's
own Jersey cows; the front garden has trestle
tables (and wasps). You can also buy milk –
but nothing else – and refreeze ice packs.

The babbling brook and rope swings next to the
millhouse are a magnet for small children, who
could happily spend the whole day splashing in
the shallows or fishing for tiddlers. The World War
II pillbox in the middle of the field, meanwhile,

Site specific

✔ The shallow river is great for children,
while everyone loves the cream teas.

✘ There's not much space between pitches,
so it can get cramped when busy.

is just the right height for scrambling over. Walk through the next field to find the Farleigh & District Swimming Club – founded in 1933, and the only remaining river swimming club in the country. There's a set of steps, a diving area and a placid pool next to a weir; non-members can join for a nominal fee.

Some of the craftspeople working in the on-site workshops welcome visitors (check Stowford Manor Farm's website for contact details), while artistic types can book a place on one of the short courses run by the Liquid Glass Centre (www.liquidglasscentre.co.uk).

All in all, it's an unhurried, traditional sort of place. Stowford Manor has been in the Bryant family for generations, and there has been a campsite here for 40 years. It's ideal for lazing about and catching up on your reading – not so good if you thrive on activity and excitement. That said, there are gardens and historic houses to visit in the vicinity, and it's only three miles to Bradford on Avon – once a booming cloth and wool centre, now a lively town with mellow, honey-coloured buildings, rows of 17th-century weavers' cottages and plenty to see and do. Bath is also an easy drive, with its museums, mannered tea rooms, gorgeous Georgian crescents and excavated Roman baths.

EATING & DRINKING

Head to Bradford on Avon for a Sainsbury's, health food stores and various independent retailers. Under ten minutes' drive from camp, Trowbridge has more choice, but makes for a less enjoyable shopping experience.

If breakfast at the tent doesn't appeal, start the day with eggs florentine or a full English at the in-store café at Woody's (01225 720006, www.woodys farmshop.co.uk), a couple of miles away. You can also buy fruit and veg, bread and deli goods.

There's a choice of three pubs nearby. The closest, less than a mile, is the Hungerford Arms (01225 754949, www.hungerford-arms.co.uk), set on a hill with a small terrace overlooking the remains of Farleigh Hungerford Castle. Drinks include Butcombe beer and Cheddar Valley cider, while the food runs from standard bar food (jacket potatoes, fish and chips) to Thai dishes.

More upmarket cooking – potted Cornish mackerel or devilled lambs' kidneys to start, perhaps, followed by venison burger with all the trimmings – is to be found at the New Inn (01225 863123, www.newinn westwood.com, closed Sun evening) in Westwood. Book if you want to partake of the Sunday roasts.

The third option is the Poplars (01225 752426, www.poplarswingfield.co.uk) in Wingfield, with its welcoming staff, Wadworth ales and adventurous

WILTSHIRE

(some might say outlandish) food menu. It's best known for having its own cricket team and field; the place is packed on match days.

For a change from pub fare, head to Bradford. The modern-looking Fat Fowl (01225 863111, www.fatfowl.com) on Silver Street serves good coffee, lunch, dinner and tapas, and hosts regular jazz nights. Next to the canal, the Lock Inn Café (01225 868068, www.thelockinn.co.uk, closed dinner Mon, Sun) is a wonderfully colourful and eccentric spot. The enormous menu caters to every craving, running from fry-ups, ciabattas and salads to hot meals (beef stew with dumplings, perhaps, or jambalaya).

ATTRACTIONS & ACTIVITIES

Walk a mile or so along the river, past the swimming club, to reach the ruined medieval towers of Farleigh Hungerford Castle (01225 754026, www.english-heritage.org.uk, closed Mon-Fri Nov-Mar). Children will enjoy the bloodthirsty tales of the Hungerford family, including one Tudor lady of the manor who burned her murdered husband's body in the castle's oven. At the back of the car park, stone steps lead up to the Hungerford Arms pub.

It's worth pottering around Bradford, taking in the Saxon church, two historic bridges, massive 600-year-old tithe barn and diminutive weavers' cottages on the hill. Narrowboat trips on the Kennet & Avon Canal

start at the lock, just south of the town centre. Or cycle along the towpath; bikes (and Canadian canoes) are available from Towpath Trail (01225 867187, www.towpathtrail.co.uk), based at TT Cycles on Frome Road.

Just over two miles from Stowford, Iford Manor (01225 863146, www.ifordmanor.co.uk, closed Mon, Fri May-Sept, all Oct-Apr except occasional Sun) is a gem. The charming Italianate garden, designed by Edwardian architect Harold Peto, is full of sculptures, terraces and surprising views, while the medieval cloisters host opera performances in summer. Note that it's open only for a few hours in the afternoon.

AMUSING THE KIDS

The river is an endless source of fascination for most kids – bring bathing suits and fishing nets.

Longleat (see p92), 11 miles to the south, is on the itinerary of most campers at Stowford Manor, and the Bryants can usually organise discounted tickets.

CAMPING NEARBY

Brokerswood Country Park (01373 822238, www.brokerswood.net, open all year) tends to be dominated by caravans and motorhomes, but its extensive facilities appeal to families. A standard pitch for two adults and two children costs £11.50-£27.50, and includes access to 80 acres of park, with play areas, a miniature railway and a fishing lake.

Abbey Home Farm

Abbey Home Farm
Burford Road, Cirencester,
Gloucestershire GL7 5HF
01285 640441
info@theorganicfarmshop.co.uk
www.theorganicfarmshop.co.uk
Map p25 ㉕
OS map SP042037

Number of pitches 50 tents/campervans. No caravans/motorhomes. 1 yurt (sleeps 5). 4 yurt camp (sleeping 18). Shepherd's hut, hut by the pond (both sleep 2, adults only).
Open Camping Easter-Oct. Huts all year.
Booking Camping: 'green field' no booking, arrive in shop hours; 'secret glade' by email, phone, online. Yurts/huts by email, online. Minimum stay 2 nights yurts/huts.
Typical cost Camping £4 adult, £1 child. Single yurt £40, £15 extra adult, £5 extra child. 4 yurt camp £550 3 days. Huts £60. Check website for latest prices.
Facilities Shop; showers (camping cold water; hut shower £1); toilets (flush and composting).
Campfires Allowed, in braziers (£5). Firewood available (£5).
Dogs Not allowed.
Restrictions No unsupervised under-18s; single-sex groups by arrangement. No amplified music, no noise after 10.30pm on the main campsite.
Getting there By road From Cirencester (south), take the A417 heading north. At the junction with the A429, turn right on to the B4425 (Burford Road) towards Barnsley. The campsite entrance is the first left after the traffic lights and is signposted for the Organic Farm Shop. Coming from the north, take the A429 to the same junction and turn left on to Burford Road. Follow the farm track to the campsite reception, on the left. **By public transport** The nearest train station is Kemble, on the other side of Cirencester. Buses are infrequent, so it's best to get a taxi, about £15, to the farm. Cirencester Taxis (01285 642767) operate from the rail station.

A far cry from the world of slick, commercial camping and caravanning sites, Abbey Home Farm is a homespun haven, set on an organic farm in the Cotswolds. Pigs, chickens and cows all live alongside the flourishing vegetable gardens and fields of grain – around which hedgerows are being planted, as part of the farm's conservation-conscious approach.

The camping area changed location in 2010: it's now an expansive, grassy, hedge-backed field, set by a broadleaf woodland and with magnificent views across the farmland. There are no designated pitches, and no vehicles are allowed, not even for unloading – but wheelbarrows are provided to help transport your stuff. Campervans and modestly proportioned motorhomes get their own area. A barn houses toilets and solar showers, with extra compost loos in the wood, and a cold water tap for washing-up. In the evenings, campers can hire a brazier and cultivate their own campfire.

For still more secluded gatherings, there's the 'secret' woodland glade. A mile from the main field and shop, it has room for four small tents (maximum eight people), its own compost loo and a stone circle at its centre. If you're lucky, you might glimpse one of the elusive resident deer.

On another hidden-away woodland clearing, the yurt camp comprises four yurts (usually hired out together), compost toilets and a charming – if chilly – outdoor shower; after heating the water over the campfire, you use a foot pump to transfer the water from bucket to overhead shower. Equipped with mattresses and not much else, these are not intended as year-round, luxury woodland retreats: aside from the wood-burning stove and gas ring in the largest yurt, it's outdoor campfires only.

The single yurt, meanwhile, is a 20-minute walk across the fields from the farm shop, in yet another patch of woodland. Close by is a hut – a wonderfully romantic hideaway, surrounded by trees and overlooking a pond. Facilities are spartan, but include a wood stove and a mattress; it also shares two showers and a flush toilet with the yurt.

If you're planning a party or family gathering, there's also a private camping area for hire, with space for up to 50 people.

The back-to-nature attitude extends to almost every corner of the farm. The site follows a 'leave no trace' ethos, which means stringent recycling policies – what's more, campers who come by car will be expected to take any rubbish that can't be recycled away with them. Noise pollution is also a no-no, with a site-wide ban on amplified music.

Regardless of what you make of the eco policies and less-is-more approach to facilities,

GLOUCESTERSHIRE

only the most churlish of campers could fail to appreciate the site's beauty – and the wonderful farm shop and café. The former is an emporium of all things organic, while the latter turns the products of the nearby vegetable gardens into luscious vegetarian fare – except on Sundays, when a magnificent roast is served.

EATING & DRINKING

The organic farm shop sells meat, fruit and veg, general groceries, eggs and dairy products, much of which is produced on the farm. There's also a cosy licensed café – like the shop, closed on Mondays. The menu is strictly vegetarian (bar the Sunday roasts).

For other food supplies and restaurants, head into Cirencester, a couple of miles away. Jesse's Bistro (01285 641497, www.jessesbistro.co.uk, closed Sun, dinner Mon) is a dependable option, serving fresh Cornish fish and meat from the butcher's next door. Run by the same owners, the latter does a fine sideline in pasties, pies and cheeses.

Locals also recommend the Twelve Bells Inn (01285 652230, www.twelvebellscirencester.com), which serves gargantuan portions of typical pub food in a warm, cosy setting. There are also a couple of Indian restaurants, along with the popular Thai Emerald (01285 654444, www.thai-emerald.co.uk) on Castle Street.

ATTRACTIONS & ACTIVITES

There's plenty of scope for walks around the farmland and woods, which seem never-ending. There are also farm tours, and the possibility of cookery classes and outdoor activities such as archery and bushcraft for groups; call for details.

Cirencester also offers much to see and do. The town's illustrious Roman heritage is brought to life in the Corinium Museum (01285 655611, www.coriniummuseum.co.uk), while a series of grassy lumps and bumps mark the site of its once-mighty amphitheatre, just west of town. In the Middle Ages, wool and weaving brought the town prosperity – and funded its fine, Cotswold stone houses and the decidedly grand Church of St John the Baptist (01285 659317, www.cirenparish.co.uk).

Chedworth Roman Villa (01242 890256, www. nationaltrust.org.uk, closed Mon, Tue Mar-Oct, all Nov-Feb), eight miles from the campsite, comprises the excavated remains of one of Britain's largest Roman villas. The site includes more than a mile of walls, along with mosaics, bathhouses and latrines.

AMUSING THE KIDS

Abbey Home Farm is wonderfully child-friendly as you might gather from the brightly painted totem pole on the new camping field. Independent exploration is encouraged, with only the farmyard off-limits; on arrival, campers are given a map of the farm, showing where the different animals live. A monthly farm walk might take in milking or cheese-making.

For excursions off-site, Cotswold Water Park (01793 752413, www.waterpark.org) is five miles away, towards Swindon. It encompasses watersport lakes, cycling and walking trails, a rare-breeds farm and two country parks – one with a lakeside beach, playground, and bikes for hire.

CAMPING NEARBY

Abbey Home Farm rarely turns campers away – but should the site happen to be full, then Mayfield Park (01285 831301, www.mayfieldpark.co.uk, open all year) is located four miles away. It offers camping and caravanning facilities for around £12 a night.

Site specific

✔ The farm shop and café are a serious draw for foodies; if you're here on a Sunday, the roast is not to be missed.

✘ If you're not keen to embrace compost loos, solar-heated showers and recycling, this might not be the campsite for you.

Doward Park

Doward Park
Great Doward, Symonds Yat,
Ross-on-Wye, Herefordshire HR9 6BP
01600 890438
enquiries@dowardpark.co.uk
www.dowardpark.co.uk
Map p25 ㉖
OS map SO548157

If you're the kind of camper who heads for the corner of the open field furthest away from everyone else, you'll love Doward Park. Set in light-filled woodland in the Wye Valley, this pretty, terraced campsite uses hedging to mark out many of the pitches, creating individual gardens that are secluded, private and sheltered, but large enough to accommodate your tent and still have plenty of chill-out space. Borrow duckboards for your porch, hire a picnic table for your dining and you're all set.

Thanks to a ban on cars in the tent fields (it's an easy walk from any of the pitches to the car park) and stern rules about children and noise, this is camping at its most tranquil, with just 27 pitches in total. Hot showers, ice pack freezing and lantern and mobile phone charging are free (although you won't get any reception here), and the small camp shop is stocked with most things you'll need – including hot drinks, milk, butter, bacon and eggs. Owner Alison Dean will even do you a same-day service wash, if you get your laundry in early enough. Gas bottles are available too.

The fenced-in woodland play area, Bluebell Woods, is terrific fun for kids, but rather than natural encounters, they'll probably favour clambering over the picturesque wooden climbing

Number of pitches 24 tents, 3 campervans/motorhomes. No caravans.
Open Mar-Oct.
Booking By phone, email. Essential weekends, school holidays. If booking, minimum stay 2 nights, 3 nights bank holidays.
Typical cost £13-£17 2 people, £3 extra adult, £2.50 extra child.
Facilities Disabled facilities (toilet); electric hook-ups (10); laundry facilities; picnic table hire (£1.50); play area; shop; showers (free); toilets; washing-up area.
Campfires Not allowed.
Dogs Allowed, on lead (£1).
Restrictions No large groups. No arrivals after 8pm, no noise after 10pm.
Getting there By road Take the A40 between Ross-on-Wye and Monmouth. From the north, turn off the A40 at the exit for Symonds Yat West. At the mini roundabout, take the second exit and follow signs for Doward Park. From the south, turn off the A40 at the sign for Crockers Ash, Ganarew and the Doward, which takes you back over the A40. Turn left at the T-junction, then take the first right after about half a mile (easy to miss). Follow signs uphill to Doward Park. Sat-nav isn't reliable. **By public transport** Train to Gloucester, from where buses 32 and 33 run daily to Ross-on-Wye (40 mins, 0871 200 2233, www.stagecoachbus.com). From there, you'll have to catch a taxi (about £10, JMC, 01600 890998).

frames and launching themselves through the air on the rope swing. Walking trails thread through the surrounding woodlands; you might spot a deer, fox or perhaps even a badger en route to the caves, rocky overhangs and quarries that are all within easy reach of camp.

The glorious setting and intimate scale of the site combine to create a rare feeling of well-being and oneness with all things – even the heads of your fellow campers, nodding amiably over the hedge.

EATING & DRINKING

Three riverside pubs are within walking distance of Doward Park, via wonderfully scenic routes. Your best bet for food is the Saracens Head Inn (01600 890435, www.saracenshcadinn.co.uk) in Symonds Yat East. It's also the most awkward – although fun – to get to, as the journey involves crossing the River Wye on a hand-operated rope ferry, run by the pub.

Easier to reach, in Symonds Yat West, are the Wye Knot Inn (01600 890501, www.wyeknotinn.co.uk) and the riverside Ye Olde Ferrie Inn (01600 890232,

www.yeoldferrieinn.com). Both are everything a good rural pub should be, with traditional grub to match.

Ten miles away on the other side of Monmouth, at the excellent Crown at Whitebrook (01600 860254, www.crownatwhitebrook.co.uk), chef James Sommerin currently holds a Michelin star; treat yourself to a blow-out meal with the money you're saving by not staying at the restaurant's accommodation. The three-course lunch menu for £29.50 is a bargain for cooking of this standard.

ATTRACTIONS & ACTIVITIES

When you arrive at Doward Park, ask for a copy of the walking map, which details routes to the impressively vertiginous Seven Sisters Rock and the spooky King Arthur's Cave, as well as various mines, quarries and pubs. Staff are always happy to suggest walks appropriate for children, frazzled parents with pushchairs or reluctant walkers.

Cyclists will appreciate the Peregrine Path, a cycleway that runs from Symonds Yat East to Monmouth, following the course of the Wye. Reach it via the track that runs past the campsite and

HEREFORDSHIRE

Site specific

✔ The peace and quiet are so intense at night as to be almost mystical, particularly when the wind rustles the surrounding woodland.

✘ The rules and restrictions can make it feel as if you have to be on your best behaviour at all times.

down to the bridge at Biblins. You can download a route map from www.sustrans.org.uk.

This being the Welsh Borders, most attractions take you up hills (the castles) or deep underground (the mines). Ten minutes' drive from Doward Park, Goodrich Castle (01600 890538, www.english-heritage.org.uk, closed Mon-Fri Nov-Mar) is an imposing sandstone edifice; children will enjoy peeking through the murder holes and finding the garderobe – a primitive toilet, whose contents were channelled into the moat. The 15th-century Raglan Castle (01291 690228, www.cadw.wales.gov.uk), 12 miles away, is more elaborate, with a hexagonal Great Tower surrounded by its own moat.

At the other extreme, Clearwell Caves (01594 832535, www.clearwellcaves.com) is an extensive natural cave system, with mine workings that date from the Stone Age. It's 20 minutes by car.

AMUSING THE KIDS

When the children tire of the woodland playground, take to the water. Wyedean Canoe Centre (01594 833238, www.wyedean.co.uk) in Symonds Yat East hires canoes and kayaks, and can arrange organised trips with guides or instructors.

For a less demanding outing, it's a half-hour drive to the Old Station (01291 689566, www.tintern. org.uk/station.htm, closed Nov-Easter) near Tintern village. Once part of the long-vanished Wye Valley Railway, it has a café and picnic areas, an exhibition about the line's history, a teeny-tiny steam train (on occasional Sun and bank holidays), art and craft shows in the former signal box, and plenty of grass to run around on. There's also a mini campsite, with room for a dozen tents, a loo, tap and hand basin, but no showers.

CAMPING NEARBY

Just over the Welsh border in the Forest of Dean, Cherry Orchard Farm (01594 832212, www.cherry orchardfarm.co.uk, open all year, adult £5, child £3) in Newland is set in a lovely part of the Wye Valley, with great facilities. It's a five-minute stroll to the acclaimed Ostrich Inn (01594 833260, www.the ostrichinn.com), and Offa's Dyke footpath is less than half a mile away.

Raglan – The Walks (01600 780257, open all year, £15 per night) is a tiny, half-acre Camping & Caravanning Club site, close to the remains of Raglan Castle. CCC members only, but you can join on site.

River Wye

Home Farm Radnage

Home Farm Radnage
City Road, Radnage, High Wycombe,
Buckinghamshire HP14 4DW
01494 484136
andrewjradford@hotmail.com
www.homefarmradnage.co.uk
Map p26 ㉗
OS map SU784968

Number of pitches 23 tents, 12 caravans, 4 motorhomes.
Open All year.
Booking Online. Essential high season. Minimum stay 2 nights.
Typical cost £12.50 family (2 adults, 2 children). Caravan/motorhome (2 people) £12.50-£17.50.
Facilities Electric hook-ups (16); laundry facilities; showers (free); toilets; washing-up area.
Campfires Not allowed.
Dogs Allowed, on lead.
Restrictions No groups of under-25s. No noise after 10.30pm.
Getting there By road From the A40 between High Wycombe and Stokenchurch, follow signs to Radnage. The campsite entrance is on City Road, on the left immediately before the Crown pub.
By public transport Saunderton train station is 5 miles from Home Farm. There's no direct bus; a taxi costs about £13 (Red Line Car Hire, 01844 343736). From High Wycombe, bus 40 (Mon-Fri, 0871 200 2233, www.arrivabus.co.uk), runs hourly and takes 15 mins to Stokenchurch. From there it's a 1.5-mile walk.

Set in beautiful Chilterns scenery, Home Farm is as delightful as it is unassuming. It's also quiet – remarkably so, given its proximity to London. The set-up is blissfully simple: two camping fields set on a hillside, with stunning views over the valleys below and across to other distant ridges. It's perfectly possible to spend hours watching the shadows of clouds chasing across the slopes, interrupted only by the soaring arc of a red kite in flight. These magnificent birds were reintroduced to the area after almost dying out in England, and are now thriving. The russet flash as they swoop down on their prey is now almost commonplace, but no less beautiful for that.

The campsite's current owners, Isabel and Andy Radford, are in the process of redeveloping it after more than 20 years of benign neglect. The improvements they've made so far have made things much more comfortable: the shower rooms have been refurbished, and there are two new washing-up stations with hot water. Also new is a laundry room with a coin-operated washing machine and tumble dryer.

Pitch-wise, the first field you come to is more convenient for the facilities, but the second has better views. In season there are plenty of pickings to be had from the blackberry bushes between the two.

Further rural charm is supplied by a small enclosure containing pigs and chickens, and by the old farm buildings. For a scenic sweep of typically English countryside, encompassing gently rolling hills, attractive woodlands and well-kept hamlets and villages, head off on a walk. Although there's little strenuous hiking to be done, country walks abound, and almost every path is a 'way' – the Ridgeway and the Chiltern Way being two of the better known long-distance paths in the area. There are bridlepaths too; horse riders and mountain bikers will appreciate the likes of the ten-mile Bledlow Circular Ride.

BUCKINGHAMSHIRE

The spread-out village of Radnage itself is nothing to write home about, although the history of the road on which the campsite sits is intriguing. When the Black Death was rife in the capital, many Londoners fled to the countryside. Locals shunned the newcomers, fearing they were already infected, and forced them to live away from the church and the village centre, in an area that became known as The City.

EATING & DRINKING

Next door to the site, the Crown pub (01494 482301, www.crownradnage.co.uk) is a good local with a value-for-money menu. The nearby Three Horseshoes (01494 483273, www.thethreehorseshoes.net, closed Mon lunch, Sun dinner) is a gem, serving excellent food and a good variety of wines by the glass, as well as real ales; set in the charming hamlet of Bennett End, it's only a few minutes walk from Home Farm. Another treat, ten minutes' drive away in Chinnor, is the Sir Charles Napier (01494 483011, www.sircharles napier.co.uk, closed Mon, dinner Sun) a destination restaurant that offers a fine – and reasonably priced – two-course lunch on weekdays. The splendid gardens are beautifully tended.

Although the campsite sells fresh eggs, the nearest place to pick up more substantial provisions is at the supermarket in Stokenchurch.

ATTRACTIONS & ACTIVITIES

You really have to make your own entertainment here: bring a kite (this is the perfect terrain), an OS map and walking boots.

Four miles away, West Wycombe is largely owned by the National Trust. As you'd expect, it's an old-fashioned, unspoilt village, with plenty of lovely timber-framed buildings, some of which date from the 17th century. Nearby is West Wycombe Park, also run by the National Trust (01494 755571, www.national trust.org.uk, closed Fri, Sat, all Sept-Mar). In the 18th century, the extravagant neoclassical mansion was home to the rakish Sir Francis Dashwood, who created its splendid landscaped gardens, dotted with temples and follies. Dashwood's grand designs didn't stop there, though. He also ordered the construction of the Hellfire Caves (01494 533739, www.hellfirecaves.co.uk, closed Mon-Fri Nov-Apr) – a series of hand-hewn, spooky subterranean chambers and passageways, where the notorious Hellfire Club once met.

Around half an hour's drive from the campsite, the village of Hambleden is beautiful, with its brick and flint cottages, traditional pub and church. It may look oddly familiar; it's starred as a location in numerous films, including *Chitty Chitty Bang Bang*.

AMUSING THE KIDS

About 13 miles from Home Farm, in Beaconsfield, Bekonscot Model Village (01494 672919, www. bekonscot.co.uk, closed Nov-mid Feb) makes for an odd but enjoyable family day out. As you walk around

the small-scale streets, don't miss the details: spotting the punning shop signs, police station escapee and moving yacht race is all part of the fun.

The Roald Dahl Museum & Story Centre (01494 892192, www.roalddahlmuseum.org, closed Mon) is in Great Missenden, a 25-minute drive. It has displays on the late, great author's life, along with free storytelling sessions and inventive hands-on activities – cook up a revolting recipe, under expert guidance, or decorate a chocolate bar Willy Wonka would be proud of. Afterwards, retire to Café Twit for lunch or a slice of Bogtrotter chocolate cake.

CAMPING NEARBY

There's not much choice in the immediate area. Well-equipped Highclere Farm (01494 874505, www.highclerefarmpark.co.uk, open Jan, Mar-Dec) is about half an hour away, near Beaconsfield, but it's rather manicured and lacking atmosphere, and aimed more at caravanners than tent campers. A tent and two people costs from £18.

BUCKINGHAMSHIRE

Britchcombe

Britchcombe Countryside Holidays
Britchcombe Farm, Uffington, Faringdon,
Oxfordshire SN7 7QJ
01367 821022
marcella@seymour82227.freeserve.co.uk
Map p26 ㉘
OS map SU307871

Number of pitches 80 tents/caravans/
motorhomes. 1 yurt (sleeps 4, possibly
more). 3 tipis (sleeping 4).
Open All year.
Booking By phone, post.
Essential weekends.
Typical cost Camping £7 adult, £3.50
5-14s. Yurt and tipi £60 1 night, £90
2 nights, £115 3 nights, plus £7 adult,
£3.50 5-14 per night.
Facilities Cream teas (Sat, Sun, Mon bank
holidays); disabled (toilet); electric hook-ups
(8); showers (free); toilets; washing-up area.
Campfires Allowed, in firepits.
Firewood available (£5).
Dogs Allowed, under supervision.
Restrictions Single-sex groups and
unsupervised under-18s by arrangement.
11pm curfew.
Getting there By road Take the A420
(Swindon to Oxford road). At Shrivenham,
turn on the B4000 towards Lambourn.
At Ashbury, turn left on to the B4507; the
campsite is 3 miles away, on the right.
If you're coming from the other direction, it's
6 miles from Wantage. **By public transport**
Train to Swindon. Buses are infrequent,
so it's best to get a taxi (Connect Cabs,
01793 238444, about £25).

Set at the foot of the Vale of the White Horse,
Britchcombe is no more than a mile from the
3,000-year-old artwork that gives the valley
its name. The creation of Bronze Age Britons,
who carved its immense outline into the hillside
then filled the trenches with chalk, the Uffington
White Horse gallops across the valley head, both
impressing and perplexing its many visitors.

Although the horse's bold, stylised curves can't
be seen from the campsite, the views over the
countryside and the steep flanks of the hills
are glorious. There are four camping fields, with
no allocated pitches, so you're free to set up
wherever you choose – though families tend to
camp in the two fields closest to the farmhouse.

The terrain slopes; in bad weather, it might be
wise to pitch in the higher areas, to avoid waking
up in a puddle. Alternatively, leave the tent at
home and book one of the newly arrived tipis or
the yurt. They're set up take four people each,
but there's room for more, especially children,
so discuss options when booking.

Britchcombe's facilities are basic but clean:
at the centre of the site, next to the farmhouse
and reception, there are a few showers, toilets
and a washing-up room that contains a fridge.
Each field has cold water taps and Portakabin
loos – more of these would be useful when the
place is busy. Campfires are permitted in the
firepits, with wood delivered to your pitch for a
fiver. For children, there's plenty of open space
to play in and slopes to roll down.

During the autumn the campsite is never
too packed, but in summer it's often heaving
with tourists and walkers, eager to explore
the prehistoric and Iron Age remains in the
surrounding area. Yet once the lights go down
and quiet descends, the setting soon reasserts
its magic. As you stargaze up at the vast, velvety
night sky, or stoke the glowing embers of the
fire, it's easy to forget your fellow campers.

EATING & DRINKING

On weekends, the campsite's owner, Marcella
Seymour, serves cream teas (3-6pm). For more
solid and regular sustenance, your best bet is one
of the nearby pubs.

Less than half an hour's walk away in Woolstone,
the White Horse (01367 820726, www.whitehorse
woolstone.co.uk, closed dinner Sun) is a good choice,
offering local real ales and a traditional menu,
supplemented by daily specials.

Marcella recommends the Fox & Hounds (01367
820680, www.uffingtonpub.co.uk) in Uffington, also
a pleasant stroll away. The gardens have magnificent
views of the Ridgeway and the White Horse, which
can be taken in while sampling the real ales and
no-nonsense pub food (own-made burgers, ham,
egg and chips, goat's cheese tart).

Another option is the Blowing Stone Inn (01367
820288, www.theblowingstone.co.uk closed dinner
Sun) in Kingston Lisle, a mile and a half from the
campsite; slightly further afield, the Woodman
(01367 820643, www.thewoodmaninn.net) in Fernham
is a pretty 17th-century inn, whose menu ranges
from simple baguettes and ploughman's lunches
to a smarter evening menu.

Should you need supplies for the barbecue, it's
six miles to the Waitrose in Wantage; alternatively,
Uffington has a general store and post office.

OXFORDSHIRE

Site specific

✔ Its proximity to the White Horse is Britchcombe's main selling point. A walk up to the Ridgeway will soon get you there, with splendid views along the way.

✗ On summer weekends, this place is full of groups and families, and noise can be a problem. For peace and quiet – and a chance to see the White Horse without the tourist hordes – consider a midweek stay.

ATTRACTIONS & ACTIVITIES

Spectacular walks and views surround the campsite, and a hike uphill to see the White Horse is a must-do (there are car parks nearby, if you'd rather drive). The Ridgeway National Trail (01865 810224, www.nationaltrail.co.uk) is also on the campsite's doorstep, running along Whitehorse Hill and connected to other, smaller footpaths.

At the top of Whitehorse Hill, Uffington Castle is the remains of an ancient hill fort, surrounded by two earth banks and a ditch. A mile or so further along the Ridgeway you'll find Wayland's Smithy (www.english-heritage.org.uk), an atmospheric and slightly spooky Neolithic burial chamber, set amid a rustling beech copse.

Ashdown House (01494 755569, www.national trust.org.uk, house open 2-5pm Wed, Sat Apr-Oct) is about six miles from Britchcombe. The 17th-century house is occupied by private tenants, but visitors

on guided tours can tackle the 100-stair climb to the roof, with its spectacular views across the Berkshire Downs. Outside are woodland walks and the remains of another Iron Age hill fort – thought to be the site of King Alfred's battle with the Danes.

The town of Hungerford is a half-hour drive; from here, the *Rose of Hungerford* (0800 1214674, www.roseofhungerford.co.uk, no sailings Nov-Mar) offers boat trips along the Kennet & Avon Canal.

AMUSING THE KIDS

Down the road in Fernham, the meet-the-animals sessions, adventure play area and pedal tractors at Farmer Gow's Activity Farm (01793 780555, www.farmergows.co.uk) should keep youngsters entertained, for a few hours at least.

If the heavens open, nearby Faringdon Leisure Centre (01367 241755, www.soll-leisure.co.uk) has an indoor swimming pool, as does Wantage Leisure Centre (01235 766201, www.soll-leisure.co.uk).

CAMPING NEARBY

This part of the world is slightly short on campsites. Some 13 miles away, just outside the Gloucestershire village of Lechlade, Bridge House Campsite (01367 252348, open Apr-Oct) has a spacious camping field, several nearby pubs and river walks along the Thames – though it is set on the road. A tent/caravan pitch costs from £7 adult, £3 child.

For a site with all mod-cons, book in at Hardwick Parks (01865 300501, www.hardwickparks.co.uk, open Apr-Oct, £15.50 for two people), a large-scale but friendly riverside holiday park near Witney, with an enormous lake for swimming and watersports.

OXFORDSHIRE

The 3,000-year-old White Horse is a mile's walk from the campsite

Vintage Vacations

Number of pitches 13 Airstream trailers (sleeping 2-4).
Open Apr-Oct.
Booking By phone, email. Essential. Minimum stay 2 nights.
Typical cost 2 nights £145-£190 midweek, £175-£255 weekend. 1 week £360-£625.
Facilities Cooker, fridge, power points, shower (in trailer), sink (in trailer); flush toilets (on site).
Campfires Log burners (free).
Dogs Not allowed.
Getting there By road From Portsmouth, take the ferry to Fishbourne (40 mins, 0871 376 1000, www.wightlink.co.uk). From there take the B3331 followed by the A3054; further directions will be provided upon booking (journey approx 15 mins).
By public transport Foot passengers can take the high-speed hover service from Portsmouth to Ryde (10 mins, 01983 717700, www.hovertravel.co.uk) or the FastCat (22 mins, 0871 376 1000, www.wightlink.co.uk). Then take a taxi (approximately £7, Ryde Taxis, 01983 811111), or hire a bike from the port (20 mins to campsite, 01983 761800 www.wightcyclehire.co.uk).

Vintage Vacations
Hazel Grove Farm, Ashey, near Ryde, Isle of Wight PO33 4BD
07802 758113
anything@vintagevacations.co.uk
www.vintagevacations.co.uk
Map p26 ㉙

Vintage Vacations kickstarted a trend when the company's creators, Helen and Frazer Cunningham, started importing vintage Airstream 'land yachts' – shiny aluminium trailers manufactured in the US in the 1950s and '60s – for use as stationary holiday rentals. Since then, several other outfits have got in on the act. However, the Vintage Vacations experience remains unique in its melding of the kitsch-tastic interiors (Helen formerly worked as a stylist in London – and it shows) and the appropriately retro Isle of Wight setting.

The trailers – long considered cult vehicles in the States – are both supremely stylish and accommodating. They range in age from a 1946 Spartan Manor to a 1966 Overlander; some come with a striped awning (don't leave it up on a windy night). The interiors have been restored to their full wooden glory, with beds (some fold-out), restored fridges and bathrooms; the 1951 Spartanette, the largest of the bunch, has the most impressive interior. Lovely touches inside range from decades-old copies of Woman's Realm and old boardgames picked up from flea markets, to colourful home-knitted blankets. Even the kitchen equipment looks the part. All bedding is provided, and complimentary cake and milk in the fridge provide a friendly welcome. Log burners and barbecues are also available.

But while aesthetics play an important role in the experience, it's in a soulful way, rather than in an attempt to impress. Vintage Vacations' trailers are not for fans of sterile designer features, nor for those who like entertainment laid on for them; although a lot of thought and effort has gone into the interiors, and plenty of information is provided on local attractions, the site itself is simple.

One major change is that all the trailers are now in the same place, on a farm just south of Ryde on the north-east tip of the island (previously, they were dotted about in different locations). This does make life a bit more comfortable: there's a good toilet block, and breakfast packs are available (£22, suitable for two people for four days).

While offering a far more comfortable experience than a tent – with proper beds and mod cons such as a fridge, stove, electricity and

Site specific

✔ The shiny, streamlined Airstreams are simply gorgeous. Sleeping in one is as far removed from the plastic caravan experience as you can get.

✘ Noisy cows may wake you in the early hours, while lighting the old-fashioned hot water tank can be slightly nerve-wracking.

hot water – a holiday in one of the Airstreams is a trip back to a seemingly more straightforward era, not only through the retro aesthetics, but also in mood. The Isle of Wight still offers that traditional English holiday idyll of Enid Blyton-esque seaside adventures, pub lunches and cream teas. Exploring the island (a manageable 23 miles by 13 miles) is easiest with a car or bike, though there are buses between the major towns. Alternatively, simply sit outside the trailer in the sunshine with tea, cake and a newspaper (deckchairs are provided) and let your cares disappear.

Vintage Vacations has other accommodation options dotted around the island, ranging from a late 19th-century tin tabernacle to an old-fashioned holiday chalet – all decorated in 1950s/60s retro-chic style.

EATING & DRINKING

Dan's Kitchen (01983 872303), on the east side of the island in the village of St Helens, prides itself on its use of local produce, with fish and seafood a speciality. Near Ventnor, on the south coast, the Boathouse (01983 852747, www.theboathouse-steephillcove.co.uk, closed Sept-May) is another excellent bet for a fishy lunch, offering freshly caught crab and lobster, while the nearby Wheeler's Crab Shed (01983 855819, closed end Oct-Easter) has superb own-made crab pasties to take away.

The Folly Inn (01983 297171, www.thefollyinn.com), north of Newport at Whippingham, provides a lovely marina setting and excellent food – but be prepared to also stomach the yachting types who frequent it. If you're after pub grub and a pint of ale, head to the Dairyman's Daughter (01983 539361, www.thedairymansdaughter.co.uk) at Arreton Old Village (www.arretonbarns.co.uk) near Newport – there are craft shops to explore too.

If you'd rather make use of the Airstream's gas stove, stock up in Newport, where you'll find branches

of Sainsbury's, M&S and Morrisons. Or buy from island producers at the farmers' market, which is held every Friday morning in the Market Square. The Real Island Food Company (01983 898817, www.realislandfood.co.uk) sells local vegetables, bakery goods, fish, meat and more, and can deliver to your trailer (minimum order £30, plus £4.95 delivery).

ATTRACTIONS & ACTIVITIES

Part of Vintage Vacations' appeal is that on-site activities are non-existent – except for the retro boardgames provided in each trailer (think Cluedo, Tiddlywinks and Beetle Drive). But walking and cycling opportunities abound in this land of green rolling hills, with bikes a particularly agreeable way to get about; try Wight Cycle Hire (01983 761800, www.wightcyclehire.co.uk).

If you're after some beach action, head south. Steephill Cove, near Ventnor, with its smugglers' coves, rocky outcrops and sandy beach, is one of the prettiest spots on the island; watch local fishermen bringing in the day's catch of crab and lobster, and then enjoy the fresh-as-can-be taste in the Boathouse restaurant. There are also some picturesque coastal walks. Ventor itself is one of the island's most attractive towns, site of the free Ventnor Botanic Gardens (01983 855397, www.botanic.co.uk) and the best bet for a mooch around local shops.

A good car boot fair is also held every Sunday at St George's Football Ground near Newport. And Osborne House (01983 200022, www.english-heritage.org.uk), Queen Victoria's family abode in East Cowes, is one of the Isle of Wight's key attractions; check the website for opening times.

AMUSING THE KIDS

The Isle of Wight provides seaside fun galore, with the most family-friendly beaches at Ventnor and nearby Shanklin. Classic sweetshops such as Lovely Traditional on Newport's High Street, with its selection of pear drops and lemon sherbet, should placate the kids.

Conservation-driven Amazon World Zoo Park (01983 867122, www.amazonworld.co.uk), off the A3056 between Newport and Sandown, is home to around 200 exotic species, including tropical birds, chameleons, tarantulas and lemurs. And good luck to any parents looking for holiday downtime once word gets out about the Toboggan Run ride at Robin Hill Countryside Adventure Park (0193 527352, www.robin-hill.com).

CAMPING NEARBY

Family-run Grange Farm (01983 740296, www.grangefarmholidays.com, open Mar-Oct) – overlooking Brighstone Bay on the south-west coast – has good facilities, including an adventure playground, and access to a pleasant sandy beach. There are micro pigs, an alpaca and water buffalo alongside farmyard animals on this working farm. A standard pitch for two adults costs £13-£18.50.

Manor Farm

Manor Farm
Blanket Street, West Worldham,
Alton, Hampshire GU34 3BD
01420 80804
info@featherdown.co.uk
www.featherdownfarm.co.uk
Map p26 ㉚
OS map SU740370

Number of pitches 7 tents
(sleeping 5 adults and 1 child).
Open Easter-Oct.
Booking By phone, online. Essential.
Typical cost Weekend (Fri-Sun) £265-£565,
midweek (Mon-Fri) £225-£515, week (Fri-Fri)
£395-£795; check website for latest prices.
Facilities Bike rental (from £8.50 per day
adult); shop; showers (free); toilets.
Campfires Allowed, in designated area.
Dogs Allowed, on lead (£5).
Restrictions No large groups unless
renting whole site.
Getting there By road From the A31 at
Alton, turn on to the B3006 (Selborne
Road). After 1.5 miles, turn left at the
crossroads signed to West Worldham.
The farm is on the left, after half a mile.
By public transport Train to Alton, from
where the site is 5 mins by taxi (£9,
Wilson Taxis, 01420 87777).

There are currently 28 Feather Down Farms
around the UK, stretching from Cornwall to
Scotland, not to mention the original cluster in
the Netherlands, and a growing number in France.
Some people might sneer that this is 'glamping'
– not the real thing – but presumably they have
yet to feel the joy of arriving at a campsite at
10pm, with the rain coming down hard and the
children tired and emotional, to find a spacious
tent complete with beds, a wood-burning stove
and candles ready for the first match.

The basic approach is consistent across all
the Feather Down sites. A handful of well-spaced
tents are spread around a working farm, with
barnyard animals at hand for petting and feeding,
and showers and a shop nearby. Nature is kept
close enough and raw enough that you can feel
you're connecting with the Great Outdoors.

The tents can sleep a family of six in three
snug bedrooms (one of which, much to the joy
of younger kids, comprises a bed inside a large
cupboard). There are proper beds and fluffy
white duvets, and a rudimentary toilet behind a
lockable door. The interior walls are wooden, as
is the raised floor, while the roof and walls are
canvas. The walls can be rolled up to provide a
refreshing breeze on hot summer days. There's
(cold) running water at the sink, and the stove
pumps out enough heat for cooking and chilly
evenings (wood is provided). Cutlery and pans
fill the cupboards, paraffin lamps swing from
the ceiling, and you eat around a wooden table
at the front of the tent. In short, you're camping,
awash with fresh air and snug under canvas,
but also strangely comfortable.

Set on the edge of the South Downs, two miles
from the town of Alton, Manor Farm (the original
UK Feather Down Farm) is run by the effervescent
Will and Anna Brock, who farm the land but also
make time to greet you with a wheelbarrow for
ferrying your kit. There are seven tents in all
(two with newly introduced open-air hot tubs),
separated by hedges: the two on the front
paddock overlook some dozy sheep (with lambs,
if you're lucky) and an area for bonfires. Send
the children out to gather armfuls of wood, collect
eggs from the chickens and visit the pair of
Gloucestershire Old Spot pigs.

At some point on the first morning, Will bounces
over on his four-wheel-drive buggy to take the
children on a tour of the farm. He dispenses milk
bottles for the lambs and delivers a newspaper.

One final point: Feather Down Farms were
designed with children in mind. You could spend
a stag night here, or even a romantic weekend,
but you will be woken early by the shrieks of
children. And, unless you've block-booked the
entire site, your neighbours in the next tent will
be a frightfully nice family from Chiswick.

HAMPSHIRE

The company also offers Victorian explorer-style tents, with a telescope and a wooden bathtub in a separate bathing tent, but located on country house estates rather than farms. See www. countryhousehideout.co.uk for details.

EATING & DRINKING

The small on-site shop sells milk, cheese, fresh veg, jams and other basics, and sometimes fantastic home-cooked dishes from Anna. There are eggs galore to be scooped up from the chicken coop, and you can hire barbecues and even a smoke barrel. Alton is the closest town for shopping, but Petersfield, Liphook and Winchester are all within easy reach too.

The area is blessed with several fine pubs. Six miles to the south, in Hawkley, the Hawkley Inn (01730 827205) is an elegant gastropub with good food, a pleasant garden and occasional live music. Slightly further off, the unfussy Harrow Inn (01730 262685, www.harrow-inn.co.uk, closed dinner Sun late Sept-late May) in Steep has tiny rooms, spectacular soup and a great garden. Best of all is the White Horse (01420 588387, www.pubwithnoname.co.uk) near Priors Dean, universally known as the 'Pub With No Name' after it lost its pub sign. It's in a field a long way from anywhere, and the food may be simple (fish and chips, steak & ale pie, fish cakes), but it's exquisite. On the other side of Alton, in Bentworth,

the Sun Inn (01420 562338) is old, dark and inviting, with a nice garden. Overlooking the cricket pitch in Lower Wield, the Yew Tree (01256 389224) is very popular. Book ahead at weekends for all of them.

If you're craving time away from muddy fields, it's a half-hour drive to Winchester and the original – and very wonderful – outpost of the Hotel du Vin (01962 841414, www.hotelduvin.com).

ATTRACTIONS & ACTIVITIES

It feels like you're buried deep in the countryside at Manor Farm. Footpaths and bridleways criss-cross the area; the Hangers Way (www3.hants.gov.uk/longdistance/hangers-way.htm), a 21-mile route through meadows, wildflowers and wooded hills, runs past Steep and Selborne. A particularly pleasant and longish walk to Steep, via the Hawkley Inn, will bring you to some great views and the Poet's Stone on Shoulder of Mutton Hill (where the poet Edward Thomas, once a local resident, is commemorated).

Selborne also contains Gilbert White's House (01420 511275, www.gilbertwhiteshouse.org.uk, closed Mon Sept-May). You can visit the charming home of the pioneering 18th-century naturalist, and also the Oates Museum, dedicated to another kind of pioneer: the polar explorer who died on Scott's ill-fated trip to the South Pole in 1911. Jane Austen's House (01420 83262, www.jane-austens-house-museum.org.uk, closed Mon-Fri Jan, Feb) in nearby Chawton is where the author spent her final years.

The New Forest and the South Downs are close enough for excursions, while your best bet for a wet day is Winchester.

AMUSING THE KIDS

No child aged under 14 is going to want to leave Manor Farm. You could tell them that the Watercress Line (01962 733810, www.watercressline.co.uk), with its glorious old steam engines, is only a few miles away, or that Marwell Zoo (01962 777407, www.marwell.org.uk) is about 40 minutes by car. But your trump card is probably Alice Holt Forest near Farnham and the local branch of Go Ape! (0845 643 9215, www.goape.co.uk), where over tens can swing through the treetops, scaring their parents witless. But when all's said and done, your brood will just want to build fires and play with the pigs. And who can blame them?

CAMPING NEARBY

Seven miles away, near Dockenfield, Mellow Farm Adventure (01428 717815, www.mellowfarm adventure.co.uk, open Apr-late Sept, £5 per person) has three camping meadows, and allows campfires on most pitches. It also offers all sorts of activities, from abseiling to archery; check the website for details.

HAMPSHIRE

Roundhill

**Roundhill
Beaulieu Road, Brockenhurst,
Hampshire SO42 7QH**
01590 624344 campsite
0845 130 8224 booking
www.forestholidays.co.uk
Map p26 ③
OS map SU335021

Number of pitches 500 tents/caravans/
motorhomes.
Open End Mar-Sept.
Booking By phone, online. Advisable high
season. Minimum stay 2 nights if booking.
Typical cost £9.50-£18.50 2 people,
£4.50-£7.50 extra adult, £2-£4 extra child.
Non-CCC/FEC members additional £3.50.
Facilities Disabled facilities (toilet
and shower); showers (free); toilets;
washing-up area.
Campfires Not allowed.
Dogs Allowed, on lead.
Restrictions No groups of unsupervised
under-18s.
Getting there By road Take the A35
(Southampton to Bournemouth road). At
Lyndhurst, head south on the A337 towards
Lymington. Turn left at Brockenhurst on to
the B3055; towards Beaulieu; the campsite
is on the right after 1.5 miles. **By public
transport** From Brockenhurst train station,
it's 5 mins by taxi to the site (Brockenhurst
Taxis, 0800 970 6863, £7).

This well-run, family-oriented campsite – one of
several Forestry Commission campsites in the
New Forest National Park – is set in a heathland
clearing, with open areas of flat grass and some
pine trees. It's the third largest campground in
the area (with 500 pitches, usually all taken
in high summer) and very popular with groups
(from extended families to teenagers doing their
DoE award), so not ideal for hardcore campers
looking for a remote, wild or especially peaceful
experience. But if you're after a traditional family
holiday vibe, it's perfect.

It's easy to feel soothed by nature at Roundhill,
thanks to the thick encircling woodland and
free-roaming New Forest ponies. The ponies
(not officially 'wild', as all have owners) are a
unique feature of camping in the New Forest
– be prepared to be woken by snorting and
snuffling outside your tent.

There are no hook-ups or hardstanding pitches,
so although caravans and motorhomes are a
feature, they don't dominate. It's a big place,
though are there some more secluded spots
among the trees (arrive early to nab these).
The facilities are excellent and well cared for,
with sparkling toilet/shower and washing-up
blocks – there's even a dogwash. Staff are
friendly, helpful and efficient.

Campers without motor vehicles should note
that if you turn up in the evening as a 'backpacker
camper' without a reservation, Forest Holidays
is obliged to find you a pitch even if the site is
officially fully booked (although you won't find
this point advertised in any of their literature).
The Forest Experience Card (FEC, £15) gives you
a discount of £3.50 per person at the campsite,
and also savings at certain local attractions.
Seven pre-erected tents are also available for
hire; contact Eurocamp (0844 406 0402,
www.eurocamp.co.uk) for prices.

With the New Forest all around, good cycling
and rambling opportunities are literally on your
doorstep: well-used trails through the forest mean
that road-free days are a real possibility. The
locality includes heathland, nature reserves,
arboretums, deer fields and meadows, as well as
plenty of chocolate-box villages to stop off at for a
well-deserved pint or pub lunch, or simply to soak
up the strong sense of local community pride.
Roundhill sits midway between two of the area's
most well-trodden villages – Brockenhurst and
Beaulieu – meaning that you won't have to go
far to stock up on provisions, or to find creature
comforts on rainy days.

EATING & DRINKING

The New Forest is prime trad English pub territory.
Brockenhurst's Foresters Arms (10 Brookley Road,
01590 623397) is one of the most popular locals, with
real ales, a large beer garden that's usually full in
sunny weather, and decent food (baguettes, jacket
potatoes, beef and Guinness pie). On the same road,
the Thatched Cottage (01590 623090, www.thatched-
cottage.co.uk) is a restaurant/B&B that serves decent
if pricey meals, including breakfast – it's a bit twee
and touristy, though. For something less contrived,
head to the nearby Rainbow Fish Bar (01590 622747)
for cod, chips and excellent mushy peas.

For a genuine country pub experience, you can't
beat the Oak Inn (023 8028 2350), in the utterly idyllic
village of Bank, near Lyndhurst. Throngs of walkers
and cyclists are drawn by the Fuller's ales and
excellent food made from locally sourced ingredients;
game and trout often appear on the menu.

ATTRACTIONS & ACTIVITIES

It would be a crime not to spend most of your time outside, exploring the natural beauty of the area – whether walking, cycling, horse-riding or birdwatching. Wildlife enthusiasts will have, er, a field day; the New Forest is the only place in Britain where the wild gladiolus grows, and is also home to the largest number of rare Dartford warblers in the UK. There are visitor information centres in Lyndhurst, Lymington and Ringwood, and the larger New Forest Centre (023 8028 3444, www.newforest centre.org.uk) in Lyndhurst. Bikes for all ages can be hired from Cyclexperience (01590 623407/624204, www.newforestcyclehire.co.uk), located next to Brockenhurst train station. Horse-riding outfits in the village include Ford Farm Stables (01590 623043, www.nfed.co.uk/fordfarm.htm). For more information on the New Forest (awarded National Park status in 2005), see www.thenewforest.co.uk.

While Brockenhurst is a pretty but workaday village, Beaulieu (01590 612345, www.beaulieu.co.uk) is the place for organised tourist attractions. There's a ruined Cistercian abbey and a stately home with gardens (Palace House, orginally the gatehouse of the abbey), but most visitors come to drool over the 250 vehicles at the National Motor Museum. Highlights include Donald Campbell's record-breaking *Bluebird* and the 1903 Napier *Gordon Bennett*, one of Britain's oldest racing cars.

Nearby is lovely Exbury Gardens (023 8089 1203, www.exbury.co.uk, closed Nov-mid Mar), created in the 1920s and known for its collection of azaleas, rhododendrons and camelias – as well as its cute miniature steam railway.

AMUSING THE KIDS

Kids will be in their element, with lots of freedom and space in which to play on the campsite itself. Rangers lead organised events, such as fishing in the small pond and nature walks.

Beaulieu has lots for (car-fixated) children, including a go-karting track, mini driving circuit and a Monorail, which travels high up through trees and into the Motor Museum itself.

CAMPING NEARBY

There are seven other Forest Holidays campsites in the New Forest, though not all are suitable for tent campers. Nearby Hollands Wood (01590 622967, www.forestholidays.co.uk, open mid Apr-Sept) may be bigger than Roundhill, with 600 pitches, but it doesn't seem like it because the plots are interspersed among trees. This means more privacy, but less open space for kids to play. Prices for non-members start at £14 for two adults.

> ## Site specific
>
> ✔ Being immersed in the ancient woodland that forms the New Forest National Park is a real privilege, and the wandering ponies are a rare delight.
>
> ✘ It's a big campsite, and the abundance of children is either a positive or a negative, depending on what you're after.

Stubcroft Farm

Stubcroft Farm
Stubcroft Lane, East Wittering,
Chichester, West Sussex PO20 8PJ
01243 671469, 07810 751665
mail@stubcroft.com
www.stubcroft.com
Map p26 ㉜
OS map SZ807976

Number of pitches 60 tents, 5 caravans/
motorhomes. B&B (2 rooms).
Open All year.
Booking By phone, email. Minimum stay
2 nights weekend high season, 3 nights
bank holiday weekends.
Typical cost Camping £7-£8 adult,
£3.50-£4 child. B&B £65-£107.
Facilities Cycle hire (£10 per day);
disabled facilities (toilet and shower);
electric hook-ups (8); showers (free);
toilets; washing-up area.
Campfires Allowed, off ground.
Firewood available (£5).
Dogs Allowed, on lead.
Restrictions No noise after 11pm.
Getting there By road From Chichester,
take the A286 towards the Witterings.
Go through Birdham village and then fork
left on to the B2198 to East Wittering and
Bracklesham. After half a mile, past the
Bell Pub, there's an S-bend; on the apex
of the second bend take a right turn down
Tile Barn Lane. After 200 yards, before the
houses, turn left on to a gravel lane. It's
another half-mile to Stubcroft Farm. Don't
rely on sat-nav. **By public transport** From
Chichester train station, buses 52 and 53
go daily to East Wittering (0871 200 2233,
www.stagecoachbus.com). Ask to get off
at Bracklesham Corner after the Bell pub;
journey takes about 15 mins.

Site specific

✔ A great spot for family camping, but
also very peaceful. Within walking distance
of sandy beaches.

✘ Hedges offer protection from breezes,
but this does mean the only view is of the
campsite itself.

There's no through traffic on West Sussex's
Manhood Peninsula. Either you live there, or
you're going to the beach. West Wittering is the
prettiest of the villages, with a stunning stretch
of sandy beach leading into Chichester Harbour,
and rolling dunes that are clear of development
thanks to the foresight of some clear-thinking
locals. Presumably, they looked at the thoroughly
unlovely mid 20th-century buildings along the
seafront at East Wittering and Bracklesham and
decided enough was enough.

There are several campsites along this stretch,
but perhaps the best for back-to-basics outdoor
living is Stubcroft Farm. Its very isolation down
vehicle-unfriendly farm tracks forces you to
slow down and leave worldly concerns behind.
Chickens cluck, bees buzz, grasses sway in the
breeze. It's almost impossible not to feel relaxed.

The campsite, set on a family sheep farm,
consists of a mown five-acre field that's been
split by tall mixed hedgerows into three small
enclosures and one large field. It's flat from
corner to corner, which is good news for tent-
owners. You can pitch wherever you like,
although farmer Simon Green suggests groups
of teenagers and twentysomethings go in the
big field furthest away, while families are
encouraged to use the smaller fields near the
farmhouse. In reality, there's a good-natured
mix of campers in all areas, and also plenty of
space for ball games and mooching. Camping
refuseniks can snuggle down in comfort in the
farmhouse's two B&B rooms.

Campfire lovers are in luck; you can borrow
portable barbecues and fire receptacles for a
tentside fire. They sell logs too. Children can
roam freely, and also enjoy visiting the farmhouse
to feed the chickens and buy eggs for breakfast.

The atmosphere is informal and friendly,
which might be why – despite Stubcroft being
less than a mile from the beach – people tend
to stick around during the day. If you do want
to explore the peninsula but prefer to leave the
car by the tent, the campsite has adults' and
children's bikes for hire.

The site is run on eco-friendly lines: ongoing
projects including hedge and wildflower planting
to attract wildlife, and campers are encouraged
to use the solar-powered composting toilets on
the camping fields, rather than the flush loos
by the house. Posters next to buckets of wood
shavings ('Use only for number twos, please!')
tell you just how much water you're saving. Kids
find the experience novel; parents just have to
get used to the smell.

EATING & DRINKING

An on-site shop sells groceries, toiletries, ice-cream and other camping essentials. Otherwise, the nearest shops are in Bracklesham and East Wittering, where there is a Co-op and a small Tesco. There's also a decent butcher and fishmonger. Local pizza restaurant Pizza Plus (01243 672537) delivers to the campsite; the menu is taped up by the sinks.

Rendezvous restaurant (01243 673584) on Shore Road in East Wittering is within walking distance of the campsite. It serves freshly caught fish and tempting meat dishes, as well as more family-friendly fodder, including fabulously tasty lasagne and spaghetti bolognese. Best for fish and chips back at the tent is the Boathouse chippy (01243 673386), also on Shore Road, although Moby's (01243 670748) on Bracklesham Lane isn't bad.

If the pubs in East Wittering don't appeal, head for the Old House At Home (01243 511234) in nearby West Wittering. It has a large attractive garden, and local seafood is a speciality.

ATTRACTIONS & ACTIVITIES

Most visitors to the Manhood Peninsula come for the associated delights of the coast: windsurfing, beachcombing, rockpooling, walking and swimming. Miles of sandy beaches stretch along Bracklesham Bay; the most attractive stretch is at West Wittering. National Trust-run East Head nature reserve is a sandy spit overlooking Chichester Harbour; it's accessible from West Wittering beach and car park.

For a dose of culture, head into Chichester, seven miles away, to the Pallant House Gallery (01243 774557, www.pallant.org.uk, closed Mon except bank holidays), which has an excellent collection of 20th-century British art, featuring work by Ben Nicholson,

Lucian Freud, Bernard Leach and Howard Hodgkin. Further north is Petworth House & Park (01798 343929, www.nationaltrust.org.uk, closed Thur, Fri and mid Nov-Feb), a huge stately home with an impressive art collection including works by Titian, Turner and William Blake, and a magnificent Capability Brown-landscaped park with lakes and deer. Petworth is a pretty town for a stroll too.

Those feeling active can cycle along the Salterns Way from Chichester to East Head; hire a boat from Itchenor Boat Hire (01243 513345, www.itchenor boathire.co.uk); or go riding from Cakeham Stables (01243 672194) in West Wittering.

Goodwood isn't far, and the campsite gets booked up for such events as the Festival of Speed (July) and Goodwood Revival meeting (Sept).

AMUSING THE KIDS

For an interesting alternative to sandy beaches, try fossil finding at Bracklesham Bay, especially after a storm. Look out for polished shark's teeth. There's also a crabbing pool at West Wittering and the appeal of having a barbecue on the beach. Children will revel in the tacky side of British seaside life at Bognor Regis, eastwards along the coast; delights include crazy golf, amusement arcades and a miniature train.

CAMPING NEARBY

If a plain grass field isn't your idea of camping heaven, the facilities at Wick's Farm (01243 513116, www.wicksfarm.co.uk, open Mar-early Nov), a couple of miles away, might serve instead. There's a shop, playground, tennis court and separate adults-only enclosure for those who don't want kids to feature in their camping experience. Tent fees are £15-£27 per night, including four people.

Woodland Yurting

Woodland Yurting
Keepers Barn, Tittlesfold, The Haven,
Billingshurst, West Sussex RH14 9BG
01403 824057
amanda@woodlandskills.com
www.woodlandyurting.com
Map p26 ㉝
OS map TQ091310

Number of pitches 7 yurts (sleeping 2, 4).
Safari tent (sleeps 4).
Open Apr-Sept.
Booking By phone, email. Essential.
Minimum stay 2 nights, bank holidays
3 nights.
Typical cost Double yurt £60 per night
midweek; £140 weekend retreat; £300
week. Family yurt £100 per night midweek;
£250 weekend retreat; £500 week. Safari
tent £90 per night midweek; £220 weekend
retreat; £450 week. £20 supplement high
season. Check website for latest prices.
Facilities Bushcraft sessions (£15);
massages (£55); showers; toilets
(composting); washing-up area.
Campfires Allowed, in fire bowls.
Firewood available (first bundle free,
then £4.50); charcoal £5.
Dogs Not allowed.
Restrictions No amplified music.
Getting there By road The site is between
the A29 and A281, about 15 miles south-
east of Guildford and 7 miles west of
Horsham. From the A281 go past the Fox
Inn at Bucks Green and turn right on to
the Haven Road; after 1.5 miles, as the
road ascends, turn left through an entrance
marked by brick pillars and the sign
'Tittlesfold'. Bear right past the converted
barn until the track forks, then bear left,
following signs for Keepers Cottage Barn.
Continue until you reach the yurts – it's a
mile from the road. From the A29, you go
though the hamlet of The Haven before
reaching the brick-pillared entrance (on
the right just before the road descends).
By public transport Billingshurst is the
nearest train station, 4 miles away. No
buses go near the campsite, so catch a taxi
(Jake's Taxis, 01403 786818, under £10).

The countryside around the Surrey/Sussex
border, on the edge of the South Downs and the

High Weald, is upmarket commuter territory;
the wealth is evident in the smart, manicured
villages and posh inns – you're as likely to meet
a Rolls on the country lanes as a tractor. But
head off the main road and you're in another
world: Shadow Woods, 65 acres of hornbeam,
hawthorn, oak, ash and maple trees, thick with
bluebells in spring and dappled with sunlight
in summer. Woodland Yurting hasn't been in
business for very long – it only opened in spring
2009 – but it's a roaring success. It's easy
to see why: it's a beautiful, tranquil spot and
although planes pass overhead and the hum
of traffic is audible, it feels very remote.

The yurts – seven will be available for the
2012 season – and the Indian-style safari tent
are tucked higgledy-piggledy amid the trees,
beside a large grassy meadow that's perfect
for kickabouts or just lolling in the sun. At one
end is the barn (built in the traditional manner,
with timber from the surrounding wood); it
houses the site's office and supplies, but isn't
for campers' use. You drive up to the barn,
drop off your stuff and then park half a mile
away down the bumpy dirt track.

The Chinese-made yurts are functional rather
than pretty, furnished with beds and bedding,
kitchen equipment and crockery. On arrival,
you're given a lantern, a one-ring gas stove and
a cooler box with ice-packs. Outside each yurt
is an umbrella-shaded sink for washing-up (cold
water only), a table and chairs, and a firebowl
for cooking and fires; the first bundle of wood is
free, and you can buy bags of charcoal, made
on-site. The 20-foot yurt is big enough for a family
of four; the others are perfect for couples, or
families if the kids sleep on the floor. Near the
barn is a communal area for group bookings
with a large firepit, earth oven and cooking plate.

The ethos is one of simplicity and respect
for nature, hence the earth toilets, housed
in wooden cabins amid the trees, with open
windows so you can view the birds while you
sit. The shower facilities have been recently
upgraded, and there's a new disabled toilet.

Most campers hang around the site, but some
of Sussex's best gardens and stately homes
are nearby. It's four miles to the nearest village,
train station and shops, at Billingshurst, and a bit
further to the busy commuter town of Horsham.

Don't miss the bushcraft taster sessions led
by resident woodsman Clive Cobie, who has
has his own camp next to the river. These
are fantastic, adding a new dimension to the
camping-in-a-wood experience; you can forage

WEST SUSSEX

for edible plants, learn about the local flora and fauna, and discover how to make fire the age-old way with a bow and spindle. Campsite manager Amanda Porter is also a holistic massage therapist and offers one-hour massages in a little glade a short walk from the yurts.

Some new accommodation – a cabin (sleeping two to six), situated on the edge of a wild flower meadow a short walk from the yurt field, and a single-decker bus (sleeping two) – is now available year round; call for details.

EATING & DRINKING

There's a pub on every village corner in these parts, but two are particularly close at hand. Half a mile from the entrance gate (turn left, then first right) is the Blue Ship (01403 822709, no dinner Mon, Sun), a proper country boozer, festooned with flowers on the outside, low-ceilinged and unpretentious inside. King & Barnes Sussex Bitter is served from a hatch, and a range of own made pies such as steak & ale and fish are available. More upmarket, and more expensive, is the Fox Inn (01403 822386, www.foxinn.co.uk) at Bucks Green. A 16th-century inn with a garden and a restaurant specialising in hefty plates of fish and seafood, it's packed most nights with well-groomed locals. You can also get takeaway fish and chips.

The Onslow Arms (01403 752452, www.onslow armsloxwood.co.uk, closed dinner Mon Oct-Apr),

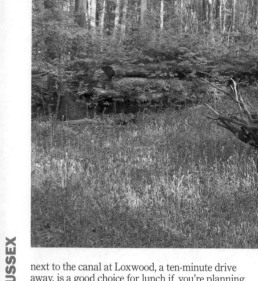

next to the canal at Loxwood, a ten-minute drive away, is a good choice for lunch if you're planning to join one of the canal boat trips.

Billingshurst has little to recommend it, but there's a bank and a few shops including a Budgens. Westons (01403 791228, www.westonsfarmshop.co.uk), off the A264 towards Horsham, sells everything from fruit and veg to chutneys and ginger cordial.

ATTRACTIONS & ACTIVITIES

Do take one of Clive's bushcraft sessions, so the next time you go camping you can make a fire without matches and firelighters. More in-depth courses in everything from coppicing to rural crafts are offered by sister outfit Woodland Skills (www.woodland skills.com). And to really relax in style, book a massage (holistic, detox, pregnancy) with Amanda (www.amandaporter.co.uk).

Also within reach are the National Trust's Petworth House & Park (01798 343929, www.nationaltrust.

Site specific

✔ It's an hour's drive from London and Brighton, yet feels remarkably isolated. Great for novice campers.

✘ Despite the yurts, this isn't a luxurious experience. Facilities are pretty basic (compost toilets, cold water), so won't appeal to everyone.

org.uk, house closed Thur, Fri, all Nov-mid Mar), with its collection of Turner paintings and Capability Brown-designed deer park; and Parham House (01903 742021, www.parhaminsussex.co.uk, closed Oct-Easter, house closed Sat, and Tue, Fri Aug), a lovely Elizabethan manor house with walled and landscaped gardens.

At weekends and bank holidays, boat trips along the Wey & Arun Canal (01403 752403, www.weyand arun.co.uk) leave from the jetty at Loxwood.

Or you can just go for a walk: the Downs Link, a 37-mile trail for walkers, cyclists and horse riders that runs along an old railway line and connects the North Downs Way and the South Downs Way, passes through nearby Rudgwick.

AMUSING THE KIDS

Exploring Shadow Woods and racing round the meadow is enough amusement for most children. For more managed entertainment, there's Fishers Farm Park (01403 700063, www.fishersfarmpark.co.uk), six miles away near Wisborough Green. Mixing farmyard fun with thrills and spills, it has indoor and outdoor play areas, tractor and pony rides, a climbing wall, goat, sheep and pig racing and theatre shows.

CAMPING NEARBY

If you like the idea of camping next to a pub, the Limeburners Arms (01403 782311, open all year, pitch £14) just outside Billingshurst has space for 40 tents, caravans and motorhomes. It's basic but clean, and the pub offers Fuller's beers, decent food and roaring fires.

Wowo

Wowo Campsite
Wapsbourne Manor Farm, Sheffield Park,
East Sussex TN22 3QT
01825 723414
camping@wowo.co.uk
www.wowo.co.uk
Map p26 ㉞
OS map TQ402232

Number of pitches 48 tents. 4 yurts
(sleeping 2, 4, 6). Shepherd's hut (sleeps
2). Small campervans by arrangement.
No caravans/motorhomes.
Open All year; 8 tent pitches only Nov-Mar.
Booking Online. Essential. Minimum stay
high season: 2 nights weekends, 3 nights
bank holidays.
Typical cost Tent £10 adult, £5 child.
Yurt 2 nights £136-£250. Shepherd's hut
check website for prices.
Facilities Freezer; fridge; laundry
facilities; shop; showers (free); toilets;
washing-up area.
Campfires Allowed, in firepits.
Firewood available (£5).
Dogs Allowed, by arrangement,
on lead (£4.50).
Restrictions No single-sex groups or
unsupervised teenagers. 11.30pm curfew.
Getting there By road Wowo is on the
A275 (Lewes to Wych Cross road), about
2 miles north of Chailey crossroads and
next door to Sheffield Park station, home
of the Bluebell Railway. The campsite is
signposted Wapsbourne Manor Farm.
By public transport The nearest station
is Haywards Heath. The 31 bus goes to
Chailey crossroads (25 mins, Mon-Sat,
0844 477 1623, from where it's a 2-mile
walk. Alternatively, arrange for the campsite
to collect you from the station (£13) or take
a local taxi (01444 440444).

Between the classic East Sussex hamlets of
Danehill and Fletchling, Wapsbourne Manor
Farm's campsite, known as Wowo, flanks either
side of Pellingford Brook on elegant, pea-green
hills. The site was originally a strawberry farm,
but a few years ago the friendly Cragg family
turned the land over to campers, with instant
and immense success.

Four fields spread along a brook contain
48 pitches, each with a firepit – unlike many

campsites, Wowo positively encourages roaring fires. The lack of caravans and motorhomes (small campervans are permitted with prior notice) aids the back-to-nature atmosphere.

If you're looking for solitude, book one of the eight pitches set along the 'tipi trail' in pretty woodland – a £10 supplement applies. This is also where you'll fine the cosy, two-person shepherd's hut (new for 2012). Four yurts offer a more secluded stay, particularly the six-berth 'Nick's Woodland Retreat' yurt. Each has a wood-burning stove (for heat), gas stove (for cooking), crockery and cool box; bedding is provided for one double bed, but you'll need to bring sleeping bags or duvets for other people.

Campers can explore the 200 acres of farmland, interspersed with substantial woodland and teeming with foxes, rabbits, hedgehogs, birds and the occasional deer. Rope swings hang from branches, and enchanting paths lead into dark groves. Families dominate the site in the holidays and there's plenty of space for kids to run and cycle and get dirty; they will make dozens of friends in no time. Musicians can stay for free, as long as they do some kind of performance.

Facilities are thorough: clean if unremarkable toilet and shower blocks, washing-up and laundry areas, fridge and freezer. If it rains, head to the barn for a game of table tennis. Campers are

Site specific

✔ Campfires are a big bonus, though the logs provided by the farm are pricey at a fiver a bundle. Wowo's proximity to Haywards Heath means it is easily accessible from London or Brighton.

✘ It's very popular with families, so can be a noisy and boisterous place until the midnight curfew if you're on a full field. A drawback for some, ideal for others.

Heaven Farm, but there are signs all along the country roads offering seasonal vegetables, meat, cider and wine. The petrol station at Chailey crossroads has a Costcutter, and there's a large Co-op in Haywards Heath, along with most other high-street shops.

Pubs are many, although none is within easy walking distance. The friendliest is the Coach & Horses (01825 740369, www.coachandhorses.danehill.biz), a couple of miles away in Danehill, which has served local ales and ciders for 150 years. It has a lovely garden with great views and an adults-only rear terrace. The food is locally sourced and excellent. The Griffin Inn (01825 722890, www.thegriffininn.co.uk) in Fletching is slightly more upmarket and also renowned for its food and the warmth of its welcome.

ATTRACTIONS & ACTIVITIES

Wowo runs courses at weekends in high season, in bushcraft, foraging and basket making; check the website for dates and details.

The steam-powered Bluebell Railway (01825 720825, www.bluebell-railway.co.uk) is undoubtedly the main attraction nearby, if not across inland Sussex. Immaculately restored Sheffield Park station, within walking distance of the campsite, is a spectacle in itself. For £13 return you can puff along the old London & South Coast line between Sheffield Park and Kingscote, half an hour away. The best time to visit is when bluebells carpet the countryside in spring, but it's attractive any time of year.

Across the road from the station is Sheffield Park Garden (01825 790231, www.nationaltrust.org.uk), which was created by Lancelot 'Capability' Brown, perhaps Britain's finest landscape architect. It was designed to show a rainbow of colour all year round, but is at its most glorious when the leaves turn in autumn. It was also the site of the first England v Australia cricket match, in 1884.

Ashdown Forest (www.ashdownforest.org), six miles north of Wowo, has endless walking trails and a llama park (01825 712040, www.llamapark.co.uk). It is also where the original Pooh Bridge is to be found – take sticks.

AMUSING THE KIDS

Wowo provides plenty for children to do, but Tulleys Farm (01342 718472, www.tulleysmaizemaze.co.uk) in Turners Hill, on the outskirts of Crawley, offers a more structured day out, with its giant corn maze, bouncy slides, tractor rides and farm animals. For horsey children, East View Riding Centre (01825 740240, www.ridinginsussex.co.uk) in Danehill caters for all abilities, from age seven upwards.

CAMPING NEARBY

The nearest campsite is Heaven Farm in Furners Green (01825 790226, www.heavenfarm.co.uk, open May-Oct, £10 adult, £5 child). It is also a caravan site (open all year). On site there's a farm shop, tea room, agricultural museum and nature trails.

encouraged to take rubbish to nearby recycling plants, and the 'leave no trace' sensibility pervades throughout.

Civilisation beckons in the form of the unlovely town of Haywards Heath, only five miles away, which has the usual high-street amenities and a mainline train station that serves London Victoria every half-hour. Options for excursions are plentiful, from walking and cycling to stately homes and gardens. The most famous (and nearest) attraction is the Bluebell Railway, located just outside the campsite entrance.

EATING & DRINKING

Wowo's shop sells all sorts of useful foodstuffs, including bread, eggs, milk, tea, ice-cream and home-grown veg. In August you can feast on pizza and paella on Friday and Saturday nights.

There are plenty of farm shops in the area. The best are the Old Dairy & Farm in Furners Green (01825 790517, www.theolddairyfarmshop.co.uk, closed Mon-Wed, Sun) and Heavenly Organics at

Blackberry Wood

Blackberry Wood
Streat Lane, near Ditchling,
East Sussex BN6 8RS
01273 890035
www.blackberrywood.com
Map p26 ③⑤
OS map TQ351146

Number of pitches 20 tents. No caravans/
motorhomes. Double-decker bus (sleeps 4).
Gypsy caravan (sleeps 2 adults). Retro
caravan (sleeps 2 adults). Helicopter
(sleeps 4).
Open All year.
Booking Online. Essential. Minimum
stay 2 nights weekends: tent Apr-Oct,
bus and caravans all year.
Typical cost Tent £5. Double-decker bus
£70. Gypsy caravan £35. Retro caravan
£20. Helicopter approx £60. All plus £5-£9
adult, £2-£4.50 3-12s.
Facilities Shop; showers (20p);
toilets; washing-up area.
Campfires Allowed, in firepits.
Firewood available (£3.50).
Dogs Allowed, on lead
(inform staff on arrival).
Restrictions Unsupervised under-18s
by arrangement. No large groups.
Getting there By road Take the B2116
between Ditchling and the A275. Turn north
up Streat Lane. Continue for a mile; go past
Sandpit Cottages and take the third turning
on the right – there's a sign, but it's not
obvious. **By public transport** Train to
Plumpton, then a 25-mins walk: from the
station, walk south down Plumpton Lane,
with the racecourse on your right. Take
the first right to Streat, then the first left
on to Streat Lane – it's then not far to the
campsite, on your left. Alternatively, a taxi
from Hassocks train station is about £12
(Five Star Taxis, 01273 846666).

interspersed with brambles and shrubs. And
the atmosphere – intimate, relaxed, homely –
is something you can't manufacture (though
many campsites would love to).

The pitches vary in size, prettiness and amount
of shade; arrive before check-in at 2pm for the
widest choice. Our favourites are Stonehenge
(enclosed and very private, but also sunny) and
Fruity (on the edge of the wood). Sirius, Humpty
Dumpty and Avalon are big enough for two or
more tents – although Avalon is next to the
toilets. The two pitches beside the parking area
are the most open, with grass rather than earth
underfoot. Park at the edge of the site, then
use the wheelbarrows provided to transport
your gear along the snaking paths.

The green hollow near the house is where
you'll find the reception caravan, along with
Blackberry Wood's newest accommodation
options: a London bus and two tiny caravans
(a traditional wooden wagon and a 1963 Dutch
model called Bubble). Just in case you thought
the repertoire of unusual beds was lacking in
variety, currently being renovated in readiness
for summer 2012 is an ex-Royal Navy helicopter.
It will come equipped with a sandbag seating
area and retro shelter, and will no doubt prove
exceedingly popular. From the hollow, steps
lead up to the shower, toilet and washing-up
block, the shop and the log shed. Most campers
favour the garden shed-style facilities by the

Blackberry Wood is one of those campsites that
made sleeping in a tent fashionable again. It's
exceedingly popular, and it's easy to see why.
There's the superb location, at the foot of the
South Downs ridge near Ditchling Beacon – just
an hour and half's drive from London, and much
less from Brighton. The setting is magical: just
20 pitches in small clearings amid a tangled
woodland of hawthorn, oak and ash trees,

EAST SUSSEX

wood; these are basic, but full of character, with showers that are open to the sky.

Staying here is like camping in your own private wood. Come dusk, the glimmer of campfires through the trees (each pitch has its own stone hearth with log seating) and murmured conversation are the only indications that you're not alone. At daybreak, the dawn chorus can be deafening, though. And pray for sunshine: muddy footpaths, dripping trees and soggy tents don't make for comfortable camping.

Just up the hill is the tiny hamlet of Streat, with its fine Elizabethan manor house, pretty church and stellar views back to the chalk ridge. Head in the other direction to access the network of walking paths that criss-cross the South Downs. Ditchling village is nearby, and the historic town of Lewes a mere five miles away.

EATING & DRINKING

The on-site shop is very basic. Ditchling has a few shops; there's more choice, including a branch of Waitrose, in Lewes.

The nearest pub, a half-hour walk via the grounds of Plumpton Agricultural College, is the Half Moon (01273 890253, www.halfmoonplumpton.com, no food Sun evening), which was tarted up a few years ago. Expect homemade country classics alongside more experimental dishes.

The best food – book in advance – is to be found in East Chiltington at the Jolly Sportsman (01273 890400,

Site specific

✔ The woodland setting is lovely. There are only 20 pitches, and each camping glade is very private.

✗ The whole site gets very muddy after rain. Bring wellies.

The South Downs Way near Ditchling

www.thejollysportsman.com, closed Sun dinner), also within walking distance. It's hard to fault: a modern-cum-rustic interior, pretty terrace, lovely garden, sterling wine list and exemplary cooking (mains might include roast monkfish with bacon and pea risotto or roast partridge with wild mushroom sauce). All this come at a price, of course, though the set lunch and dinner menus are a bargain.

Ditchling has the old-fashioned Ditchling Tea Rooms (01273 842708), the recently refurbished General café/resturant (01273 846638), and the Bull pub (01273 843147, www.thebullditchling.com) for fancier and more expensive meals, with a focus on local ingredients. Lewes is home to Harveys brewery, so real ale fans will be happy.

ATTRACTIONS & ACTIVITIES

It's a 20-minute stroll down Streat Lane to the foot of the South Downs, and miles of fantastic footpaths. (The prominent 'V' of trees on the hillside was planted to celebrate Queen Victoria's golden jubilee in 1887.) If you don't want to tackle the stiff walk to the top, you can drive to the National Trust car park at Ditchling Beacon – via the famously steep, winding hill that is the bane of every cyclist on the London to Brighton bike ride – and strike out from there.

The South Downs Way (www.southdownsway. co.uk) runs along the chalk ridge, with a particularly pleasant walk to the Jack and Jill Windmills. The latter (www.jillwindmill.org.uk) is open most Sundays 2-5pm May-Sept. In early summer, cowslips cover the slopes, and hawthorn, cow parsley and campion are in flower. Listen out for skylarks on the ridge.

Lewes is an idiosyncratic town, with a long history of non-conformism: 18th-century American revolutionary Tom Paine lived there, and its anti-Catholic Bonfire Night celebrations still draw headlines every year. It's even got its own currency, the Lewes pound. There's an imposing Norman castle (01273 486290, www.sussexpast.co.uk), an antiques arcade and plenty of second-hand bookshops.

East Sussex is also Bloomsbury Group territory. Monk's House (01323 870001, www.nationaltrust. org.uk, closed Nov-Mar), Virginia Woolf's country retreat, is at Rodmell, just outside Lewes. More enticing are the vibrantly painted interiors of Charleston (01323 811265, www.charleston.org.uk, closed Nov-Mar), home of Woolf's sister, Vanessa Bell, and her husband Duncan Grant. It's about 12 miles away, near the village of Firle. Drop into nearby Berwick Church to see the wall paintings by Bell and Grant. Both houses are open only in the afternoon a few days a week, so plan ahead.

AMUSING THE KIDS

There's no open space for ball games at Blackberry Wood, although small children love the winding paths and the tyre swings. For seaside fun, the beach, amusement arcades and ice-cream parlours of Brighton are less than 30 minutes by car.

CAMPING NEARBY

The luxurious bell tents of Safari Britain (07780 871996, 07974 266108, www.safaribritain.com), are a fun option, particularly if there are a few of you. Prices vary depending on when you go: weekdays are considerably cheaper (about £45 per adult) and larger groups often book the whole site at weekends (£1,800 for 20 people). For smaller group bookings, it's best to contact the owner directly. The site occupies a lovely spot beneath Firle Beacon, and all sorts of guided activities, such as foraging, bushcraft and falconry are included in the weekend rate. It's perfect for families.

Welsummer

Welsummer
Chalk House, Lenham Road,
Harrietsham, Kent ME17 1NQ
01622 844048, 07771 992355
bakehousemail@yahoo.co.uk
www.welsummercamping.com
Map p26 ㊱
OS map TQ866505

Number of pitches 20 tents. No caravans/motorhomes. 2 bell tents (sleeping up to 6). 1 ridge tent (sleeps up to 4). Minimum stay 2 nights bank holidays and school holidays in pre-erected tents.
Open Apr-Oct.
Booking By phone, email. Essential weekends and school holidays.
Typical cost £12 small pitch, £20 large pitch, £45 pre-erected tent. All plus £3 adult, £1 3-13s.
Facilities Café; laundry facilities; shop; showers (free); toilets; washing-up area.
Campfires Allowed, in designated areas. Firewood available (£3.50-£5).
Dogs Allowed, on lead (book ahead).
Restrictions No noise after 10.30pm.
Getting there By road Take the A20 from Maidstone to Harrietsham. At Harrietsham, turn right on to Fairbourne Lane towards Ulcombe, then left on to Lenham Road towards Platts Heath. After half a mile, you'll go past Greenhill Lane and the sign for 'Chalk House free-range eggs'; the entrance is the next gate on the right, signposted Welsummer. **By public transport** The campsite is a couple of miles from Harrietsham or Lenham rail stations. Bus 59 from Maidstone (Mon-Sat, 0871 200 2233, www.arrivabus.co.uk) takes 35 mins to Kingswood, which is slightly closer. A taxi from Maidstone costs about £7 (Streamline Taxis, 01622 750000).

This lovely campsite is named after a breed of chicken, and its location is marked by a sign that depicts a cartoon chicken looking quizzically at an egg that has appeared between its legs. It's a charming start, and an indication of the welcoming, unpretentious nature of the place; returning here after a day in the Kent countryside feels like coming home. The approach is on small country lanes, but the site is just south of the M20, and conveniently close to a couple of train stations.

Welsummer is a small site – two fields and some woodland – dotted with fruit trees. The owner used to camp on this land with her family when she was a child, before opening up the campsite, and it retains an appealingly intimate feel. The atmosphere is laid-back, with helpful staff and very few rules – just enough to stop the site becoming unruly. Thoughtful touches include the hand basin at children's height in the shower block, and the fact that cars are parked in a large field away from the tents. There's also a new family shower room and a two-acre play area.

Campfires are allowed in firepits (most with fire bricks and backplates), creating a cosy, inviting glow at night – enhanced, on our last visit, by children clutching glow sticks. There are some beautiful woodland pitches (carry a torch at night, or you'll struggle to find your tent), but most of the woodland is untouched and there are no plans to extend into it – it's a joy to walk through, and a magical, safe place for children to run wild.

Various footpaths run past the site and the Greensand Way long-distance path is nearby. Slightly further afield are the North Downs. Though, in truth, Welsummer is such a pleasant place that sitting under a damson tree with a book might be all the relaxation you need.

Respect for the environment is a big factor. Welsummer aims for low impact, and as this is more than just a token gesture, not all campers will be happy with the results. The slightly ramshackle shower and toilet block is quite basic (John Grisham paperbacks aside), while hot water is heated centrally by a wood-burning stove and therefore isn't always available; washing-up water is allowed to run cold during peak demand on the showers, for example. All rubbish must be sorted, there are no electric hook-ups and there's a ten per cent discount for campers who arrive on foot, by bike or by public transport – in other words, not by car. For eco-conscious campers in search of a low-key getaway, this is pretty much paradise.

KENT

Site specific

✔ The shop sells excellent bacon butties and fresh coffee in the morning, and fruit (apples, plums) straight from the trees.

✘ The environmental approach means that facilities are pretty basic, and hot water for washing-up isn't guaranteed.

EATING & DRINKING

Open daily, the campsite shop sells fresh eggs, milk, fruit, cheese and bread, along with home-made goodies to cook over the campfire; foil-wrapped, raisin and cinamon-stuffed apples, say, or stuffed marrows, grown in the garden. Ten minutes' drive away, the village of Lenham has a deli, butcher's and bakery; a little further out, Headcorn has a wider range of shops and a supermarket.

A pleasant ten minutes' stroll (20 minutes if you take the footpaths rather than the road), the Pepperbox Inn (01622 842558, www.thepepperboxinn.co.uk, closed Sun evening) has a pleasant atmosphere, Shepherd Neame beers on tap and the best food in the vicinity. The pub is marked on the local footpath map available at the campsite, along with the King's Head (01622 850259, closed lunch Mon-Thur) in Grafty Green, which has a large beer garden and a children's play area.

Just over five miles away, Headcorn is home to the George & Dragon (01622 890239), a characterful pub with good beers and ciders. It also serves food – though you might be lured in by the Headcorn ashop (01622 890682) instead, with its enticing array of own-made cakes.

It's worth driving the ten miles to Biddenden and the pretty Three Chimneys (01580 291472, www.the threechimneys.co.uk). Set in atmospheric, low-ceilinged, 15th-century premises, with a lavender-lined garden, the restaurant specialises in seasonal dishes sourced from local suppliers.

ATTRACTIONS & ACTIVITIES

Bring hiking boots and an OS map; a nearby path connects with the Greensand Way – a waymarked trail that meanders through a gentle landscape of orchards, copses and agricultural land.

An 11-mile drive brings you to Biddenden Vineyards (01580 291726, www.biddendenvineyards.com, closed Sun Jan, Feb). Two paths lead through the vineyards, and there are samples of the wines, cider and apple juice in the shop. Better still, take one of the twice-monthly free guided tours, which culminate with a tasting. Combine a visit to the winery with a trip to exquisite Sissinghurst Castle Garden (01580 710701, www.nationaltrust.org.uk, closed Wed, Thur, closed Nov-mid Mar). Designed in the 1930s by Vita Sackville-West and laid out in a series of garden 'rooms', divided by yew, boxwood and hornbeam hedges, it's an irresistibly romantic place, brimming with colour and fragrance.

AMUSING THE KIDS

Children create their own fun at Welsummer, climbing trees or running amok in the huge playing field (bring equipment for rounders, cricket or other games).

Nearby Leeds Castle (01622 765400, www.leeds-castle.com) makes for a cracking day out. Built on two islands in the River Len, it rises from the water like a fairytale castle. Along with the opulent interiors and beautifully landscaped gardens, there's an aviary, a magnificent yew maze, a lovely wooden playground and, at weekends, falconry displays. The castle's wooded grounds are also home to an outpost of Go Ape! (0845 643 9215, www.goape.co.uk, call for opening times), where older kids can hurtle along zip-wires to their hearts' content.

CAMPING NEARBY

Ten miles south, on the other side of the M20, Dunn Street Farm (01233 712537, open Easter-Oct, £6 adult, £4 child is a low-key, informal site on a working farm with 40 pitches for tents, camper vans and caravans. Facilities are basic but ultra-clean, and the owners make everyone feel welcome.

KENT

Debden House

Debden House
Debden Green, Loughton, Essex IG10 2NZ
020 8508 3008/6770
debden.house@newham.gov.uk
www.debdenhouse.com
Map p26 ③⑦
OS map TQ439983

Number of pitches 350 tents/caravans/
motorhomes.
Open May-Sept.
Booking By phone, online.
Typical cost £7.50 adult, £3.50 child.
Facilities Bike hire; café; electric hook-ups
(55); laundry facilities; play area; shop;
showers (free); toilets; washing-up facilities.
Campfires Allowed, in firepits (book in
advance). Limited firewood available (free).
Dogs Allowed, on lead (£1).
Restrictions Single-sex groups by
arrangement. Gate closed at 10pm,
no noise after 10.30pm.
Getting there By road From the North
Circular (A406) take a short trip up the M11,
coming off at the next exit (junction 5) for
the A1168 northbound. Turn right on to the
A121, then right again on to Clay's Lane,
and left on Debden Lane. The house and
campsite are straight ahead. **By public
transport** Debden, the nearest tube station,
is around 1.5 miles away; Loughton is 2
miles. Both stations are on the Central line.

Camping at Debden House on a Saturday night
is like being at Glastonbury, without the music.
There are Essex girls in skinny jeans and glittery
tops, a group on a hen weekend dressed as
American Indians, quite literally whooping it up,
and a gang of teenagers sack-racing up the gentle
slope of the fire field in their sleeping bags, then
rolling back down. There are chickens, goats and
two amiable, sleepy pigs in the animal enclosure.
And everywhere, groups of laid-back friends and
families are gathered around the firepits on their
generously sized pitches, tossing logs on the fire
and drinks down their throats with the kind of
merry abandon and bonhomie you're unlikely to
find outside a festival. In such circumstances,
it's hard to feel anything but love for your fellow
campers and the wider world beyond.

Of the seven fields at Debden's 50-acre
grounds, three are reserved for pre-booked
groups, leaving four sizeable fields for other
campers. Fields one and four (no booking – just
turn up) have playgrounds and large open spaces,
where kids can play safely and happily until
sunset; extended London and Essex families
come back year after year, drawn by the friendly
atmosphere. Fields two and five (which must
be booked ahead – bring photo ID) are the ones
with the giant firepits.

Facilities are adequate – there's a small shop,
a great café and just about sufficient toilets.
A limited amount of firewood is stored on site,
which campers can use for free; when that runs
out, a genial Aussie turn up to sells logs at £5
a wheelbarrow.

Pitches are large, well marked (with a numbered bin) and filled with all manner of unlikely people – a much wider mix than you'd find on an average campsite. You're just as likely to be camping next to a local Essex family as you are a plumber commuting into central London on a contract for a fortnight. In the group fields, French, German and inner-city English students play football in games that anyone can join. The feeling is very much of a campsite that reflects multi-generational, multicultural Britain; one that is essentially London in a field – or seven. Which in our view, makes it one of the best campsites in the country.

EATING & DRINKING

The campsite's shop offers very basic basics, so it's best to make a stop at one of the nearby supermarkets for your barbecue provisions; the closest is in Debden, just over a mile away. Alternatively, pig out on a full English breakfast at the site's excellent café (open until 7pm), which also serves decent sandwiches and jacket potatoes, and saves you from having to venture out to Debden's suburban pubs.

At High Beach in Epping Forest, the Green Hut tea room on Fairmead Road offers a sterling range of snacks. With tea costing 35p and filled rolls from 75p, it does a roaring trade (quite literally; just follow the sound of motorbikes to find it). Nearby, the Kings Oak pub (020 8508 5000) on Nursery Road is a great spot for a well-earned lunch and pint if you're spending the day rambling in the woods, with a play area for children, a pleasant restaurant and a prime location in the heart of Epping Forest.

ESSEX

ATTRACTIONS & ACTIVITIES

Epping Forest (www.eppingforest.co.uk/forest.html) is a short walk from Debden, offering ample opportunity for long, rural rambles through ancient woodland and open heathland, as well as heaps of activities including boating, cycling and horse riding. If you're of a literary persuasion, make a pilgrimage to High Beach churchyard, where Alfred Lord Tennyson wrote part of 'In Memoriam' (he lived in the area); it's about three miles away, and a lovely walk.

Around six miles away is the riverside Lee Valley Regional Park (0845 677 0600, www.leevalleypark. org.uk), where attractions include an ice-skating rink, two city farms and assorted birdwatching hides (it's a prime spot for kingfishers), along with a riding centre.

But don't discount Debden House's own natural charms. Its extensive forest, ten minutes' walk from the campsite, is home to a deer sanctuary, and camp staff can provide a map detailing this and other areas of interest in the 50-acre grounds. And if it rains, jump on the Central line and head into London.

AMUSING THE KIDS

The Epping Forest Visitor Centre in High Beach (020 8508 0028, www.cityoflondon.gov.uk) organises a range of child-oriented activities, including nature trails. If older children relish ghostly goings-on, a midnight stroll here might be rewarded with a sighting of the ghost of Dick Turpin; the highwayman used to shelter in secret hideouts in the depths of the forest, and various spooky sightings and paranormal activity have been reported.

CAMPING NEARBY

At Lippitts Hill, near High Beach, the pretty and intimate Elms Caravan & Camping Park (020 8502 5652, www.theelmscampsite.co.uk, open Mar-Oct) has 50 pitches and a well-stocked camp shop. Prices start at £15.50 for a tent pitch with two adults.

Lee Valley Campsite (020 8529 5689, www.leevalley park.org.uk, open Mar-Jan, £12.90-£18.20 2 people) in Chingford is a half-hour ride (bus 215) from Walthamstow Central station. It offers great facilities, friendly staff and campers, many taking advantage of affordable digs with easy access to central London.

Site specific

✔ The fascinating mix of people, and the proximity to London. Debden House is just 20 miles from London's West End, and the only campsite within walking distance of not one, but two tube stations

✘ The location of the toilets is frustrating. The two blocks are easily accessible if you're in the family fields, but a long hike from the fire fields, with lengthy queues when you get to the nearest one.

Harbour Camping

Harbour Camping & Caravan Park
Ferry Road, Southwold, Suffolk IP18 6ND
01502 722486 enquiries
01502 588444 bookings
lucy.aldman@waveney.gov.uk
www.waveney.gov.uk
Map p26 ⑱
OS map TM504749

Number of pitches 100 tents/caravans/
motorhomes.
Open Apr-Oct.
Booking By phone. Essential.
Typical cost £16.50-£22.50 2 adults,
£2.20 extra adult, £1.10 child.
Facilities Disabled (toilet and shower);
laundry facilities; showers (free); toilets;
washing-up area.
Campfires Not allowed.
Dogs Allowed, on lead.
Restrictions No unsupervised under-18s.
Getting there By road Take the A12 to
the Suffolk coast. Turn off on to the A1095
between Blythburg and Wangford, following
signs to Southwold; it's about 4 miles to
the town centre. From there, follow signs
south to the harbour. **By public transport**
Train to Lowestoft. Bus 99 (First Buses,
www.firstgroup.com) runs at 13 mins past
the hour from Lowestoft bus station; it takes
about 50 mins to Southwold's Market Place.
From there, walk a mile to the harbour,
catch bus 601 (every hour) or get a taxi.

SUFFOLK

Southwold's many delights have been well
known to holiday-makers for several centuries;
it's a picture-perfect vision of a traditional
English small town and the jewel in the Suffolk
coast's crown. There are no retail parks or
suburban sprawl, just a higgeldy-piggeldy ramble
of small streets here, candy-coloured beach
huts there, a tasteful pier, and an understated
seafront promenade. If it wasn't so soulful,
you'd call it twee.

Londoners come here for the simple life,
but their presence is felt, not just in the shops
(the Black Olive Deli stocks sausage rolls from
Marylebone's renowned butcher, Ginger Pig),
but in the high percentage of holiday homes.
The only blot on the landscape is Sizewell's
nuclear power plant just down the coast,
though from Southwold it just looks like a
daring futuristic sculpture.

The Harbour campsite is about a mile out of
town, next to the small-scale and picturesque
harbour, and a mere hop, skip and jump over the
dunes from an expansive sandy beach that is
safe for swimmers of all ages. For an evening
stroll into town, you can walk along the road or
the beach or take the path through the dunes
between the two. The campsite is, unusually,
run by the local council, so its feel is municipal
rather than intimate (although the staff in the
office are friendly and helpful enough).

On arrival, you drive through a field of static
mobile homes (so sought after that there's a
waiting list for the waiting list) and into another
large field divided in two by a hedge. The prime
spots for privacy and shelter are anywhere
along the inland side of the hedge, but places
are allocated, so it's pot luck. Caravans are in
a minority, as there no electric hook-ups.

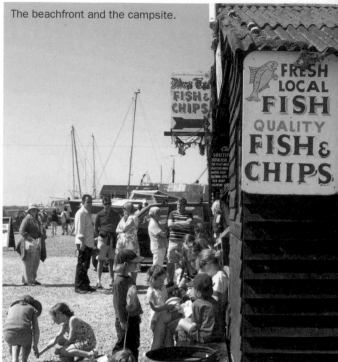

The beachfront and the campsite.

Considering the lack of trees, the site isn't particularly windswept since it's surrounded by large dunes and scrubby banks. There's a loo and shower block in each section of the field, but the larger half would benefit from more showers. The pitches are marked on the grass and aren't huge, but there is room around most to park a car. This is wholesome camping at its old-fashioned best and it's quiet too, as most people have kids in tow and go to bed when the sun disappears to make the most of the morning. It's also very popular, so booking is crucial.

Site specific

✔ The sunsets in the huge Suffolk sky are incredible, and waking up to the sound of skylarks singing ain't bad either. The campsite is surrounded on one side by the sea, on another by the harbour and on the others by cows grazing in salt marsh meadows, so it's very peaceful.

✗ There aren't enough showers to cope when the campsite is full, and the facilities need cleaning more often.

EATING & DRINKING

There are no on-site facilities, although Willie the Milk arrives at about 9am (too late for most campers' breakfasts) with milk, bread, yogurt, newspapers and a few other staples.

Along the harbour front on Blackshore, just around the corner from the campsite, you'll find Mrs T's Fish & Chips (01502 724709, closed Mon except bank holidays). You can take your own bread and wine to accompany the seafood platters at the Sole Bay Fish Co (01502 724241, www.solebayfishco.co.uk, restaurant closed Mon), or score some fresh fish for the barbecue from its shop. The shack-like little café next to the chandlery provides hearty breakfasts, and tasty fare throughout the day.

Further along Blackshore, the Harbour Inn (01502 722381) serves good platefuls of grub, while, across the water in Walberswick, the Anchor (01502 722112, www.anchoratwalberswick.com) is a top-end gastropub with a locally sourced menu. Southwold is the home of the Adnams brewery, so most local pubs and hotels serve its ales. A pint or two of Broadside will certainly help campers get a good night's sleep.

A stroll into Southwold opens up many more possibilities. For spectacular ice-cream sundaes, visit Tilly's tea room (01502 725677, www.tillysof southwold.co.uk) on the High Street. The Lord Nelson (01502 722079, www.thelordnelsonsouthwold.co.uk)

SUFFOLK

on East Street is understandably one of the town's most popular pubs, serving exceptional fish and chips, sandwiches and kids' meals inside a cosy bar and outside in a pleasant courtyard.

ATTRACTIONS & ACTIVITIES

Southwold has attractions galore. Visit tiny Southwold Museum (9-11 Victoria Street, 01502 726097, www.southwoldmuseum.org, closed Nov-Easter) to enjoy imaginative displays exploring the social history of the town. It was recently refurbished and they've done a fine job.

You can climb the steps to the lamp room of the Lighthouse – a classic old-fashioned white tower – for great views of the coastline and to marvel at the tiny lightbulbs. It's open most Wednesdays and weekends from Easter to the end of October.

The marvellously tasteful pier has Tim Hunkin's clock and playful water sculpture performing on the half hour and some zany hand-built rides and games in its curate's egg of an arcade. Play 'Whack the Banker', take a mock deep-sea dive in the Bathyscape or get some unusual photos for the family album in the Expressive Photobooth. Those wanting a quiet moment should head for the Sailors' Reading Room on East Cliff, where they can peruse a book or newspaper in an armchair and listen to the waves pounding the shore outside. The more actively inclined might prefer

a 30-minute power-boat blast around Sole Bay or a longer trip as far as Orford Ness with Coastal Voyager (07887 525082, www.coastalvoyager.co.uk).

If you wish to explore Walberswick, the best (and cutest) way to get there is on the tiny rowing boat ferry across the River Blyth, which leaves from the campsite end of the harbour.

AMUSING THE KIDS

The beach provides guaranteed fun. The sand is the perfect consistency for bucket-and-spade building projects; alternatively, there's always crab fishing along the harbour. You'll need a line, a bucket and something to entice the crustaceans; the Sole Bay Fish Co is usually happy to provide free bait. Then it's just a case of getting the crabs into the bucket… Keen crabbers can enter the British Open Crabbing Championship, held every August in Walberswick.

CAMPING NEARBY

If you want to go one step more basic, there's a tiny, 20-pitch campsite at Walberswick. It's only open during the six-week summer holiday, but it's intimate and fun if you like surviving with one cold tap and no loos (you can dash across to the village hall if that's just too much to contemplate). Book well ahead with Norma Boyle on 01502 478019. Prices range from £6-£16 per night, depending on the size of tent.

Bags packed, milk cancelled, house raised on stilts.

You've packed the suntan lotion, the snorkel set, the stay-pressed shirts. Just one more thing left to do – your bit for climate change. In some of the world's poorest countries, changing weather patterns are destroying lives.

You can help people to deal with the extreme effects of climate change. Raising houses in flood-prone regions is just one life-saving solution.

**Climate change costs lives.
Give £5 and let's sort it *Here & Now***

www.oxfam.org.uk/climate-change

Oxfam is a registered charity in England and Wales (No.202918) and Scotland (SCO039042). Oxfam GB is a member of Oxfam International.

Be Humankind (☿) **Oxfam**

The Orchard

The Orchard Campsite
28 Spring Lane, Wickham Market,
Woodbridge, Suffolk IP13 0SJ
01728 746170
info@orchardcampsite.co.uk
www.orchardcampsite.co.uk
Map p26 ③
OS map TM306560

Number of pitches 15 tents, 5 caravans/
motorhomes. 2 Gypsy caravans (sleeping 4).
Open Mar-Nov.
Booking By email. Essential.
Typical cost £16-£22 per pitch (up to
6 people; large tents may be charged for
2 pitches). Gypsy caravan £170 2 nights.
Facilities Cycle hire (from £7); disabled
facilities (toilet and shower); electric hook-
ups (22); fishing rod hire (£5); laundry
facilities; play area; shop; showers (free);
toilets; washing-up area; Wi-Fi.
Campfires Allowed. Firewood available
(£3.50 bag, £15 wheelbarrow).
Dogs Allowed, on lead.
Restrictions Groups (maximum 6)
of under-18s by arrangement only.
No amplified music after 11pm.
Getting there By road Head north on the
A12 (Ipswich to Lowestoft road). About 9
miles north of Ipswich, take the second exit
to Wickham Market, then the third left on
to Spring Lane. The campsite is on the left,
after 500 yds. **By public transport** Train to
Ipswich, then bus 63 to Wickham Market
(takes 50 mins, Mon-Sat, 0871 200 2233,
www.firstgroup.com). It's then a 10-mins
walk to the campsite. Wickham Market rail
station is not in the town itself, but near
Campsey Ash, a 30-mins walk away –
though you can arrange for the campsite
to collect you.

You don't come to the Orchard for peace and
quiet; this family-run campsite in Suffolk is an
unabashedly lively, fun place. The haphazard,
higgledy-piggledy arrangement of tents, vehicles
and campfires fills a pleasant site that was once
an orchard; a few venerable fruit trees remain,
and new ones are being planted.

Up and running for almost 20 years, the site
has excellent facilities. A well-maintained toilet
block has power-showers, washing machines
and driers, while the washing-up area features
a microwave oven, kettle, fridge and freezer.
The camping field, meanwhile, comprises three
interconnected areas. Closest to the toilets and
with electric hook-ups, the meadow is a sunny,
open expanse; this is where families tend to set
up camp. The pond area is slightly more tucked
away, and a favourite with groups. Finally – and
furthest from the toilet block – there's the
woodland area, where tents nestle in clearings.

The meadow also has a well designed pitch
for campers with disabilities, close to the site's
amenities and accessed by a paved path. There
are also two hand-built Gypsy caravans, each
with a double bed and two singles, and heated
by a pot-bellied stove.

The latest innovation – and very useful – is
the on-site general store and off-licence, where
you can stock up on local foodstuffs, including
meat, jams and tinned goods, as well as a fine
selection of beer, cider and wine. Fresh bread
and croissants are delivered daily. For other
supplies, Wickham Market is a five-minute
walk away. Clustered around the village square
are two small supermarkets, a pharmacy and
various restaurants.

The 11pm music curfew nothwithstanding,
there are few rules here. Large groups, including
hen and stag parties, are welcome, though overall
it's very family-oriented, with games of all sorts
played between the tents (often perilously close
to campfires). There's a popular playground, and
a table-tennis hut next to the barbecue area.

The result is a noisy, exuberant atmosphere
where you're as likely to have a football land
on your tent as you are to be invited for a drink
'next door', or a child's birthday party three tents
away. That said, there are plenty of spots for
peaceful contemplation, and less boisterous
pursuits such as Pooh sticks can be played by
the river. There are various walks through the
pleasant Suffolk countryside too – including a
two-and-a-half-mile ramble to Easton, home to
the prettiest pub in the area.

What really sets the Orchard apart from other
sites, though, is the small observatory, with its
sliding roof and telescope. Historically, the local
area is a UFO hotspot (centred around nearby
Rendlesham Woods), and spooky stories of
sightings abound – although, alas, there were
no extra-terrestrial visitors during our stay.

EATING & DRINKING

The Orchard's shop, supplemented by deliveries
from the excellent Ufford Produce (01394 460813,
www.suffolk-produce.co.uk), means you can be

SUFFOLK

SUFFOLK

Site specific

✔ On nights with good visibility, the sights captured by the observatory telescope are displayed on a plasma screen for all to marvel at. In winter, Alien Encounter weekends fill the orchard with sky-gazing campers.

✘ The noise, from both people and vehicles. The proximity of the A12 makes getting to the Orchard very easy, but also means you can always hear traffic.

perfectly well provided for without leaving camp. Ufford Produce also has a shop in Lower Ufford, a couple of miles away.

That said, bestirring yourself to tackle the short walk to Wickham Market is an effort worth making. The Teapot (01728 748079) is a charming café, with a sweet summer patio and bric-a-brac to browse next door. For takeaways, there's also a decent chippie, Eat Inn (01728 746361, closed Sun) and Indian and Chinese restaurants.

The village pub, the George (01728 746306) isn't overly welcoming, but is fine for a pint. Further afield in Ramsholt, the Ramsholt Arms (01394 411229) is a much nicer spot, with a riverside beer garden. Better still is the picturesque, 18th-century White Horse (01728 746456) in Easton, with real ales, a good choice of wine by the glass, and seating overlooking the village green.

ATTRACTIONS & ACTIVITIES

Bicycles can be hired on site, as can fishing rods; the river that runs along the lower end of the campsite is populated by impressively large pike.

The coast is an easy, 30-minute drive. Aldeburgh is a charmer, with its fishing boats, shingle beach and traditional high street. A few miles inland, near Snape, the restored brewery complex of Snape Maltings (01728 688303, www.snapemaltings.co.uk) can provide entertainment, food and shelter on inclement days, as well as birdwatching and river trips; it's also the centre of the Aldeburgh Music Festival (www.aldeburgh.co.uk) every June.

There are lovely walks to be had in and around Orford, a pretty village with a 12th-century castle; take a ferry ride across the river to the former military test site of Orford Ness (01728 648024, www.national trust.org.uk, open Tue-Sat July-Sept, Sat Apr-June, Oct), now an eerily atmospheric nature reserve. Five miles from the campsite, just outside the market town of Woodbridge, is the famous Anglo-Saxon

burial site of Sutton Hoo (01394 389700, www. nationaltrust.org.uk, open all year but days vary).

AMUSING THE KIDS

Easton Farm Park (01728 746475, www.eastonfarm park.co.uk, closed mid Sept-mid Mar except for half-term and 2 weeks Dec) keeps children occupied with a play barn, playground, pony rides and animals to pet. On the outskirts of Ipswich, the indoor track at Anglia Karting (01473 240087, www.angliakarting. com) should amuse speed fiends on a rainy day.

Just over six miles from the Orchard, Framlingham Castle (01728 724189, www.english-heritage.org.uk, closed Mon-Fri Nov-Mar) is a splendid crenellated fortress. There's a children's audio tour along the ramparts, and an exhibition explains its various incarnations, from Tudor stronghold to poorhouse.

CAMPING NEARBY

Ten miles from the Orchard, in Shottisham, St Margaret's Camping & Caravan Site (01394 411247, www.stmargaretscampsite.co.uk, open Easter-Oct, £12 for two people) is a vision of rural tranquillity, with a daisy sprinkled camping field, simple facilities, and a friendly local pub, the thatched Sorrel Horse, in the village.

SUFFOLK

Woodside Farm

NORFOLK

Woodside Farm
Common Lane, Thurne, Great Yarmouth,
Norfolk NR29 3BX
01692 670367
ajfjtf@hotmail.com
www.woodside-farm.co.uk
Map p26 ㊵
OS map TG403165

Number of pitches 10 tents,
2 caravans/motorhomes.
Open All year.
Booking By phone, email.
Typical cost £21.50 4 people,
£3 extra adult.
Facilities Disabled facilities (shower
and toilet); electric hook-ups (8);
fishing lake (free); showers (free);
toilets; washing-up area.
Campfires Not allowed.
Dogs Allowed, on lead.
Getting there By road From the A47
(Norwich to Great Yarmouth road), turn off
at Acle on to the A1064, heading towards
Caister. Turn left on to the B1152 and
then follow signs to Thurne. Go through
the village, past the Lion Inn on the Street;
the campsite is just after the dead-end sign
to the right. **By public transport** The nearest
train station is at Acle. From there, take
a taxi (Acle Taxi Service, 01493 752223,
about £8).

Woodside Farm is set amid the rivers and lakes
of the Norfolk Broads, 20 miles from Norwich
in the village of Thurne. Located at the edge of
the village – which sees more boats than cars
passing through – and at the end of a dead-end
lane, it's a very peaceful spot. With just a dozen
pitches on a site that could easily accommodate
twice that number, you're sure to have plenty
of space as well as peace and quiet; a braying
donkey or distant barking dogs may be all you
hear at night.

The helpful owners, Julia and Andy Furr, took
over the place – previously a caravan site – in
2004. Surrounded by fairly new hedges, the
single camping field is almost flat, so the pitches
are comfortable and well drained – a bonus for
campers tired of lumpy, bumpy, sloping fields. The
pitches are around the edge of the field, leaving
plenty of space for ball games in the middle. The
shower and toilet block is in fine nick: very clean,

with water that is generally piping hot. There's
only one male and one female shower, mind,
so there can be queues. A small shed provides
drinking water and washing-up space.

There's no shop on site, but the Lion Inn is just
five minutes' walk away. As well as serving good
pub grub (including breakfast), you can also find
milk, bread and other basic provisions here in
the summer months. If you've forgotten the tent
pegs or need other equipment, there's a Norwich
Camping store (01603 717600, www.norwich-
camping.co.uk) ten miles away in Blofield.

Woodside Farm is popular with families, and
also with those who like to combine boating
with camping. Thurne is in the heart of Broads
country. Those travelling by water can moor
overnight at the village staithe, then stroll down
to the campsite for a blissful night's sleep.

EATING & DRINKING

The Lion Inn (01692 670 796, www.lion-inn-thurne.
co.uk) in Thurne is more than just a pub: it also has
a shop, an arcade, pool tables, a restaurant and music
nights in summer. The food is a cheerful selection
of pub grub favourites (steaks, sausage and mash);
there are also vegetarian dishes and a children's menu.
It's a lively spot, popular with locals and visitors.

There's a shortage of lovely pubs in the area,
but it's worth visiting the Ship Inn (01603 270049,
www.theshipsouthwalsham.co.uk) in South Walsham,
a 20-minute drive away. Food is a mix of homespun
British flavours – steak and kidney pie, battered
fish with home-cut chips, rack of lamb – and more
Mediterranean-inspired dishes, such as monkfish
tail wrapped in prosciutto with roasted vegetables.
Real ales include Adnams.

Site specific

✔ It's a relaxed and tranquil spot, with easy access to the Broads.

✗ There's not much to do on the site itself, and facilities are limited.

For a serious blow-out, head 12 miles inland to Brundall, to the Lavender House (01603 712215, www.thelavenderhouse.co.uk). Housed in a 16th-century thatched cottage and run by Richard Hughes, a chef dedicated to Norfolk produce, the restaurant is idiosyncratic and welcoming, the menus creative (including a tasting menu, £58). The four-course Sunday lunch, featuring the likes of slow-cooked brisket of Barnard's beef, smoked mash and roasted root veg among the mains, is great value at £25. There's even a cookery school.

ATTRACTIONS & ACTIVITIES

You can stride straight from your tent on to the Weavers Way, a 58-mile footpath that wiggles through the Broads from Cromer to Great Yarmouth. It runs through the village, adjacent to the River Thurne; heading south brings you to Acle, while four miles north is Potter Heigham – one of the main boating centres, where you can hire boats for a day trip. There's also a Broads Authority information centre (www.broads-authority.gov.uk, closed Nov-Mar). To explore the area without taking to the water, rent a bike from the campsite at nearby Clippesby Hall (01493 367800/369221, www.thebroadsbybike.org.uk).

The Broads are home to a rich and diverse collection of wildlife, especially birds. Some of the Broads themselves are nature reserves, such as Hickling Broad, where you'll discover walking and water trails, boat trips and a visitor centre (01692 598276, closed Oct-Mar except weekends and half-term). At How Hill reserve, near Ludham, a jaunt aboard

the *Electric Eel* (01692 678763, no trips Nov-Easter) leads through a variety of landscapes from fen to grazing marsh to woodland.

Windmills – used for both grinding grain and drainage – are as much an integral feature of the Broads landscape as waterways. The whitewashed dyke drainage mill standing proud in Thurne is open on occasional Sunday afternoons from April to September; more accessible is the National Trust-run Horsey Windpump (01263 740241, www.national trust.org.uk, closed Mon-Fri Feb-Mar, all Nov-Jan), eight miles from the campsite. Clamber up the five-storey pump for striking views across Horsey Mere to the coast.

The Museum of the Broads (01692 581681, www.northnorfolk.org/museumofthebroads, closed Oct-Mar) at Stalham Staithe, 15 minutes' drive away, is a small gem that illuminates the traditional way of life in this unique part of Britain.

AMUSING THE KIDS

Turn the children loose at Bewilderwood (01603 783900, www.bewilderwood.co.uk, closed Nov-Mar, and some Tue and Wed), a wonderful and curious fantasy world of woodland mischief, inhabited by boggles, twiggles and thorny crocklebogs. It's in Hoveton, ten miles from Thurne.

If beachside fun is required, Sea Palling, a 25-minute drive, has a vast, sandy and under-used beach. Horsey's beach is equally wide and dramatic, and backed by dunes; seals sometimes can be found sunning themselves on the sand. Further south, Great Yarmouth is a proper old-fashioned seaside resort, with three piers and the Pleasure Beach amusement park along the 'Golden Mile', the seafront promenade.

CAMPING NEARBY

Clippesby Hall (01493 367800, www.clippesby.com, open all year, £11.50-£30.50 per pitch) offers a variety of areas for camping, plus holiday cottages. Some pitches sit close to facilities with hook-ups; others are set in woodland and are exclusively for tents.

NORFOLK

Deer's Glade

Deer's Glade Caravan & Camping Park
White Post Road, Hanworth,
Norwich, Norfolk NR11 7HN
01263 768633
info@deersglade.co.uk
www.deersglade.co.uk
Map p26 ④①
OS map TG216335

Set in a woodland clearing in the heart of the north Norfolk countryside, around five miles from the coastal town of Cromer, Deer's Glade may be fairly easy to reach, but has a wonderful sense of isolation.

There's an atmospheric fishing lake on site, drawing swooping swallows in summer, as well as anglers. The deer after which the site is named tend to be winter visitors, keeping away from the area when it's full of campers – but they can always be spotted on the neighbouring Gunton Hall estate, which has a deer park.

With caravans and campervans easily outnumbering tents, Deer's Glade is not a site for pastoral solitude. Instead, it's a highly organised operation, with a whole raft of amenities including electric hook-ups, laundry facilities, TV points, a shop and even dog kennels. You can check your email without leaving your tent (if you really have to), thanks to the site-wide Wi-Fi. Pitches are flat, spacious and well drained; the shower and toilet blocks are squeaky-clean. Most pitches are numbered, although there's an area by the lake that offers more flexibility for larger groups. Four wooden pods, set in woodland just off the main park, arrived in 2011; they're unfurnished, but have heating, lighting, water and even a TV.

Parents flock here as there's plenty for their offspring to do. Many families rent bikes and tear around the woods; there are also organised activities such as storytelling in a special tipi, and family-oriented facilities such as baby-changing and play areas.

Number of pitches 25 tents (75 during Aug). 100 caravans/motorhomes. 4 pods (sleeping up to 5).
Open All year.
Booking By phone, online, email. Essential high season. Minimum stay 2 nights weekends Apr-Oct, 3 nights bank holiday weekends.
Typical cost Camping £12.50-£16.50 2 people, £5.25-£7.25 extra adult, £1.50-£2 extra children (minimum £10). Muntjac Meadow (Aug only) £14 2 people, £6.50 extra adult, £2 extra child. Pod £30-£35 2 people, £7-£9 extra adult, £2-£4 extra child.
Facilities Cycle hire (£10 per day); disabled facilities (toilet and shower); electric hook-ups (100); fishing lake (£4.50 per day); laundry facilities; play area; shop; showers (free); toilets; washing-up area; Wi-Fi (£1 per hour).
Campfires Allowed, off ground.
Dogs Allowed, on lead (£1).
Restrictions No unsupervised under-18s. No arrivals after 11pm.
Getting there By road From Norwich: take the A140 towards Cromer. Five miles beyond Aylsham, turn right towards Suffield Green, along White Post Road. The site is half a mile on the right. From Kings Lynn: take the A148 towards Cromer. Turn right on to the B1436 towards Roughton. Then join the A140 going towards Norwich. Two miles beyond Roughton, turn left towards Suffield Green, along White Post Road. The site is half a mile on the right. **By public transport** Bus 44 between Cromer and Aylsham stop at the Alby Horseshoes pub, a 10-mins walk from the campsite. Runs Mon-Sat, journey time 15 mins (01263 712800, www.sanderscoaches.com).

Site specific

✔ It's great for families, with plenty of activities to keep youngsters entertained.

✘ Lovers of basic camping will find it too organised – unless you visit in August and stay at Muntjac Meadow.

If that all sounds a bit too holiday-parkish, during August it is possible to have a more low-tech, back-to-nature camping experience. Another field opens up just over the road from the main site: it's a quiet, secluded spot that overlooks a farm. Muntjac Meadow is exclusively for tents and there are no fixed pitches or electric hook-ups, although the site has its own shower and toilet area. At night, campers can gather around the communal campfire and toast marshmallows.

EATING & DRINKING

The nearest pub to Deer's Glade is the Alby Horseshoes (01263 761378, www.users.waitrose.com/~albyhorseshoes, closed Mon-Thur lunch), just over a mile away on the A140. Food is superior pub grub (including the likes of lamb and apricot pie and home-boiled hams) and the beer is well-kept Norfolk ale. The landlord and several locals have their own pewter mugs and play vinyl records on a hi-fi. There's a spacious back garden too.

Cromer, a ten-minute drive, is a faded Victorian bucket-and-spade resort, so yearnings for fish and chips are easily satisfied – try Mary Janes Fish Bar (01263 511208) on Garden Street. For a proper sit-down meal, the Courtyard restaurant (01263 515419)

at the Wellington pub on New Street serves excellent, reasonably priced bistro-style food with an emphasis on fish and seasonal local produce.

Further west along the coast, in Sheringham, No.10 (01263 824400, www.no10sheringham.com, closed Mon, Tue, Sun) has won a reputation for its Mediterranean-oriented cooking, again featuring first-class ingredients from Norfolk's farmers and fishermen. Brunch is served on Saturdays.

ATTRACTIONS & ACTIVITIES

Deer's Glade is sandwiched by two National Trust properties, both about five miles away. North lies Felbrigg Hall (01263 837444, house closed Thur, Fri, all Nov-Feb), an elegant country mansion with a Stuart exterior, Georgian interiors and Victorian gardens. The hall stands in 1,700 acres of parkland, with plenty of woodland trails – ideal for walking and cycling. To the south is Blickling Hall (01263 738030, house closed Mon except summer school holidays, Tue, all Nov-Feb), a preposterously grand Jacobean behemoth renowned for its Long Gallery, rare books and tapestries and for the ghost (headless, of course) of Anne Boleyn. There are superb formal gardens, and another huge park that includes meadows, woods and an artificial lake surrounding the house.

If such stately pleasure grounds don't suffice, there's also Sheringham Park (01263 820550, www.national trust.org.uk), ten miles from the campsite. Designed in 1812 by Humphry Repton, the gardens are noted for their spectacular rhododendron and azalea displays.

Next door is the small town of Sheringham. Its many flint-covered houses are picturesque, its high street bustling and its Blue Flag beach popular. For something a little different, the beach at Overstrand, a mile from Cromer, is wide and a lot quieter. Cromer is also the unlikely setting for the Amazona Zoo (01263 510741, www.amazonazoo.co.uk, closed Nov-Mar); it's not quite the steaming tropical jungle of popular imagination, but the macaws, squirrel monkeys and assorted big cats are exotic enough.

AMUSING THE KIDS

Cromer beach is the obvious choice for sunny days; if it rains, head for the pier and the arcades.

Alternatively, it's a ten-minute drive south to the market town of Aylsham, where you'll find Aylsham Fun Barns (01263 734108, www.aylshamfunbarns.co.uk) and the Bure Valley Railway (01263 733858, www.bvrw.co.uk). The former features an indoor play barn, outdoor adventure playground and petting zoo, while the latter offers an 18-mile round trip aboard a narrow-gauge steam train to Wroxham, in the Broads.

CAMPING NEARBY

Manor Farm (www.manorfarmcaravansite.co.uk, open Easter-Oct) caters for both caravans and tents on a clifftop site overlooking the sea at East Runton, just west of Cromer. A standard pitch for two adults cost £13.50-£16.50. It's about 20 miles to High Sand Creek (see p152), near Wells-Next-the-Sea.

High Sand Creek

There's no website, no email address, no on-site activities and definitely no Wi-Fi. But you'll be hard pressed to get a pitch at High Sand Creek without booking, because this site has something special: a wonderful view. Looking towards the coast, you'll see nothing but salt marshes for miles to either side, and beyond that a golden sandy beach, stretching far into the distance at low tide. At high tide, the water floods into the many creeks that lead almost up to the campsite. A profusion of birds, including avocets, godwits and redshanks, make the marshes their home.

The campsite itself, near the village of Stiffkey (pronounced 'stoo-key'), consists of a sloping field with a facilities block. If you're in a campervan, the best pitches are at the top of the slope, to ensure the finest views. Those under canvas may want to trade the panorama for some shelter (there's a reason for the profusion of windmills in these parts); the line of trees at the bottom provides relief.

The shower and toilet block is remarkably clean, considering its location is beside a huge muddy marsh. There's a pleasant old pub and a great shop in the village, which is five minutes on foot. You can buy a few necessities such as gas bottles from reception, and also recharge your phone there.

This is a family-friendly campsite: kids love climbing the trees and getting covered in mud on the marshes. However, parents might want to balance the joy of proximity to the coast with the lack of facilities on site. There's a ban on noise after 11pm, so this is not a spot for party people.

EATING & DRINKING

There are several good eateries along this stretch of the coast, from low-key crab shacks to high-end restaurants. In Stiffkey itself, the Red Lion (01328 830552, www.stiffkey.com) has bags of charm, a friendly atmosphere and some enterprising dishes on the daily-changing blackboard menu, such as pan-fried salmon and curried chickpeas, or apple,

Site specific

✔ The miles of pristine salt marsh just outside your awning, plus a string of lovely seaside villages to explore.

✘ The site is exposed to the wind. This is basic camping, so the weather will be key to your enjoyment, especially if kids are involved.

High Sand Creek Campsite
Greenway, Stiffkey, Norfolk NR23 1QF
01328 830235
Map p26 ㊷
OS map TF962435

Number of pitches 80 tents/motorhomes. No caravans.
Open Mid Mar-mid Oct.
Booking By phone. Essential high season.
Typical cost £12-£18 2 people, £3-£4 extra adult, £2 extra child
Facilities Disabled facilities (toilet and shower); play area; showers (free); toilets; washing-up area.
Campfires Not allowed.
Dogs Allowed, on lead.
Restrictions No unsupervised under-18s. No noise after 11pm.
Getting there By road High Sand Creek is off the A149, the north Norfolk coast road running between Hunstanton and Cromer. The campsite is next to the village of Stiffkey, about 13 miles west of Sheringham; there's a signpost near the Red Lion pub. **By public transport** The Coasthopper bus (01553 776980, www.coasthopper.co.uk) runs daily between King's Lynn and Cromer, stopping at Stiffkey. It takes about 50 mins in either direction.

---

leek and blue cheese risotto. Further into the village, the superb Stiffkey Stores (01328 830489, www.stiffkeystores.com) sells croissants, cakes and cappuccinos. Pub-lovers can detour inland to Warham to the Three Horseshoes (01328 710547) for a classic aged interior, well-kept ales and a decent menu.

To the east is a string of small, attractive villages. In Blakeney, five miles away, the White Horse Inn (01263 740574, www.blakeneywhitehorse.co.uk) serves excellent, quite pricey, Modern European food, with a fish and seafood bent. Local produce (Morston mussels, Norfolk meat and game, real ales) is to the fore. A cheaper, down-to-earth bar menu is available at lunchtime. For a more traditional vibe, squeeze into the tiny, low-ceilinged rooms at the King's Arms (01263 740341, www.blakeney kingsarms.co.uk) and sample the local whitebait or steak and ale suet pudding.

Just beyond Blakeney, Wiveton Hall (01263 740525, www.wivetonhall.co.uk) has a pretty café that makes impressive use of produce from its own farm. As well

as cakes and daily lunches, tapas is available on Thursday, Friday and Saturday evenings in summer (6-8pm). You can also pick your own fruit and veg, or take in one of the regular arts and crafts shows.

Further east, in Salthouse, Cookies Crab Shop (01263 740352, www.salthouse.org.uk) is a smashing seafood café. After lunch here – soup, sandwiches or a seafood salad – you might want to pop into the Dun Cow (01263 740467) on the village green for a pint.

There are more options in Morston and Cley, and in the opposite direction, in Wells-Next-the-Sea.

ATTRACTIONS & ACTIVITIES

You can spend days exploring the area's coastal paths, big sandy beaches, nature reserves, unusual flint churches and picturesque villages. The North Norfolk Coast Path runs all along the coast, joining up with the Peddars Way cycle trail for the stretch from Cromer to Holme. Walking any distance is a great way to get close to the varied terrain (sand, shingle, marsh) and abundant birdlife that distinguishes this part of East Anglia.

Of the villages, Cley is a beaut. It has a delicatessen, a smokehouse (superb smoked salmon), a bookshop, a fabulous pottery, a couple of galleries and nice pubs, as well as a famous windmill (now a B&B). Its 13th-century church is an impressive reminder of a time when the village was a prosperous port. Cley Marshes (01263 740008, www.norfolkwildlifetrust.org.uk) is a nature reserve renowned for its birding opportunities, with a handsome new visitor centre, four hides, a café and stupendous views across the marshes.

Blakeney village is another attractive spot, with narrow streets and a handful of pubs, shops and restaurants, including a deli and a fishmonger. Blakeney Point is an important breeding ground for common and grey seals; seal-watching trips (Apr-Oct) are available from Blakeney quay, and also in Morston with Beans Boat Trips (01263 740038, www.beansboattrips.co.uk). You can also walk to the point from Cley – it's a desolate but wonderful four-mile return trip.

AMUSING THE KIDS

If children tire of the endless beaches and marshland, take them to the Muckleburgh Collection (01263 588210, www.muckleburgh.co.uk, closed Nov-Mar), Britain's largest privately owned military museum, where they can ride in a Gama Goat, a US personnel carrier. It's ten miles away, en route to Sheringham.

CAMPING NEARBY

Deepdale (see p154) is 11 miles west along the A419, in the village of Burnham Deepdale.

NORFOLK

Deepdale

Number of pitches 82 tents/motorhomes. No caravans. 6 tipis (sleeping up to 6). 2 yurts (sleeping up to 6 & 8). Bunk barn (sleeps 19). Hostel (sleeps 40).
Open All year.
Booking By phone, email, online, post. Minimum stay 2 nights weekends.
Typical cost Camping £9-£18 2 people, £4.50-£9 extra person. Tipi £40-£80 1-2 people, £72-£114 3-6 people. Yurt £50-£95 1-2 people, £80-£125 3-6 people. Bunk barn £150-£250. Hostel from £10.50-£15 dorm, from £30-£60 double.
Facilities Café; disabled facilities (toilet and shower); internet access; laundry facilities; shop; showers (free); toilets; washing-up area.
Campfires Not allowed.
Dogs Allowed, on lead. Not allowed in tipis, yurts or hostel.
Restrictions No noise after 10pm.
Getting there By road Burnham Deepdale is on the A149, 9 miles east of Hunstanton and 8 miles west of Wells-Next-the-Sea. The site's entrance is on the inland side of the main road, opposite St Mary's Church.
By public transport Train to King's Lynn. From there, the Coasthopper bus (01553 776980, www.coasthopper.co.uk) runs hourly to Burnham Deepdale; journey time 70 mins. There's a more frequent service from Hunstanton.

Deepdale Backpackers & Camping
Deepdale Farm, Burnham Deepdale,
Norfolk, PE31 8DD
01485 210256
info@deepdalebackpackers.co.uk
www.deepdalebackpackers.co.uk
Map p26 ⑬
OS map TF804442

On the north Norfolk Coast, towards the edge of the Wash, is the clutch of villages known as the Burnhams. Burnham Deepdale is one of these, set close to the coast. This multifaceted campsite sits on the main road in the middle of the village, at the foot of a huge wheat field with a view to an impressive wooded ridge. The salt marsh coast, the sandy beaches of Brancaster and Holkham, and the North Norfolk Coast Path are nearby. The area can be explored on foot, by bike and via the excellent Coasthopper buses.

Deepdale's facilities are relatively basic, although the presence of a fair-sized reception and shop – both well run – testify to effective organisation. Pitches are on the small side, but perfectly adequate for a reasonably sized tent. Some lie on a gentle slope, though the well-drained land is pretty flat in general. The site covers five fields, with vans, tipis and tents intermingled throughout. The site has a particularly good reputation among classic VW campervan owners; you'll usually find a few of these on site. More yurts and extra-large tent pitches are planned for 2012.

The fields get bigger and more exposed the further you get away from reception; on the other hand, the view is better from the more distant fields. An ongoing landscaping programme involves planting more trees and hedges, dividing paddocks and beautifying the site.

The site's hostel adds to the air of organised adventure. It has accommodation in double/twin, triple, quad and family rooms, all ensuite, as well as dorms. There's also a barn for groups.

Deepdale is eco-aware – solar panels are used for the buildings' water and underfloor heating, for example – and has received an award from the Green Tourism Business Scheme. The vibe is laid-back and friendly; check the notices above the washing-up area for ideas about what to do locally. With a 10pm curfew, this is not a party campsite, but a haven for lovers of peace and quiet.

EATING & DRINKING

Deepdale Café (01485 211055, www.deepdale cafe.co.uk, open 7.30am-4pm daily) is perfect for big breakfasts and brunches. There are also enticing sandwiches, salads, omelettes and cakes, and the Sunday roasts are highly recommended.

It's a short walk along the main road to the White Horse (01485 210262, www.whitehorsebrancaster. co.uk) for lovely views across the marshland. A daily-changing menu of good gastropub food is available at the bar, with more formal cooking in the restaurant. Ingredients are locally sourced where possible (shellfish comes from the beds at the bottom of the garden). For a more family feel, head another half mile west to the Jolly Sailors (01485 210314, www.jollysailorsbrancaster.co.uk). The children can romp in the garden and play area, and meals include stone-baked pizzas and local seafood. The pub produces its own Brancaster Brewery ales. Further west still, in Thornham, the Lifeboat Inn (01485 512236, www.lifeboatinn.co.uk) is a ramshackle 16th-century pub serving crowd-pleasing bar meals.

If you're going in the other direction, to Holkham, the Victoria (01328 711008, www.victoriaat holkham.co.uk) is a vibrantly decorated gastropub-cum-boutique hotel offering the likes of Holkham steaks and organic chicken. You'll need to book. Also on the Holkham Estate, the Marsh Larder Tearooms (01328 711285) is excellent for tea and cakes, and serves good breakfasts and lunch.

A few miles inland at Burnham Market, the yellow-painted Hoste Arms on the Green (01328 738777, www.hostearms.co.uk) has often been credited (or blamed) for being the restaurant that brought Londoners to north Norfolk. The setting is smart and the menu stylish, with homely dishes such as steak and kidney pud sitting alongside more international flavours. If you'd prefer a proper old-fashioned boozer, head to the Lord Nelson (01328 738241, www.nelsonslocal.co.uk) in nearby Burnham Thorpe – the naval hero was born in the

village. Sink into a high-backed wooden settle with a pint and tuck into the superior pub food.

ATTRACTIONS & ACTIVITIES

Six miles east along the coast road, Holkham (www.holkham.co.uk) pretty much has it all. Holkham Hall itself (01328 710227, www.holkham.co.uk, closed Wed, Fri, Sat, all Nov-May) is the most stately of stately homes, Palladian in style, with perhaps the finest collection of Roman statuary in a private house in Britain. The splendid grounds include a large lake, a deer park and various overblown monuments.

Holkham National Nature Reserve (which stretches along the coast from Burnham Norton to Blakeney) is a typically Norfolk maze of creeks and salt marshes, and incredibly rich in birdlife; it also includes much-lauded Holkham Beach, a gorgeous four-mile stretch of golden sand, backed by pinewoods. Access is via the car park opposite the north entrance to the Hall. Brancaster beach, a couple of miles west

Holkham Beach

of the campsite, is similarly dramatic. For more birdwatching – a major attraction in these parts – the RSPB's Titchwell Marsh reserve (01485 210779, www.rspb.org.uk) attracts all manner of sea birds, particularly in spring, to its lagoon and foreshore. There's a visitor centre, shop and a café. There are also boat trips to the Scolt Head Island National Nature Reserve (01328 711183, www.natural england.org.uk) between April and September. Ferries leave from Burnham Overy Staithe.

Site specific

✔ Deepdale is a fine example of a simple, well-organised campsite with a variety of accommodation that should suit all-comers.

✘ It's not far from the sea, but you have to go through the village to reach the salt marsh coast. The nearest beaches are a drive or bus trip away.

For boutiques not birds, stroll around the handsome village of Burnham Market, with its long, tree-lined green. It has been more or less taken over by second-homers, whose money has allowed some intriguing independent shops to flourish. Food is a highlight, though there are also clothing, antiques and gift shops in the mix.

AMUSING THE KIDS

For a traditional English seaside experience, genteel Hunstanton, aka 'Sunny Hunny', is a 20-minute drive west. The Sealife Sanctuary (01485 533576, www.sealsanctuary.co.uk) on the promenade features seals, sharks, otters and penguins, and there are also pony rides on the beach.

CAMPING NEARBY

Pinewoods (01328 710439, www.pinewoods.co.uk) is a large family-oriented caravan and camping site, near the beach at Wells-Next-the-Sea. For a tent without hook-up, expect to pay £11-£30, depending on season and time of the week.

High Sand Creek (*see p152*) in Stiffkey has a great location by the salt marshes.

Middle Woodbatch Farm

Number of pitches Approx 10 tents. No caravans or motorhomes. B&B (3 doubles).
Open Mar-Oct. B&B all year.
Booking By phone. Minimum stay 2 nights weekends.
Typical cost Tent £7 adult, £3 5-16s. B&B from £30 per person.
Facilities Kitchen with fridge and freezer; showers (£.1); toilets; washing-up area.
Campfires Allowed, in fire bowls only. Firewood available (£3).
Dogs Allowed, on lead (£1).
Restrictions No single-sex groups or unsupervised under-18s.
Getting there By road Take the A488 (Shrewsbury to Knighton road). Turn on to the B4385 to Bishop's Castle (approx 22 miles from Shrewsbury, 13 miles from Knighton). Continue straight past the church, not right to the town centre. After about 250 yards, turn left on to Woodbatch Road and follow it to the end, about 1.5 miles. **By public transport** Train to Shrewsbury. From there, a Minsterley Motors bus (www.minsterleymotors.co.uk) runs every 40 mins to Bishop's Castle; the journey takes an hour. Then either ask for the town's only taxi driver – Ivor Davies – or walk 1.5 miles.

Middle Woodbatch Farm
Woodbatch Road, Bishop's Castle,
Shropshire SY9 5JT
07989 496875
steve.austin5@btinternet.com
www.middlewoodbatchfarm.co.uk
Map p27 ⓸
OS map SO314883

Middle Woodbatch Farm, climbing up to Reith Top along the Shropshire Way, isn't designed for working holidays, but don't be surprised if you are asked to help bring in the cows, shear a sheep or even deliver a lamb. The delightful owners, Mary and Steve Austin, have run this campsite and B&B for only a few years (although the farm has been in the family for generations), but already the warm welcome, spotless facilities and startlingly dramatic views across the vast valley to Colebatch Hill is attracting regulars – some even book specifically for the lambing season.

The farm is a couple of miles from the small market town of Bishop's Castle, which has some fine Elizabethan buildings, a couple of convenience stores, pubs and high-end gift shops. It's 22 miles to Shrewsbury, the nearest major town, and the Welsh border is a hop, skip and a jump away.

Although there are two large fields for tent campers (no caravans or motorhomes are allowed), pitches are restricted to a sparse ten

or so. There's plenty of space, but the far field has the best views down the valley. Campfires are allowed in the fire bowls (firewood available to buy from the farm). Amenities comprise two very clean showers and toilets, and a kitchen with kettle, fridge, freezer and microwave; Mary and Steve can also rustle up breakfast or supply a dash of milk. You might even find yourself sharing a bottle of red on the patio and chatting about rural life. As much as possible is recycled, and the farm supports the 'Buy local, be sustainable' movement.

The B&B option (three well-appointed en suite rooms) is popular with grandparents whose offspring are camping outside. Stabling facilities are also provided for visitors who want to bring their own horses; Mary, a keen rider, can recommend routes, look after the animals and provide riding advice if needed.

Most campers are walkers enjoying Shropshire's many paths, in particular the 139-mile Shropshire Way, which circumnavigates the county and goes directly through the farmyard. For the more adventurous, the campsite is a popular stopping point along the mammoth hike from Land's End to John O'Groats. Cyclists will find routes from technical single-tracks to meandering quiet lanes, and maps are available.

EATING & DRINKING

The best pub in Bishop's Castle is the Six Bells (01588 638930, www.sixbellsbrewery.co.uk), a proper country pub with friendly locals and staff, and own-brewed, award-winning ale. The other good pub in town, the Three Tuns (01588 638797, www.threetuns

Site specific

✔ The friendly, family welcome sets the tone for your stay. Whether or not you feel like helping around the farm, you'll get a fine insight into a side of rural life that few people experience. Really clean toilets and showers too.

✗ Getting to the farm by public transport is tricky. And the nearest pub and restaurant is a couple of miles away in Bishop's Castle.

brewery.co.uk), also has its own brewery. For eating, try the Castle Hotel (01588 638403, www.thecastle hotelbishopscastle.co.uk) at the high end of the town. All the food is cooked by Nicky, the landlady, and the desserts are particularly delectable. Superb views from the beer garden too.

Ludlow, 18 miles away, is renowned as an eating and drinking mecca, with numerous independent shops and more Michelin starred-restaurants than anywhere in the UK except London. Standouts include Mr Underhill's (01584 874431, www.mr-underhills.co.uk, closed lunch and Mon, Tue) and Restaurant La Bécasse (01584 872325, www.la becasse.co.uk, closed Mon, Tue lunch, Sun dinner). The Food & Drink Festival in September attracts thousands of foodies.

ATTRACTIONS & ACTIVITIES

Walcot Stables (01588 680514, www.walcotstables. co.uk), in nearby Ledbury North, offers lessons and hacks around Shropshire for all ages and levels. Long Mynd, the largest hill in the area, is a magnet for adventure sports fans. You can ride down it, walk up it, fly off it and drive up it – if you dare: it's the steepest road we've ever encountered.

History buffs will find some beautifully preserved castles in the area. One of the best is Stokesay Castle (01588 672544, www.english-heritage.org.uk), thought to be England's finest remaining fortified medieval manor house. Ludlow Castle (01584 873355, www.ludlowcastle.com) is attractively ruined, and Powis Castle (01938 551944, www.nationaltrust. org.uk), just across the Welsh border, is famed for its gardens.

Fans of the BBC2 series *Victorian Farm* can visit the Acton Scott Historic Working Farm(01694 781307, www.actonscott.com closed Nov-Easter and Mon except bank holidays), where the series was filmed. There is traditional home cooking in the School House Café and plenty of trails and paths around the farm buildings, which include a working blacksmith, a wheelwright and a farrier. Staff offers courses in woodland crafts, building skills, animal husbandry and jam making – all with an early 1900s emphasis.

AMUSING THE KIDS

Mickey Miller's (01588 673800, www.mickeymillers. com), 11 miles away in Craven Arms, is a large play barn with a rural vibe.

CAMPING NEARBY

Although aimed mainly at caravans and motorhomes, Green Caravan Park (01588 650605, www.green caravanpark.co.uk, open Easter-Oct) in nearby Wentor is a good alternative, particularly for families. It costs £13 for two people and tent.

Acton Scott is the setting for a posh, Victorian-style explorer's tent, equipped with furniture, pot-bellied stove and an outdoor tub for bathing. It's from the same people as Featherdown Farms; see www.countryhousehideout.co.uk for details.

New Hall Farm

New Hall Farm
New Hall Lane, Edingley,
Nottinghamshire NG22 8BS
01623 883041
www.newhallfarm.co.uk
Map p27 ④⑤
OS map SK660549

Number of pitches 10 tents,
25 caravans/motorhomes.
Open Mar-Oct.
Booking By phone, online, email, post.
Minimum stay 2 nights weekends July, Aug.
Typical cost Tent, caravan or motorhome
incl 2 people £12-£16. Extra adult £4.
Facilities Electric hook-ups (25);
laundry facilities; showers (free);
toilets; washing-up area.
Campfires Not allowed.
Dogs Allowed, on lead.
Restrictions No under-16s. Groups by
arrangement. No noise after 10pm.
Getting there By road The campsite is
14 miles from Nottingham and 3 miles
from Southwell. From Southwell, follow
signs to Edingley and turn into New Hall
Lane at the top of the hill. Follow the road
for half a mile. **By public transport** Train
to Nottingham. Bus 100 (www.nctx.co.uk)
runs frequently from Nottingham to
Southwell (journey 50 mins), from where
bus 29 (www.stagecoachbus.com) runs
every hour to Edingley (journey 10 mins).
It's then a short walk to the site.

Inspecting the new additions to the pedigree
Limousin cattle at New Hall Farm, David Brown
explains he is at least the fourth generation of
his family to work this land, perched high on a
hill north of Nottingham. 'At the churchyard in
Edingley, gravestones with Brown on them date
back to the 1700s; we don't move around much,'
he laughs. Three hundred years ago, the Browns'
farm would have been surrounded by the mighty
Sherwood Forest – now long gone, though
pockets of woodland can be still seen across
agricultural north Nottinghamshire.

David and his wife Jill diversified into farming
campers and caravanners in 2005: 'We had
such a beautiful plot that we thought campers
would like to see it as well.' The inspiration
was one particular field, which slopes steeply
towards the village of Edingley and provides a

grand view over to what remains of Sherwood
Forest. A small wooden gantry provides a
sheltered spot for watching the sunset.

A narrow road leads from Edingley to the
compact campground, set near the main
farmhouse and an 18th-century stone threshing
barn. The always-open reception area contains
a fridge stocked with delicious local ice-cream,
and provides leaflets about the area. There's
a modern and spotless toilet block and laundry
facilities, and that's about it. Tents can be
pitched further down the field, away from the
caravans. Pitches 9 and 10 – which have electric
hook-ups but are not hard-standing, so are
suitable for tents – are the most popular because
they are slightly raised and offer lovely views.
Visitors rave about the songbirds.

It is very peaceful – partly because of the no
under-16s policy. That's for health and safety
reasons as it's a working farm, but also because
the Browns want to be a quiet site.

New Hall is increasingly popular with
ramblers, and as a consequence, Jill is collecting
a useful series of walks in the locality. The
biggest draw, however, is the excellent Sherwood
Forest visitor centre. The attractive Minster
town of Southwell has plenty of shops, pubs
and restaurants.

EATING & DRINKING

The campsite is fairly remote, so it's best to bring
provisions. Careful barbecues are allowed, and Jill
and David serve roast beef cobs on selected weekends.

Hill's Farm Shop (01623 882664, closed Mon, Tue,
Sun) in Edingley sells meat, vegetables and fruit
(pick your own in June and July). The only pub is the
Old Reindeer (01623 882253, www.oldreindeer.co.uk),
which offers a fine selection of cask ales and a
carvery, alongside the usual pub food. For a wider
range, Farnsfield, a couple of miles away, has a
Co-op, a Spar, a post office and a couple of pubs.

Site specific

✔ It's adults only on this working farm,
meaning that it is a quiet and relaxed
site. Also, there are fantastic views over
Sherwood Forest and plenty of walks
through the countryside.

✘ Most of the plots, particularly those with
electric hook-ups, are on the small side and
there are few hedge barriers for privacy.

A view from New Hall Farm, looking north over Nottinghamshire towards Sherwood Forest.

NOTTINGHAMSHIRE

The most famous pub in the area is the Saracens Head (01636 812701, www.saracensheadhotel.net) in Southwell. This 16th-century coaching inn twice sheltered Charles I during the Civil War. On a warm day, the cobbled courtyard is a prime spot for a pint and a bite to eat. In Rolleston, on the other side of Southwell, the Crown Inn (01636 819000, www.the crownatrolleston.co.uk, closed dinner Sun) is popular for its smart cooking, modish design and slick service.

An upmarket option is the Clumber Park Hotel's Courtyard Restaurant (01623 835333, www.clumberparkhotel.com), 15 miles to the north: choose from Modern British cuisine in the courtyard restaurant (dinner only, Fri and Sat, booking essential) or cheaper fare in the Normanton inn.

ATTRACTIONS & ACTIVITIES

Fulfil your childhood fantasy by becoming Robin Hood or Maid Marian at the Sherwood Forest National Nature Reserve (01623 823202, www.robinhood.co.uk). The entrance and visitor centre is on the B6034 just north of Edwinstowe, about 11 miles from the farm. Set among 450 acres of forest and heathland, the 'Playground of Kings' has immense significance for both its cultural and natural history. The key sight is the aptly named Major Oak, thought to be at least 800 years old, though it's unlikely that Robin Hood and his Merrie Men ever lived within the tree. Three miles away is medieval Rufford Abbey, now in ruins; set in a lovely park, it's much quieter than its famous neighbour. It has a good craft centre too.

It's hard not to love Southwell, a charming market town and the birthplace of the bramley seedling apple. Beautiful Southwell Minster (01636 812649, www.southwellminster.org.uk), an outstanding example of Norman and Early English architecture with its distinctive 'pepper-pot' spires, is the usual starting point for historical walking tours around the town that also take in the Burgage common land surrounded by stone houses – one of which was briefly occupied by Byron.

CAMPING NEARBY

Located on the other side of Southwell, Meadowfield Gardens Campsite (01636 813064, open all year depending on weather, £4-£12 per night) in Rolleston is a family-run site. Tents, caravans and motorhomes are welcome.

North Lees

North Lees Campsite
Birley Lane, Hathersage,
Derbyshire S32 1BR
01433 650838
Map p27 **46**
OS map SK235832

Number of pitches 60 tents.
No caravans/motorhomes.
Open All year.
Booking By phone. Advisable high season.
Typical cost £6 adult, £5 student,
£4 child, £2 car, £1 motorbike.
Facilities Showers (free); toilets;
washing-up area.
Campfires Not allowed.
Dogs Allowed, on lead.
Restrictions No unsupervised under-18s.
Quiet time after dark.
Getting there By road From the main street
in Hathersage, don't take the A6187 to
Castleton but fork right on Jaggers Lane,
then first right up Coggers Lane and right
again on to Birley Lane. The campsite is on
the left, after about half a mile. Note that
the postcode isn't accurate for sat-nav use.
By public transport It's a long walk uphill
from the nearest station at Hathersage,
where bus 272 (0871 200 2233,
www.firstgroup.com) from Sheffield also
stops. So get a taxi instead (Grindleford
Private Hire, 01433 630360, £6).

Run by the Peak District National Park Authority,
North Lees is the epitome of a small, unfussy,
tent-only campsite that knows the things its
campers like and provides them with aplomb.

There's not much to it: a series of neat little
fields, divided by drystone walls and surrounded
by tall trees, with a fenced-off stream running
along one side. An attractive stone building
houses the men's and women's showers
(just one apiece) and toilets – all in immaculate
condition, with freshly whitewashed walls and
spotless tiled floors – and a roofed-over
dishwashing area. The site office is here too,
though the friendly wardens are usually only
around in the mornings and evenings. Cars
are parked at the top of the site's dirt track.

The grass is short, springy and generally flat
(apart from the patches that have been left
to grow wild, and are full of meadow flowers
in summer), and you can pitch where you like.

The walls and trees keep the wind at bay, and
wooden pallets are provided to keep barbecues
and cooking stoves off the ground. Noisy groups
and rampaging dogs are forbidden; the focus is
on appreciating the beauty of your surroundings
in peace. What more do you need?

Nothing, according to the regulars who've
been camping here for years. Walkers,
mountain bikers and hardy outdoor types love
the place – especially climbers. A short walk
through the woodland at the top of the site,
or along the adjacent road, brings you to one of
the country's best rock climbing areas. Stanage
Edge is a sight to behold: a four-mile gritstone
escarpment that carves its way across the top
of the moor like a medieval fortress. It swarms
with climbers throughout the year, and is a
magical spot at sunset.

A mile and a half away is Hathersage, a classic
Peak District village of grey gritstone houses, with
enough cafés and pubs to satisfy most campers
(though no big supermarket). Something of a
mecca for outdoors enthusiasts, it is also famed
for its Charlotte Brontë connections. She visited
a friend here in 1845, and the Elizabethan tower
of North Lees Hall – once the home of the Eyre
family, and now used for upmarket holiday lets
– is thought to be the model for Rochester's
Thornfield Hall in *Jane Eyre*. The village's other
claim to fame is that Robin Hood's right-hand
man, Little John, was supposedly born in the
village; his 'grave' is next to the church door.

Some of the Peak District's most popular
destinations, such as Castleton and its
showcaves, are within easy reach. And if you're
craving a taste of urban life, it's only 20 minutes
by car to bustling Sheffield.

EATING & DRINKING

Hathersage has a petrol station, a bank, a small Spar
and an unfeasible number of outdoor equipment
shops, including old-timer Outside (01433 651936,
www.outside.co.uk),whose upstairs café serves pies,
cakes, jacket potatoes and other climber-friendly nosh.

Other cafés on the main street include homely
stalwart Cintra's (01433 651825, www.cintras
tearooms.co.uk) for breakfast, lunch and cream teas,
and a bucolic back garden. You can sit also outside
at more modern newcomer Elliott's (01433 659911)
and order decent coffee, cakes, numerous breakfast
dishes and local Hope Valley ice-cream from the
super-friendly staff. The local pubs are pretty
mediocre, though acceptable for a quick pint –
the Millstone Inn (01433 650258, www.millstoneinn.
co.uk) probably has the best range of real ales.

PEAK DISTRICT

and caper salad, for instance, or a bacon and brie sandwich). There's also a shop – handy if you're after some new knives and forks, for camping or otherwise – and the factory is open for tours.

But the most famous eating establishment in the area is Grindleford Station Café (01433 631011), five miles away by Padley Gorge. Dishing out massive portions of caff food (baked beans and chips with everything), it is renowned for its grumpy handwritten notices and monosyllabic staff.

ATTRACTIONS & ACTIVITIES

Walking, climbing, potholing, hang-gliding and other strenuous pursuits are what bring most people to this area. If you'd rather not go it alone, or want to take up a new sport, Hathersage-based Peak Activities (01433 650345, www.iain.co.uk) runs courses for novices and families.

Six miles away, the picture-postcard village of Castleton is one of the honeypots of the Peak District, drawing daytrippers galore to its tea rooms, craft shops and, most of all, its network of vast subterranean caves. Speedwell (01433 620512, www.speedwellcavern.co.uk) is famous for its underground boat trips; the Blue John Cavern (01433 620638, www.bluejohn-cavern.co.uk) is where Blue John stone, a local variety of fluorspar, has been mined since Roman times; Treak Cliff (01433 621487, www.bluejohnstone.com) has the most impressive displays of stalactites and stalagmites; and the Devil's Arse, aka Peak Cavern (01433 620285, www.peakcavern.co.uk) is the only wholly natural cave system.

If you'd prefer to go up rather than down, the ruined Norman keep of Peveril Castle (01433 620613, www.english-heritage.org.uk) perches fetchingly on a hill above Castleton. Visit the National Park visitor centre (01629 816572, www.peakdistrict.gov.uk) in the middle of the village for more ideas; it also houses a local museum.

AMUSING THE KIDS

Unless they're budding rock climbers, there's not much for children at the campsite – ball games are forbidden – so take the plunge and spend an afternoon at the lovely open-air swimming pool in Hathersage (01433 650843, www.hathersageswimmingpool.co.uk, closed Oct-Mar). The water is heated to a balmy 84°F (29°C) whatever the weather, and there's also a sunbathing lawn, a café and even a bandstand.

Alternatively, the caverns around Castleton should appeal: how can any kid resist somewhere called the Devil's Arse?

CAMPING NEARBY

Rowter Farm (01433 620271, open Easter-Oct) offers back-to-basics camping on two fields at the top of Winnats Pass, above Castleton. It's a working farm, and rather exposed, but the views to Mam Tor are fantastic. Adults pay £6, children £3. It's about 11 miles to Upper Booth Farm (see p168) at Edale.

The smartest place to eat is the Walnut Club (01433 651155, www.thewalnutclub.com, closed Mon), where 'West End contemporary cooking meets Peak District lifestyle' (their words). There are even jazz nights at weekends; hiking boots probably won't cut it. At the other extreme, the tiny bakery, up a side street, serves fabulous bacon butties and Spam sandwiches.

Just south of Hathersage, on the Bakewell Road, David Mellor's award-winning cutlery factory (01433 650220, www.davidmellordesign.com, factory closed Sat, Sun) is housed in a striking circular building. The glass-walled café is a lovely spot for coffee, superior cakes or lunch (smoked trout with cucumber

Stanage Edge

PEAK DISTRICT

Site specific

✔ Low-key camping at its best, with some of Britain's best walking and climbing at hand. And it's tents only.

✗ Campfires are forbidden, and the midges can be a nuisance on warm, still evenings. And there's not much for children to do.

Haddon Grove

Haddon Grove Caravan & Campsite
Haddon Grove Farm, Bakewell,
Derbyshire DE45 1JF
01629 812343
Map p27 ⑰
OS map SK180661

Number of pitches 60 tents/caravans/
motorhomes.
Open Mar-Oct.
Booking By phone, but not necessary.
Typical cost £4 adult, £2 6-12s, £2 vehicle.
Facilities Electric hook-ups; showers (free);
toilets; washing-up area.
Campfires Not allowed.
Dogs Allowed, on lead.
Getting there By road From the A515
(Ashbourne to Buxton road) turn on to the
B5055 to Monyash. Go through Monyash
and after another 2 miles turn right at the
top of the hill, at the sign for Haddon Grove.
The campsite is at the bottom of the lane.
You can also come on the B5055 from
the opposite direction, from Bakewell.
By public transport Train to Buxton. From
there, catch the Transpeak bus to Bakewell
(www.transpeak.co.uk, journey 30 mins),
then the 178 to Monyash (01246 582246,
www.hulleys-of-baslow.co.uk, 15 mins),
which goes along the B5055. Ask to be let
off at Haddon Grove, just 5 mins on foot
from the campsite. Alternatively, a taxi from
Buxton costs around £22 (Buxton Radio
Taxis, 01298 23457).

Haddon Grove sits in the heart of the White
Peak, the southern limestone section of the
Peak District that is characterised by verdant
green hills, steep-sided dales and spectacular
caves; it's a softer and gentler landscape than
the harsh gritstone fells of the Dark Peak to the
north. A couple of attractive villages, Monyash
and Over Haddon, are within walking distance.

It's a typical farm campsite – perfectly adequate
but nothing special. There are three camping
fields: the largest, near the farmyard, has
mildewy caravans moored permanently around
the edge, but plenty of space for tents. To the
right is a walled field that's popular with school
groups, and at the end is the family field, the
nicest, backed by trees (providing much-needed
shelter from the wind) and with views to the
south. From there, it's a bit of a trek to the

facilities, which are in outbuildings next to the
rose-covered farmhouse: toilets and showers
(freshly painted, if spartan) and a separate
washing-up area, with a phone-charging point.

The low-key, ramshackle vibe has appeal,
and it's popular with families from Sheffield
(a 40-minute drive). You're very much left to
your own devices – it can be hard trying to find
someone to pay – and the only rules seem to
be that you can't have fires and the bottom field
is for families.

What is special is Haddon Grove's location:
it's a few hundred yards from the rim of Lathkill
Dale, a mesmerisingly gorgeous limestone gorge
that snakes for three miles from Monyash via
Over Haddon to Conksbury Bridge. One of the
five major Derbyshire Dales, it's an enchanting
spot, particularly in spring and early summer
when the overhanging rocky cliffs and lush river
valley are awash with wild flowers, including
cowslip, orchids, honey-scented meadowsweet
and the rare violet-blue Jacob's Ladder.

The honey-coloured stone buildings of Bakewell,
three miles away, are full of expensive cafés and
souvenir shops; the effect is twee and rather
smug, and it's overrun with visitors in summer.
The Victorian spa town of Buxton, ten miles to
the north-east, is more down to earth.

EATING & DRINKING

Monyash, a couple of miles away by road, has
two great options next to each other on the
handkerchief-sized village green. The Old Smithy
Café (01629 810190, www.oldsmithymonyash.co.uk)
is a cracking spot, serving everything from ice-cream,
bacon baps and sandwiches to full meals, with hot
chocolate, wine and beer (including draught ales from
the Peak Ales brewery, based on the Chatsworth
estate) on the drinks menu. The ramshackle interior
is appealing, but the best seats in sunny weather are
at the two tables outside the front.

Next door, the Bull's Head (01629 812372, www.
thebullsheadmonyash.co.uk) is a snug den for
hearty cooking (lasagne, lamb casserole, stew
with dumplings), good beer and a game of pool.
It also has a back garden next to a playground.

Over Haddon, in the opposite direction, isn't as
picturesque as Monyash, but the Lathkil Hotel
(01629 812501, www.lathkil.co.uk) at the far end
of the village is well worth a visit for its sterling
selection of real ales, above-average pub grub and
killer view over sheep-studded fields to Lathkill Dale.

There are plenty of tourist-oriented eateries in
Bakewell, including various outlets competing to be
the 'original' purveyor of the town's famous Bakewell

PEAK DISTRICT

Lathkill Dale

pudding. It's also the nearest place for supplies, whether food, walking gear or camping equipment.

ATTRACTIONS & ACTIVITIES

There's some fabulous walking in the area, not least through Lathkill Dale itself. Follow the path from the right-hand camping field to the top of the dale, then descend the precipitous steps. The walk to Monyash is particularly lovely – and you can have a pint as a reward. It leads through a variety of terrain, from wide open to narrow and wooded, and past industrial remains: an abandoned watermill, former lead mines and Ricklow Quarry (where 'Derbyshire marble' was once dug). It's a habitat for the endangered water vole, unusual butterflies and all manner of birds.

You can hire bikes from the National Park's Parsley Hay Centre (01298 84493, closed Nov-Feb) on the A515, ten minutes' drive from the campsite, then head straight out on the Tissington and High Peak Trails, which follow the course of various ex-railway lines. Another route, the Monsal Trail, starts in Bakewell. The town's tourist information centre (01629 816558, www.peakdistrict.gov.uk) is on Bridge Street.

It's five miles to Haddon Hall (01629 812855, www.haddonhall.co.uk, closed Tue-Fri Apr, Oct, all Nov-Mar), a wonderfully preserved medieval manor house. A few miles further on, beyond Bakewell, is Chatsworth (01246 565300, www.chatsworth.org, closed mid Dec-mid Mar), the Duke and Duchess of Devonshire's country pile, and probably the most famous stately home in the country thanks to its appearance in numerous costume dramas – most notably in the 2005 film of *Pride and Prejudice* with Colin Firth's 'wet shirt' scene. The extensive park is free to visit, but you'll have to pay to see the house's jaw-dropping interiors and the renowned, fountain strewn gardens.

AMUSING THE KIDS

Charging round the camping fields, petting the Shetland ponies by the farmyard and playing on the tyre swings keeps most children happy. If that palls, the treetop walkways, zip-wires and Tarzan swings of Go Ape! (0845 643 9215, www.goape.co.uk, closed Tue in term-time, Mon-Fri Nov, all Dec-Mar) are just outside Buxton – assuming you haven't already been to one of the company's 20-plus sites around the UK.

CAMPING NEARBY

Just down the road from Haddon Grove, Mandale House (01629 812416, www.mandalehouse.co.uk, open May-Sept) offers an open field for tents (£4.75 adult, £3.25 under-12s), and a camping barn.

Lathkill Dale Campsite (01629 813521, 07971 038702, www.lathkilldalecampsite.co.uk, open Mar-Oct) is in the middle of Monyash village. Tents (approx £5-£25 depending on size) and VW campervans are welcome, but not caravans. Pitches are flat and sheltered, but on the small side.

> ## Site specific
>
> ✔ Haddon Grove's location, at the top of one of Derbyshire's most beautiful dales, is sublime.
>
> ✘ It's a bit rough and ready, and the moored caravans in the main field are unsightly.

Upper Booth Farm

Upper Booth Farm & Campsite
Edale, Hope Valley, Derbyshire S33 7ZJ
01433 670250
mail@heliwell.info
www.upperboothcamping.co.uk
Map p27 ④⑤
OS map SK102852

Number of pitches 30 tents/campervans.
No caravans/large motorhomes. Barn
(sleeps 12).
Open Mid Feb-Nov.
Booking By phone, online. Advisable.
Typical cost Camping £4-£5 adult, £3-£5
under-12s, £2 vehicle. Barn £6 per person,
£60 sole use.
Facilities Café; shop; showers (free);
toilets; washing-up area.
Campfires Not allowed.
Dogs Allowed; must be kept under control.
Restrictions No unsupervised under-18s.
No noise after 10.30pm.
Getting there By road Take the A6187
(Hope Valley Road). If you're coming from
the west, from Chapel-en-le-Frith, after
about 4 miles turn left to Edale and Barber
Booth. Head down a steep hill, then take
the first left, signed to Upper Booth. From
the other direction (east), turn right in
the village of Hope on to the Edale Road.
Continue for 6 miles (past the turn to Edale
village); the road bends to the left and over
a river bridge. Turn right immediately after
the bridge, following signs to Upper Booth.
By public transport Train to Edale and then
bus 200 (01298 812204, www.bowers
buses.com, journey 15 mins), which takes
you to the door of the farm. It's a school
bus, so there are 3 buses a day in the
afternoon, and no service at weekends
or in the holidays.

Edale village has been a tourist hotspot since the
railway arrived in the 1890s, bringing the masses
from crowded and polluted northern cities to enjoy
fresh air and exercise on the surrounding moors.
These days, the walking is just as good, the views
just as magnificent and the village – strung along
a thin spur off the main road through Edale Valley,
with a train station and car park at one end, and
the start of the Pennine Way at the other – just as
popular. A couple of miles west of the village, up a
winding road, is Upper Booth Farm.

There are two camping fields: a small walled
plot next to the farm buildings (favoured by
Duke of Edinburgh groups) and, above that,
a larger, sloping field with moorland views.
You can pitch where you like – the choice spots
are at the top of the big field or next to tumbling
Crowden Brook. Numbers are kept down, so
it never feels too packed. The occasional
campervan turns up, but the site is not suitable
for caravans or large motorhomes. There's
also a bare-bones camping barn (no electricity,
heating or water).

Most visitors are hardened walkers, not
bothered by such niceties as hand soap and
fresh towels – so the minimal washing facilities
haven't deterred campers in the past. But that's
all about to change: a handsome new toilet and
shower block, situated between the two fields,
should be ready in time for the 2012 season.

The Pennine Way runs though the farm; come
summer, the place is heaving with ramblers,
stopping off for a refreshing cuppa and a slice
of own-made cake at the 'café' – a jumble of
tables and chairs outside the kitchen door.

Upper Booth is a conservation-conscious
National Trust farm – perhaps the reason that
the cluster of stone buildings around the historic
farmhouse and its lovely walled garden is so
attractive. Herds of belted Galloway cattle and
Swaledale sheep are reared on the surrounding
uplands. You can taste the results: the farm's
own meat is for sale, along with eggs from the
most definitely free-range chickens (look out
for the handsome Derbyshire Redcaps).

Edale itself is pretty, though lacking in facilities
and horribly crowded in high season. Pop into
the Moorland Visitor Centre (01433 670207,
www.peakdistrict.gov.uk), with its sedum roof
and entrance waterfall, for information and
displays about the Peak District.

EATING & DRINKING

There are two pubs in Edale, at either end of the
village. At the foot of the Pennine Way is the Old
Nag's Head (01433 670291); next to the station is
the Rambler Inn (01433 670268, www.therambler
inn.com). Neither are as good as they should be,
thanks to the stranglehold they have over Edale's
crowds of footsore hikers and daytrippers, but they're
fine for a pint and large platefuls of heart-warming,
if undistinguished, food; there might be changes at
the Nag's Head as it's under new management. It's
the more historic (founded 1577) and characterful
of the two pubs, while the Ramblers has more outdoor
space for families.

PEAK DISTRICT

Otherwise, there are a couple of daytime cafés – the National Trust-run Penny Pot Café (01433 670293, closed Mon, Tue Mar-Oct, Mon-Fri Nov, Dec, all Jan, Feb) opposite the station; and Coopers Café (01433 670401, closed Tue-Thur Oct, Mon-Fri Nov-Mar), a good spot for a wholesome breakfast before heading for the hills. Next to the latter is the village's only shop (and post office), but it's very basic.

The farm sells its own beef, lamb and eggs, and local ice-creams. At weekends and bank holidays more food is available, including bacon, cakes, packed lunches and a full-blown meal for two comprising meat, bread, salad and a disposable barbecue. Before you arrive you can also book online a hamper of local produce – a good idea considering the lack of food shops nearby.

ATTRACTIONS & ACTIVITIES

If you're not here to walk, you're in the wrong place. On one side of Edale is the Iron Age hill fort of Mam Tor, a popular hang-gliding spot; on the other the bleak gritstone plateau of Kinder Scout (spiritual home of the ramblers' movement), and most visitors

Site specific

✔ The farm is a couple of miles outside Edale, so far from the madding crowds, but still on the Pennine Way.

✘ It's a long walk to the nearest pub, and a drive to the nearest proper shop.

are here to tackle the Pennine Way, or at least part of it. Numerous paths criss-cross the land.

A good afternoon's hike leads straight from Upper Booth Farm along the Pennine Way towards Edale, then strikes north over a wide meadow laid with paving slabs and up Grindsbrook Clough, which gets rougher, narrower and steeper as it ascends before topping out on Kinder Scout. The plateau can be dangerous, especially in bad weather, when it's easy to lose your bearings. Less arduous is the route to Mam Tor ('shivering mountain') for panoramic views over the Edale and Hope Valleys. Add in Rushup Edge and Hollins Cross for a fine circular walk back to Edale.

For hang-gliding or paragliding taster days or longer courses, contact the Derbyshire Flying Centre (0845 108 1577, www.d-f-c.co.uk).

If the weather turns, or you just want a change of scene, Castleton (see p164) is about five miles away. It's as popular as Edale, but for underground caves rather than hilltop hikes.

AMUSING THE KIDS

Ladybooth Equestrian Centre (01433 670205, www.ladybooth.co.uk), three miles away, offers trekking and farm rides and is well set up for children.

At the Chestnut Centre Otter, Owl & Wildlife Park (01298 814099, www.chestnutcentre.co.uk, closed Mon-

Grindsbrook Clough, leading to Kinder Scout.

Fri Jan), 11 miles away near Chapel-en-le-frith, sleek Asian, North American and European otters tumble in streams and 15 species of owl peer owlishly out. There are Scottish wildcats and foxes too, along with a nature trail and café.

CAMPING NEARBY

Just up the street from the Old Nag's Head, Coopers (01433 670372, open all year, pitch from £6) has space for 120 tents and 15 caravans on open fields. The on-site café is a bonus.

In the middle of the village, Fieldhead (01433 670386, www.fieldhead-campsite.co.uk, open all year, £5-£6.50 adult, £3-£4.50 under-16s) provides tent camping only in a series of tiny plots set around the Peak District visitor centre building. It's picturesque when empty, but very cramped when busy. A noticeboard by the visitor centre lists other campsites in and around Edale – there are plenty.

Gordale Scar

Gordale Scar Campsite
Gordale Farm, Malham,
North Yorkshire BD23 4DL
01729 830333
www.malhamdale.com/camping.htm
Map p27 ⑲
OS map SD914634

Number of pitches 40 tents/caravans/
motorhomes.
Open Apr-Oct.
Booking By phone.
Typical cost £3 adult, £1.50 child,
£3 tent, £3 vehicle.
Facilities Electric hook-ups (2); showers
(10p/2 mins); toilets; washing-up area.
Campfires Not allowed.
Dogs Allowed.
Restrictions Single-sex and unsupervised
under-18 groups by arrangement.
Getting there By road From the A56
between Skipton and Long Preston, look
out for signs to Malham from either
Gargrave or Coniston Gold. Both routes
run through the villages of Airton and
Kirkby Malham before reaching Malham.
At Malham, turn right on to Finkle Street
and then on to Gordale Lane; it's about a
mile to the campsite. **By public transport**
The nearest train station is Skipton.
Various local buses, including Little Red Bus
(01756 795666, www.littleredbus.co.uk)
and DalesBus (www.dalesbus.org), run
from Skipton to Malham. The journey takes
45-60 mins, and then it's a 20-mins walk
to Gordale Scar. Transport details (and
numbers of local taxi firms) are available
on the Malhamdale website.

Gordale Scar is one of the most wondrous natural
sights in the Yorkshire Dales. Eighteenth-century
watercolourist Edward Dayes certainly thought
so, as a sign by the Scar attests: 'Every object
conspires to produce one of the grandest
spectacles in nature. The rocks dart their bold
and rugged fronts to the heavens, and impending
fearfully over the head of the spectator, seem to
threaten his immediate destruction.' Nowadays,
easy access to foreign landscapes may have
lessened the thrill of the British countryside,
but the 300-foot high limestone ravine and
two waterfalls of the dramatic gorge are still
a truly impressive sight.

As a result the Scar attracts a lot of visitors –
luckily for the famers who own the land through
which Gore-Tex-clad hikers make their pilgrimage.
The final half-mile section of path that leads
to the ravine passes through the middle of
Gordale Scar campground. Rising high on each
side are ragged cliffs, and winding past the
tents is Gordale Beck, the stream that forms
after falling through the Scar.

Actually, there's not much else to the site,
except some very basic toilets, a couple of
showers and a washing-up area. From the
condition of the toilet block, it seems that farming
still dominates the owners' interest. Still, this
means that rules are few, and you can pitch
pretty much anywhere you like. There is, however,
a constant stream of hikers, school groups
and climbers heading up to the Scar from dawn
to dusk. You'll have to camp midweek or in the
off-season to avoid the crowds.

Malham, a mile away, is the nearest village;
it's a pretty little spot, complete with a babbling
brook, a couple of good pubs and a café – but

it does get overrun with tourists on summer weekends. There's also a superb National Park Visitor Centre (01969 652380, www.yorkshiredales.org.uk – Malhamdale is at the southern end of the park), with plenty of information on walks and other activities, and some camping gear.

Just north of the village, Malham Cove is another majestic natural feature: a curving amphitheatre of limestone cliffs, 260 feet high, capped with a classic eroded limestone pavement. Elsewhere in the dale are some picturesque hamlets, Norman churches and waterfalls such as Janet's Foss – thought to be named after the fairy queen who lives in a cave behind the foss (a Nordic word for waterfall). Drop a penny in one of the tree stumps nearby and make a wish.

EATING & DRINKING

Stock up with groceries before you get to Malham. The village has just a newsagent and shop selling basic camping supplies, although there are plans to sell more food in the future.

There are two pubs. Both are reasonable, but the choice pint and best food is to be found at the characterful Lister Arms (01729 830330, www.listerarms.co.uk), a 17th-century coaching inn opposite the green that's popular with climbers who have just attacked the tougher routes on the local limestone cliffs. You'll find a good selection of Thwaites cask ales (Original, Wainwright, Nutty Black, Lancaster

Bomber) and a large inglenook fireplace that's wide enough to take some chairs. Posh pub food made with local ingredients, such as bangers and mash, and steak and ale pie, is available. Hot and cold sandwiches are served between noon and 3pm. It also has some attractive B&B rooms.

Tucked away behind the Lister is Beck Hall (01729 830332, www.beckhallmalham.com), a B&B with an excellent daytime-only tea room (closed Mon) offering sandwiches and 'cyclists favourites' such as sausage, egg and chips. On weekend evenings from March to October it also has an evening meal option (7-9pm). The garden is a pleasant place for tea.

ATTRACTIONS & ACTIVITIES

Hiking and mountain biking are by far the most popular activities in the area, and the 150-strong population of Malham expands dramatically in summer when the holiday-makers pour in. The Pennine Way passes through the village, but there are plenty of shorter routes criss-crossing the area. Climbers are attracted to Gordale Scar and Malham Cove: both have routes for learners, but it is the highly technical climbers that get their kicks among the towering limestone crags.

Much more accessible, and great for children, is 'geocaching' – a kind of hi-tech treasure hunt based around GPS coordinates, which often includes some problem-solving first. The Yorkshire Dales National Park Authority has embraced this new sport with enthusiasm – probably more so than any other area in the country. You can hire GPS receivers from the National Park visitor centres in Malham, Grassington, Hawes and Reeth. Simply tap in the postcode or area you want to explore and it will draw up a list of containers planted by other geocachers. Solve the problem, find the coordinates and head outdoors looking for the hidden treasure. A good alternative to a pre-programmed receiver is a car sat-nav or a mobile phone with GPS capabilities. More information on www.geocaching.com.

Birdwatchers also love Malham Tarn National Nature Reserve, three miles north of the village, with its populations of willow warblers, spotted flycatchers and pipistrelle bats.

AMUSING THE KIDS

There isn't much to do on rainy days, so take a ride into Skipton, 12 miles away. The Castle (01756 792442, www.skiptoncastle.co.uk) is a wonderfully preserved medieval fortress with a Tudor courtyard, a café, picnic area and plenty to keep children amused.

CAMPING NEARBY

Riverside Campsite (01729 830287, open Easter-Oct), located at Town Head Farm next to Malham Cove, is a good alternative. It's also pretty basic, but the toilets are clean and the farmer's wife is friendly. A tent for two costs £15, £3.50 extra adult, £2 extra 5-13s.

Masons Campsite (see p174) near Appletreewick is about 15 miles away.

Site specific

✔ The campsite is set within the gorge of one of the most beautiful places in the Yorkshire Dales, and near the walking centre of Malham. On a quiet day with few campers and visitors, it's a magical spot.

✘ The toilet block is poorly maintained and the area around the main house is piled high with discarded throwaway barbecues and fold-away chairs. There are also lots of people walking through the land.

The campsite (top) and Malham village, including the Lister Arms (centre left).

Masons

Masons Campsite
Appletreewick, Skipton,
North Yorkshire BD23 6DD
01756 720275
masonscampsite@btinternet.com
www.masonscampsite.co.uk
Map p27 ⑤⓪
OS map SE052600

The River Wharfe runs through the Yorkshire Dales, skirting the quaint village of Burnsall and flowing around the rocky meander by Masons Campsite, before continuing its journey to the River Ouse and the North Sea. The river, which has carved its way through the Dales, also dominates this idyllic campsite. On summer evenings, anglers wait for grayling and trout to bite (fly-fishing permits are sold on-site), while families paddle in the shallows and catch crayfish to grill on the barbecue.

The site consists of a three-and-a-half-acre field, with a smaller overspill field for particularly busy periods – which also provides plenty of room for kite-flying, boules and games. Owners Georgie and Grant Hinchliffe, who took over the site at the end of 2007, have greatly improved the facilities, adding more showers, new toilets (with underfloor heating, no less) and washing machines. There's also a small shop, housed, along with the office, in a gleaming Airstream trailer.

On summer weekends, most visitors are families; as the sun comes out, it can feel rather like a school sports day. The site is also popular with outdoor enthusiasts: guests arriving on foot

Number of pitches 40 tents. No caravans.
Open Easter-Oct.
Booking By phone. Minimum stay 2 nights weekends, 3 nights bank holidays.
Typical cost £17-£27 2 people, £6 extra adult, £3.50 extra child.
Facilities Electric hook-ups (40); laundry facilities; shop; showers (free); toilets; washing-up area.
Campfires Open fires not allowed. Firepits for hire (£15 incl wood). Extra wood £5.
Dogs Allowed, on lead.
Restrictions No single-sex groups, no unsupervised under-18s. Quiet time 11.30pm-7.30am.
Getting there By road Follow the A59, Harrogate to Skipton road. At the Bolton Abbey roundabout, take the B6160 signposted to Burnsall. After about 6 miles, turn right at the Red Lion Hotel in Burnsall and head over the bridge; the campsite is on the right. **By public transport** Train to Ilkley. Bus 74 to Grassington (www.pride ofthedales.co.uk/ilkley.htm) runs every couple of hours or so, stopping outside the campsite. The journey takes about 30 mins.

or by bike qualify for a discount, and the owners promise to squeeze in hikers and cyclists, even in peak season.

There's glorious walking on your very doorstep here: the 80-mile Dales Way passes by the bottom of the campsite, and a network of paths and bridleways leads up into the Dales. The prosperous little town of Grassington, with its cobbled main square, cafés and shops, is an hour-and-a-half's walk away along the river; in the opposite direction lies the lovely woodlands and ruined priory at Bolton Abbey.

The beauty of this place, though, is that you can be as lazy as you please. Appletreewick's two excellent pubs are a mere five minutes' walk from the site. A 15-minute stroll along the riverbank brings you to 'bonny Burnsall', with its magnificent five-arch bridge – and another splendid pub, set on the village green.

EATING & DRINKING

Milk, bakery goods and other items are available at the small campsite shop. Otherwise, the well-stocked Shop on the Green (01756 720000) in Burnsall has all the essentials. Better still, its enterprising owners have launched a mobile shop, which calls at the campsite at 8.30am each day during busy periods, and every Saturday and Sunday in low season. An ice-cream van also materialises on sunny summer afternoons, so save your change for a cornet.

In Grassington, Relish (01756 753339, www.relish caterers.co.uk) is a charming little deli and grocer, whose shelves and counters are crammed with local jams and preserves, cheeses, pâtés, farm-baked bread and fresh fruit and veg.

There's no shortage of excellent pubs in the area. In Appletreewick, the Craven Arms (01756 720270, www.craven-cruckbarn.co.uk) is a traditional country pub with decent grub and excellent beers – which are also sold in takeaway cartons. In April, the pub's folk festival attracts acoustic musicians from around the country, and in October it hosts the annual Craven Beer Festival. Another option in the village is the New Inn (01756 720252, www.the-new-inn-appletreewick. com). The food is hearty and unpretentious, and there's a fine selection of draught beers and lagers, along with dozens of Belgium blends. It's popular with mountain bikers, with a bike livery and workshop next door.

Across the five-arch bridge in Burnsall, the 16th-century Red Lion (01756 720204, www.redlion.co.uk) is a pretty place; the reliable food menu ranges from ploughman's lunches to braised beef with

horseradish mash. Muddy boots and dogs may have to remain in the beer garden.

The foodie highlight in this part of the Dales, though, is the Angel Inn (01756 730263, www.angel hetton.co.uk) in Hetton, a 25-minute drive away. It has won a formidable reputation – and a clutch of awards – for its fine, locally sourced food. The bar and restaurant menus are strictly seasonal, but might include the likes of pan-roasted wild turbot with samphire and scallops or roasted chump of Yorkshire lamb. Invest in a bottle of wine to take home at the inn's 'wine cave', just across the road, or book in for a wine tasting.

ATTRACTIONS & ACTIVITIES

The Yorkshire Dales National Park (0300 456 0030, www.yorkshiredales.org.uk) is a 660 square mile sweep of open fells, valleys, hills and pastures, dotted with pretty, stone-built villages and isolated farmhouses. With miles of footpaths, bridleways and winding country lanes to explore, this is prime terrain for ramblers, cyclists and horse riders – and Wharfdale is one of the most popular areas. Still, even on busy weekends, it is easy to escape the crowds, especially around Appletreewick.

A scenic two-hour walk from the campsite, the village of Bolton Abbey (01756 718009, www.bolton abbey.com) is part of the Duke of Devonshire's estate. The ruins of the 12th-century priory, overlooking the River Wharfe, are the main draw, and there are glorious rambles through the ancient woodland to the Strid, where the river rushes through a narrow (and very slippery) chasm; in early spring, when the bluebells are in flower, it's even more magical. There are plenty of places to picnic, and the village itself has a handful of shops, and several tea rooms and restaurants.

Set on the B6265, five miles from the campsite, Stump Cross Caverns (01756 752780, www.stump crosscaverns.co.uk) were discovered by miners in 1860 – who also found the remains of wolverines, reindeer and bison. The weird, twisted rock formations and glistening stalactites are eerily otherworldly; above ground, there's a pleasant café and a visitor centre.

AMUSING THE KIDS

Playing on the campsite's rope swings and paddling in the river provide endless entertainment; children can also set sail in dinghies (sold by the Shop on the Green, if you haven't brought your own). The river is also a popular spot for wild swimming – though youngsters should, of course, be supervised.

Bolton Abbey makes for a busy day out; intrepid kids can pick their way over the 57 stepping stones that cross the river to the priory, play on the sandy 'beach' or follow colour-coded nature trails through Strid Wood.

CAMPING NEARBY

It's a 30-minute drive to Gordale Scar campsite (*see p171*) in Malhamdale.

YORKSHIRE DALES

Site specific

✔ Families adore it here. Children soon find new friends, leaving the adults free to relax over the barbecue and take in the views.

✘ It's pricey, with supplements payable for having a gazebo, bank holidays, arriving early, leaving late…

Jerusalem Farm

Jerusalem Farm
Jerusalem Lane, Booth, Halifax,
West Yorkshire HX2 6XB
01422 883246 (Easter-Sept)
edward.ashman@calderdale.gov.uk
Map p27 ⑤
OS map SE035278

Number of pitches 30 tents.
No caravans/motorhomes.
Open Easter-Sept.
Booking No booking.
Typical cost £5 adult, £3 5-15s.
Facilities Disabled (toilet); play area;
shower (free); toilets.
Campfires Not allowed.
Dogs Allowed, on lead.
Restrictions No unsupervised under-18s
or single-sex groups of under-25s. No
admission after 8pm. No noise after 10pm.
Getting there By road From the A646 at
Luddenden Foot, head uphill on Luddenden
Lane. After three-quarters of a mile, turn
right (signposted Booth). Go through Booth,
following the road downhill, then turn left
and immediately left again into Jerusalem
Lane. Continue between stone walls;
Jerusalem Farm is the first building on the
right, with the car park just beyond. Don't
rely on sat-nav. **By public transport** Train to
Halifax. Buses 573, 574 and 575 (08450
260099, www.firstgroup.com) stop at Booth,
half a mile from the campsite. Service
operates Mon-Sat, journey takes 35 mins.

Cooking breakfast outside your tent, with only
chattering birds and a gurgling stream to disturb
the reverie, and nothing but grass and trees in
view, it's hard to believe that Jerusalem Farm
is only seven miles outside Halifax. The tranquil
setting helps: the campsite is tucked at the
bottom of a narrow little gorge in the Calder Valley,
with Luddenden Brook and Wade Wood on one
side, and steep grassy banks on the other.

You can pitch where you want on the long,
thin, undulating grass strip – but it's best to
be near a picnic table and, if you want a
barbecue, one of the stone slabs. There's no
vehicle access, so you have to carry all your
gear down (and back up) the knee-achingly
steep paths from the car park. That's where
the facilities are too: separate men's and
women's toilets, and one press-button shower.

Fortunately, there are drinking water taps and
washing-up points on the camping field.

There's been a campsite here since the end
of World War II. Unusually, it's council-run, which
adds a municipal touch to proceedings: the grass
(mown once a week) is as close-cropped as a golf
course, and the warden, a wonderfully friendly
and chatty Yorkshireman, makes sure the toilets
and flower beds are in shipshape condition.

The site is part of a local nature reserve to
which the public have open access – so you may
have the disconcerting experience of dog walkers
or canoodling couples strolling past your tent,
or a family setting out their sandwiches on one
of the picnic tables. Consequently, it doesn't
feel very private or secure. Mosquitos can be
a problem too: bring midge repellent, or be
resigned to evenings trapped inside your tent.

The place runs on a first come, first served
basis – mainly because there's parking for only
21 cars – though that shouldn't cause a problem
during the week. The other drawback is that the
car park isn't reserved for campers, and can get
filled by daytrippers on sunny weekends. The
parking area is closed overnight, although you
can get a key. The warden is around in the
morning and evening, and full-time at weekends.

The brook is crossed at one end by a stone
bridge and at the other by giant stepping stones.
Walk over to explore the paths winding through
the woods – beech, birch and holly – and into the
moorland beyond. Look out for golden plovers,
Pennine finches and red grouse in the uplands.

Three miles away is Hebden Bridge: vibrant,
creative, gay-friendly and with a reputation as
a mecca for free spirits. It draws tourists in
numbers, but also supports a healthy number
of quirky cafés, traditional pubs, smart fashion
boutiques, health food shops and homeopaths.
There's a small camping shop too.

EATING & DRINKING

Two pubs are within a mile and a half's walk of
the campsite. Head through the woods and across
farmland to Saltsonstall and the Cat i' th' Well (01422
244841, www.catithwell.co.uk), aka the Caty, or down
to Luddenden village to the historic Lord Nelson
(01422 882176, www.thelordnelson.uk.com, one-time
haunt of Branwell Brontë. The Nelson offers the likes
of own-made pies and roasts at the weekend, while
the Caty provides lunch and dinner, with game
(pheasant, wild boar) a seasonal speciality.

Hebden Bridge is the best place for food shopping
and has no less than four markets: on Wednesday
(second-hand), Thursday (general), the first and third

Sunday of the month (farmers'), and the second Sunday (crafts). It's also crammed with cafés, tea rooms, pubs, restaurants and takeaways. Two favourites are Market Street's funky Mooch Café Bar (01422 846954, www.moochcafe.co.uk, closed Tue) for coffee, wine, Mediterranean platters and a sweet back garden, and AJ's (01422 846755) on Bridge Gate, a modern chippie with veggie dishes and burgers alongside traditional fish and chips.

ATTRACTIONS & ACTIVITIES

There's lots of good walking in the vicinity, from the paths that snake through the adjoining woods and out into the countryside to long-distance routes. Jerusalem Farm is on the Calderdale Way, a 50-mile circular path that follows former packhorse trails across the gritstone hills and villages that encircle Halifax, Hebden Bridge and Todmorden. The Pennine Way isn't far either, on the other side of Hebden Bridge.

This is also Brontë country. Ten miles to the north you'll find the steep cobblestone streets of Haworth, now overrun with tourists following every move of Charlotte, Emily and the other sister that no one can remember. The main attraction is the Brontë Parsonage Museum (01535 642323, www.bronte.org.uk, closed Jan), where the family lived and the sisters wrote most of their novels. On the windswept moor above the town, the desolate ruin of Top Withens, reputedly the inspiration for *Wuthering Heights*, is so popular with Asian fans that the footpath signs are in Japanese.

At Haworth, you can also jump on the five-mile long Keighley & Worth Valley Railway (01535 645214, www.kwvr.co.uk, closed weekdays), which runs full-size steam trains between Keighley and Oxenhope. If you can remember the 1970 film

The Railway Children, it might all seem rather familiar. The literary connections continue at nearby Mytholmroyd, birthplace of poet Ted Hughes. It's also home to Britain's last clog factory, Walkley Clogs (01422 885757, www.clogs.co.uk). Tour the factory, then buy yourself a chunk of Yorkshire history.

AMUSING THE KIDS

On site, follow the stepping stones across the brook to find a small adventure playground.

A day trip to Halifax is in order to visit Eureka! (01422 330069, www.eureka.org.uk), the best children's museum in the country, with hundreds of inspiring, hands-on exhibits in six galleries. It sits next to the railway station, so the quickest way to get there is by train from Hebden Bridge or Mytholmroyd.

CAMPING NEARBY

Options are limited, with a preponderance of caravan parks. Just over eight miles away, Elland Hall Farm (01422 372325, www.ellandhallfarm.co.uk, open all year, £9 for two people) is a modest, family-run site with Portakabin loos and showers. There's space for ten caravans or tents.

WEST YORKSHIRE

Spiers House

Spiers House Caravan Park & Campsite
Cropton, Pickering, Yorkshire YO18 8ES
01751 417591 campsite
0845 130 8224 booking
spiers.house@forestholidays.co.uk
www.forestholidays.co.uk
Map p27 ⑤
OS map SE757918

Number of pitches 60 tents, 100 caravans/
motorhomes. 21 cabins (sleeping 4-6).
Open All year.
Booking By phone, online. Advisable
high season. Minimum stay 2-3 nights
if booking; cabin 3 nights.
Typical cost Camping £11-£17 2 people,
£4.75-£6.25 extra adult, £2.50-£4 extra
child. Non-CCC/FEC members additional
£3.50. Cabin £182-£1,545.
Facilities Cycle hire (£18 per day);
disabled facilities (toilet and shower);
electric hook-ups (100); laundry facilities;
play area; shop; showers (free); toilets;
washing-up area.
Campfires Not allowed.
Dogs Allowed, on lead.
Restrictions Unsupervised under-18s by
arrangement. No arrivals after 10.30pm,
quiet time 10pm-8am.
Getting there By road From the A170
between Pickering and Kirbymoorside, turn
off north towards Wrelton, Cropton and
Rosedale. About 1.5 miles after Cropton,
turn right into the forest at the sign to
Spiers House. **By public transport** From
Pickering train station, catch the M50
Moor Bus (01845 597000, www.northyork
moors.org.uk) directly to Spiers House;
the journey takes 20 mins. It runs daily
in Aug, but only on bank holidays and Sun
Apr-July, Sept, Oct. Otherwise a cab from
Pickering costs around £7.50 (Elite Cars,
01751 477319).

Spiers House is set deep within 10,000 acres
of Forestry Commission-managed woodland,
high on the North York Moors National Park.
After following the signs down a winding lane,
overarched by pine and spruce trees, you may
find the scale of the site a bit of a surprise.
With 160 pitches, 100 of which have electrical
hook-ups, it seems vast. Yet after a few minutes'
walk, even along the main woodland paths,

you'll hear the chirping of jays and the tapping
of woodpeckers.

The site is run by Forest Holidays, which
manages various camping and caravan sites
around the country for the Forestry Commission
(others featured in this book are Roundhill in the
New Forest – *see p122* – and Cashel on Loch
Lomond – *see p287*). As a result it can
sometimes feel like a rural holiday camp, and
may not suit those in search of solitude. If you
have children, though, or fancy an easy
introduction to camping, the facilities are superb.

Divided into standard, premium, select and
select-plus categories, the pitches are equipped
with various extras (electric hook-ups, picnic
tables and the like). If in doubt, book the

standard camping on the lower field, which is perfectly pleasant. For those keen to avoid guy rope tangles and sagging canvas, five pre-pitched tents are available through Eurocamp (0844 406 0402, www.eurocamp.co.uk). Camping & Caravanning Club members or holders of a Forest Experience Card get a discount.

The truly camping-averse can book into a cabin. Much grander than that description might suggest, these are brand new eco-lodges, equipped with full kitchens, flatscreen TVs and DVD players, modern art on the walls and an outdoor hot tub in which to wallow.

The Forest Retreat office and shop is a hub of information, dispensing maps marked with mountain bikes trails and walking routes, along with details of the park's historical sites. Best of all are the ranger-led events and guided talks. For a mere £6 (£5 for a child), you can learn how to make a shelter and other forest survival techniques, try a spot of tree identification, or take a wildlife safari. The nightly dusk watch, which heads out into the forest to find owls, moths and bats, is an experience not to be forgotten. Alternatively, hire a pair of night vision goggles (£12 per night) and creep up on the badgers, red deer and roe deer.

EATING & DRINKING

In addition to camping equipment, the Forest Retreat shop sells fresh bread every morning, to go with your newspaper, gas and essential provisions. It also stocks a reasonable selection of wines, and locally produced Cropton's bottled beer. Campfires are not allowed on site, but you can bring raised barbecues.

The closest town for food and convenience stores is Pickering, just over six miles away. On Eastgate Square, the Organic Farm Shop (01751 473444, www.theorganicfarmshop.com, closed Sun) stocks meat and seasonal produce from Standfield Hall Farm and two other local farms, along with home-baked bread and assorted groceries.

Close to the entrance of Spiers House, in Cropton village, is the large New Inn (01751 417330, www. newinncropton.co.uk). This family-friendly pub has a beer garden and modern, airy restaurant, but the

---

Site specific

✔ Qualified, knowledgeable Forestry Commission rangers lead guided walks through the unspoilt woodland, with tours for all ages.

✘ With 160 pitches (a fifth of which are seasonal pitches) and a busy schedule of organised events, Spiers House can feel slightly corporate.

real reason to head here is for Cropton's Brewery (01751 417330, www.croptonbrewery.com). Its ales and porters have won dozens of awards and are sold across the region; die-hard fans can book in for a brewery tour.

For an authentic country pub, head to the Blacksmiths Arms (01751 417247, www.blacksmiths lastingham.co.uk) in Lastingham – around an hour's walk away. A CAMRA favourite, it serves Theakston's Best and a selection of guest ales, along with sterling portions of hearty, home-made grub. The interior is cosy, with beamed ceilings; out front, a handful of outdoor tables face the church.

ATTRACTIONS & ACTIVITIES

Cropton Forest is the prime attraction for campers. Wildlife enthusiasts come to spy on a large population of badgers, roe deer, jays and woodpeckers; the red deer, lizards and pine martins tend to be more elusive. Well-signposted trails and bike paths interweave through the trees, and mountain bikes can be hired at the Forest Retreat shop. The shop also stocks nature books and 'iRanger' MP3 tours for independent forays into the forest. Laser combat (less painful than paintball) is also offered.

Pickering offers several museums for a rainy day. The Beck Isle Museum (01751 473653, www.beck islemuseum.co.uk, closed Nov-mid Feb) explores the agricultural history of the area, and provides a snapshot of early life on the moors.

About 14 miles from the campsite is the market town of Helmsley, with its shops, restaurants, arts centre and 12th-century castle (01439 770442, www.english-heritage.org.uk); from here, it's a three-and-a-half mile walk to the atmospheric ruins of Rievaulx Abbey. Both Scarborough and Whitby are under an hour's drive away across the moors.

The steam trains of the North Yorkshire Moors Railway (01751 472508, www.nymr.co.uk) chuff along 18 miles of track from Pickering to Grosmont. En route is Goathland station, which may look curiously familiar to acolytes of a certain boy wizard; with a few judicious tweaks and otherwordly props, it stood in for Hogsmeade in the film of *Harry Potter and the Philosopher's Stone*.

For information on the North York Moors National Park as a whole, visit www.northyorkmoors.org.uk.

AMUSING THE KIDS

There are lots of child-friendly organised events around the site and forest, from 'young explorer' ranger-led treks to the occasional magic show; note that charges apply. To enjoy the great outdoors for free, bring a bike and cycle around the trails. The site also has a small play area for younger children, with swings, slides and a climbing frame.

CAMPING NEARBY

For a completely different kind of camping experience, the vintage caravans of La Rosa (*see right*) are half an hour's drive north.

La Rosa

La Rosa
Murk Esk Cottage, Whitby,
North Yorkshire YO22 5AS
01947 606981
info@larosa.co.uk
www.larosa.co.uk
Map p27 ⑤
OS map NZ816026

Number of pitches 9 vintage caravans.
Open Apr-Oct.
Booking By phone. Minimum stay 2 nights
July, Aug.
Typical cost £60 per caravan per night.
Facilities Showers (free); sweet shop;
toilets; washing-up area.
Campfires Allowed, in designated areas.
Firewood available (free).
Dogs Not allowed.
Getting there By road Goathland is clearly
signposted off the A169, about 15 miles
north of Pickering and 8 miles south of
Whitby. From Goathland, take the Egton
Bridge/Roman Road turn-off near the
Mallyan Spout Hotel; the mile-long track to
La Rosa is on the right after about 2.5
miles. The only sign is four roses on a
gatepost. **By public transport** Get to
Goathland by taking the Coastliner bus 840
(01653 692556, www.coastliner.co.uk) from
Whitby (25 mins) or Pickering (40 mins), or
catch the steam train from Pickering on the
North Yorkshire Moors Railway (01751
472508, www.nymr.co.uk). From Goathland,
it's a 20-mins walk through woodland to the
site; call for directions before you arrive.

There is, quite simply, no other campsite like
La Rosa. This astonishing fantasy land, down
a rabbit hole somewhere near Whitby, is a
riot of kitsch caravanning in glorious technicolour.
There's a roll-top bath out in the orchard,
under the twinkle of fairy lights strung from
the trees; the common area is a circus tent,
decked out like a vaudeville theatre with
candelabras, bunting and a dressing-up rail.
The compost loo is in a shepherd's hut, with
a fortune teller's sign propped outside, and the
showers are housed in a former cow byre lit
by candles. There is a tipi with a fire inside for
soggy evenings, a sweet-shop caravan, and a
tiny caravan for the farm cats. And then there
is the accommodation.

The nine vintage caravans, mainly acquired
from travellers and circus performers, have
names like Psycho Candy, Viva Espana and
Shanty Shell; each has a totally different
theme, linked only by the overblown whimsy
that permeates the whole site. Vegas Vice
features all manner of glitter balls, casino
games and memorabilia, while Psycho Candy
is very, very pink. All are cosily heated, sleep
two in a double bed, and have gas burners for
cooking (crockery, pots and pans are provided,
along with sheets and eiderdowns).

The site's valley setting, deep in the North
Yorkshire Moors, is wonderfully secluded. It
is on National Park territory, so much of the
area is untouched and there is an enticing
network of footpaths and bridleways to explore.
A lovely 15-minute walk through the woods
takes you to the Birch Hall Inn, which dates
from the 1600s and doubles as a shop. This
diminutive pub has won awards for its guest
ales, and offers a snapshot of moorland life
of bygone times.

The nearest village is Goathland, a picturesque
– if sometimes tourist-filled – little place, where
flocks of sheep nibble the village green and stray
into people's front gardens. The fishing port of
Whitby is the closest town of any size, and the
place to come for fish and chips, provisions
and walks along the blustery North Sea coast.
It's also home to La Rosa's quirky B&B, which
overlooks the harbour and Whitby Abbey. Once
again, each room has a different theme; the
Lewis room is named in honour of the *Alice in
Wonderland* author, who stayed in the house
on several occasions. The Stoker room pays
homage to the town's most famous literary
connection: in Bram Stoker's dark masterpiece,
Count Dracula came ashore at Whitby before
stalking his unfortunate victims.

Site specific

✔ The site is utterly unique, and
unforgettable. It's also very sociable, with
the caravans dotted around two campfires
– perfect for groups of friends.

✘ Despite the extremely comfortable
caravans, this is not glamping. You'll
still have to collect firewood, walk to the
shared toilet, bathe outside and pack a
pair of wellies.

EATING & DRINKING

Sitting on the pier, spearing chips with a wooden fork, is the quintessential Whitby experience. If you want to start an argument here, ask two locals which chippy serves the best fish and chips. The Magpie Café on Pier Road (01947 602058, www. magpiecafe.co.uk, closed Jan) is the best-known establishment, although this is reflected in the prices. The Quayside (01947 602059, www.fuscowhitby.com) is also good – but you can't really go wrong at any chip shop in town if there's a queue outside.

Also in Whitby is the award-winning Green's (01947 600284, www.greensofwhitby.com), which specialises in seafood. It's very reasonably priced, given its reputation, and the Whitby turbot with seared queenies, and halibut with steamed mussels are boat-fresh.

For tea and cakes, visit the tea room at La Rosa's new guesthouse on East Terrace. Five miles outside Whitby, is the recently refurbished Falling Foss Tea Garden (Sneaton Forest, 07723 477929, www.falling fossteagarden.co.uk, closed Mon-Fri Oct, all Nov-Mar), set in tranquil woodland next to a waterfall.

The only pub within walking distance of the campsite is the tiny Birch Hall Inn (01947 896245, www.beckhole.info, closed Mon evening Sept-May, closed Tue Nov-May). It's at its best on a balmy evening, when you can sit outside with a beer before heading back for a few more bottles around the campfire. The menu is short and to the point: superb pies, made by the local butchers, the Beck Hole Butty (a sandwich with a large chunk of cheese, pâté, beef or ham), scones and beer cake. It has a basic shop too.

ATTRACTIONS & ACTIVITIES

Harry Potter fans jump on their broomsticks and fly en masse to Goathland train station, which appeared as Hogsmeade station in some of the Harry Potter films and is served by the steam trains of the North Yorkshire Moors Railway (01751 472508, www.nymr.co.uk). And, as any diehard fan of *Heartbeat* will know, Goathland village is where the TV series was filmed. Despite the hordes of peak-season visitors, it's an appealing place.

The ancient port of Whitby is one of Britain's most charming coastal towns. Its ruined 13th-century abbey, perched high on a sea-battered cliff, dominates the landscape; there has been a religious settlement on this site since 664. From the town, 199 steps lead up to the parish church of St Mary's, with its gravestones for lost mariners. Immediately behind the church stand the dramatic remains of the once-mighty abbey (01947 603568, www.english-heritage.org.uk, closed Tue, Wed Oct, Mon-Fri Nov-Mar, all Jan).

In the 18th century, Whitby was central to the whaling industry – and home to an ambitious young naval apprentice, James Cook, who would later captain the *Endeavour* and find fame and fortune as an explorer. In the 19th century, jet mining and carving bought prosperity to the town, especially after a bereaved Queen Victoria took to wearing the stone. You can admire some intricate pieces in Whitby Museum (01947 602908, www.whitbymuseum.org.uk), whose collections also include fossils, natural history exhibits and Captain Cook memorabilia.

Dracula is, of course, an inevitable theme around town, and fans of the gothic novel will find all manner

of souvenirs. One rather tacky offering is the Dracula Experience (01947 601923, www.draculaexperience. co.uk, closed Mon-Fri Nov-Feb): 'See him rise from the dead and hear his screams.' Ghost walks are also popular; try Whitby Walks (www.whitbywalks.com).

The busiest weekend in Whitby is in late August, when the Regatta (www.whitbyregatta.co.uk) takes over the harbour for three days, culminating in a colourful fireworks display.

AMUSING THE KIDS

Children love Whitby. The famous whale jawbone arch on the West Cliff, the fossilised, Jurassic-era marine reptiles in Whitby Museum, the atmospheric, brooding abbey and the *Dracula* links all exert a powerful appeal. Equally enticing are the magnificent steam trains of the North Yorkshire Moors Railway: the nearest stations are Goathland and Grosmont. Keep an eye out for special events such as teddy bears' picnics and family days.

CAMPING NEARBY

Five miles south of Whitby, near Robin Hood's Bay, much-loved Hooks House Farm (01947 880283, www.hookshousefarm.co.uk) is a picturesque coastal option. Showers, washrooms, toilets and sinks, together with the use of an electric kettle, are included in the modest prices (from £6 adult, £3 child).

Spiers House (*see p178*) in Cropton Forest is about 15 miles away, near Pickering.

Whitby: the beach and the ruined abbey looming above the harbour.

Clitheroe

LANCASHIRE

Clitheroe Camping & Caravanning Club
Edisford Road, Clitheroe,
Lancashire BB7 3LA
01200 425294
www.campingandcaravanningclub.co.uk/
clitheroe
Map p27 ⑤
OS map SD727411

Number of pitches 32 tents, 54 caravans/
motorhomes.
Open Apr-Nov.
Booking By phone, online (members only).
Typical cost Members £5.90-£9.05 adult;
£2.65-£2.85 child. Non-members additional
£7.10. CCC membership £39 per year.
Facilities Disabled (toilet and shower);
electric hook-ups (34); laundry facilities;
showers (free); toilets; washing-up area;
Wi-Fi.
Campfires Not allowed.
Dogs Allowed, on lead.
Restrictions No single-sex groups
and unsupervised under-18s.
Getting there By road Clitheroe is just
off the A59 between Preston and Skipton.
Either way you come in, follow the signs
to the town centre and look for the B6243.
The campsite is on Edisford Road, on the
left just before the narrow stone bridge.
By public transport There's a train station
at Clitheroe, from where it's about a mile
to the site, so walk or grab a taxi. Bus 280
(www.dalesbus.org) runs hourly Mon-Sat,
less frequently Sun, between Skipton and
Preston via Clitheroe.

The carefully manicured lawns of the Camping &
Caravanning Club site at Clitheroe illustrate the
high standards set by the CCC. It's about as far
from wild camping as you can get, but for those
looking for a few luxuries, and the chance to
explore the often-overlooked Forest of Bowland,
this clean and tidy campground is a good option.
Clitheroe is known for its Norman keep, which
still dominates this picturesque town. It also has
plenty of independent shops, restaurants and
pubs, with more quality eating establishments
spread out along the Ribble Valley.

Walkers, cyclists, birdwatchers and anglers are
drawn to the remote gritstone fells of the Forest
of Bowland – no longer wooded – that extend
west to Lancaster. The area doesn't pull in nearly
as many visitors as the more famous Dales to the
north, and you don't need to go far outside town
to feel you're in the middle of nowhere. One of
the better trails is the well-signposted Ribble Way,
running for 70 miles from Longton near Preston,
through Clitheroe and Gisburn, and ending in
Gavel Gap. Lovely parts of the trail through the
Ribble Valley can be walked from Clitheroe.

Rising from the east is the mighty Pendle Hill.
To climb it – in good weather, mind – it's best to
set off from Barley (about seven miles away);
once the peak has been conquered, return to
Barley for a pint and a bite in the Pendle Inn
(01282 614808, www.pendle-inn.co.uk).

The campsite is located within Clitheroe itself.
Campers are outnumbered by caravanners, but
the tent area is tucked towards the back of the
site, away from the hard-standings and caravans;
even on busy weekends there is enough distance
from your neighbour. Many visitors are regulars,
giving the place a friendly, community vibe. The
toilets, showers, washing-up and laundry facilities
are spotless (Clitheroe won the CCC loo of the
year award in 2008), and extras include Wi-Fi
and a disabled toilet and shower.

You don't have to be a CCC member to camp
here, although non-members pay slightly more.

EATING & DRINKING

All the usual convenience stores, petrol stations
and pubs can be found within walking distance in
Clitheroe. The nearest pub is the family-friendly
Edisford Bridge Inn (01200 422637), a very short
stroll across the bridge. Regulars at the campground
rave about the reasonably priced lunches, and the local
CAMRA association recommends its Jennings ales.

The Ribble Valley is also becoming known for its
good gastropubs and restaurants, many specialising
in local produce. At the centre of this local revival is
Nigel Haworth's much-lauded – and Michelin-starred
– Northcote (01254 240555, www.northcote.com) in
Langho, seven miles to the south. It's probably the
most expensive offering in the area, but it's worth the
spend (and worth checking the website for special
deals). The langoustine ravioli and Lancashire hot
pot (order ahead) are lovely options.

For a more down-to-earth hostelry, the Three Fishes
(01254 826888, www.thethreefishes.com) in nearby
Mitton offers Morecambe Bay shrimps and a generous
ploughman's, perfectly matched by local bitters.

ATTRACTIONS & ACTIVITIES

The Forest of Bowland, taking in the fells and the
Ribble Valley, covers more than 300 square miles.
Dozens of waymarked paths pass through, or near,

Clitheroe, and horse riders and cyclists have an equally prodigious network of bridleways. Inhabitants are few, particularly on the high peat moorland, so care must be taken under the (often) brooding skies.

As you may note from the number of witch logos found hereabouts, including at the campsite, this area has an intriguing Wiccan history. The villages around Pendle Hill were the scene of Britain's most notorious witch trials. In 1612, 12 suspected witches were charged with killing ten people using witchcraft. Nine women and two men were eventually hanged. The story still threads through local folklore and has attracted a large pagan community, and witchy images abound on souvenirs and beers. There's even a Pendle Witch Camp (www.penwitchcamp.co.uk), held over the summer solstice weekend in June.

The recently remodelled Clitheroe Castle Museum (01200 424568, www.lancashire.gov.uk/museums) is a child-friendly place, charting the history of the 800-year-old Norman castle, and the keep built by Robert de Lacy. Keeping with the theme, a ghost walk can be taken from the castle gates (07543 326215, www.ahauntingexperience.co.uk).

Fans of *The Lord of the Rings* can follow the five-mile Tolkien Trail in nearby Hurst Green. The author was a regular visitor to the area while writing his masterpiece; the Shire's Buckleberry Ferry is thought to be based on the old ferry at Hacking Hall.

Permits for fishing in the River Ribble are available from the campsite reception.

AMUSING THE KIDS

There is a small playground and a large, fenced green space next to the campsite. Clitheroe Castle has a good display for children, while the Bowland Wild Boar Park (01995 61554, www.wildboarpark.co.uk) just outside the village of Chipping, nine miles to the west, is tailor-made for youngsters. Llamas, deer and goats play alongside the boar, and there are tractor rides and a play area too.

CAMPING NEARBY

A few minutes away, on the other side of the River Ribble, is Edisford Bridge Farm (01200 427868, www.edisfordbridgecaravanandcamping.co.uk, open Mar-Dec) with room for 20 caravans and more tents (from £10 per night). It is still a working farm, and feels a bit earthier than the CCC site. Kids and well-behaved dogs are welcome.

Site specific

✔ Being a CCC site, the campground is well organised, very clean and has good facilities. It's also very close to Clitheroe's pubs, shops and restaurants.

✘ The site feels rather urban – the nearest field is a public green with a playground. But a sense of wilderness is not far away.

Gibraltar Farm

Number of pitches 50 tents,
60 caravans/motorhomes.
Open Mar-Oct.
Booking By phone, email. Advisable.
Typical cost Tent £9-£16 (£6 without car).
Caravan/motorhome £16 (£11 without
hook-up).
Facilities Disabled (toilet); electric
hook-ups (18); laundry facilities;
showers (free); toilets; washing-up area.
Campfires Not allowed.
Dogs Allowed.
Restrictions No unsupervised under-21s.
No noise after 11pm.
Getting there By road From Carnforth
(off the M6, at junction 35), drive west on
the B5282 towards Silverdale. After about
4.5 miles, you go over a level crossing; turn
left at the next T-junction and then take the
next left on to Hollins Lane; Gibraltar Farm
is at the end of this road, and clearly signed.
By public transport Silverdale train station,
with regular links to Lancaster, is a couple
of miles from the campsite. The Silverdale
Shuttle bus is a hail-and-ride service that
links the village with the station, coinciding
with train arrival/departure times. More
information on www.lancashire.gov.uk.

Gibraltar Farm Campsite
Gibraltar Farm, Silverdale, Carnforth,
Lancashire LA5 0UA
01524 701736
camping@gibraltarfarm.co.uk
www.gibraltarfarm.co.uk
Map p27 ⑤⑤
OS map SD462741

While it is almost impossible to describe
Morecambe Bay without the adjective 'windswept',
it is also usually accompanied with 'beautiful',
'stunning' or 'gorgeous'. Hanging on to the
cliffs just north of the quintessential British
seaside town of Morecambe is Gibraltar Farm,
a working dairy farm on the southern edge of the
village of Silverdale.

Descending into the site opens up views across
Morecambe Bay to Barrow-in-Furness, the outlets
for the Rivers Kent, Leven and Wye and the Lake
District beyond. Depending on the tide, the views
will be dominated by vast mudflats or choppy
waves that have built up height rolling from the
Isle of Man and Ireland.

The campground consists of two stone-walled
fields – one with electric hook-ups for caravans,
the other for campers – although other fields
are opened when it gets busy. All the fields slope
down towards the sea, offering extensive views
of the dairy cow pastures below (the farm's

ice-cream is sold in a hut on-site) and the coastline across the bay. The camping field includes an attractive rocky copse – a good spot for sheltering tents against the breeze. There is also a wooded area that can be hired (£100 minimum) for private groups. A network of paths wind through the surrounding woodland; one, which leads to sheltered Jack Scout Cove and a rocky outcrop popular with climbers, is great for exploring or picnicking. On clear days, the sunsets are wonderful.

It's a ten-minute walk to the quaint village of Silverdale, with its post office, newsagent, Co-op, Italian restaurant, art gallery and couple of pubs – including the unmissable Woodlands. The largest town is Morecambe, 12 miles away, a holiday destination for Lancashire's workers since Victorian times. Like any proper seaside resort it has its tacky elements, but with the £11m refurbishment of the art deco Midland Hotel, its rollercoaster fortunes appears to be rising up again. If nothing else, it's worth going to sing 'Bring Me Sunshine' by the Eric Morecambe statue on the promenade.

Most campers, however, will be attracted to Gibraltar Farm because of the rugged coastal walks around the Arnside and Silverdale Area of Outstanding Natural Beauty, and superb birdwatching opportunities. A delightful location – though, be warned, it is windy.

Site specific

✔ The dramatic coastline that can be seen from the campsite has abundant birdlife, and makes for exciting blustery walks exploring sandflats and hidden coves.

✘ There aren't enough showers, especially when the campsite is full.

EATING & DRINKING

Just up the road, the Wolfhouse Gallery (01524 701405, www.wolfhouse-gallery.co.uk, closed Tue, closed Mon Feb-Easter, all Jan-early Feb) so called because it is thought the last wolf in England was shot outside the building – has a daytime café serving snacks, soups and tasty own-made cakes. Paintings, ceramics, glassware and jewellery by local artists are on display and for sale.

Silverdale's drinking highlight is the Woodlands (01524 701655), known to locals as 'Woody's'. Located on Woodlands Drive, just over a mile and a half from Gibraltar Farm, the pub occupies two converted rooms in an old and spooky-looking manor house. Inside, the welcome is as warm as the roaring wintertime fire. A cross between a hotel bar and a working man's boozer, the place oozes character and, once locked into conversation with a local farmer, you'll find it almost impossible to leave. There's a revolving selection of ales on tap, with Black Sheep as standard. To eat, there are sandwiches made by Dave, the owner, and crisps.

The only other pub of note is the Silverdale Hotel (01524 701206, www.thesilverdalehotel.co.uk), which serves decent pub grub, and has a pleasant conservatory and beer garden. The village's sole restaurant is L'Amico (01524 784191, www.lamico-restaurant.co.uk, closed Mon). Italian owners Ciro and Vanessa Cappiello make their own pasta and pizza on site, and their steaks are renowned locally.

There are a few places to get basic provisions, including Burrow & Son butchers (01524 701209, closed Sun), which is run by the Gibraltar Farm family. For a Tesco and more shops, head to Carnforth.

ATTRACTIONS & ACTIVITIES

The area is a birdwatcher's Eden. Only a mile away is RSPB Leighton Moss Nature Reserve (01524 701601, www.rspb.org.uk), the largest reed bed in north-west England and home to bitterns, bearded tits, marsh harriers and all manner of wading birds. It's open daily from 9am to dusk, and you can hire binoculars for use in the hides and along the nature trails. There are regular guided walks and a tea room.

Film buffs can pay homage at Carnforth station (01524 735165, www.carnforthstation.co.uk), where David Lean shot his masterpiece *Brief Encounter*: there's a visitor centre, the iconic station

LANCASHIRE

Jack Scout Cove; and (below) the Woodlands pub in Silverdale.

clock and, most nostalgic of all, a replica of the refreshment room where Trevor Howard removed grit from Celia Johnson's eye.

Stately homes nearby include Levens Hall (015395 60321, www.levenshall.co.uk, closed Fri, Sat and Oct-Easter), nine miles to the north. The Elizabethan mansion is very fine, but it's the astonishing topiary gardens – designed in the 1690s and considered the best in the country – that fascinate visitors.

AMUSING THE KIDS

Children will love bounding across the rocks by the sea, but be careful of the turning tide and mudflats.

Morecambe's traditional seaside amusements appeal to kids, while Lancaster, 12 miles to the south, offers a 1,000-year-old castle (01524 64998, www.lancastercastle.com) – still used as a court and prison today – and Lancaster Maritime Museum (01524 382264, www.lancashire.gov.uk/acs/sites/museums), which hosts craft sessions for children in the summer holidays.

CAMPING NEARBY

Hollins Farm (01524 701767, www.hollinsfarm.co.uk, open Mar-Oct), on the northern side of Silverdale, towards Arnside, is highly respected. It has recently teamed up with nearby Holgates Holiday Park, and campers and caravanners can use the park's gym, pool and restaurant. A tent or caravan with two adults and two children costs £37.

Low Wray

Low Wray Campsite
Low Wray, near Ambleside,
Cumbria LA22 0JA
015394 63862
campsite.bookings@nationaltrust.org.uk
www.nationaltrust.org.uk/campsites/
lakedistrict
Map p27 56
OS map NY373010

Number of pitches 130 tents/campervans.
Small motorhomes allowed. 10 pods
(sleeping 2). Also 2 yurts, 3 bell tents,
7 pre-erected tents, 12 tipis (not run by NT).
Open Easter-Oct.
Booking By phone, email, online. Essential.
Minimum stay 2 nights high season
weekends, 3 nights bank holidays.
Typical cost Camping £8-£23.50 1 adult,
£5 extra adult, £2.50 extra under-16.
Pod £30-£47.50.
Facilities Disabled facilities (toilet and
shower); laundry facilities; play area; shop;
showers (free); toilets; washing-up area.
Campfires Not allowed.
Dogs Allowed, on lead (£1-£1.50).
Restrictions No groups over 4 people;
other groups by arrangement. No noise
after 11pm.
Getting there By road Take the A593 from
Ambleside, then turn left at Clappersgate
on to the B5286. Turn left at the sign for
Wray. The site is less than a mile on the left.
By public transport The 505 bus (Coniston
Rambler, 0871 200 2233, www.stagecoach
bus.com) goes from the nearest train station
at Windermere, and can drop you within a
mile of the site. It runs daily Apr-end Oct
and takes 30 mins.

Admiring Britain's longest lake from one of the
many boats that ply its waters is all very well,
but to see Windermere in all its moods, you
can't do better than to camp at Low Wray. Set
on the lake's wooded north-western shore, this
picturesque, National Trust-run site affords
magical views – especially if you steel your
resolve and set your alarm in time for sunrise.

One of four National Trust campsites in the
Lake District, Low Wray is perfectly located for
exploring the area's charms. The nearest big
town is Ambleside, located at the head of
Windermere, around ten minutes' drive away;

the undeniably lovely tourist honeypots of
Bowness, Grasmere, Coniston and the Langdale
Valley are also close.

The site is large, but peaceful – thanks, in
part, to the NT's rules and regulations, which
are firmly enforced. You have to leave a 20-foot
gap between tents, 'quiet time' is from 11pm to
7am, and group sizes are restricted. No cars are
allowed on the grass, so it can be a bit of a walk
from the car park to your pitch; choose your spot
with care if you're lugging lots of equipment.

On arrival, you'll most likely be directed to
one of two fields, Vic's Meadow or Ransoms.
Vic's, a pleasant, open meadow, is the main
camping area. Closer to the lake, and incurring
a £10 surcharge for the privilege, is Ransoms.
Smaller, and slightly more densely wooded, it's
a wonderfully quiet place to camp; you might see
ducklings waddling to the water's edge in the
mornings, or hear herons calling. Mosquitos
also congregate here, so pack some repellent.

There's also a large wooded area with lake
access, across a little beck from Ransom's;
outside peak season, it's generally used by
groups. Your other option is Woodhouse Meadows
– furthest from the lake, and hence the quietest
area of the campsite.

For campers prone to getting their guy ropes
in a twist, there are cute wooden pods, insulated
with sheep's wool. You'll need to bring all your
standard camping equipment (except for a tent,
of course), as they're unfurnished. Other options
not booked via the NT are: seven pre-erected
Eurocamp tents (0844 406 0402, www.euro
camp.co.uk); 12 brightly painted canvas tipis
(01539 821227, www.4windslakelandtipis.co.uk);
and two yurts and three rather lovely bell tents
(01539 731089, www.long-valley-yurts.co.uk), all
with solar-powered fairy lights and wood-burning
stoves. More yurts perch in woodland next to the
lake (07909 446381, www.wildinstyle.co.uk).

Site specific

✔ The widely spaced pitches and the
peaceful atmosphere mean that the
camping fields seldom feel overcrowded,
even in high season.

✗ Despite the helpful staff, the site does
have a slightly impersonal feel. The ground
is uneven and rocky in places, so expect
some bent tent pegs.

LAKE DISTRICT

Facilities have had an upgrade recently; the rather rundown toilet and shower blocks have been refurbished. And, as planned, the shop has expanded and been moved, along with reception, to the centre of the site – making it easier for all concerned. The chidren's play area is also being spruced up, in anticipation for a new wave of boisterous youngsters.

EATING & DRINKING

The on-site shop sells the basics, though its opening hours and stock are somewhat restricted, and a catering van, run by a local farm, can provide sandwiches, burgers and other hot snacks.

For more choice, head to Ambleside, which is stuffed with eateries. The Mediterranean-influenced menu at the Priest Hole restaurant (015394 33332, www.thepriesthole.co.uk) offers pasta, substantial meaty mains and a few fish and vegetarian dishes. Then there's Zefferelli's (015394 33845, www. zeffirellis.com), a cinema and jazz bar with a splendid sideline in vegetarian food: think wholemeal pizzas, butternut squash lasagne or gorgonzola and chive

soufflé with walnut and pear salad. For the simpler, salty charms of a fish and chip supper, head to the Walnut Fish Bar (015394 32521).

In the hamlet of Outgate, a good half hour's walk from Low Wray, the Outgate Inn (015394 36413, www.outgateinn.co.uk) dispenses Robinson's ales from its gleaming taps and serves good, old-fashioned pub grub and Sunday roasts. A mile outside Outgate, the Drunken Duck Inn (015394 36347, www.drunkenduckinn.co.uk) is an acclaimed, if pricier, option. At lunchtime, fill up on superior sarnies and sturdy ploughmans; in the evening, splash out on grilled plaice with cobnut and caper butter, or braised venison haunch with red cabbage and garlic mash.

ATTRACTIONS & ACTIVITIES

The lake is easily accessible from any of the site's fields; sit and watch the boats, feed the ducks or just admire the lovely scenery. Fishing is allowed on Windermere, Blelham Tarn and Esthwaite Water.

A four-mile drive away is the pretty village of Hawkshead. Strolling its car-free centre makes

for a relaxing morning; pop into the Old Grammar School Museum (www.hawksheadgrammar.org.uk, closed Nov-Mar) to see the desk once occupied by a young William Wordsworth, who carved his name into the wood, then peruse the watercolours and sketches on display at the Beatrix Potter Gallery (015394 36355, www.nationaltrust.org.uk, closed Fri, all Nov-Jan). Another stop-off on the Potter trail is the 17th-century farmhouse where she wrote many of her stories, Hill Top (015394 36269, www.nationaltrust.org.uk, closed Fri, all Nov-Jan), which is near Sawrey.

Vast Grizedale Forest Park (01229 860010, www.forestry.gov.uk/grizedalehome), some six miles away, is criss-crossed with walking and cycle paths, and has bikes for hire (01229 860369), there's also a brilliant sculpture trail.

There are numerous places to walk to from the site – not least around Windermere itself. You can buy map of local walks and cycle routes from the campsite for £2. For a more challenging fell walk, drive to Great Langdale and tackle the Langdale Pikes. The route from the New Dungeon Ghyll Hotel to Stickle Tarn and Pavey Ark is the best, taking in Harrison Stickle and Pike O'Stickle, and returning via Loft Crag.

AMUSING THE KIDS

Low Wray's playground has swings and a climbing frame, and is the starting point for several family-friendly walks. Many campers bring boats or canoes to explore Windermere, and you can swim. Rowing and motor boats are for hire, while the less energetic can take a cruise from Ambleside (015394 43360, www.windermere-lakecruises.co.uk).

Children familiar with Peter Rabbit and Mrs Tiggy-Winkle may also enjoy the Beatrix Potter sites.

CAMPING NEARBY

An easy stroll across the fields from Hawkshead, Hawkshead Hall Campsite (015394 36221, www.hawksheadhall-campsite.com, open Mar-Oct, £15 for two people) is a relaxed, unspoilt site with spotless showers; just avoid the steeper pitches. There's another National Trust site at Great Langdale (015394 63862), with superb walking and climbing nearby. Two adults pay £12-£15 and it's open all year.

LAKE DISTRICT

Eskdale

Eskdale Camping & Caravanning Club
Boot, Holmrook, Cumbria CA19 1TH
01946 723253
www.campingandcaravanningclub.co.uk/
eskdale
Map p27 ⑤⑦
OS map NY190009

Number of pitches 80 tents/motorhomes.
No caravans. 10 pods (sleeping 4).
Camping barn (sleeps 8).
Open Mar-Jan
Booking By phone, online (members only).
Minimum stay 2 nights school holidays.
Typical cost Members £7.50-£9 adult,
£2-£3 child. Non-members additional £7.15.
CCC membership £39 per year. Pods
£42.50. Camping barn £125.
Facilities Disabled facilities (toilet and
shower); drying room; electric hook-ups (35);
laundry facilities; play area; shop; showers
(free); toilets; washing-up area.
Campfires Not allowed.
Dogs Allowed, on lead.
Restrictions Groups by arrangement. No
unsupervised under-18s. No car access
11pm-7am; no noise after 11pm.
Getting there By road Take the A595
(Broughton in Furness to Whitehaven road).
About 17 miles north of Broughton, just
before Holmrook, turn right towards Eskdale
Green, then right again to Beckfoot and
Whillan Beck. The campsite is on the left
after 3 miles. **By public transport** Train
to Ravenglass, then catch the Ravenglass
& Eskdale Railway steam train (01229
717171, www.ravenglass-railway.co.uk,
open mid Mar-Oct and winter weekends) to
'Dalegarth for Boot'. It's aimed at tourists,
but is also a working train line, though it
is slow: the 7-mile journey takes 80 mins.
The campsite is a mile to the east.

Getting to Eskdale can be quite an adventure,
should you elect to arrive via the twisting,
tortuous Hardknott Pass. One of England's
steepest roads, its unrelenting gradients, hairpin
bends and sheer drops are a tough challenge
for both cars and drivers. The more roundabout
route from the A595 may be a wise choice, no
matter what sat-nav says.

On arrival, however, you'll be rewarded by a
landscape of unsurpassed beauty. For Alfred

Wainwright, Eskdale was 'one of the loveliest
of Lakeland's valleys'; surveying its craggy
mountains, rolling fells and oak woodland, you'll
be inclined to agree. Sellafield nuclear site is only
a dozen or so miles away, but you'd never know.

The campsite sits towards the eastern end,
just off the main valley road and close to the
picturesque little village of Boot. As with many
Camping & Caravanning Club sites, it's admirably
organised and well groomed, with exemplary
facilities. Two level fields are set among trees,
along with a car-free strip for backpackers,
reached via a slate bridge across the beck.

The modern, immaculately clean toilet block
is nearby. The showers are a joy: power-showers,
spacious cubicles and plenty of hooks, plus a
separate shower room for families and disabled
visitors. There are indoor and outdoor washing-up
areas, a laundry room with washing machine,
tumble dryer and spin dryer, a playground and
a thoughtfully stocked shop, with long opening
hours. The drying room is handy for walkers.

As an alternative to camping, you could book
one of the pods – ten cosy, bow-roofed wooden
huts, dotted around two neatly kept little
clearings with a picnic table at the centre. Each
pod can comfortably fit two adults, or a family
of four; you'll need to bring your own camp beds
or inflatable mattresses. If the wool insulation
doesn't keep the cold out, you can borrow a
heater from reception.

For larger groups, there's a camping barn,
with its lovely (and fully equipped) stone-flagged
kitchen, wood-burning stove and central heating;
up a spiral staircase, the sleeping area has
comfortable folding camp beds. Which, after
a hard day following in Wainwright's footsteps,
are nothing short of blissful.

EATING & DRINKING

The on-site shop has a good selection of local produce
including fruit and veg, meat, and fresh bread from a
nearby bakery, plus camping spares.

Boot, a couple of minutes' walk away, has several
pubs, a shop and a post office. The Brook House Inn
(01946 723288, www.brookhouseinn.co.uk) prides
itself on its well-kept ales and hearty home-made food;
booking is recommended. The Boot Inn (01946 723224,
www.bootinn.co.uk) serves traditional food with a
focus on local ingredients, and has a good-sized beer
garden with two play areas. Your third option is the
Woolpack Inn (01946 723230, www.woolpack.co.uk)
for own-made casseroles and ploughmans at lunch,
pizzas in the café and more ambitious fare in the
evenings (a new restaurant opened in autumn 2011).

For snacks or a light lunch, pop into Fellbites Eatery (01946 723192, closed when Ravenglass Railway not operating) at Dalegarth station, which also stocks a fine selection of Lakeland ice-creams; don't miss the sublime – and beautifully named – 'Thunder & Lightning' flavour.

Around three miles away in Eskdale Green, Eskdale Stores (01946 723229, www.eskdale stores.co.uk) sells organic food, alcohol and local produce – including the justly celebrated Waberthwaite cumberland sausage. Nearby, the 17th-century Bower House Inn (01946 723244, www.bowerhouseinn.co.uk) impresses with dishes such as pork belly with black pudding mash and caramelised vegetables. It also offers afternoon tea.

ATTRACTIONS & ACTIVITIES

Boot is a photogenic cluster of stone and whitewashed cottages, with a small art gallery (Fold End Gallery, 01946 723316, closed Nov-early Mar) and a beer festival (www.bootbeer.co.uk) in June. Cross the 17th-century packhorse bridge over Whillan Beck to visit 16th-century Eskdale Mill (019467 23335, www.eskdalemill.co.uk, closed some Mon & some Sat Apr-Sept, open by appointment Oct-Mar), one of the oldest water-powered corn mills in England.

From Dalegarth station, catch the 'La'al Ratty' miniature steam train (01229 717171, www. ravenglass-railway.co.uk). The seven-mile route runs through woodland, then drops into a valley and chugs across marshes to the coast at Ravenglass.

The Brook House Inn (top) and the Ravenglass & Eskdale Railway (right).

There are plenty of inspiring walks from the campsite, with maps available in the shop; choose from a trip to Burnmoor Tarn or the dramatic waterfall at Stanley Ghyll – a red squirrel stronghold. There's good access to the Scafell range and Scafell Pike, although you'll need to set aside a whole day. Try Harter Fell for a more manageable climb, and great views of Eskdale, the Duddon Valley and beyond to Coniston.

At the western end of Hardknott Pass, a short but steep walk from the small car park leads to the remains of Hardknott Roman Fort (www.english-heritage.org.uk), founded in the second century. The ruins are splendidly sited, and the views stretch far across the valley towards Scafell.

Site specific

✔ Full marks for the spotlessly clean and tidy facilities and the impressive attention to detail – from the excellent showers to the children's trampoline.

✘ When the place is busy, you may well have to wait in line for a shower. It's also quite pricey if you're not a member of the Camping & Caravanning Club.

If you're camping at the end of September, the Eskdale Show (www.eskdale.info) offers hound trailing, fell racing, local crafts and sheep-judging, fuelled by refreshments from tea and beer tents.

AMUSING THE KIDS

Children fare well with the on-site swings, adventure playground and tremendously popular trampoline. They'll also love the Ravenglass & Eskdale Railway; even if you don't travel on it, it's fun to watch the train puffing into the station, then being turned around for its return journey.

Near Ravenglass, Muncaster Castle & Gardens (01229 717614, www.muncaster.co.uk, closed Sat, all Nov-Mar) makes for a satisfying family day out. Ghostly tales should keep the kids' attention from wandering. There are also extensive gardens, an owl centre and indoor MeadowVole maze.

CAMPING NEARBY

A mile or so away, Fisherground Farm Camping (01946 723349, www.fishergroundcampsite.co.uk, open Mar-end Oct) is a quiet, family-friendly site with an adventure playground and rafting pond. It costs £6 adult, £3 child, £2.50 car.

There's another CCC site at Ravenglass (01229 717250, from £7.10 adult, £2.45 child), run by the same people as Eskdale. Just 500 yards from the sea, it covers six peaceful wooded acres and is open all year.

Wasdale Head

Wasdale Head Campsite
Wasdale Head, Seascale,
Cumbria CA20 1EX
01946 726220
www.nationaltrust.org.uk/campsites/
lakedistrict
Map p27 ⑤⑧
OS map NY183076

Number of pitches 120 tents/
campervans/motorhomes. No caravans.
4 pods (sleeping 2, 4).
Open All year.
Booking Online.
Typical cost Camping £8-£12 adult,
£5 extra adult, £2.50 extra under-16.
Pod £25-£47.50.
Facilities Disabled (toilet and shower);
electric hook-ups (6); laundry facilities;
shop; showers (20p); toilets; washing-up
area.
Campfires Not allowed.
Dogs Allowed, on lead (£1.50).
Restrictions No single-sex groups;
no groups larger than 4 on weekends
summer holidays, other groups by
arrangement. No noise after 11pm.
Getting there By road Take the A595
(Broughton in Furness to Whitehaven road).
Just past Holmrook, turn right towards
Santon Bridge and follow signs to Wasdale
Head. If you're coming from the north,
turn left at Gosforth. **By public transport**
Seascale train station is about 12 miles
away, on the coast. A taxi from there
costs about £19 (Gosforth Private Hire,
019467 25308).

The drive along the northern edge of Wastwater
to the head of the Wasdale Valley must be one of
the most scenic approaches to any campsite in
the country. Ahead is 'Britain's favourite view' –
the glorious grouping of Yewbarrow, Great Gable
and Lingmell fells. Across the water to the right
are the precipitous slopes of Wastwater Screes,
tumbling down into England's deepest lake;
beyond is the immense Scafell massif.

Just after the end of the lake, a bridge
across Lingmell Beck leads to the site, which is
sheltered from the elements by the surrounding
woodland, with mountains looming on all sides.
The large, level camping field is interspersed with
trees, and has some pleasantly secluded pitches

around the edges. The lake is not visible from
the site, but is a short walk away; its proximity
means that midges can be a problem. On one
side of the field, screened by shrubbery, are
four unfurnished wooden camping pods, with
sheep's wool insulation and french doors.

Wasdale is much loved by climbers and
walkers, whose compact tents give the place
a spacious feel. Simplicity is key, with people
cooking out in the open on small stoves and
barbecues. Drinking water taps are dotted
about, and the central shower block is clean
and well lit, if slightly dated. Bring a stash of
20-pence pieces for the showers; each coin buys
you around five minutes' worth of hot water.

Wasdale is classified as a 'quiet site', which
means any campers making too much noise late
at night may be asked to leave. To add to the
tranquil atmosphere, and the look of the place,
cars must be parked away from the camping
ground. The campsite is open year round – and
outside the school holiday rush, there are few
families staying here. For those prepared to brave
the cold, an off-season stay offers a wonderfully
peaceful getaway, and the chance to see the
magnificent surroundings at their best.

EATING & DRINKING

Campers can stock up on fresh, tinned and frozen
food at the on-site shop – although it is quite pricey.
For further supplies, it's a nine-mile drive back along
Wastwater to the A595 and the village of Gosforth.

It's a 20-minute walk to the Wasdale Head Inn
(01946 726229, www.wasdale.com) towards the head
of the valley. A down-to-earth, traditional pub with
stone flooring, wooden booths and well-polished horse
brasses, it has a large selection of ales from the in-
house Great Gable Brewing Company. Food includes
baguettes, jacket potatoes, soups and main meals.

Five miles away in Nether Wasdale, the Screes
Inn (01946 726262, www.thescreesinnwasdale.com)
and the Strands Inn (01946 726237, www.strands
hotel.com) are both recommended for their food.
The latter has a more elaborate menu, along with
its own microbrewery, which produces the niftily
named 'Errmmm' bitter.

ATTRACTIONS & ACTIVITIES

People camp at Wasdale for the outstanding walking
and climbing in the vicinity. Setting off from the
campsite, you can tackle Scafell Pike, England's
highest mountain at 3,210 feet – either following
the main route via Brown Tongue, or conquering
Lingmell first (a steep climb, but worth it for the
excellent views of Great Gable from the top).

LAKE DISTRICT

Another challenging day out is the Mosedale Horseshoe, a hike of more than ten miles across the peaks of Yewbarrow, Red Pike, Scoat Fell, Steeple and Pillar. Seek out the stone 'chair' on Red Pike, near the summit, for a vantage point overlooking Wastwater. From Steeple, there are fine views across Ennerdale. Walk back via the Wasdale Head Inn for a restorative pint.

The lovely St Olaf's is the smallest church in England. It can be found among the yew trees, along a footpath opposite the Wasdale Head Inn.

AMUSING THE KIDS

There are no on-site facilities for children, and unless they enjoy walking, there is little else to do. You can launch canoes from further down Wastwater, although only a certain number are allowed on the lake at a time. Further afield, there's the Ravenglass & Eskdale Railway steam train (*see p193*), which runs for seven miles between Eskdale and Ravenglass on the coast.

CAMPING NEARBY

The nearest option is a camping field opposite the Wasdale Head Inn, run by the Barn Door Shop (www.barndoorshop.co.uk) – itself a useful spot if you need any outdoor equipment. It's very basic, but

Site specific

✔ The tranquil and sheltered woodland location is in stunning surroundings, with unrivalled access to the Lake District's high fells.

✘ If you're not a walker or climber, there's little else to do in the area.

very cheap: just £2.50 per person. Barbecues and open fires are not allowed. You can't book in advance – just pay in the shop on arrival, or the next morning.

In Nether Wasdale, Church Stile Farm Holiday Park (01946 726252, www.churchstile.com, open Apr-Nov, £14 for two adults plus £2 car) has a large, level camping field surrounded by woodland, with modern facilities and a children's playground.

The Old Post Office Campsite (01946 726286, www.theoldpostofficecampsite.co.uk, open Mar-Oct), is seven miles away in Santon Bridge. Bordered by the River Irt, it's a delightfully pretty place, and the proximity of the village pub is a bonus. A pitch for two adults with a standard size tent costs £14.

LAKE DISTRICT

Side Farm

Side Farm
Patterdale, Penrith, Cumbria CA11 0NL
01768 482337
andrea@sidefarm.fsnet.co.uk
www.lakedistrictcamping.co.uk/campsites/
northeast/side_farm.htm
Map p27 ㊙
OS map NY394160

Side Farm campsite is situated directly below
the steep side of Place Fell, next to the southern
shore of Ullswater, one of the Lake District's
most glorious lakes. From Patterdale village,
follow the bumpy farm road past the school and
over a little bridge to the farm. After booking in
at the tea room (if it's closed, ring the bell at
the farmhouse), follow an even more pot-holed,
rocky track to the campsite entrance.

Here you'll find a well-tended field with stunning
views over the chilly waters and the surrounding
fells. There are flat pitches by the shore, but
you'll need to arrive early to nab one, especially
at weekends. The rest of the field is on a slope;
there are no marked pitches, so campers tend
to spread randomly across the hillside. The lower

Number of pitches 70 tents/motorhomes.
No caravans.
Open Easter-Oct.
Booking No booking.
Typical cost £8 adult, £3 child, £2 vehicle.
Facilities Laundry facilities; showers (free);
tea room; toilets; washing-up area.
Campfires Not allowed.
Dogs Allowed, on lead.
Restrictions Single-sex and large groups
by arrangement. No entry 10.30pm-7am.
Getting there By road Patterdale is on the
A592, about 12 miles north of Windermere
and 14 miles south of Penrith. Turn right
in the village between the school and the
church and head over the bridge; Side Farm
is signposted. **By public transport** Train to
Penrith, from where Stagecoach bus 108
(0871 200 2233, www.stagecoachbus.com)
runs 4 times a day to Patterdale. It takes
about 45 mins. From Windermere, the 517
bus runs daily July, Aug, at weekends and
public holidays Apr-June, Sept-Oct.

section is partly shielded from the lake by trees, so if you want an unimpeded view head to the far end. Note that the ground is more steeply angled here and you may struggle to manoeuvre your car, especially if the site is full.

The facilities, like the prices, are modest. The basic but adequate stone-built toilet block by the entrance has four free showers, with ample hot water (they're the sort that operate in bursts, at the press of a button). There's also a washing-up area and a laundry room, with a coin-operated washing machine and dryers.

For the most part, the site attracts families, young couples and walkers. In the daytime, you can wander up to the tea room to sample the owner's superb fruit flapjacks and ginger cake, or sit and daydream by Ullswater's pebbly shore, watching the green- and white-painted steamers sailing to and fro. This being the Lake District, there are also plenty of opportunities to get active: messing about on the water in canoes, pony-trekking across the windswept fells and, above all, walking – from leisurely lakeside strolls to serious, day-long treks.

As the sun slowly disappears behind Glenridding Dodd, and a pan of hot chocolate bubbles away on the camping stove, sit back and tune into the site's atmosphere of quiet contentment – before planning the next day's adventures.

EATING & DRINKING

For tea and cakes, look no further than Side Farm's tea room, five minutes' walk from the camping field.

Patterdale's Village Store (017684 82220, www.patterdalevillagestore.co.uk), around 15 minutes

on foot, crams an impressive array of goods into its modest premises, from bacon or sausage sarnies and fresh bread to beer, wine and barbecue supplies. It's also the post office. At the White Lion Inn (017684 82214), cheery staff serve well-kept ales and simple, filling food, geared towards hungry walkers. The Place Fell Inn (0845 305 2111, www.patterdale hotel.co.uk) has a pleasant beer garden.

Just over a mile away, Glenridding is home to several food shops and half a dozen eating places. Fellbites Café & Restaurant (017684 82781, www.fellbites.co.uk) offers lunchtime snacks and an inviting evening menu, with hearty crowd-pleasers (lamb shanks and mash, say, with sticky toffee pudding to follow). For coffee, cakes and panini, there's Greystones Coffee House (017684 82392, www.greystonesgallery.co.uk), which doubles as a contemporary art gallery.

At the Inn on the Lake (017684 82444, www.lake districthotels.net/innonthelake) – magnificently set on the edge of Ullswater, with lawns leading down to the lake – you can choose between the formal restaurant and more casual ramblers' bar, where steak and stout pie or local cumberland sausage head the menu. There's a playground too.

ATTRACTIONS & ACTIVITIES

The campsite has direct access to the lake, so campers are welcome to bring canoes and boats (vehicles can't drive to the water's edge, though, so it's smaller craft only). If you haven't got your own boat, don't worry; there are plenty of places to hire one. St Patrick's Boat Landing (01768 482393, www.stpatricksboatlandings.co.uk) rents motorboats, rowing boats and bicycles, while Glenridding Sailing

Site specific

✔ The uplifting lakeside location and views, and wonderfully sustaining own-made cakes.

✘ The majority of pitches are on a slope and the ground is quite stony; expect some bent tent pegs. Facilities are basic, and the staff aren't always available.

LAKE DISTRICT

Centre (017684 82541, www.glenriddingsailing centre.co.uk) has sailing boats, canoes and kayaks, and can arrange lessons and weekend courses. Alternatively, take a cruise to Howtown or Pooley Bridge from Glenridding on one of the little steamers (017684 82229, www.ullswater-steamers.co.uk).

You can also fish for brown trout and perch – get a rod licence at the tourist office in Glenridding.

As for walking, there are no end of options. At the top of the campsite, cross the ladder stile to reach a wonderfully scenic lakeside path. Directly behind Side Farm is Place Fell (2,155 feet); you can reach the top in around 90 minutes. The route is steep and rocky in parts, and reaching the summit feels like a real achievement – the vistas are magnificent. Another steep route leads to the Boredale Hause crossroads and on to Angle Tarn Pikes (1,860 feet) and Angle Tarn itself, an idyllic spot with views to Helvellyn, Brothers Water, Kirkstone Pass and Dovedale. And it's a relatively easy two-hour hike to the spectacular waterfalls at Aira Force.

For something completely different, drive 11 miles to the top of Ullswater and beyond to find Dalemain House (01768 486450, www.dalemain.com, closed Fri, Sat, all Nov-Mar). Behind its stately Georgian facade the interiors are a historical hotch-potch, mixing medieval and Tudor elements with opulent

18th-century additions. Outside, the old-fashioned Rose Walk is in full scented bloom in June and July.

AMUSING THE KIDS

Children can spend a happy afternoon pootling about by the lake and paddling in the shallows (it's rocky terrain, so best wear water shoes). Bring – or hire – bicycles or canoes, and a world of possibilities awaits.

Sockbridge Pony Trekking Centre (01768 863468) and Park Foot Trekking Centre (01768 486696, www.parkfootponytrekking.co.uk), both around half an hour's drive away, provide horse and pony rides for all ages and abilities. In Troutbeck, seven miles from Patterdale, Rookin House (01768 483561, www.rookinhouse.co.uk) also offers horse riding, along with indoor go-karting and archery.

CAMPING NEARBY

The closest alternative is Gillside Farm (01768 482346, www.gillsidecaravanandcampingsite.co.uk, open Mar-Nov), just outside Glenridding. It has lovely views, simple facilities and a welcoming atmosphere. A tent and two adults costs £14. Near Hartsop and Brothers Water, Sykeside (01768 482239, www. sykeside.co.uk, open all year, tent £7 plus £5 per adult in high season) has a perfectly flat camping field, set against a gorgeous backdrop of hills.

Wales

Cae Du, Snowdonia, p247.

Three Cliffs Bay

Three Cliffs Bay Holiday Park
North Hills Farm, Penmaen, Gower,
Swansea SA3 2HB
01792 371218
info@threecliffsbay.com
www.threecliffsbay.com
Map p28 **❶**
OS map SS534886

Number of pitches 75 tents, 20 caravans/
motorhomes.
Open Apr-Oct.
Booking By phone. Essential. Minimum stay
2 nights weekends, 3 nights bank holidays.
Typical cost Tent £13 1 person, £20
2 people, £20 4 people. Caravan/
motorhome £23 up to 2 adults, 2 children.
Facilities Disabled facilities (toilet and
shower); electric hook-ups (35); laundry
facilities; shop; showers (30p); toilets;
washing-up area.
Campfires Not allowed.
Dogs Allowed, on lead.
Restrictions No single-sex groups.
Getting there By road From Swansea take
the A4118 west towards the Gower. Turn left
on to North Hills Lane just before Penmaen;
it's a few hundred yards to the campsite,
which is clearly signposted. Motorhome
and caravan owners should note that the
lane is very narrow. **By public transport**
Train to Swansea. Gower Explorer bus 118
to Rhossilli runs every couple of hours,
stopping on the A4118 at the top of the
lane to the campsite. The journey takes
about 30 mins. More information on
www.visitswanseabay.com.

Three Cliffs Bay and its campsite have been
swamped with accolades in recent years, including
'Number one view from a campsite in the world'.
There is a certain amount of hyperbole to all
this, but it is undoubtedly a beautiful view and a
beautiful beach – and if you snag the right pitch,
you'll enjoy a breathtaking vista across the bay
as you unzip your tent door each morning.

That said, most of the pitches with the best
views are on a serious gradient, so you may also
have spent the night rolling downhill in your sleep
(the caravan and motorhome pitches are on level
ground in a separate field). Campers flock to stay
here regardless of their angle of repose, though,
thanks to the site's stellar location – and if you're

willing to sacrifice the spectacular sea views,
there are level pitches in a third overflow field.
This is also the best spot in inclement weather,
as hedgerows provide a modicum of shelter.

The site's facilities are excellent and well
maintained, but the real draw is the proximity to
Three Cliffs Bay. Surveyed from the clifftop, it's
an idyllic scene: an impressively craggy headland,
rolling blue waves and a vast, golden beach. Set
back from the beach is a meandering stream,
forded with stepping stones; adding to the air of
enchantment, a ruined castle overlooks the bay.

From the campsite, it's a ten-minute walk to
the beach down a steep, rocky footpath – which
can be tricky to negotiate if you're carrying a
stack of beach paraphernalia (and a long slog
back up at the end of the day). Once you reach
sea level, though, all will be forgiven.

Be cautious in the water, as there is a strong
undertow and powerful rip currents at high tide.
The limestone cliffs in the middle of the beach
that give the bay its name are popular with
climbers. At low tide you can walk west around
the cliffs to Oxwich Bay, another sheltered,
sweeping curve of sand, backed by dunes
and woodland. The water here is shallow and
calm, but watch out for boats and jet-skiers
around the slipway.

Another footpath leads from the campsite
to the hamlet of Parkmill, about a mile to the
east – a diminutive spot with, usefully, a pub,
restaurant, general store and café.

In summer, Three Cliffs Bay, the campsite and
the local access roads become extremely busy.
To see the place at its best, and most tranquil,
visit in spring or autumn.

EATING & DRINKING

The on-site farm shop sells milk, groceries and
fresh bread, along with ice-creams, own-made cakes,
disposable barbecues and beach gear.

Site specific

✔ The stunning panoramic view and easy
access to one of Wales' loveliest beaches.

✘ The sloping pitches: they really do
spoil an otherwise faultlessly located
campsite. The footpath to the beach is
also troublesome – the youthful and nimble-
footed won't mind it, but families with lots of
beach clobber may not enjoy negotiating it.

GOWER

In Parkmill, the child-friendly Gower Inn (01792 233116) offers a wide range of bar meals – they're chain-pub in style, but tasty and filling. If you don't fancy pub fare, the ever-busy, daytime-only Shepherd's Store (01792 371228) has a coffee shop and café, along with a decent deli, an off-licence and ice-creams for the kids. The tea room at the Gower Heritage Centre also has a solid, dependable menu, kicking off the day with bacon sarnies and cooked breakfasts before moving on to home-made chilli, paninis and plates of ham, egg and chips.

The village's smartest offering, though is Maes yr Haf (0845 085 0610, http://maes-yr-haf.com). At lunchtime, sample the good-value set menu. Come evening, splash out on carefully sourced and beautifully cooked mains, such as pan-fried organic sewin with wild fennel bisque, or rack of salt-marsh lamb with minted peas.

Mumbles, overlooking Swansea Bay and 20 minutes by car, has some decent pubs and restaurants. At the end of the promenade, Verdi's (01792 369135, http://verdis-cafe.co.uk) is an institution. Pizza and pasta are on the menu, but most customers are here to take in the views and deliberate over the enormous array of own-made Italian gelati. Also on the seafront, Patrick's (01792 360199, www.patricks withrooms.com, closed dinner Sun) offers polished cooking in smart, airy surroundings; steamed local mussels with taffy apple cider to start, say, followed by chicken with chilli baby coriander butter.

ATTRACTIONS & ACTIVITIES

Outdoor options on the Gower are almost unlimited, with sailing, waterskiing, kite-surfing, stand-up paddle surfing and windsurfing all available in nearby Oxwich Bay.

There's also some great walking in the area, either along the Pembrokeshire Coast Path (www.visit pembrokeshire.com) or inland along the spine of Cefn Bryn (also good for mountain bikers). This is the highest point on the Gower Peninsula, and on a clear day the superb, 360-degree panorama encompasses the Black Mountains and, across the Bristol Channel, the coasts of Devon and Somerset.

Mumbles is a good option for lazier days. You can fritter away your change in the pier's amusement arcade, meander around the shops and, if you feel a burst of energy, climb the hill to survey the sea views. The remains of 12th-century Oystermouth Castle dominate the skyline; during the summer, it provides an atmospheric backdrop for open-air Shakespeare performances.

AMUSING THE KIDS

Paddling, sandcastle-building and investigating the caves and rock pools around Three Cliffs Bay will keep most children occupied indefinitely.

In Parkmill, the Gower Heritage Centre (01792 371206, www.gowerheritagecentre.co.uk) is a good option whatever the weather. Its attractions include a puppet theatre, adventure play areas and an animal enclosure; look out for themed special events such as medieval fun days and music festivals. The restored 12th-century corn mill and La Charrette, the smallest cinema in Wales, will be of more interest to adults.

CAMPING NEARBY

Oxwich Camping Park (01792 390777, http://oxwich campingpark.hotels.officelive.com/default.aspx, open mid Apr-early Sept, £16 for two adults) is fuss-free and relaxed, and within easy walking distance of Oxwich Beach. It's relatively basic, but well organised and peaceful; children enjoy the small on-site swimming pool.

Hillend Camping Park (*see right*) is about nine miles away at Rhossili Beach.

Hillend

Hillend Camping Park
Llangennith, Gower, Swansea SA3 1JD
01792 386204
Map p28 ❷
OS map SS419910

Hillend keeps its number one attraction well hidden from view – it's only when you've clambered over the sand dunes in front of the site's three flat, grassy fields that you encounter the magnificent three-mile arc of golden sand and blue-green surf that is Rhossili Bay.

Few beaches in Britain can compare with this. Located at the westernmost edge of the Gower peninsula, it's a stunning sight whatever the weather. If you're into surfing or sunbathing in a cheerful, bustling environment, you'll love Hillend with its mix of families, wannabe surfers and the occasional 'real' waverider toting surfboards, boogie boards and wetsuits in an endless procession to and from the waves. A huge expanse of sand opens up at low tide, perfect for kite-flying and sandcastle-building. The stiff breezes also attract hang-gliders and paragliders. It isn't a great swimming beach, however: the undertow can be dangerous.

The owners ensure that the site's three fields (four when it's busy) are organised to accommodate like-minded individuals, which

Number of pitches 300 tents/motorhomes. No caravans.
Open Apr-Oct.
Booking No booking.
Typical cost Up to 3 adults or 2 adults, 3 under-16s £12-£18 Mon-Thur, Sun; £15-£22.50 Fri, Sat. Extra person £3-£5.
Facilities Disabled facilities (toilet and shower); laundry facilities; play area; restaurant; shop; showers (free); toilets; washing-up area.
Campfires Not allowed.
Dogs Not allowed.
Restrictions Groups and unsupervised under-18s by arrangement.
Getting there By road Take the B4295 or B4271 to Llanrhidian, then follow signs to Llangennith (about 5 miles). The turn to the campsite is on the left at the end of the village; motorhome owners should note that the road is very narrow in places. **By public transport** Train to Swansea. Catch Gower Explorer bus 116 to Llanrhidian (30 mins) and then the 115 to Llangennith (15 mins), from where it's just under a mile to the site. Buses are infrequent. More information on www.visitswanseabay.com.

means younger groups camp in the first field, while families and those looking for a little less action are offered the second and third fields, the latter being the quietest. However, the term 'quiet' is relative (though rowdy campers do get kicked off). Hillend is an extremely popular site and as you can't book, you have to be here early to ensure a pitch in high season: 'We're usually full by 3pm on a Friday afternoon in summer,' warns the warden.

The section of beach at the northern end of Rhossili Bay has been at the heart of the Gower surf scene for decades, with former European surfing champion Pete Jones running one of Wales' oldest established surf shops (PJ's) in Llangennith village. For visiting surfers this is probably the most popular beach in Wales, as the number of campervans and board-bedecked cars parked on the road above will testify.

The campsite is well equipped for the surfers it attracts: the clean, modern shower and toilet blocks mean you can freshen up in comfort after a day in the surf; there are outside showers where you can rinse your 'wettie'; and Eddy's Coffee Shop & Bistro is a good spot to re-energise and take in the views in between surf sessions. It's a shame about the large static caravan site next door, which is far from friendly on the eye.

The dunes provide a certain amount of shelter from the elements if the weather turns foul, though you can expect a thorough blasting from wind, rain and sand if a full-on gale hits. Shipwrecks were common here, thanks to the Atlantic swells and fierce storms that can batter the coast; the remains of the *Helvetia*, which ran aground in 1887, are visible at the southern end of the beach at low tide.

EATING & DRINKING

On-site Eddy's Coffee Shop & Bistro (01792 386606) is an attractive, airy café with a large outside deck, lovely views and a pretty decent menu. It's worth knowing it can also host private functions, from kids' birthday parties to wedding receptions. However, it closes early (around 8.30pm) and has much reduced opening times outside peak season, so for evening dining and/or beer, the obvious option is the King's Head pub (01792 386212, www.kingsheadgower.co.uk) in Llangennith. You'll find great home-cooked food, a decent range of beers, a sunny terrace and allegedly the largest collection of malt whiskies in any pub outside Scotland.

ATTRACTIONS & ACTIVITIES

Watersports are the big draw, of course, and surfing in particular. The Welsh Surfing Federation (01792 386426, www.wsfsurfschool.co.uk, closed Nov-Mar, and Mon-Fri during term-time) runs a surf school at the campsite. You can hire all the required gear.

This is also prime walking territory. At the very least, you should make the round trip along the beach to the southern end, where the village of Rhossili looms above the headland, and return via Rhossili Down (or vice versa). Note that it's a seriously steep slog to the summit, more than 600 feet above the beach, but the views of the bay, the curving spit of land known as Worm's Head, and across the water to St Govan's Head in Pembrokeshire and the coast of north Devon are sensational. There's a National Trust shop and visitor centre in Rhossili.

If the weather closes in, there's not that much to do locally, but the half-hour drive to Swansea is worth it for a visit to the National Waterfront Museum (01792 638950, www.museumwales.ac.uk/en/swansea). Housed in a listed waterfront warehouse linked to a new, ultra-modern slate and glass building, it has informative displays about Swansea's surprisingly rich maritime and industrial heritage. Many are interactive and will appeal to youngsters.

AMUSING THE KIDS

Children will find endless amusement on the beach. You could also head to Mumbles, 16 miles away, for its famous ice-cream parlours – Joe's, and Verdi's – on the seafront walk known as the 'Mumbles Mile'. When the ice-cream is finished, they can spend their pocket money at the various amusement arcades on Mumbles Pier.

CAMPING NEARBY

Llanmadoc (01792 386202, www.gowercampsite. co.uk, open May-Oct) has space for around 250 tents and 50 caravans or motorhomes in a fantastic location next to the huge sandy beaches of Broughton Bay and Whiteford Sands, at the very top of the Gower peninsula. On the downside, facilities are on the basic side, the tent fields aren't very flat and you could find a cheaper place to stay.

GOWER

Site specific

✔ You couldn't get any closer to the sand and the surf, and the facilities are good. The views from the hill above the campsite are superb.

✘ It can get very busy and you can't book, so there's no guarantee of a pitch. However, if you do call to check availability, the owners are good at getting back to you.

Trefalen Farm

Trefalen Farm
Bosherston, near Pembroke,
Pembrokeshire SA71 5DR
01646 661643
trefalenfarm@yahoo.co.uk
Map p28 ❸
OS map SR966945

PEMBROKESHIRE

Number of pitches Approx 40 tents, 15 campervan/motorhomes.
Open All year.
Booking By phone, email. Essential summer.
Typical cost Tent £5 adult, £2.50 child. Campervan £12 1-2 people, motorhome £14 1-2 people, £5 extra adult, £2.50 extra child.
Facilities Toilets; washing-up area. No showers.
Campfires Allowed, off ground; must be put out at 11pm.
Dogs Allowed.
Restrictions No single-sex groups or unsupervised under-16s.
Getting there By road From Pembroke take the B4319 south. After about 3.5 miles, turn left; go through Bosherston and follow signs to Broad Haven. The campsite is on the right after a mile. **By public transport** Train to Pembroke, from where the Coastal Cruiser bus 387 runs three times a day. It takes about an hour to Broad Haven beach car park, next to the campsite. More information on www.pembrokeshire.gov.uk.

Pembrokeshire has a wealth of beaches and few are lovelier than the clean, sandy cove and limpid blue waters of Broad Haven South. Seawards lie impressive sea cliffs and the solitary spire of Church Rock, thrusting above the breakers; inland, dunes slope down to the Bosherston Lily Ponds, home to otter, heron and kingfisher. Part of a tranquil nature reserve, the clear, still ponds are covered with lilies in late spring and summer. It's a stunning setting – and all within a couple of minutes' walk of Trefalen Farm.

Trefalen is a very basic campsite, and the owners are happy to keep it that way. One small but clean toilet block, drinking-water taps and washing-up sinks are all you get in the way of facilities, and there is no hot water or showers. Byt there is a phone-charging point and ice packs are available. The best pitches on the site's fields offer views out to sea; if the weather takes a turn for the worse, though, there's little shelter.

The location and relative solitude are the main draws; visit on a warm, sunny weekday in mid June, and there probably won't be more than a half-dozen other campers. It does get busy at the height of the season and on bank holidays, so you won't always get it all to yourself.

The limestone cliffs on either side of the bay provide some of the finest sea cliff climbing in Europe (they're south-facing, so are warmed by the sun even in winter). Half a mile to the west, tiny and enigmatic 13th-century St Govan's Chapel is perched amid the rocks at the base of the cliffs. (According to legend, it's impossible to count the roughly hewn steps leading to the chapel; each time you try, you'll get a different total.) These days, the chapel is surrounded by land owned by the Ministry of Defence, so check path opening times before setting off.

Children can surf, swim and bodyboard on the beach, while outdoor types can rock climb, hit Wales' best surf spot (nearby Freshwater West) or paddle around the coast in a sea kayak. Meanwhile, visitors wanting to relax and let life drift by can bask on the beach and stroll around the lily ponds, before popping into nearby St Govan's Inn for an afternoon pint.

EATING & DRINKING

It's a one-mile walk, cycle or drive to the two nearest places to eat, both in the village of Bosherston. Family-friendly St Govan's Inn (01646 661311, www.stgovanscountryinn.webeden.co.uk) serves excellent home-cooking, with fresh fish, cawl (a traditional Welsh stew), Sunday roasts and delicious puddings, as well as a decent selection of guest ales. It's not open every day in winter. Next door is the Olde World Café (01646 661216, closed Oct-Apr), long a popular stop with climbers, who know a thing or two about where to get good tea and cakes. The owner, 'Ma' Weston, recently received an MBE after 70 years' service at the café. Bosherton also has a shop, although for a decent range of supplies you'll need to drive six miles to Pembroke.

Three miles away, in Stackpole Quay, you can get a light lunch or cream tea at the Boathouse Tearoom (01646 672687, closed Mon-Fri Oct-Easter).

Tenby is less than 30 minutes by car, with an assortment of cafés, restaurants, pubs and shops to make the journey worthwhile.

ATTRACTIONS & ACTIVITIES

Here's a tip – you may well head to Broad Haven South toting all your surf paraphernalia, but

Tenby

Church Rock

St Govan's Chapel

PEMBROKESHIRE

the waves are almost always better a few miles along the coast at Freshwater West.

The Pembrokeshire Coast Path (www.visit pembrokeshire.com) passes the campsite – look out for the acorn sign on posts. It's a three-mile walk east to the tiny harbour at Stackpole Quay, past the inviting turquoise waters and soft, pale sands of Barafundle Bay. In the other direction, towards Castlemartin, lies a Ministry of Defence firing range, so you'll need to check access in advance (type 'Castlemartin firing notice' into the search box on www.mod.uk for a schedule). Castlemartin is also a spectacular place to try sea-cliff climbing. Contact a local outfit such as Tenby-based Alun Richardson's climbing school (07749970612, www.alunrichardson. co.uk) if you're new to the sport and need lessons.

Site specific

✔ This is back-to-basics camping in a superb location, with easy access to glorious beaches, sea cliffs and inland walks.

✘ If you like plenty of facilities, this is not for you. The MoD's firing range at nearby Castlemartin can be a noisy irritation too, with the sound of tank fire, machine guns and helicopters.

Tenby is an elegant if slightly faded Victorian seaside resort. With its pastel-painted Georgian houses, maze of narrow streets and handsome harbour, it's a delight to stroll around; what's more, there are three Blue Flag beaches. Boats run from Tenby to Caldey Island (01834 844453, www.caldey-island.co.uk, closed Nov-Easter), home to a thriving Cistercian monastery and a ruined medieval priory.

AMUSING THE KIDS

Eleventh-century Pembroke Castle (01646 684585, www.pembroke-castle.co.uk), perched above two tidal inlets, certainly looks the part, with massive crenellated walls interspersed by round towers. There are falconry displays, Civil War re-enactments and other special events throughout the summer.

For something more modern, Oakwood Theme Park (01834 891376, www.oakwoodthemepark.co.uk, closed Nov-Mar) has all manner of activities and rides.Don't miss Megafobia: a fast and furious wooden rollercoaster, which speeds its way around a fearsome tangle of tracks.

CAMPING NEARBY

Just south of Pembroke, Windmill Hill Caravan Park (01646 682392, www.windmillhillcaravanpark.co.uk, two-man £10 £3.50, caravan £11.50) is a spacious, family-run site with good facilities, set by a working dairy farm. It's open year-round.

Pembroke Castle

Newgale

Newgale Beach

Newgale Camping Site
Wood Farm, Newgale,
Pembrokeshire SA62 6AR
01437 710253
enquiries@newgalecampingsite.co.uk
www.newgalecampingsite.co.uk
Map p28 ❹
OS map SM855220

Number of pitches 120 tents/motorhomes.
No caravans.
Open Fri before Easter-Sept.
Booking No bookings.
Typical cost £5 per person.
Facilities Disabled facilities (toilet
and shower); showers (50p); toilets;
washing-up area.
Campfires Not allowed.
Dogs Not allowed.
Restrictions No single-sex groups,
other groups by arrangement. No noise
after midnight.
Getting there By road Take the A487
from Haverfordwest towards St Davids;
Newgale Beach is adjacent to the road,
after about 9 miles. **By public transport**
Train to Haverfordwest. Bus 411 (Richard
Bros, 01239 613756, www.gobybus.net)
runs approximately every hour and takes
25 mins to Newgale.

It's a balmy summer morning and you're camping
at Newgale. Unzip your tent, slip into your
swimming gear, and 30 seconds later you can
be neck deep in the Atlantic, enjoying a wake up
call like no other. The campsite certainly couldn't
get much closer to the waves; you just have to
cross the A487 coast road (take care, it can be
busy) to get to the beach, and during particularly
fierce storms, the sea has been known to invade
the tent fields.

The simple, grassy camping area has a relaxed
feel even when it's thronged with visitors – which
it almost always is in summer, thanks to the
terrific location. There are no marked pitches
and no advance bookings, so you turn up and
take your chances – something of a gamble on
glorious weekends. After paying your dues at
the owner's caravan, simply choose a spot. Most
of the site is perfectly flat, aside from a small
hill at the southern end. Opting for the sloping
terrain does have its benefits: the views are
better, and you'll avoid waking up in a puddle
if it rains heavily. The closer you are to the road,
the noisier it is, of course.

The simple but adequate facilities are kept
in pristine condition, and the wardens are cheery
and obliging. Indeed, the entire site exudes
a welcoming, friendly feel, with tents and
motorhomes aflutter with colourful flags and
banners, children punting balls and flying kites,
and a steady procession of surfers marching
to and from the beach, bearing their boards.

If you like waves and water, you could hardly be in a better spot. Backed by a steep pebble bank, the Blue Flag-winning sands of Newgale Beach are perfect for sandcastle-building, lounging or engaging in more active pursuits; this is one of the best beginner's surf spots in Wales. The two-mile long beach is patrolled by lifeguards in summer; children, in particular, should swim and surf between the red and yellow flags, which means they'll be under constant surveillance.

If the surf isn't co-operating, the marvellous Pembrokeshire Coast Path (www.visitpembroke shire.com) is on the site's doorstep. It runs for 186 miles from St Dogmaels in the north to Amroth in the south, past a variety of landscapes. There are lighthouses and prehistoric forts to explore, and a wealth of birds, plus grey seals and other maritime wildlife, to be spotted. Even if you have no intention of walking any great length along it, it's worth tackling the short, steep clamber to the top of the hill at the northern end of the beach for sensational views along the golden sands.

Although Newgale attracts a young and sporty crowd, it's also very family-oriented. Single-sex groups are not welcomed, as the owners like to have everything calm and quiet by midnight – which means keeping the noise down as you wander back from the pub, which is all of 50 yards from the site.

EATING & DRINKING

On-site facilities are limited to a burger van, but there's a shop selling basic groceries next door. A few hundred yards north, Sands Café (01437 729222) serves basic – albeit not terribly inspiring – café food throughout the day. The Duke of Edinburgh pub (01437 720586) is also next to the site, and serves bar meals. Slightly lacking in atmosphere, it has a large-screen TV and a depressing array of fruit machines.

Four miles to the south, the Druidstone Inn (01437 781221, www.druidstone.co.uk) is an eclectic establishment perched on the cliffs above Druidstone Beach. It has sensational views, a funky little bar, regular themed 'feast nights' and occasional live

entertainment; it's also quite child-friendly. Another good bet is the Ship Inn (01437 721247) in the village of Solva, five miles in the other direction. A cosy pub, it has excellent beer and a fine curry house out back, manned by Bangladeshi cooks and staff. Solva is also home to the Old Pharmacy (01437 720005, www.theoldpharmacy.co.uk,closed dinner Jan-mid Feb, closed lunch Nov-Mar), a convivial, low-key place with a sun-dappled riverside garden. Local produce takes pride of place on the menu; bouillabaisse with olive bread is a house speciality.

Slightly further afield, the pint-sized cathedral city of St Davids caters to a steady steam of visitors with traditional tea rooms, independent cafés and a decent assortment of restaurants (*see p214*). The daytime-only Refectory at the Cathedral (01437 721760, www.stdavidscathedral.org.uk) occupies a beautifully converted medieval hall, with an airy mezzanine level and sleek, stripped-down decor. The menu offers soups and superior sarnies, along with daily-changing specials: cottage pie made from local beef and Welsh ale, perhaps, or a slice of sumptuous quiche.

ATTRACTIONS & ACTIVITIES

Nolton Stables (01437 710360, www.noltonstables. co.uk) can arrange a gallop along the beach at Druidstone Haven – or, at high tide, a ride though a 35-acre private valley, criss-crossed with trails. Based in the village of Nolton, it's just over three miles from the campsite.

It's also well worth taking a day away from the beach to visit one of Pembrokeshire's islands. Skomer is one of only three Marine Nature Reserves in the UK, and is home to the world's largest population of manx shearwaters – peculiar little birds that nest in underground burrows. You can take a boat to the island (Apr-Sept) from Martin's Haven, 15 miles away (01646 603110, www.pembrokeshire-islands.co.uk).

AMUSING THE KIDS

Newgale Beach is patrolled by lifeguards; next to the campsite, Newsurf Surf Shop (01437 721398, www.newsurf.co.uk) can rent or sell wetsuits, boogie boards, surfboards and kayaks as well as providing surfing, windsurfing and kite-surfing lessons. Note that you do have to cross the relatively busy A487 to reach the beach, so children should be supervised.

There aren't very many indoor attractions in these parts, although the new leisure centre in Haverfordwest (St Thomas Green, 01437 776676, www.pembrokeshire.gov.uk/leisure), about eight miles inland, has a 25-metre swimming pool, toddlers' pool and, for the grown-ups, a sauna and steam room.

CAMPING NEARBY

Newgale Farm Campsite (01437 721505, open Easter-Sept) is half a mile away up the hill on the A487 to St Davids, and charges £5 per person. Facilities are very basic (no hot showers), as you would expect at that price, but the views across St Brides Bay are stunning. On the other hand, beach access is not that good.

Site specific

✔ The proximity to sea, sand and surf. There's also a great buzz on the site – if you want to meet fellow wave riders this is a great place to be, especially if you're a beginner.

✘ The site is exposed to any gales that blow in from the sea, and becomes waterlogged after heavy rain. The main road passes the site, so certain pitches can be a bit noisy.

PEMBROKESHIRE

Caerfai Farm

Caerfai Farm Campsite
St Davids, Pembrokeshire SA62 6QT
01437 720548
chrismevans69@hotmail.com
www.cawscaerfai.co.uk
Map p28 ❺
OS map SM758243

Number of pitches 70 tents/campervans
(90 Aug). No caravans/motorhomes.
Open Late May-late Sept.
Booking By phone. Advisable; essential
school holidays. Minimum 7 nights
school holidays.
Typical cost £7 adult, £3.50 child.
Facilities Electric hook-ups (6); laundry
facilities; shop; showers (free); toilets;
washing-up area.
Campfires Not allowed.
Dogs Allowed, on lead (£3).
Restrictions No large groups.
Getting there By road Take the A487 from
Haverfordwest to St Davids. Turn left at
the Oriel y Parc/St Davids visitor centre
just before the town, following signs for
Caerfai. Follow the road for three-quarters
of a mile until you reach the farm office,
with a red phone box on the left. **By public
transport** Train to Haverfordwest. From
there, bus 411 (Richard Bros, 01239
613756, www.gobybus.net) runs approx
every hour and takes 45 mins to its terminus
at St Davids New Street. Follow the road
directions above from the visitor centre.

St Brides Bay

A few years ago a national newspaper dubbed
Caerfai Bay one of the '100 Best Beaches in
the World'. Hyperbole, perhaps. But there's no
doubting that when the sun is shining, Caerfai
Bay is a stunning location by anyone's standards,
with deep purple cliffs plunging down to golden
sands and jade-green waters ideal for swimming.

And Caerfai Farm Campsite is just a minute's
walk from all this magnificence. Its panoramic
clifftop location has views across the huge sweep
of St Brides Bay, and the Pembrokeshire Coast
Path runs along the edge the site. There are
three fields (four in August), all well maintained,
with water standpipes at 100-yard intervals.

The site owners will do their best to reserve
you a pitch, but can't guarantee that at busy
times. If you do get the right spot, you can unzip
your tent in the morning and gaze out across the
blue waters of the bay without having to get out of
your sleeping bag. Perfect! On the downside, the
fields have a slight slope in places and there's
very little shelter – a few trees on the right-hand
side and low stone walls dividing the fields – and
the site can receive a good old battering when an
Atlantic gale rolls ashore. In such circumstances
you really do need to ensure everything is well
secured: every summer, tents get ripped to

shreds by the elements on the Pembrokeshire coast. The bottom field nearest the beach has the best views, but is also the most exposed.

Caerfai Farm's owners are very eco-aware, and their 180-acre organic dairy farm uses various forms of renewable energy. Produce from the farm (including three kinds of cheese: cheddar, caerphilly, and caerphilly with leek and garlic) is available in the shop, which is always busy first thing in the morning.

The beach – well sheltered from the wind and something of a sun-trap – is the campsite's main attraction. The waves are rarely big enough to cause anything other than screams of delight, and the rock pooling at low tide is excellent; it's one of the best beaches in the area for families. It's small by Pembrokeshire standards, however, and can get crowded on sunny summer days, and at high tide the whole beach is submerged.

A walk along the Pembrokeshire Coast Path – which winds its way along 186 miles of some of the best coastal scenery in the country – is a good alternative to the beach. It's at its most beautiful in early summer, when the wildflower displays are sensational. You can wander into St Davids via the path in around half an hour: Britain's smallest city is a real gem, with a huge and impressive 11th-century cathedral and bishop's palace, as well as a decent selection of outdoor and surf shops, restaurants and cafés. It is also home to the Oriel y Parc gallery (01437 720392, www.orielyparc.co.uk), with works by Graham Sutherland, Picasso and Van Dyke. Attached to the gallery is a Pembrokeshire Coast National Park information centre.

EATING & DRINKING

On-site facilities are limited to the farm's small shop, selling its own organic produce and basic groceries.

Head into St Davids (ten minutes' walk along the road) for excellent coffee at Pebbles Yard (01437 720122) on Cross Square near the cathedral – it's a great spot to sit in the sun and people-watch in summer. For a relaxed meal in rustic-minimalist surroundings, there's Cwtch (01437 720491, www. cwtchrestaurant.co.uk) on the High Street. The kitchen uses plenty of locally sourced ingredients, preparing them with the minimum of fuss and

pretension, to produce nostalgic British flavours. Or, for hustle, bustle and a cheerful Italian flavour, head across the road to the Bench Bar (01437 721778, www.bench-bar.co.uk) for pizza, pasta and own-made Italian ice-cream.

Sadly, St Davids is lacking in characterful pubs – most locals head to the Farmers Arms (01437 721666, www.farmersstdavids.co.uk) on Goat Street for beer and bar meals; its main advantage is its deck overlooking the Cathedral, a good spot for catching the evening sun.

ATTRACTIONS & ACTIVITIES

The magnificent medieval cathedral and the evocative ruins of the bishop's palace (01437 720199, www.stdavidscathedral.org.uk) are St Davids' centrepiece. A visit can easily keep you occupied for a morning, and in early summer a music festival is held here, along with theatre, in the palace grounds.

Coasteering is the latest craze in outdoor activities. Supposedly 'invented' by the guys at TyF Adventure (01437 721611, www.tyf.com), it's a guide-led, wetsuit- and trainer-clad mix of scrambling, climbing, jumping and swimming around the coast. It's an activity that people of all ages can enjoy and is especially popular with families.

The islands that you can see from the campsite (the nearest is Ramsay Island) are internationally important wildlife habitats, home to everything from puffins and shearwaters onshore, to seals, whales and dolphins offshore. You may see any or all of these on a jet-boat trip with Thousand Islands Expeditions (01437 721721, www.thousandislands.co.uk, closed Nov-Mar), based at Cross Square in St Davids.

AMUSING THE KIDS

The ideal activity for children whatever the weather is surfing – after all, it doesn't matter if it's raining, they're already wet. Surf lessons can be taken at Whitesands Beach through Ma Simes Surf Hut (01437 720433, www.masimes.co.uk). It has an office on the High Street in St Davids, or you can book at the beach or by email.

CAMPING NEARBY

Two alternatives are within a few hundred yards of Caerfai Farm. Just across the road, Caerfai Bay Caravan & Tent Park (01437 720274, www. caerfaibay.co.uk, open Mar-Nov, £11-£17.50 per night for two people) has a more manicured feel and takes caravans, though the views are equally fabulous. And just up the road, but not adjacent to the sea, Glan-y-Mor Campsite (01437 721788, www.glan-y-mor.co.uk, open Apr-Sep) is slightly smaller and has a generally younger clientele. Prices are £12-£18 for two people with a tent, caravan or motorhome.

Further along the coast, Porthclais Farm Campsite (01437 720256, www.porthclais-farm-campsite. co.uk, open all year, £7 adult, £3 child) occupies five fields on the cliffs above Porthclais Habour and St Brides Bay.

Site specific

✔ The location: great sea views, a lovely beach and some of the best coastal walking in Britain on your doorstep.

✗ Both the campsite and the beach can get packed in summer. And if the weather turns nasty, you'll get a real hammering from wind and rain, even if you're in a campervan.

Ty Parke

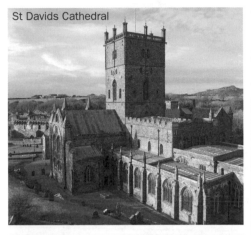

St Davids Cathedral

Strumble Head

Ty Parke
Llanreithan, Pembrokeshire SA62 5LG
01348 837384
camping@typarke.co.uk
www.typarke.co.uk
Map p28 ❻
OS map SM863286

Number of pitches 10 (10 tents
or 5 campervans or a mix). 3 yurts
(sleeping 4-6).
Open May-Sept.
Booking By phone, online. Essential.
Minimum stay 1 week school holidays.
Typical cost Camping £11 adult, £5.50
child. Yurt 3 nights weekend £225-£265;
4 nights midweek £275-£335; 1 week
£450-£540 (high season £500-£600).
Facilities Fridge-freezers; laundry facilities;
showers (free); toilets; washing-up area.
Campfires Allowed, in fireplts.
Firewood available (£2.50)
Dogs Allowed (£2.50).
Restrictions No single-sex groups
or unsupervised under-18s.
No noise after 10pm.
Getting there By road Take the A487
(St Davids to Fishguard road). About 6 miles
from St Davids, turn inland at Croes-goch
on the B4330; after about 3 miles look
out for a small slate sign for Ty Parke on
the left. The campsite is half a mile down
the dirt track. Sat-nav users, beware: you'll
end up at a farmhouse about half a mile
west of Ty Parke. **By public transport**
Train to Haverfordwest. Bus 414 to St
Davids leaves hourly until 7.45pm and
takes 45 mins. From St Davids, a taxi to
the campsite (Tony's Taxis, 01437 720931)
will cost about £18. More information on
www.pembrokeshire.gov.uk.

PEMBROKESHIRE

Observant readers will notice that there's no
street name in Ty Parke's address. Neither are
there bus services, shops, pubs or any other
modern 'amenities' around the campsite – a
compact, cosy place that sits happily with its
solitude in the heart of the north Pembrokeshire
countryside. This is not the wild, coastal
Pembrokeshire of the guidebooks, although that
is within easy reach. Ty Parke is simply a flat,
green field, surrounded by leafy hedgerows,
other equally green fields and a burgeoning

area of woodland. Since, for all its charm, the
Pembrokeshire coast can become rather hectic
in high season, the campsite provides a bucolic
escape from the beach-bound masses.

Space is what's key here. Only ten tents are
allowed at one time, so you're never going to feel
cramped. Pitches are dotted around the boundary
of the generously sized main field, so you can
spread out and relax with just the sound of the
birds and the wind for company – along with the
occasional hen and, quite probably, excitable

PEMBROKESHIRE

children, since this is a very family-oriented site. For more privacy, there are five 'hideaway' pitches – three in clearings with newly planted trees, two in their own fields – booked on a first come, first served basis.

Newly arrived are three yurts, one in a corner of the main field, two in more secluded settings (the latter will have their own compost toilets by 2012). Offering the last word in luxury, these come with wooden floors, a double bed and two single futons (duvets and bedding are provided), a table and four chairs, solar-powered lighting and a wood-burning stove. Adjacent to each is a fully equipped tented kitchen area.

Bring your wellies to explore the five-acre nature trail, and keep an eye out for wildlife. Buzzards and kestrels soar overhead, while owls and badgers venture out at dusk (there are several badger setts nearby). The site is run on eco-conscious lines; recycyling is encouraged, light bulbs are low-energy, and the barn roof sports solar panels, providing hot water for the impeccably kept showers and washing-up area.

Children can run wild here – the field is easily big enough for ball games and Frisbee-throwing. There's not even the danger of scuffed paintwork on your car, as once camping gear has been unloaded, visitors are encouraged to leave their cars in a separate parking area, which gives the site a much more pleasant look and feel.

Although the field is quite open, it is reasonably well sheltered simply by dint of being inland – unlike coastal campsites, you don't have to worry about being battered by onshore winds if the weather turns nasty. If it's sunny, the sturdy picnic tables and benches and small firepits – provided on every pitch, regardless of location – invite alfresco dining. The fires act as a focal point for long evenings spent chatting with friends and sipping wine, while the smoke helps to keep midges at bay (pack midge repellent too).

Away from Ty Parke there's plenty to explore, although you will need a car or bike to get around. For cliff jumping and coasteering enthusiasts, Abereiddi beach is a lovely three-and-a-half-mile cycle ride away. Its famous lagoon is a flooded former slate quarry, with brilliant, deep blue-green waters. From here, a 12-mile clifftop walk along the Pembrokeshire Coast Path (www.visitpembrokeshire.com) leads past Porthgain, Longhouse and Abercastle to the quiet shingle beach at Abermawr, backed with woods and marshland.

EATING & DRINKING

Other than free, freshly laid eggs, which the owners leave by the barn doorway for your breakfast omelette, no food is available on the campsite. Head to Porthgain, about four miles away on the coast, for two good options.

The harbourside Sloop Inn (01348 831449, www.sloop.co.uk) is open from breakfast to late, and serves quality beer and decent bar meals; local sausages with mash and caramelised onion gravy, say, or ribeye steak with creamed leeks and Caerfai cheese. The Shed (01348 831518, www.theshed porthgain.co.uk, call to check opening times) is a pricier affair, with lovely views over the quay. Downstairs is a wine bar, while the intimate first-floor bistro is known for its local seafood.

It's a 20-minute drive to the diminutive cathedral city of St Davids, which has a good assortment of shops, cafés and restaurants (*see p214*).

ATTRACTIONS & ACTIVITIES

You're inevitably going to end up on north Pembrokeshire's beautiful coastline, so why not explore it properly with a sea kayak trip or a coasteering adventure? Either can be organised through Preseli Venture (01348 837709, www.preseliventure.co.uk). An eco-friendly outdoor centre, based about four miles away in Mathry, it offers lessons, equipment hire and guided trips.

A little further north along the coast is spectacular Strumble Head, where the Irish Sea churns past in a vortex of blue-green eddies. You're almost guaranteed to see grey seals and possibly even dolphins, porpoises and whales from the headland or the wildlife observatory on the low cliffs. Strumble Head Lighthouse (the beam of which you'll see at night in the light- and pollution-free skies above the campsite) is also open to visitors, on occasion.

Britain's smallest city, St Davids, makes for a pleasant day trip. The city – more of a large village, if truth be told – centres on the medieval cathedral (01437 720202, www.stdavidscathedral.org.uk), with its superb choir, oak ceiling and intricately carved misericords; the refectory café is a lovely lunch spot.

AMUSING THE KIDS

Children can watch wildlife along the nature trail, meet the farm animals or make friends with the site's resident collies, Daisy and Poppy, who never tire of a game of fetch.

A good option on wet days is the Ocean Lab (01348 874737, www.pembrokeshire.gov.uk) at the seafront in Goodwick, about nine miles away. Children can 'explore' the sea through hands-on displays and activities, and there is an internet café, a soft play area and an exhibition on the history of Goodwick and its twin town, Fishguard. Look out too for the Irish Sea ferries entering and leaving port.

CAMPING NEARBY

Trellyn Woodland Camping (01348 837762, www.trellyn.co.uk, open May-Sept) at nearby Abercastle has just five tent pitches, plus a tipi, a dome and two yurts – all new – and an eco-friendly approach. Only weekly bookings are taken: a tent, two adults and one car costs £189, the tipi sleeping up to six is £385-£540.

PEMBROKESHIRE

Site specific

✔ The solitude. Since the owners strictly control the number of people camping, there's no chance of overcrowding. It's also great for families.

✘ The solitude. You need a car or bicycle to get here and should arrive equipped with groceries and other supplies, as the nearest supermarket is several miles away. There is no pub close at hand, either.

Rhydhowell Farm

Rhydhowell Farm
Boncath, Pembrokeshire SA37 0LA
01239 841267
enquiries@rhydhowellfarm.co.uk
www.rhydhowellfarm.co.uk
Map p28 ❼
OS map SN206375

Number of pitches 10 tents/caravans/
motorhomes (maximum 5 caravans/
motorhomes).
Open All year.
Booking By phone, email.
Typical cost £10 2 adults,
£5 extra adult, £2.50 extra child.
Facilities Showers (free); toilets;
washing-up area.
Campfires Allowed, in firepits.
Dogs Allowed.
Restrictions Late arrivals by arrangement.
Getting there By road From the A487
(Fishguard to Cardigan road) take the
B4332 from Eglwyswrw, or the A478 from
just outside Cardigan, turning left on to the
B4332. In Boncath village turn right after
the Boncath Inn, towards Bwichgroes. After
half a mile, turn right along a narrow lane
signposted Rhydhowell Farm. Note that
the track is rough in places. **By public
transport** Long-winded but just about
possible. Train to Carmarthen, from where
Richard Bros bus 460 or 461 (01239
613756, www.gobybus.net) takes 80 mins
to Cardigan. The service operates every
2-3 hours Mon-Sat, less frequently on Sun.
From Cardigan, bus 430 takes 25 mins
(no service Sun) to get to Boncath, from
where it's a mile on foot.

North Pembrokeshire and the Preseli Hills are
two of Wales' best-kept secrets, and Rhydhowell
Farm sits right at the heart of this green, rolling
expanse of countryside. Woodland covers almost
a third of its 72 acres, and the weathered 18th-
century stone farmhouse and outbuildings are
Grade II-listed and gloriously pretty.

The small, sheltered campsite nestles between
hedgerows and trees, where there's a constant
twitter of birdlife. Buzzards and red kites soar
high above (the name of the nearby village of
Boncath is Welsh for buzzard), and a nature
trail wends from the campsite through ancient
woodland and wildflower meadows, with evocative
names such as Cwm Rhew-erwyll (Valley of
the Frosts). You may be joined along the trail
by Sally, the farm's affable sheepdog.

Aside from the main field and peak-season
overflow meadow, there are a scattering of
smaller pitches, hidden amid the trees; the Firs
is big enough for three tents, while the romantic
Willows, set by a dew pond, takes just one.
Although there's space for more campers, friendly
owner John Quinn deliberately keeps numbers
down to preserve the site's tranquillity. There are
designated campfire areas on the main site and
at the hideaways, while campers in the overflow
field can borrow portable fire trays.

Facilities on-site and in the surrounding
area are minimal – which means visitors can
experience the peace and quiet of a part of the
countryside little changed in millennia. The past
is palpable throughout the area; Europe's oldest
living language, Welsh, is the predominant tongue
locally, and the nearby Preseli Hills are home
to standing stones and remains that date from
Neolithic times. You can walk past the site from
where Stonehenge's bluestones were quarried.

Alternatively, a short drive or bike ride along
quiet country roads will bring you to the dramatic
cliffs and blustery coast path of Pembrokeshire's
marvellous coastline.

EATING & DRINKING

There are tables and chairs in the barn; on rainy
days, campers retreat here to make tea over their
camping stoves. On Wednesdays, the Preseli Green
Dragon minibus (0845 686 0242, www.prta.co.uk –
book ahead) can call by and take you to Cardigan,
where there is a Tesco's.

Half a mile away, Boncath's post office doubles as a
well-stocked general store, while the CAMRA award-
winning Boncath Inn (01239 841241) is a splendid spot
for a pint of real ale and a plate of proper pub grub.
A few miles further, beside the river at Abercych, the
Nag's Head (01239 841200, closed Mon) is heartily
recommended by locals. Again, it has great ales and
serves excellent own-made food, including local sea
trout and steak and ale pie.

ATTRACTIONS & ACTIVITIES

Head to the Preseli Hills, where you can follow the
5,000-year-old 'Golden Road' across the spine of the
hills on foot or mountain bike, and enjoy some of
the finest views in South Wales. On a clear day, you
can see as far as Snowdonia in the north, the Gower
Peninsula to the east and Ireland's Wicklow Hills to
the west. On Sundays, the Preseli Green Dragon runs
a handy bus service to the hills, aimed at walkers.

Just outside Cilgerran village, a ten-minute drive, is the Teifi Marshes Nature Reserve (01239 621600, www.welshwildlife.org), whose freshwater marshes, reedbeds and tidal mudbanks are home to herons and otters, along with various insects and amphibians. The Welsh Wildlife Centre (a striking wood and glass building, closed Jan-Mar) has interactive displays, a café and an adventure playground. Guided canoe excursions (01239 612133, www.cardiganbay active.co.uk) also run from here; spot the brilliant blue flash of a kingfisher, hunt for otter tracks and brave the gentle – but bumpy – river rapids.

The Pembrokeshire Coast Path (www.visit pembrokeshire.com) is at its most spectacular in this corner of the county, with remarkable features such as the massive folds in the cliffs of Cemaes Head, and the churning waters of the Witches' Cauldron (where you'll find a cave, blowhole and arch). Both are accessible on an afternoon's walk from Ceibwr Bay, near the village of Moylgrove, around half an hour's drive from the farm.

The nearest large town is Cardigan, six miles to the north. Passable for a morning coffee and a brief wander, it's somewhat short on visitor interest; in the evening, however, Theatr Mwldan (01239 621200,

www.mwldan.co.uk) offers arthouse movies and an eclectic range of music, theatre and dance.

AMUSING THE KIDS

There's plenty going on around the farm. Children are warmly welcomed, and can visit the Welsh mountain ponies, help to feed the chickens and ducks, or pet the rabbits and guinea pigs. Alternatively, set them to work foraging for firewood in the woodland.

Castell Henllys (01239 891319, www.castell henllys.com), is a reconstructed Iron Age village near Eglwyswrw, about five miles away. Set amid woodland and lush river meadows, four thatched roundhouses and a granary have been built on prehistoric foundations. There's a turf-topped education centre, along with guided tours; even better, the site hosts storytelling sessions, Celtic festivals, 'living history' events and craft workshops.

CAMPING NEARBY

The campsite at Llwyngwair Manor Holiday Park (01239 820498, www.llwyngwair.co.uk, open Easter-Oct, from £15) in Newport is well located for the coast and the Preseli Hills. Facilities include a tennis court, snooker tables and a small games room.

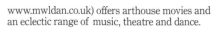

Site specific

✔ Wildlife watching is blissfully easy, even for hardened city-dwellers, thanks to the nature trail. Seeing butterflies flit by in the wildflower meadow or spotting buzzards overhead is a wonderfully relaxing way to spend an afternoon.

✘ The pitches are on a gentle incline, which won't suit all campers, and access to the site is tricky for larger vehicles and caravans. If it rains, there's little to do in the immediate vicinity.

Fforest

Fforest
Fforest Farm, Cilgerran,
Pembrokeshire SA43 2TB
01239 623633
info@coldatnight.co.uk
www.coldatnight.co.uk
Map p28 ❸
OS map SN188451

PEMBROKESHIRE

Number of pitches 8 domes (sleeping 2). 8 nomad tents (sleeping 4). 5 kåtas (sleeping 4-6). 4 crog lofts (sleeping 4). 3 bell tents (sleeping 4-5).
Open Easter-Oct (crog lofts all year). Minimum stay 3 nights; 1 week Easter and summer holidays.
Booking By phone, email, online. Essential.
Typical cost Dome £455-£530 weekend (3 nights), £680-£825 week (7 nights). Nomad tent £270-£350 weekend (3 nights), £400-£470 week (7 nights). Bell tents/kåta £335-£400 weekend (3 nights), £450-£605 week (7 nights). Prices are for two people; add £10 extra adult, £7 extra 4-15. Crog loft £450-£650 weekend (3 nights), £690-£1040 week (7 nights).
Facilities Communal lodge; pub; sauna; shop; showers (free); toilets; washing-up area; Wi-Fi (lodge).
Campfires Allowed, in firepits. Firewood available (first bundle free, then £4).
Dogs Allowed (£4).
Restrictions No unsupervised under-18s. Quiet time after 10pm.
Getting there By road The campsite is a few miles south of Cardigan. From the A478, follow the signs for the Welsh Wildlife Centre in Cilgerran. Fforest is signposted along the entrance road. **By public transport** From the rail station at Narberth, the 430 bus runs three times a day, Mon-Sat, to Cardigan (01239 613756, www.richardsbros.co.uk). Ask the driver to drop you at the turning for the Wildlife Centre at Cilgerran (journey 50 mins) – it's a half-mile walk to Fforest's entrance.

Walking through the flap of one of Fforest's 'domes', it's clear that this is no common or garden tent. It's a sleekly modern, geodesic structure, with pale wood flooring, a dapper little wood-burning stove and a custom-made double bed, complete with Welsh wool blankets and a cosy duvet. The clear plastic front looks out across the horizon-filling valley and nearby Cilgerran Castle; outside is a wooden deck and covered cooking space, with kitchen equipment, a table and chairs and a water butt.

Elsewhere on the 200-acre farm are more domes, plus kåtas (traditional Sami tipi tents), bell tents and large tunnel-shaped 'nomad' tents. Still more luxurious are the four crog lofts, housed in a converted barn. These mini cottages are beautifully appointed, with underfloor heating, slate floors, a wet room, a double bed and two bunks. All the accommodation options have an outdoor eating and cooking area.

Key to the site's friendly atmosphere, though, are its communal areas. The wooden lodge, with a gorgeous west-facing terrace, is the focal point for breakfast. It also offers sofas, tables and chairs, games, books and music. In another covered area, you can buy produce from a local farm once a week in high season; the innovative Do Lectures (www.dolectures.co.uk) are also held here in September. The shower and toilet block is in the woods above the lodge; this is also where you'll find the cedar-barrel sauna, big enough for six.

During peak season, there's also a Thursday-evening film night; if the weather doesn't allow for an outdoor screening, attendees perch on hay bales in the barn, munching popcorn. The crofter's cottage-turned-pub is another highlight. Serving local ales, ciders and a surprisingly good wine selection, its roaring fire, candlelit chandeliers and liberated church pews positively ooze good cheer.

Fforest's glorious setting – by the magnificent Teifi gorge, and next to the Teifi Marshes Nature

Reserve – means there are all sorts of activities to try. On site, you can have a go at archery, orienteering and bushcraft, and a few miles away, courses specifically for Fforest guests include climbing, white-water rafting (available in winter and after heavy rainfall, and highly recommended), canoeing and coasteering.

Around 20 minutes' drive away, adjacent to little-known Penbryn Beach, the newer Manorafon sea camp is an alternative to the main site. This has just three domes and three nomad tents, along with a handful of cabins (inherited from the previous campsite, but updated in accordance with Fforest's design sensibilities). Not as well established as the original site, it doesn't quite have the same atmosphere, but it's getting there. The camp's social hub is in place too: a sympathetically converted stable, where wonderful breakfasts of own-made bread, jams, granola and fresh fruit are served.

EATING & DRINKING

There are two hobs in each covered outdoor area, no matter what sort of lodging you choose. Pans and

tableware are provided, as is a cool box. A wholesome breakfast, served in the lodge, is included in the price, and there are usually two excellent evening barbecues every week (for which you pay extra).

The village of Cilgerran has a convenience store and an off-licence. Cardigan, ten minutes by car, is the largest town in the area, and has a supermarket, banks, butchers and grocers. Here too is Fforest's own store, Fforest Outdoor (01239 615286, closed Sun Sept-July), which sells climbing, kayaking and general outdoor gear, and includes a lovely café.

A popular brunch option in Cardigan is the Castle Café (01239 621882) on the High Street. Its downstairs Cellar Bar offers an impressive programme of roots and blues artists, spoken word and poetry events and open-mic nights; check www.myspace.com/castlecafecellarbar for events.

To experience one of the area's best restaurants, drive 25 miles up the coast to the quaint port of Aberaeron. The Harbourmaster (01545 570755, www.harbour-master.com) is a lively, upmarket restaurant serving impeccably fresh seafood, including lobster from Cardigan Bay. Meat eaters can gorge on prime Welsh Black fillet steaks. The

Site specific

✔ This is about as luxurious as camping can get. Nonetheless, the outdoor cooking areas and rural location mean you still get a feel for the outdoor life.

✘ On arrival, it can feel a bit like checking into a hotel: there's an inventory and disclaimer to sign, and credit card details to hand over.

room, split between bar seating and tables, lends itself to a chatty lunch with a bottle of white.

ATTRACTIONS & ACTIVITIES

Fforest runs dozens of activities for all ages; these vary seasonally, but include all manner of water sports, both on the river and in the sea. Non-guests are welcome to participate too; contact the booking office in Cardigan for more details (01239 613961, www.fforestoutdoor.co.uk).

The Fforest camp is on the Ceredigion Coast Path (www.ceredigioncoastpath.org.uk), which undulates between the Teifi and Dyfi estuaries and is rich in wildflowers, birds and sealife. The steep, hour-long hike to Llangrannog, a picturesque fishing village with a decent pub, is recommended.

Fforest also borders the Teifi Marshes Nature Reserve (*see p219*), with its architecturally impressive wildlife centre overlooking the River Teifi and the woods towards Cardigan. Free walking tours are held on Wednesday and Sunday afternoons, and the café serves organic dishes made with local produce.

For rainy days, Cardigan has most to offer, with plenty of shops, cafés and restaurants.

AMUSING THE KIDS

The organised activities include plenty of stuff for children, and there are usually lots of other kids

to play with. Clambering around the romantic ruins of nearby Cilgerran Castle (01443 336000, http://cadw.wales.gov.uk, unstaffed Nov-end Mar) will while away a few hours.

CAMPING NEARBY

If Fforest is full, then its newer sister site, Manorafon sea camp, may have spaces.

Alternatively, about six miles south, diminutive North Lodge Eco-Camping (01239 841401, http://eco-camping.co.uk, open all year) has space for just five tents (from £15 per pitch) plus two pre-erected canvas bell tents (from £30) and a log cabin (from £40). Gardening courses are available, and dogs and horses are welcome.

Ynysfaen

Ynysfaen
Cwmwysg, Trecastle,
Brecon, Powys LD3 8YF
01874 636436
ynysfaencamping@btconnect.com
www.campingatynysfaen.co.uk
Map p28 ⑨
OS map SN857282

As basic as a campsite can be, Ynysfaen is heaven for campers who like to get as close to rural simplicity and the great outdoors as this tiny, industrialised island will allow. It's basically a very pretty field behind a very pretty farm on the banks of the Usk. Your immediate companions are likely to be sheep and chickens – the same birds that provide the free-range eggs on sale for a pound per half dozen – meaning nothing will detract from your enjoyment of the huge, inky Usk Valley skies at night and the peaceful seclusion by day.

Chances are, of course, that you won't be here much during the day, with the whole of the Brecon Beacons within easy range. Still, it's worth simply sitting and appreciating the peace and quiet – and, as the sun sets, lighting a fire in the small firebasket provided and listening to the sounds of nature. Although the site is rarely empty it is

Number of pitches 20 tents.
No caravans/motorhomes.
Open All year (call ahead for winter camping).
Booking By phone, email. Advisable.
Minimum stay 2 nights bank holiday weekends.
Typical cost £8 adult, £6 5-11s.
Facilities Showers (free); toilets; washing-up area.
Campfires Allowed, in firepits.
Firewood available (£5).
Dogs Allowed (£1).
Restrictions No noise after 10.30pm.
Getting there By road Take the A40 west from Brecon for about 11 miles. At Trecastle, turn left to Cwmwysg just after the Castle Coaching Inn and before the Antiques Centre. Continue for 1.5 miles; Ynysfaen is on the left, beside the River Usk. **By public transport** The nearest train station is at Llandovery. From here, bus 64 (Roy Brown, 01982 552597, Mon-Sat) to Brecon stops at Trecastle, taking 20 mins. The site's owners can provide lifts from Trecastle, by arrangement.

often quiet, and owners Jane and Nigel Matthews like to keep numbers down to ensure their guests' tranquillity. There's a 10.30pm noise curfew; all the better to hear the tawny owls calling amid the trees. The couple also think that Ynysfaen should be a campsite rather than a car park, so no vehicles are allowed on the field. Their son Tom can give campers with larger tents and lots of gear a helping hand with his tractor, while smaller loads can be transported via good old-fashioned wheelbarrows.

You can store milk and perishables in a large fridge in the always open pumphouse, fish for trout on the river (if you have a rod licence), enjoy water from a spring-fed supply and, in season, eat freshly picked garden vegetables grown by the Matthews. The brand-new shower and toilet block (three showers, three loos) is a bonus.

The site is relatively new (it came into being in spring 2009, when guests to a family birthday party couldn't find accommodation in the area, and instead brought tents and pitched camp in the meadow), but it probably won't remain a secret idyll for much longer. Make the most of it while you can.

EATING & DRINKING

Eggs, occasional veg and even a cooked breakfast (ordered in advance) are available at Ynysfaen, but for any other supplies you'll have to drive to nearby Sennybridge, just over five miles away. It has various food shops, along with the Camp Shop (01874 638145, www.campshop.co.uk) that's been selling camping essentials to military personnel and civvies for more than 50 years from inside the Sennybridge Army Camp.

Real ale fans should pay homage at the friendly Tanners Arms (01874 638032, www.tannersarms pub.com) in Defynnog, just beyond Sennybridge – it's got a staggering number of brews to try, plus pub grub and Sunday roasts.

En route you'll pass Trecastle, where the Castle Coaching Inn (01874 636354, www.castle-coaching-inn.co.uk, closed lunch Mon-Fri) has a deserved reputation for its food. Its concise but inviting menu focuses on local ingredients such as Welsh Black beef and lamb chops; eat in the cosy bar, or the elegantly understated restaurant (dinner only).

Site specific

✔ The isolated location and lack of facilities put lots of campers off, which means that camping here is often akin to being in the wild – with the added bonus of a cooked breakfast delivered to you in the morning, on request.

✘ The 10.30pm noise curfew means early nights are par for the course.

BRECON BEACONS

ATTRACTIONS & ACTIVITIES

As you criss-cross the western Brecons you'll notice raptors soaring over the mountains; chances are they're red kites. For a closer look, spend an hour in the hide at the Black Mountain Red Kite Feeding Station (01550 740617, www.redkiteswales.co.uk), next to the Cross Inn in Llanddeusant and a ten-minute drive from Ynysfaen.

Anglers will be in their element. The scenic Usk Reservoir (www.breconbeacons.org), just five minutes from the campsite, is considered one of Wales' best fisheries. Fishing for brown and rainbow trout is open to all; just buy a day pass from the hut on the bank at the western side of the dam wall. A five-mile cycling and walking track also runs around the reservoir.

If you're here for the walking, don't miss Llyn y Fan Fach, a glacial lake set against the stunning Bannau Sir Gaer ridge in the Fforest Fawr Geopark (www.fforestfawrgeopark.org.uk). A four-mile circular walk to the lake – and much higher, if you're up for it – is an exhilarating experience.

If it's raining, take shelter on the southern rim of the Brecons at the Dan yr Ogof National Showcaves Centre for Wales (01639 730284, www.showcaves. co.uk, closed Nov-Mar). Set two miles north of Abercrave, it's an extensive eerie world of caves and underground lakes.

AMUSING THE KIDS

Pootling around the site occupies many a happy hour: there are chickens to feed, warm eggs to hunt out, and a bevy of friendly dogs: Scooby the jack russell, and Ozzy and Dylan the spaniels. Children can also play in the shallows of the river, building dams and catching tiddlers.

There's not much in the area to beat the National Showcaves Centre for Wales for child-friendliness. As well as the thrill of the caves, the complex's above-ground attractions include a dinosaur park, where full-scale models lurk amid the undergrowth, and a farm with more domestic beasts (Shetland ponies, alpacas, rabbits, ducks). There are also two indoor play areas.

Children also love the Brecon Mountain Railway (01685 722988, www.breconmountainrailway.co.uk, weekends only, closed Nov, Jan, Feb), a vintage steam engine that pulls its observation coaches through miles of the Brecons, taking in the mountain foothills, castle ruins and a disused quarry.

CAMPING NEARBY

Just five minutes' walk along the river from the market town of Brecon, Priory Mill Farm (priory mill@btinternet.com, www.priorymillfarm.co.uk, open Mar-Oct, £7 adult, £4 under-11s) has a gorgeous setting in a riverside meadow. Firepits with locally produced charcoal and firewood means you can have a campfire, and the shower block is insulated with sheepswool. Very cosy. The excellent Bull's Head pub is less than ten minutes' walk away, and the start of the walk up Pen y Fan (at 2,907 feet, the highest mountain in South Wales) is close by.

Llanthony Priory

Llanthony Priory
Court Farm, Llanthony, Abergavenny,
Monmouthshire NP7 7NN
01873 890359
courtfarm@llanthony.co.uk
www.llanthony.co.uk
Map p28 ⑩
OS map SO286279

Number of pitches Approx 100 tents/
campervans. No caravans. Bunk barn
(sleeps 16). Self-catering cottage (sleeps 5).
Open All year.
Booking Not needed for camping,
essential for cottage. By phone, email.
Typical cost Camping £4 adult, £3 child.
Bunk barn £10 per person.
Cottage £320-£440 per week.
Facilities Pub; toilets. No showers.
Campfires Not allowed.
Dogs Allowed.
Getting there By road Take the A465
(Abergavenny to Hereford road). About7 miles
north of Abergavenny, turn into the village of
Llanvihanglo Crucorney. At the Skirrid Inn follow
the signposts to Llanthony, about 6 miles away.
By public transport The nearest train station
is Abergavenny, from where it's a 13-mile/
£22 taxi ride (Brian's Taxis, 01873 858597).

Campsite proprietor and sheep farmer Colin
Passmore describes Llanthony Priory as 'just
a field with a tap'. And essentially that's what it
is. But that description grossly undervalues the
site because it misses one vital ingredient –
its superlative location. The field is next to the
extensive ruins of a 12th-century priory in the
centre of the Black Mountains in the Brecon
Beacons National Park. The valley walls, rising
sharply from the ground, constantly change colour
as clouds, sun and, yes, rain pass overhead.
Mountain bikers, horse riders and walkers delight
in the remote paths and bridleways that criss-
cross some of the loveliest scenery in Wales.

Perhaps the highlight of the campsite is
the priory cellar, which has been turned into
a pub. The chance to drink a locally brewed
ale while sitting outdoors on 800-year-old
ruins and looking up the Llanthony Valley is
an unforgettable experience. The priory is
managed by Welsh Heritage and has a liberating
hands-off approach, meaning you are free to
wander the priory (holding a pint) and imagine

how life was for those 12th-century monks.
The pub also serves good food.

The lack of facilities (no showers, for example)
means the site is only recommended for campers
who don't mind getting a little dirty, or for one-
night stays. There are no set pitches in the field
– just put up your tent on the deepest and most
comfortable grass available. Don't forget to
take wellies: the grass is long, and wet weather
almost guaranteed. the rain is heavy and flooding
a possibility, It's best to camp at the top of the
field on a slight slope. The site can fill up in
summer with groups doing Duke of Edinburgh
award schemes, but any noisy campers will be
told to shut up or leave.

There are two toilet options. The cleanest are
those attached to the priory pub, but they open
and close according to pub hours. Others are
by the car park; these are for visitors to the
priory, but they are open 24 hours. They're not
particularly pleasant, however. A bunk barn is
also available, but needs to be booked well ahead.

EATING & DRINKING

The Undercroft Bar, in the cellar of the priory, is
fabulous. It is actually part of the Llanthony Priory
Hotel (01873 890487, www.llanthonyprioryhotel.co.uk,
closed Mon except summer school holidays), known
locally as the Abbey Hotel, which has four B&B
rooms. Alongside well-kept local ales, ciders and a
great perry, the bar has a deserved local reputation for
its food, cooked by the owner. The actual bar is tiny,
with limited table seating, but when the sun shines
most drinkers find an ancient stone to sit on. Diners
can either eat in the bar area or in a small dining room.

The next nearest pub is the Half Moon Inn
(01873 890611), just a two-minute walk across a
field. It offers good beers and ciders and a pleasant
bar area. The remarkable Skirrid Inn (01873 890258,
www.skirridmountaininn.co.uk, closed lunch Mon,
dinner Sun) is just off the A465 in Llanvihangel
Crucorney, on the corner at the turn-off to the priory,
and six miles from the campsite. Thought to have
been built in 1110, it's Wales' oldest inn, and one of
the most ancient in Britain. It has gained notoriety
from its use as a courtroom – and gallows – and has
even featured in the *Most Haunted* TV series. It is
thought that one John Crowther was the first of 180
people to be hanged in the pub, after being found
guilty of stealing sheep in 1110. There are some
excellent beers and the food is perfectly passable.

ATTRACTIONS & ACTIVITIES

Built by Sir William de Lacy in 1118, Llanthony
Priory was one of the first Augustinian priories in

BRECON BEACONS

Site specific

✔ The location next to Llanthony Priory is stunning. There aren't many places in Britain where you can stand among medieval ruins with a drink and watch the sun sink over mountains.

✗ The lack of facilities – just toilets and a tap, no showers – is a drawback, but that shouldn't put you off spending at least one night here.

Britain. But being 'fixed among a barbarous people', its monks were forced out and returned to Gloucester. It was rebuilt around 1200, with a large and impressive church for the monks, who regained their foothold in Wales until Owain Glyndwr, the last Welsh Prince of Wales, led a revolt against the English, finally emptying the priory in the early 1500s. What remains today is of great historical value and a major attraction for the area. Admission is free.

Offa's Dyke Path, which runs for 177 miles along the Welsh border, passes close to the priory; the campsite is a popular stopping point for walkers on the path. The Llanthony Riding & Trekking Centre (01873 890359, www.llanthony.co.uk, open Apr-Oct)

is run by the campsite's owner, Court Farm. It offers day and half-day hacks into the Black Mountains. All levels of riding ability can be catered for.

The winding road from the Skirrid Inn north to Hay-on-Wye is a beautiful drive, especially at the northern end around the wonderfully named Lord Hereford's Knob, which has commanding views.

The nearest town is Abergavenny, 13 miles away. It has two good bike shops, an outdoors outfitter, banks and supermarkets. For a bad-weather day, the Abergavenny Museum (01873 854282, www.abergavennymuseum.co.uk, closed Sun Nov-Feb), in the grounds of a Norman castle, traces the tumultuous history of Mid Wales.

AMUSING THE KIDS

There's nothing specifically aimed at children at the campsite, though they'll love exploring the priory ruins. If the heavens open, a trip to Abergavenny may be the best option.

CAMPING NEARBY

Tan House Farm (01873 860221, www.camping 4us.co.uk, open all year) is just over the English border and very close to the Offa's Dyke Path. This popular site has views over the Black Mountains, and the farmer runs a shop in nearby Longtown village. Only tents are allowed (from £5 per person). There's a pub five minutes away.

BRECON BEACONS

Hollybush Inn

**Hollybush Inn & Campsite
Old Brecon Road, Hay-on-Wye,
Herefordshire HR3 5PS**
01497 847371
hollybushcamping@gmail.com
www.hollybushcamping.co.uk
Map p28 ⑪
OS map SO200399

Number of pitches Approx 800 tents/
caravans/motorhomes. 4 tipis
(sleeping 2, 4, 6, 10). B&B (5 rooms).
Open All year.
Booking By phone.
Typical cost Camping £7 adult,
£3.50 child. Tipis £15 per person.
B&B £55-£65 per room.
Facilities Canoe hire (£20/half-day,
£30/day); electric hook-ups (28);
laundry facilities; play area; pub;
shop; showers (50p); toilets.
Campfires Allowed. Firewood available (£5).
Dogs Allowed, on lead (£2).
Restrictions Unsupervised under-18s
by arrangement.
Getting there By road From Hay-on-Wye,
head west on the B4350 (Old Brecon Road)
for about 3 miles. The pub is just before
the village of Glasbury-on-Wye. **By public
transport** Train to Hereford. From there,
bus 39 (Stagecoach, www.stagecoachbus.
com) runs about six times a day to Hay-on-
Wye and then on to Glasbury-on-Wye. The
inn is just before the village – ask the driver
to let you off at the Hollybush.

Rising steeply from the broad River Wye, the coniferous woods beside the Hollybush Inn in Glasbury-on-Wye – just inside the Welsh border – shelter a secluded campsite, albeit with a pub within stumbling distance. The river is the highlight of this wooded camp. Canoes and a couple of kayaks can be hired for frolicking along the Wye (one great trip is down to nearby Hay-on-Wye, stopping at the pubs en route).

There are two main camping plots set beneath the trees, their leaves making a spongy natural mattress. Pitches aren't allocated in advance, but you will be asked to choose between the 'top wood', which can be reached by car, or the 'bottom wood', which is a short walk down steps near the river bank. Both are shaded, but the bottom wood is nearer the river, quieter and a little more open. The walk down to the river is a bit steep, however. There are also four tipis of varying sizes pitched in the woods above the river. A gorgeous trail runs along the river bank, with rope swings hanging from the trees en route. Most people are happy simply to enjoy the views over the river: it's particularly lovely at sunset.

The campsite is centred around a homely pub, the Hollybush Inn. However, if you're looking for more amenities, then Hay-on-Wye, of literary festival fame, is a couple of miles away. This charming town is well known for being home to more than 30 secondhand bookshops, attracting bibliophiles throughout the year, but particularly during the annual Guardian Hay Festival at the beginning of June.

You might also want to make the most of the facilities in Hay, as the two toilet and shower blocks on the campsite leave much to be desired, particularly when it is busy (the more modern ones nearer the shop are better kept). There are also several hard-standing sites, and some caravans that look as if they haven't been on the move for quite a while.

Nevertheless, Hollybush is a reasonable place to stay if you're canoeing down the Wye, or simply out to enjoy the area's outstanding natural beauty without expecting too much by way of amenities.

EATING & DRINKING

The quirky interior of the Hollybush Inn is a pleasant place to relax, and serves a good range of local bitters, perries and ciders. Food is good gastropub style – the likes of a halloumi wrap for a snack and local lamb shank for a main course. Service can be slow.

The best food in the area is in Hay-on-Wye. The Three Tuns (01497 821855, www.three-tuns.com) in Broad Street is a 16th-century alehouse serving robust mains such as pan-roasted pork tenderloin with black pudding and mash, or monkfish tail poached with vermouth and fennel. Decent bar snacks include filled ciabattas or salmon and smoked haddock fish cakes. The wine list is varied and impressive.

Kilvert's Inn (01497 821042, www.kilverts.co.uk), in the Bullring, named after a 19th-century priest, is a small hotel highly recommended for its food and particularly its exemplary ales – including local brew Kilvert's Gold. The menu is traditional pub grub (steak and ale pie, own-made burgers), but the portions are large and the cooking good.

A small shop on the campsite sells basic provisions and toiletries. If you need a supermarket, the nearest (a Co-op) is in Hay-on-Wye.

ATTRACTIONS & ACTIVITIES

The biggest attraction in the area is Hay-on-Wye and its many bookshops. The Butter Market, held every Thursday in Memorial Square, is handy for picking up local produce, before heading off for a picnic along the river. The campsite is on the northern border of the Brecon Beacons National Park, and near the Black Mountains; both areas are popular for walking and cycling. The Offa's Dyke Path – a 177-mile trail along the border – passes through Hay-on-Wye heading south across the Black Mountains.

At the Hollybush Inn, owner Barbara Lewthwaite runs courses on healing and occasionally even a sweat lodge in the tipis. There are music events throughout the year, including a bluegrass festival every July.

The Glasbury House Outdoor Education Centre (01497 847 231, www.glasburyhouseoec.co.uk), on the other side of the river from the campsite in the centre of Glasbury village, has dozens of courses and activities for all ages, including hill walking, canoeing, caving and mountain biking.

AMUSING THE KIDS

The river provides all the entertainment a child could need, and you can hire canoes at the campsite. Rope swings are dotted throughout the wood, and there's a trampoline in the pub garden. For youngsters, the Play Barn (01874 623480, www.

Site specific

✔ The River Wye, beneath the camping woods and opposite the foothills of the Brecon Beacons, is beautiful. Camping here will give you the opportunity for an early-morning swim, or a canoe trip. There is also a lovely path alongside the river that's worth exploring.

✘ The toilets and showers. When we visited they were flooded and filthy: we found it best to use the pub facilities. Ask if there are any parties or events happening – they could make a restful stay impossible.

brynich.co.uk) is an indoor soft-play centre in Brecon, about 12 miles away; it's closed Mon and Tue in term-time, but open daily in the holidays.

CAMPING NEARBY

Radnors End Campsite (01497 820780, www.hay-on-wye.co.uk/radnorsend, open Mar-Oct, £6) is very close to Hay-on-Wye – it can be seen from Hollybush – and has views over the Cambrian Mountains. The site has toilets, showers, a fridge-freezer and kids' play area.

River Wye

Rhandirmwyn

Number of pitches 90 tents/caravans/
motorhomes.
Open Apr-Oct.
Booking By phone, online (members only).
Minimum stay 2 nights weekends if booking.
Typical cost £5.90-£9.05 adult,
£2.65-£2.85 child. Non-CCC members
additional £7.10.
Facilities Disabled facilities (toilet and
shower); electric hook-ups (50); laundry
facilities; play area; shop; showers (free);
toilets; washing-up area.
Campfires Not allowed.
Dogs Allowed, on lead.
Restrictions No noise after 11pm.
Getting there By road Take the A40 from
the south or east, or the A483 from the
north, to Llandovery. In the town centre,
by the railway level crossing, follow the
sign for Builth Wells, and then turn left
for Rhandirmwyn. When you reach the
village, turn left at the post office – the
campsite is on the left just before the
bridge. **By public transport** No buses go
near the campsite from the closest train
station at Llandovery, so a rather pricey
taxi is the only option. Try Llangadog Taxis
(01550 777924, around £20).

Rhandirmwyn
Llandovery, Carmarthenshire SA20 0NT
01550 760257
www.campingandcaravanningclub.co.uk/
rhandirmwyn
Map p28 ⑫
OS map SN779435

Set in the Towy Valley, in the foothills of the
Cambrian Mountains, Rhandirmwyn is a vision
of rural tranquillity. It's hard to convey just how
lovely this spot is; the River Towy runs along one
side of the campsite, and beyond wooded slopes
rise the dark outlines of the mountains. The
modern world suddenly feels far away – all the
more so as mobile phone reception is lacking.

With level, good-sized pitches and grass as
soft and springy as a newborn Welsh lamb, the
neatly mown camping field is delightfully trim and
tidy; it's as if Mary Poppins had been holidaying
here. There's a small playground with swings
and slides. It's a Camping & Caravanning Club
site, so the facilities are spotlessly clean and
the managers enthusiastic and helpful.

The Towy Valley is a former lead mining area,
and Rhandirmwyn (pronounced ran-dee-mo-n),
means Valley of the Minerals. Thanks to the
fertile soil and river, it's home to a terrific range
of wildlife. It's particularly rich in birds; the
patches of woodland shelter song thrushes,

great tits and blue tits, and by the river you might glimpse the vivid blue flash of a kingfisher in flight. The upper valley is a stronghold of red kites, along with ravens and buzzards.

Your fellow campers will likely include a twitcher or two, along with footsore walkers; a section of the 275-mile Cambrian Way (www.cambrian way.org.uk) follows the Towy Valley, and passes directly by the campsite. For less ambitious ramblers, there are plenty of shorter walks from the site, including a lovely wooded trail leading to the shop and tea room in Rhandirmwyn village.

Indeed, one of the site's strengths is that it is wonderfully remote, without feeling lonely. During the day, you can wander through unspoilt countryside in blissful solitude; in the evening, a ten-minute walk will take you to the convivial 16th-century Royal Oak Inn, with its polished real ale pumps and crackling log fire. Then it's back to the quiet of the campsite, and the sound of the passing river.

EATING & DRINKING

Although the camp shop is well stocked with maps, second-hand books and all manner of camping accessories, it doesn't sell food. To lay in supplies, you need to head ten minutes up the steep woodland trail to Rhandirmwyn. Here, the village store and

Ty Te Twn tea room (01550 760139) can provide provisions to cook back at your tent, along with sandwiches, ready-made picnics and own-made cakes and scones. This is also where you'll find the Royal Oak Inn (01550 760201, www.theroyaloak inn.co.uk) – and, in the evening, most of your fellow campers. It's a pleasingly traditional pub, with a lovely back garden, no music, lots of CAMRA awards for its impressive range of beers, and the kind of food you'd expect: burgers, steaks, ploughmans and sandwiches, as well as a small range of more exotic dishes in the evening.

From here, you can follow a delightful circular walk to the Towy Bridge Inn (01550 760370), a couple of miles away. Sampling the extensive range of ciders while sitting on the riverbank or in the teeny lounge bar is an enjoyable way to build an appetite for dinner at the Royal Oak (the Towy doesn't serve food).

ATTRACTIONS & ACTIVITIES

Run by the RSPB and famous for its red kites, Dinas Nature Reserve (01654 700222, www.rspb.org.uk) is about four miles from Rhandirmwyn and includes a wonderful two-mile walk to the waterfalls of the upper Towy Valley.

Six miles away, Llyn Brianne Reservoir offers more fine walks, spectacular views and some excellent mountain biking trails, as does the woodland at

nearby Cwm Rhaeadr (0845 604 0845, www.forestry. gov.uk). The latter has a great all-ability trail for cyclists, along with striking views of the falls that tumble over rocks and crevices into the valley.

Near Llandovery are two impressive feats of engineering. Cynghordy Viaduct is a soaring, 18-arch railway viaduct, built by the Victorians and still in use today, while Dolauhirion Bridge is a graceful, 17th-century single-span bridge across the Towy. (Just under the bridge is a stretch of rapids, where

intrepid canoeists occasionally come a cropper.) Llandovery itself is an appealing market town on the edge of the Brecon Beacons National Park, with a sprinkling of shops, cafés, pubs and a heritage centre.

About 20 miles to the south, in Llangathen, the 15th-century Aberglasney Gardens (01558 668998, www.aberglasney.org) features calm pools, a cloister walk, a heart-stoppingly lovely yew tunnel and hundreds of rare plants.

AMUSING THE KIDS

Gold panning, caves, wooded hillsides, creepy mines and nature trails should please all-comers at the Dolaucothi Gold Mines (01558 650177, www.nationaltrust.org.uk, closed Nov-Feb) in Pumsaint, around 11 miles away. First exploited by the Romans and now run by the National Trust, it holds regular events aimed at children.

CAMPING NEARBY

Within walking distance of Llandovery and founded in the 1950s, Erwlon Caravan & Camping Park (01550 721021, www.erwlon.co.uk, open all year) is a cheery, family-run park. Its stellar facilities include a heated toilet and shower block, with designated family rooms, a play area and Wi-Fi. A tent or caravan with two people costs £13-£16.

Site specific

✔ The walks in the immediate area, from leisurely riverside strolls to more strenuous ascents of the surrounding peaks, mean you could spend a few days here without the need for a car.

✘ The site is popular with campervan and RV owners, so if you prefer your camping to feature picturesque tents rather than rows of white vans, you might opt to go elsewhere – though you'll miss out on meeting some of the nicest campers around.

Fforest Fields

Fforest Fields Caravan & Camping Park
Fforest Fields, Hundred House,
Builth Wells, Powys LD1 5RT
01982 570406
office@fforestfields.co.uk
www.fforestfields.co.uk
Map p28 ⑬
OS map SO100535

Number of pitches 50 tents,
50 caravans, 20 motorhomes.
Open Apr-Oct.
Booking By phone, email, online.
Typical cost £4.50 per pitch,
£4 adult, £2.50 child.
Facilities Electric hook-ups (80);
laundry facilities; showers (free);
toilets; washing-up area.
Campfires Allowed. Firewood available (£5).
Dogs Allowed.
Getting there By road Fforest Fields is just
off the A481, about 6 miles north of Builth
Wells and 7 miles south of the junction with
the A44. **By public transport** The nearest
train station is tiny Builth Road (2 hrs from
Swansea), a couple of miles from the site.
No buses go nearby, so get a taxi (Dowse's
Taxis, 01982 551159).

Diving into the campsite's mirror-flat lake, with the hamlet of Llansantffraed to the west, the wooded Glascwm Hill rising steeply to the north and an endless patchwork of fields and lakes to the south, is a divine splash into Wales at its best. The Fforest Fields campsite (the Welsh often spell forest with a double 'f'), teetering on the Powys side of the Welsh/English border, is a surprisingly well-equipped spot given its remote location along a winding road between Builth Wells and the pleasant village of Hundred House. After a dip in the lake, take time to explore the surrounding woods and moors, to discover some of the flora and fauna that inspired the grand duke of British nature, David Bellamy, to give the site a gold award for conservation on behalf of the British Holiday & Home Parks Association. Owners George and Katie Barstow are inspiringly eco-minded and encourage a strong recycling ethos.

Set back half a mile off the A481, the seven-acre plot includes two large man-made lakes: one for fishing and one for swimming. Many of the reasonably sized pitches are semi-secluded by thoughtfully landscaped trees and shrubs.

And despite the number of pitches – a hefty 120 – there is a real sense of serene wilderness wherever the eye is cast.

The facilities are superb and the common areas immaculately clean. The toilet and shower blocks are currently fine, though there are plans to modernise them. There is also a well-equipped laundry room and an electrical block (more of a shed, actually) that has fridges, freezers and – very thoughtfully – charging plugs in lockable boxes, so that you can leave your mobile phone or laptop while they're charging. The site contains a mix of hard-standings for caravans and motorhomes, and tent areas. Ingeniously, there are 18 standings for long-term tents, which have a spongy ground and special gravel on top (the soft, manufactured kind found in playgrounds), to avoid ruining the grass.

The reception area has a fridge full of dairy products and bread, with an honesty box on top; it also offers a wealth of leaflets and information about things to do in the locality and across Mid Wales. If you need extra tent pegs, Wayfarers (01587 825984, www.the

campingshop.co.uk) is a comprehensive camping shop in the nearby village of Llandrindod Wells.

EATING & DRINKING

The nearest pub is the Hundred House Inn (01982 570231) in the hamlet of the same name, about a mile to the north. The local ales are worthy of attention, but it's not the best venue for food. More substantial meals are available at the Seven Stars Inn (01982 560494, www.7-stars.co.uk) in Aberedw, about ten minutes by car. This lovely pub, with original beams, is recommended by the Barstows as a pleasant lunch spot during a 12-mile round-trip walk around the country lanes and over the Aberedw Valley. It's standard pub grub, but will sustain you for the walk back. The pub is also at the head of the River Edw Valley – superb for walks and bike rides.

Another ten-minute drive away is the 500-year-old Roast Ox (01497 851398, www.roastoxinn.co.uk) in Painscastle. This traditional stone country pub is dog- and family-friendly and has an excellent locally sourced menu, but it isn't a budget option.

The historic market town of Builth Wells, first settled by the Romans, has plenty of convenience stores, cafés, takeaways and shops and is the nearest place for last-minute supplies. The Drovers Tea Rooms (01982 552056, closed Sun) is particularly recommended for a fabulous breakfast.

ATTRACTIONS & ACTIVITIES

The nearby Elan Valley, north of Builth Wells, well known for its Victorian dams, is popular with hikers and day-trippers, but you can head off in any direction from the campsite and discover wonderfully atmospheric views over the Cambrian Mountains. George and Katie can provide maps and route suggestions for day-long walks.

The campsite appeals to paragliders, who launch themselves from the top of the surrounding hills. There are plenty of landing fields around the site and it is often used by the Welsh Borders Paragliding Club (01982 570736, www.flywelshborders.org.uk).

Kathy Bufton at Underhill Farm (01597 851890, www.underhillridingstables.co.uk) can organise hacks

and lessons for those who want to explore the area on horseback. And if you prefer two wheels to four legs, there's plenty of good mountain biking; the Edw Valley is particularly popular with cyclists.

The busiest time to visit Fforest Fields is during the Royal Welsh Show (01982 553683, www.rwas.co.uk), held in Builth Wells towards the end of July. This famous agricultural event attracts 250,000 people for its livestock competition, and accommodation quickly gets booked up. A winter fair is held in November.

AMUSING THE KIDS

Wholesome fun – swimming in the lake, hunting for creepy crawlies – means that children will find more than enough to occupy themselves on-site, despite the lack of a playground. And for those without children, who'd like a bit of peace and quiet, the site has a child-free area.

CAMPING NEARBY

New House Farm (01497 851671, www.new-house-farm.co.uk, open Easter-Oct) in the Radnorshire Hills, 15 miles from Builth Wells, and seven from Hay-on-Wye, is a friendly and basic rural campsite. Breakfast is served in the farmhouse conservatory, and the owners can provide a three-course dinner. Tents and caravans cost £3.50 per person.

MID WALES

The swimming lake at Fforest Fields; there's a separate fishing lake, stocked with trout.

The Yurt Farm

The Yurt Farm
Crynfryn, Penuwch, Tregaron,
Ceredigion SY25 6RE
01974 821594
info@theyurtfarm.co.uk
www.theyurtfarm.co.uk
Map p28 ⑭
OS map SN585621

Number of pitches 1 21ft yurt (sleeps 8).
2 18ft yurts (sleeping 6). 1 18ft yurt &
1 14ft yurt (sleeping 6, 2).
Open April-Oct.
Booking By phone, email. Minimum stay
3 nights weekend; 1 week July, Aug.
Typical cost 18ft 1 night £60; 3 nights
£165-£240; 1 week £350-£550.
21ft or 18ft & 14ft 1 night £80; 3 nights
£195-£270; 1 week £420-£600.
Bedding £10 per person.
Facilities Kitchen; play area; shop;
showers (free); toilets (composting).
Campfires Allowed, in designated areas.
Firewood available (free).
Dogs Not allowed.
Getting there By road Take the A487 coast
road (between Aberaeron and Aberystwyth)
to Llanrhystud. Turn inland on the B4337;
after 4 miles turn right at the village of
Cross Inn towards Penuwch on the B4577.
At Penuwch turn right on the B4576. After
1.5 miles, take a left when you see the sign
for the Yurt Farm; follow the arrow on the
woodpile down the track to the car park.
By public transport Train to Aberystwyth.
Bus 588 (Mid Wales Motorways, 01970
828288) runs three times a day to Penuwch
(about 50 mins). The campsite owners are
happy to collect guests from there.

There are few more joyous ways to spend a
night than under the creaking wood and flapping
canvas of a yurt. The Yurt Farm is hidden away
deep in the Welsh county of Ceredigion, set
between a field full of sheep and a large copse,
with a remarkable view over the Aeron Valley.
It's an idyllic location for a weekend of country
walks, fruit-picking, egg-collecting, cosy pubs
and fluffy pillows – all totally off-grid.

Laurie and Thea Murton and their daughter
Mossy assembled the camp in a peaceful corner
of their 150-acre family farm in 2009. There
are five yurts in total (though one pair is always

rented out together). Each is equipped with
futon beds, two-ring gas hob, hurricane lamps
and a battery of cooking utensils. Sheets are
provided, but bring your own duvets and pillows
(you can also hire these). A wood-burning stove
crackles away, warming the space and heating
a kettle for nettle tea.

Outside, there is a picnic table and firepit.
The Murtons also provide a welcome pack of
organic vegetables and eggs, all either from the
farm or a nearby producer. It is this local focus
that is at the core of the Yurt Farm ethos; the
yurts themselves were built a couple of villages
away, using timber cut on the farmland.

The yurts are spread across a meadow site,
leaving vast amounts of space for very few
people. The only place where you're likely to
meet fellow-campers is in the communal log
cabin. Hand-built by Laurie and Thea, it has a
sofa, table, leaflets about the locality and a small
library of cooking and woodcraft books. It also
houses a wood-burning stove and a communal
cooking area. The two showers are heated by
solar panels, and there are compost toilets.

There's no denying that the location is remote,
although there are some good pubs nearby.
The dramatic coastline, a 20-minute drive away,
is a highlight, and the charming seaside town
of Aberaeron has a number of good seafood
restaurants. But more likely than not, you'll find
yourself lying back in the cosy yurt, dreaming
of erecting your own timber-framed retreat in
the back garden at home.

EATING & DRINKING

It's worth taking provisions if you're staying for
more than a couple of days, as the cooking facilities
are top-notch. There are good pots and pans, cutlery,
plates, condiments and olive oil in the yurt and
communal cabin, as well as teas. Once you've
devoured the contents of the welcome basket, you
can buy fresh veg in the farm shop, along with farm-
reared pork, lamb and beef (the lamb chops are
superb). When fruit is in season, you can pick it
off the branch, or see what the hens have laid.

The nearest towns with supermarkets and post
offices are Tregaron, Lampeter and Aberaeron, all
of which are within ten miles. Of the three, Aberaeron
has the best restaurants and services. La Cuccina
(35 Alban Square, 01545 571012, closed Sun) is a
lovely little café; you could lunch on a deliciously
light mushroom, tomato and feta pie, or make straight
for the superb carrot cake. The most upmarket
restaurant in town is the Harbourmaster on Key
Parade (01545 570755, www.harbour-master.com),

MID WALES

which serves freshly landed fish, along with local lamb and Welsh Black beef. The Hive (01545 570445, www.hiveonthequay.co.uk, (ice-cream parlour closed Oct-Mar) is renowned for its seafood, including lobster, but the honey-sweetened ice-cream is the star turn, we recommend the hazelnut and honey.

The only pub in walking distance of the farm is the Penuwch Inn (formerly the Last Invisible Dog). It's fine for a pint and a game of pool, and the Sunday lunches are good. But the Rhos Yr Hafod Inn (01974 272644, www.rhos-yr-hafod-inn.co.uk) in nearby Cross Inn is the best choice for ales and food.

ATTRACTIONS & ACTIVITIES

Although this is a working farm, visitors are encouraged to explore. Various trails meander through the marshland, meadows and coppices, and there's much to do. Depending on the season, you can pick your own fruit and vegetables, dig up carrots with which to feed the cattle, and admire the majestic rare-breed pigs. The site can be slippery underfoot after rain, so take wellies.

Penuwch, the nearest hamlet, is at the top of the valley, and numerous paths and bridleways descend into the horizon-filling Aeron Valley. For cyclists

Site specific

✔ The yurts are extremely cosy, while the remote location instills a feeling of really getting away from it all.

✘ Although there are plenty of walks close at hand, you really need a car to explore the area to its full potential.

(bikes can be hired through the farm), the Ystwyth Trail rolls through the Teifi Valley between Tregaron and Aberystwyth; much of the route follows a disused railway line.

In Tregaron, the Red Kite Centre & Museum (01974 298977, closed weekdays Oct-Mar) covers local history and is set in an old schoolhouse. You can also explore the Cors Caron reserve (01974 298977, http://cors-caron-national-nature-reserve.wales.info), an ancient bog that's rich in wildlife. Red kites have been successfully reintroduced here, with feeding sessions held from October to March.

The artist who made the mugs and bowls in the farm's log cabin, Dan Boyle (01570 423596, www.danielboyleceramics.com), is happy to show visitors his studio, three miles outside Lampeter, where he makes the salt-glaze ceramics.

AMUSING THE KIDS

With pigs, chickens and cattle around the farm (and an immense eagle owl that frequents the area), there is plenty to keep children absorbed. For wobbly-legged baby lambs, visit in lambing season (Mar-Apr). There's also a small – but expanding – play area; if it rains, retreat to the communal lodge for board games.

On sunny afternoons, jaunts to the seaside at Aberaeron or Aberystwyth are a must. Another great day out is a trip along the Vale of Rheidol Railway (01970 625819, www.rheidolrailway.co.uk, closed Oct-Easter): a narrow-gauge steam train that runs between Devil's Bridge and Aberystwyth.

CAMPING NEARBY

Outer Bounds Camping (01974 272444, www.camping.artizen.me.uk, open end Mar-Oct) is tranquil, secluded and an idyllic spot to get away from it all. There are only six pitches (£5 adult, £1 child), and a small shower and toilet block. The nearest village, four miles away, is Llanrhystud, on the coast.

Owners Laurie and Thea, with their daughter Mossy, and the cosy communal log cabin

Tyllwyd Farm

Tyllwyd Farm
Cwmystwyth, Aberystwyth,
Ceredigon SY23 4AG
01974 282216 campsite
01970 630281 cottage
clare@welshaccommodation.co.uk
www.welshaccommodation.co.uk
Map p28 ⑮
OS map SN806746

Number of pitches 20 tents, 16 caravans/
motorhomes. Cottage (sleeps 6).
Open All year, but call in advance
about winter camping.
Booking By phone, email, online, post.
Typical cost Tent £12 2 people.
Caravan £13 2 people. £5 extra adult.
Cottage phone for details.
Facilities Electric hook-ups (16); play area;
showers (free); toilets; washing-up area.
Campfires Allowed, in designated areas.
Firewood available (£4).
Dogs Allowed, on lead.
Getting there By road Take the A4120
(Aberystwyth to Ponterwyd road). At Devil's
Bridge turn on to the B4574 to Cwmystwyth
village. When you reach the village, follow
signs towards Hafod. Pass by Hafod and
a derelict lead mine, and Tyllwyd is on the
right. **By public transport** Not really viable.
The nearest train station is 18 miles away
in Aberystwyth, from where it's an expensive
taxi ride – around £25-£30 (Domino's Taxis,
01970 625888).

Although it's only half an hour from Aberystwyth,
the sense of remoteness is palpable in this
little-visited part of Mid Wales. The SAS regularly
practise manoeuvres in the area, across what
is some of the most difficult terrain in the British
Isles – and even the cows look a little nervous
about the size of the mountains. Travelling along
the twisting, stomach-churning, single-track
road between Aberystwyth and Rhayader, past
deserted lead mines, vast Forestry Commission
conifer woods, one-pub villages, and fields full
of stoic sheep, it's a relief to reach Tyllwyd
campsite, set in the middle of a steep valley
above the fast-flowing River Ystwyth.

The small site is popular with hikers, who
brave the dark surrounding hills of Allt, Neint
and Graigwen. The nearby Hafod Estate,
described as a 'restored 18th-century landscape',
is popular with less adventurous walkers, and
most people make the effort to hike to the lively
Peiran Falls. Anglers seem happy to spend the
day hoicking trout out of the river.

Tyllwyd is run by James and Clare Raw, and
James Jr, who one day will become the seventh
generation to farm the land here. The farm
covers a vast area, 3,000 acres in all, rising
from 800 to 1,800 feet in elevation, and is
home to 40 Limousin suckler cows and 1,000
Welsh Mountain sheep (which are reared on
the hill so they never wander far).

The campsite has been open since the 1960s;
a couple of regulars have been coming since the
early days. There are hook-ups for enterprising
caravan and motorhome owners who dare to
drag their vehicles along the winding mountain
road, but the site is dominated by hikers and
bikers in tents. Another field is opened on busy
bank holiday weekends, but most of the time
there is plenty of space – and no one has ever
been turned away.

The clean toilet and shower block behind the
Raws' whitewashed house (once a drover's inn),
has a spring-fed water supply. A small play area
with swings sits next to several brick barbecues
and picnic benches, from where you can drink
in the gorgeous views of the stony river and the
valley it created. It's a tranquil spot and far-
removed from the modern world (don't expect
to get reception on your mobile).

EATING & DRINKING

There is very little in the immediate vicinity, and
no pub within walking distance.

The nearest village that is set up for visitors is
Devil's Bridge, five or so miles west, best known
for the Vale of Rheidol Railway and the trio of
bridges and waterfalls that give it its name. Feeding
the tourists is the imposing Hafod Hotel (01970
890232, www.thehafodhotel.co.uk), built as a
hunting lodge by Thomas Johnes of the Hafod
Estate in 1787. The restaurant serves good local
produce (there's a bar menu too), though service
can be a little too relaxed.

The best pub in the locality is the Miners Arms
(01974 282238, www.minersarms.net, closed lunch
Tue-Sat, dinner Mon, Sun) in Pontrhydygroes, a ten-
minute drive away. While the menu is pretty average
pub food – all own-made, mind – the locally sourced
meat makes it worth the visit. They also take pride
in their real ales, and have a good selection of wines
and whiskies (including Wales's own Penderyn).

Aberystwyth, on the coast, is the nearest major
town, with plenty of shops and supermarkets.

MID WALES

ATTRACTIONS & ACTIVITIES

Plenty of hiking routes cross the valley (take care when venturing out, especially in poor weather). A more relaxed stroll heads along the old water leat – a watercourse, constructed in 1876, which carried water from the River Ystwyth to drive the crushing wheels at the now disused lead mine. A few miles away, the Hafod Estate (01974 282568, www.hafod. org) offers a glimpse into the eccentric world of Thomas Johnes (1748-1816), who built a mansion and landscaped the area in keeping with the 'Picturesque' aesthetic, planting more than three million trees. The sentiment is carried through today, and although the mansion was destroyed, some interesting buildings and ruins remain. The highlights are the five walks, two created by Johnes, that explore the rocky gorge and cross several bridges.

Birdwatchers are also in their element. Red kites, kestrels and peregrine falcons hunt small mammals and birds along the valley, while rarer pied and grey wagtails and tree creepers inhabit the wooded areas.

Mountain bikers head off in all directions from Tyllwyd, including a renowned route to Llangurig. For more organised riding, the Bwlch Nant Yr Arian mountain biking centre (01970 890453, www.forestry.gov.uk/bwlchnantyrarian), two miles west of Ponterwyd, has some superb single-track cycle trails. Run by the Forestry Commission, it also has a visitor centre, café, adventure playground and gift shop. Don't miss the red kite feeding sessions at 3pm daily (2pm winter).

AMUSING THE KIDS

There is a small play area on campsite, but it is the river that is the centre of attention.

Another popular distraction is the Vale of Rheidol Railway (01970 625819, www.rheidolrailway.co.uk, closed Nov-Mar) – miniature puffing trains chug the 12 miles to Aberystwyth twice a day.

CAMPING NEARBY

Glangwy Farm (01686 440232, www.llanidloes.com/glangwy_farm, open all year) has some of Tyllwyd's rural charm. Located just off the main A44 in the village of Llangurig, it has room for 25 tents, and some tourers and caravans. Expect to pay £3-£5 per person. There are restaurants and pubs in the village, and all amenities in Llanidloes.

> ## Site specific
>
> ✔ Tyllwyd is real rural Wales. It's perfect for walkers and mountain bikers who enjoy spending their days outdoors on windswept mountains.
>
> ✘ Like anywhere in Britain, the weather can be a problem, but given the remote location, the winter months can be brutal.

Gwerniago Farm

Gwerniago Farm
Pennal, Machynlleth, Powys SY20 9JX
01654 791227
contact@gwerniago.co.uk
www.gwerniago.co.uk
Map p28 ⑯
OS map SH712002

MID WALES

Number of pitches 20 tents, 12 caravans/
motorhomes.
Open Mar-Oct.
Booking By phone, online, email, post.
Advisable.
Typical cost £14 2 people. £5 extra adult,
£2-£3 extra child.
Facilities Electric hook-ups (3); fridge;
freezer; pony rides (from £2); showers
(50p); toilets; washing-up area.
Campfires Allowed. Firewood available (£3).
Dogs Allowed, on lead (£1).
Restrictions Single-sex groups by
arrangement.
Getting there By road The campsite is
3 miles west of Machynlleth, off the A493.
From Machynlleth, head north on the A487
and turn left immediately after Dyfi Bridge.
Follow the road for 2 miles, then turn left
at the campsite sign and follow the lane to
the farm entrance on the right. **By public
transport** Train to Machynlleth, then bus
28 or 30 (0871 200 2233, www.arrivabus.
co.uk) to Pennal. It runs daily and takes
8 mins to village, from where it's a 15-mins
walk to the farm. The 28 also runs from
Aberystwyth (Mon-Sat, journey 1 hr).

The landscape of the Dyfi (or Dovey) Valley is
very different from that of Snowdonia to the
north. It's gentler, more welcoming: the bleak
jagged mountains, drystone walls and slate
slag heaps have been replaced by lush farmland,
honeysuckle-filled hedges and wide river
estuaries. Even the air seems softer. In the middle
of all this is Gwerniago Farm, a small campsite
on a working farm, with room for just 20 tents
and a dozen caravans. Visit midweek at the end
of June and you might have the place to yourself.
Come during the school holidays and it will be full
of children, rampaging around the camping fields
or waiting for pony rides in the farmyard.

On arrival, check if Mair Jones, the welcoming
owner, is in residence at the white farmhouse, so
that you can pay upfront. If not, head to the right,
around the back of the farmhouse, and down to
the camping fields: a small upper field, a middle
field with a majestic oak on one side, and a
bottom field with low-slung hedges and views
across the valley. There's also a separate field
for caravans. Campfires are allowed, as long
as you use one of the existing stone hearths.
There's a cold-water sink for scrubbing the pots,
but it's a bit of a drag walking uphill to the loos.

If you go left from the farmhouse, you'll get
stuck among the static caravans – a dozen in
all, in regimented rows with neat little gardens.
This is also where the ablutions block is located:
a couple of toilets and a shower for each sex –
just about adequate, but not exactly the height
of luxury (a new toilet block should be completed
by 2012). A fridge, a freezer and the recyling bins
are in the garage next door.

To avoid sleeping on a slope, set up in the
centre of the lower field, or next to the verdant

hedgerow – which is also where you'll get the best views. In the evening you can watch the farmer and his collies round up the sheep across the valley, or tune into the ever-present birdlife.

Gwerniago is an unfussy place, without irritating regulations or beady-eyed wardens watching your every move. You'll need a car to explore the area – there are sandy beaches, seaside resorts and nature reserves within a 15-minute drive. And most visitors take the water-powered railway up to the Centre for Alternative Technology (CAT), five miles north up the A487. Also worth a visit is Machynlleth, three miles away, a workaday rural town with new age overtones and an extremely ugly (but much-loved) clocktower.

EATING & DRINKING

The nearest pub is the Riverside Hotel (01654 791285, www.riversidehotel-pennal.co.uk) in Pennal, a 15-minute walk down the back lane. New owners arrived in 2010 and have completely transformed the place: it's now a stylish bar and restaurant, with an estimable selection of real ales and an appealing menu that takes in houmous and flatbread, chicken pie and chips, and fish stew with prawns

---

Site specific

✔ The atmosphere is wonderfully relaxed and calming. Tents outnumber caravans.

✘ The toilets and showers could do with some TLC. And the statics, though ever so trim, are still an eyesore.

---

and chorizo. Work by local artists adorns the walls, and a log-burning stove warms the snug.

Locals also favour the atmospheric, low-beamed Black Lion (01654 703913, closed Mon Sept-June) in Derwenlas. It's a good idea to book.

Otherwise, Machynlleth has assorted cafés, pubs and restaurants, including the lively Wynnstay Hotel (01654 702941, www.wynnstay-hotel.com, pizzeria closed Sun), which manages to multi-task as a hotel, bar, restaurant and pizzeria. Its produce comes from an impressive array of local suppliers, and the beers from across Wales. For cakes, snacks and hot dishes, try the Quarry Café (01654 702624, closed some Sun, a wholefood café and shop run by the Centre for Alternative Technology. There's also a couple of

small supermarkets and a good butcher's. The Wednesday street market is an institution (it's been going for 700 years), offering quality food stalls, second-hand books, CDs and household goods.

ATTRACTIONS & ACTIVITIES

Perched high above the Dulas Valley on top of an old slate quarry, the Centre for Alternative Technology (01654 705950, www.cat.org.uk) provides an inspiring – if chaotic – jumble of displays on everything from solar power to composting, alongside gardens, eco-houses, a straw-bale theatre, a wholefood café and a great shop. It's currently undergoing major renovations, which should make it even more of a must-visit.

Machynlleth's long main street is worth a potter. As well as a small information centre (closed Thur afternoon, Sun), there's an ultra-fashionable homewares store (the Deco Shop) and some other browsable shops. The Museum of Modern Art (01654 703355, www.momawales.org.uk, closed Sun) combines rotating exhibitions of modern Welsh art with performing arts in the adjacent Tabernacle, a former Wesleyan chapel.

The hills around Machynlleth are a playground for mountain bikers. Three cross-country routes (Mach 1, 2 and 3) start in the town, while a more challenging purpose-built technical trail (cli-machx) runs through the Dyfi Forest to the north. The Holey Trail bike shop (01654 700411, www.theholeytrail.co.uk, closed Sun) has maps of local routes and bikes for hire.

For less energetic pursuits, drive eight miles along the winding road adjacent to the wide Dyfi estuary to Aberdovey (Aberdyfi in Welsh). A low-key seaside resort of pastel-painted Victorian villas, it has all the fish and chip shops you could need and a vast sandy beach, fringed by low dunes, that stretches north for miles. On the south side of the estuary is the RSPB's Ynys-hir nature reserve (01654 700222, www.rspb.org.uk, closed Mon, Tue Nov-Mar), an unusual mix of wet grassland, Welsh oak woodland and salt marsh. Next door, Borth Sands reveals the shin-high stumps of an ancient petrified forest at low tide.

AMUSING THE KIDS

The Centre for Alternative Technology is well set up for children, and makes for a brilliant day out. Five miles north of town, the diminutive Corris Railway (01654 761303, www.corris.co.uk, closed Oct-Easter) runs at weekends and bank holidays. The return trip, including a guided tour, takes about 50 minutes. Also in Corris is King Arthur's Labyrinth (see p253). Otherwise, a trip to the seaside at Aberdovey is always a winner.

CAMPING NEARBY

A five-minute walk from CAT, Llwyngwern Farm (01654 702492, open Apr-Oct, £12 for two people) has room for tents, caravans and motorhomes in a flat field next to a river. Facilities are basic and it can get muddy after rain, but campfires are allowed and the closest pub is only a mile away.

Dyfi Valley

MID WALES

Cae Du

Cae Du Campsite
Rhosllefain, Tywyn, Gwynedd LL36 9ND
01654 711234
Map p28 ⑰
OS map SH571060

Number of pitches 40 tents,
15 caravans/motorhomes.
Open Easter-Oct.
Booking By phone, post. Advisable.
Typical cost Tent £15-£20 2 adults.
Caravan/motorhome £15-£20.
Facilities Freezer; laundry facilities;
showers (£1); toilets; washing-up area.
Campfires Allowed, in designated areas.
Firewood available (£5).
Dogs Allowed, on lead (£1).
Getting there By road Take the A493 south
from Dolgellau towards Tywyn. Just under
3 miles beyond Llwyngwril, the road bends
sharply to the left; turn right (carefully)
immediately on the bend and drop down
into Cae Du. It's a tricky manoeuvre if
you're coming from the other direction.
By public transport Train to Shrewsbury,
then the Cambrian Coast Line (0845 606
1660, www.arrivatrainswales.co.uk) via
Machynlleth to Tonfanau (journey 2 hrs),
a couple of miles from the site. Also, bus
28 runs between Machyllneth and Dolgellau,
past the campsite entrance (50 mins).

South of Barmouth, at the bottom of Snowdonia National Park, the narrow coast road twists upward, with nothing but the twinkling sea to your right and green, sheep-studded hills to your left. As the road bends sharply inland, turn right and drop down past a farmhouse, then follow the bumpy single-lane track under the railway bridge to one of the most blissfully located campsites you'll ever find.

It's a simple spot. Ahead stretches the wide blue sea. Uphill on either side are the two camping fields, sloping but flattening out at the cliff edge and at the back. Pitch where you like; there's plenty of space. For some reason, campervan and caravan owners tend to prefer the left-hand field, though there's not much to differentiate them. The lush grass is dotted with clover and buttercups (and sheep droppings), and stone circles indicate where you can build fires – wood is available from the farm, but it's not great quality, so bring your own or

forage for driftwood. At beach level, between the two fields, stand a derelict cottage and an old barn, which houses the blue- and white-painted showers and toilets (spotless, with hairdryers, hand soap and piping hot water). There's also space for a few tents, right next to the shore. The open side of the barn has a sofa and tables in case of bad weather. You'll be fighting to scrub the dishes, so lovely is the view from the sinks.

Seaweed and rocks carpet the beach, alongside grey boulders weathered into strange Henry Moore-esque shapes, and the occasional patch of sand. It's not great for swimming, though the water is shallow and fine for paddling.

A sense of peace and isolation pervades – despite the fact that the Cambrian Coast Line between Pwllheli and Aberystwyth runs past the back of the site. Every couple of hours a two-carriage diesel pootles by, but you won't even notice after a while. Cae Du's owners aren't

much in evidence, but can usually be found at the farmhouse if needed. Messing about on the beach, walking the dog, or simply gazing at the sea keeps most campers relaxed and happy for days, and the sunsets are spectacular.

The only drawback (apart from the chemical-tasting drinking water) is that the the clifftop site is very exposed; there are no trees, although the drystone wall next to the train track offers some protection. If a gale blows in, you'll know it.

Should you feel the urge to move from your tent, the resort town of Tywyn is less than 15 minutes by car. From there, you can hop on the narrow-gauge steam trains of the Talyllyn Railway or catch the scenic coast train north past Cae Du to the seaside amusements of Barmouth. Driving takes 40 minutes (longer if you don't use the Penmaenpool toll bridge) as you have to go quite a long way inland around the Mawddach estuary. Much closer is Fairbourne, where there's yet another miniature railway (see p253). Inland lie some beautiful

steep-sided valleys and glacial finger lakes, and the challenge of Cader Idris mountain.

EATING & DRINKING

The farm sells eggs and excellent lamb burgers, but that's all; there are no shops nearby, so it's best to bring supplies. The nearest pub is the Peniarth Arms (01654 711505) in Bryncrug, about three miles away, which does perfectly decent pub grub – there might be changes, as it was about to change management.

Site specific

✔ Sea views, fabulous sunsets and campfires: it doesn't get much better than this.

✗ You're on a cliff and the wind can be vicious. Bring a windbreak, and make sure everything is battened down.

Tywyn, a few miles further on, has a Spar, a butcher, assorted cafés and a chippy.

For more choice, head to Barmouth, where there's another Spar, a Co-op, plenty of old-fashioned tea rooms and assorted restaurants, including Bistro Bermo (01341 281284), a cosy and informal little place that serves modern Welsh food using local fish and lamb. The drawback? It's open for dinner from Tuesday to Saturday, and for Sunday lunch.

There are more eateries in the historic market town of Dolgellau at the start of the Mawddach estuary. For other suggestions in the area, *see p252*.

ATTRACTIONS & ACTIVITIES

Bucket-and-spade fun awaits at Barmouth, where the wide, sandy beach is overlooked by an amusement arcade and funfair. Pottering around the shops or strolling across the wooden footbridge over the mouth of bay should fill a couple of hours. For stupendous views across the estuary, ascend to the Panorama Walk (www.mawddachway.co.uk/panorama-walk.html) behind the town, which has been popular since Victorian times. A steep five-mile circular route starts at the railway station, or you can cheat by driving up to the car park. Look out for climbers scaling the nearby Barmouth Slabs.

It's not far to Cader Idris, the highest mountain in Wales after the Snowdon massif. The most popular ascent is the Pony Path from Ty Nant, about three miles south of Dolgellau. Drive there via the B4405; it's not the most direct route, but it is the most scenic. Following the course of the Talyllyn Railway, it offers a heart-stirring vista as you approach the glacial blue waters of Lyn Mwyngil (also known as Tal-y-llyn Lake). The shorter but much steeper Minffordd Path starts at the north end of the lake, climbing past deep Llyn Cau and along the dramatic rim of Craig Cau to the summit at Penygadair. Cader is often shrouded in mist, but on a clear day the views are breathtaking.

From Tywyn, it's a picturesque seven-mile ride inland on the Talyllyn Railway (01654 710472, www.talyllyn.co.uk). Get off halfway to see the pretty Dolgoch Falls or stop at Abergynolwyn, where there's a tea room; fortified by refreshments, you can walk through the forest to the final stop at Nant Gwernol.

AMUSING THE KIDS

Scrambling over boulders, messing around in rock pools, building sandcastles, paddling – it's hard to get children off the beach. You'll find more sand at Twywn and Barmouth beaches, but they have none of the wild beauty of Cae Du.

Of the various restored steam railways nearby, the Talyllyn is probably the best choice because of its *Thomas the Tank Engine* connections – the train-obsessed Reverend Awdrey volunteered here.

CAMPING NEARBY

About seven miles north, Graig Wen (*see p251*) overlooks the Mawddach estuary at Fairbourne.

Graig Wen

Graig Wen
Arthog, Dolgellau, Gwynedd LL39 1BQ
01341 250482
hello@graigwen.co.uk
www.graigwen.co.uk
Map p28 ⑱
OS map SH651157

Number of pitches Mid July-Aug: 20 tents,
8 caravans/motorhomes. Jan, Mar-mid July,
Sept-Dec: 12 tents/caravans/motorhomes,
2 yurts (sleeping 2-5). B&B (5 rooms).
4 cottages (sleeping 4-6).
Open Jan, Mar-Dec.
Booking By phone, email.
Essential high season.
Typical cost Camping £7-£10 adult, £3-£5
5-15. Yurt £60-£100. B&B £75-£130.
Cottage £315-£700 per week.
Facilities Electric hook-ups (8); play area;
shop; showers (free); toilets (flush and
composting); washing-up area.
Campfires Allowed. Firewood available (£5).
Dogs Allowed, on lead.
Restrictions Groups by arrangement.
No arrivals after 8pm, no noise after 11pm.
Getting there By road Turn off the A470
Dolgellau bypass, and take the A493
towards Tywyn/Fairbourne. About 5 miles
from Dolgellau and 1 mile before Arthog
village, look out for a postbox on the right-
hand side. Graig Wen is 200 yds further
on, on the right, on the brow of a slight hill.
By public transport Morfa Mawddach is
the nearest rail station, a mile away. You
can walk from there (details on the website)
or arrange to be picked up. The 28 bus
runs between Aberystwyth and Dolgellau;
ask to be dropped at Graig Wen, between
Penmaenpool and Arthog. The journey
takes 2 hrs from Aberystwyth, 15 mins
from Dolgellau (0871 200 2233,
www.arrivabus.co.uk).

Combining eco-friendly credentials with
contemporary comforts, the bewitching Graig Wen
represents camping at its very coolest. Its green
ethos is evident throughout, from the compost
toilet known as the tree bog to the car-free field
and recycling bins. Set up camp in the grassy
glades and meadows, or book one of the fully
furnished yurts, with a wood-burning stove. The
B&B accommodation, housed in a converted

Victorian slate-cutting mill, is even more stylish
– and, after a few nights' rough weather camping
around North Wales, sorely tempting.

Graig Wen commands sublime views over
wooded green slopes all the way across the
Mawddach estuary. The vista from the aptly
named panorama pitches, not far from the house,
is jaw-droppingly beautiful. The lower camping
fields – verdant pastures, fringed by woodland
– take you a little closer to the estuary, where
gulls and waders soar and dip with the tide.
At night, it's magical; a velvety silence pierced
by seabirds' cries and owl hoots.

Close to the main house and touring field (open
all year except Feb) are the toilets, sink block and
two showers. The shower room also contains an
honesty shop, with a fridge filled with local bacon
and sausages, free-range eggs and milk, and
a shelf stocked with pasta, beans and soup –
and, most importantly, bags of marshmallows.

The best time for tent campers to visit is in
the middle of summer, when the lower camping
fields, accessible by a rough, steepish track,
are open. A couple of standpipes and the tree
bog are your only ablutionary aids. The latter
is as clean as a whistle and free from pongs –
as you sit on the throne in the handsome wooden
hut, you can gaze out through the shoulder-high
window on to your woodland kingdom.

To go a little wilder still, head for the car-free
area. Equipment and provisions have to be
carried to the pitches using a wheelbarrow
– although the site's owners will transport
overladen campers in their Land Rover, if
necessary. A grassy slope and stile lead almost
to the water's edge; only the Mawddach Trail
stands between you and the estuary shore.
Each pitch is named after a native tree, and has
its own rock-encircled campfire (a large bag of
logs and kindling is yours for a fiver, and should
last for two nights).

SNOWDONIA

EATING & DRINKING

You can get away with staying put, thanks to the honesty shop; otherwise, the nearest civilisation is down the road in the little coastal town of Fairbourne, whose shops include a grocer, butcher, post office and general store. Just opposite Fairbourne station, Indiana (01341 250891, www.indianacuisine.co.uk, closed Tue) is terrific. It's run by a former Bollywood film actor and his wife, and offers a pan-Indian menu that's served with panache.

Three or four miles along the estuary in Penmaenpool, just by the toll bridge to Barmouth and easily accessible via the Mawddach Trail, the George III Hotel (01341 422525, www.georgethe third.co.uk) is a great place for a pint and a slap-up feed. Perched in the hills above the estuary, in a Victorian mansion, the Penmaenuchaf Hall Hotel (01341 422129, www.penhall.co.uk) is special occasion territory. Its modish but unfussy menu is rich in local produce, set off nicely by a distinguished wine list. From Penmaenpool, it's a short drive to the market town of Dolgellau, which also has a variety of cafés and restaurants.

Award-winning chef Ifan Dunn runs the smart but reasonably priced Mawddach restaurant (01341 424020, www.mawddach.com, closed Mon, Tue, dinner Sun) in Llanelltyd, a 20-minute drive from Graig Wen. Dunn bakes his own bread and champions local produce, including lamb from his brother's farm.

ATTRACTIONS & ACTIVITIES

Birdwatching on the estuary, swimming and building sandcastles on the beaches of Fairbourne, and crossing the lovely old wooden bridge to Barmouth for a pint and a fish supper are just a few of our favourite activities in these parts.

The more energetically inclined can scramble past the Arthog waterfalls all the way to Cadair Idris – Snowdon's junior, but a mountain to be taken seriously, nonetheless. You can head straight from the campsite to cycle or walk the Mawddach Trail (www.mawddachtrail.co.uk), which runs for nine and a half miles along a disused railway line on the southern edge of the estuary. If stirrups rather than pedals appeal, there's beach riding and trekking from Bwlch Gwyn Farm (01341 250107, www.bwlchgwynfarm.co.uk), located between Arthog and Fairbourne.

In Dolgellau, Welsh traditional music is promoted by Ty Siamas (01341 421800, www.tysiamas.com), the National Centre for Welsh Folk Music, with its interactive exhibition, workshops, gigs and café. A few miles' walk from the town, Cymer Abbey was founded by Cistercian monks in 1198, though never completed. Set in a remote valley, surrounded by streams and woods, it is wonderfully serene; ask for directions at Dolgellau Tourist Information Centre (01341 422888, closed Tue, Wed Nov-Easter).

AMUSING THE KIDS

Children relish King Arthur's Labyrinth (01654 761584, www.kingarthurslabyrinth.co.uk) in Corris, 18 miles away. The subterranean boat ride takes intrepid visitors through a waterfall and into a series of vast caverns and tunnels, accompanied by tales of King Arthur and other Welsh legends.

Steam trains are usually a prerequisite of a child's holiday in Wales. Close to Graig Wen, in Fairbourne, the locomotives of the Fairbourne & Barmouth Steam Railway (01341 250362, www.fairbournerailway.com) chuff the short distance to Penrhyn Point. Note that trains don't run every day, especially out of season.

CAMPING NEARBY

In Arthog, Garthyfog (01341 250254, www. snowdonialogcabins.co.uk, open all year, tents £10-£15, caravans £15-£20) has a campsite as well as log cabins and caravans. Just over six miles away in Llanelltyd is Vanner (01341 422854, www.vanner.co.uk, open mid Mar-Oct, £8-£10 for two people), which forms part of a working hill farm surrounding Cymer Abbey; the camping site, though caravan-dominated, also caters for tents.

Cae Du (*see p247*) is just lovely – a small, simple beauty looking out over the sea at Llwyngwril – while Cae Gwyn Farm (*see p258*) is on the A470 ten miles north of Dolgellau.

SNOWDONIA

Discover the best of Britain...

Shell Island

Shell Island
Llanbedr, Gwynedd LL45 2PJ
01341 241453
enquiries1@shellisland.co.uk
www.shellisland.co.uk
Map p28 ⑲
OS map SH557267

Number of pitches 800 tents/motorhomes.
No caravans.
Open Mid Mar-end Oct.
Booking Online (but only for 20% of
pitches, 80% is for walk-ins). Minimum
stay 3 nights Whitsun, Aug bank holiday.
Typical cost £6.25-£7.25 adult,
£2.50-£3 child.
Facilities Bar; café; disabled facilities
(toilet and shower); laundry facilities;
restaurant; shops; showers (free);
toilets; washing-up area.
Campfires Allowed, off ground.
Firewood available (£4).
Dogs Allowed, on lead (£2).
Restrictions No single-sex groups or
unsupervised teenagers. Midnight curfew.
Getting there By road Shell Island is
about two miles west of the A496, which
runs along the coast between Barmouth
and Harlech. At Llanbedr take the turn just
after the bridge; signs point to the campsite
and RAF airfield. **By public transport** The
nearest train station is at Llanbedr, which
is a 30-mins walk from the campsite. There
are no buses, but a taxi will cost around £4
(Id'Z Taxis, 07811 259307).

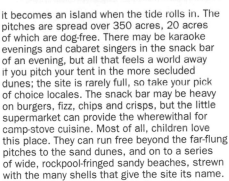

If the children's spirits soar as they're driven
along the causeway to this huge, bells-and-
whistles campsite, adult campers may be forgiven
for feeling a corresponding plummet in mood.
But give Shell Island a chance. Alright, it is
supposedly the largest campsite in Europe, a
claim to fame that surely quashes any hopes of
peaceful evenings under the stars. As you drive
past the unprepossessing huts of the RAF cadet
base, images of 1950s holiday camps may pop
unbidden into your head. Then there's the garish
welcome to Shell Island: its busy reception area,
café/bar and evening entertainment schedule
all laid out before you as you register. It may not
bode well, but it deserves further inspection.

Set on a tongue of land (also known as
Mochras) that's crossed by the River Artro,
it becomes an island when the tide rolls in. The
pitches are spread over 350 acres, 20 acres
of which are dog-free. There may be karaoke
evenings and cabaret singers in the snack bar
of an evening, but all that feels a world away
if you pitch your tent in the more secluded
dunes; the site is rarely full, so take your pick
of choice locales. The snack bar may be heavy
on burgers, fizz, chips and crisps, but the little
supermarket can provide the wherewithal for
camp-stove cuisine. Most of all, children love
this place. They can run free beyond the far-flung
pitches to the sand dunes, and on to a series
of wide, rockpool-fringed sandy beaches, strewn
with the many shells that give the site its name.

The site has been owned by the Workman
family since 1958, and each sibling has his
or her own area of responsibility: a couple of
sisters take care of the supermarket, gift shop
and camping shop, while the brothers run the
licensed snack bar and deal with day-to-day
front-of-camp duties. Further development of
Shell Island is carefully restricted as it's part
of Snowdonia National Park, and the few rules
that have been laid down are designed to
keep this Site of Special Scientific Interest
scientifically interesting. Caravans are banned,

SNOWDONIA

there are no electric hook-ups, and campfires and barbecues are permitted as long as they are raised from the ground, and cleared up afterwards. And we approve of the rule that forbids pitching within 20 metres of another tent; that way, there's plenty of room for everyone.

A small supermarket supplies groceries and other essentials, and the camping shop stocks spare pegs, guy ropes, gas canisters and cooking utensils and offers a replacement-pole fitting service. If your tent has really suffered in the winds and the staff can't fix it, Cartwright Upholstery in nearby Llanfair (01766 781030) can repair tents. It's usually closed at weekends, but can open on Saturdays by arrangement.

EATING & DRINKING

The snack bar's burgers, chips and white bread sandwiches will soon pall, although it's nice to be able to sit down with a pint in the evening.

In Llanbedr, around two and a half miles away, the Victoria Inn (01341 241213, www.victoriainnllanbedr. co.uk) can provide an evening drink and a bar menu with children's choices; expect fish and chips, steak pies, burgers, jacket potatoes and sandwiches. Set on the banks of the River Artro, it also has a children's play area. Decent bar meals are available at Ty Mawr Hotel (01341 241440, www.tymawrhotel.com), and the restaurant at the smart Bryn Artro Country House (01341 241619, www.llanbedr-brynartro.com) is open to non-residents at the weekend. Many campers love Yr Hen Feudy (01341 241555, closed lunch), a family-friendly, traditional restaurant that specialises in hearty Welsh dishes such as slow-cooked local lamb with seasonal vegetables.

Bear in mind that if you venture off site at night, you must check the tides; a noticeboard at the start of the causeway indicates safe times to cross.

ATTRACTIONS & ACTIVITIES

Exploring the beach and rockpooling are the most popular activities on site, while anglers can fish for grey mullet, bass and plaice from the shore beyond the harbour (tackle and bait are sold in the shop). In peak season, the evening entertainment in the snack bar runs from karaoke to magic shows.

Just south of Shell Island, Morfa Dyffryn is a huge, sandy beach – and a well-known naturist spot. As well as nudity, the beach is renowned for regular sightings of dolphins. Another attractive beach, popular with anglers and birdwatchers, is Llandanwg, a 15-minute drive north.

About two miles from Shell Island is the prime walking terrain of Nantcol Valley, with its waterfalls, babbling brooks, riverside walks and nature trails. For more rugged hikes, head into the Rhinog mountains. Rhinog Fawr from Cwm Bychan is a challenging eight-mile route, outlined on the Walk Snowdonia website (www.walkeryri.org.uk).

The lovely town of Harlech, dominated by its towering fortress, is a few miles north of Llanbedr – and if there's one castle you shouldn't miss in Wales,

Site specific

✔ A fantastic spot for families. Thanks to the café, snack bar, mini supermarket and camping shop, you won't have to leave the campsite unless you want to.

✘ It does feel like a holiday camp, especially if you linger around the snack bar and shops for too long. Don't come here if you're allergic to young children; anklebiters are everywhere.

it's Harlech (01766 780552, www.cadw.wales.gov.uk). Perched high on a rock, this was one of Edward I's 'iron ring' of fortresses, designed to keep out the barbaric Welsh. It didn't. Hum 'Men of Harlech' as you explore the castle and feel stirred by the story of Owain Glyn Dwr, set out in an exhibition here.

Keen golfers, preferably from a recognised club and with low handicaps, can have a round at Harlech's top-notch Royal St David's Golf Course (01766 780361, www.royalstdavids.co.uk). Theatr Harlech (01766 780667, www.theatrharlech.com) hosts a lively mix of dance, drama, stand-up and music. Prettily placed with Snowdonia's mountains centre-stage and sand dunes as a backdrop, the theatre also shows family-friendly films in the school holidays.

AMUSING THE KIDS

Children can easily entertain themselves: crabbing on the causeway, rockpooling, swimming and shell collecting on the beach, scampering around the playground and squandering their holiday money on penny sweets, fudge and ice-cream, crab lines, buckets and all manner of brilliant beachy tat. Those that are game for a walk will enjoy the Nantcol waterfalls, where the Children's Island Nature Trail traces a short circular route around a small island in the river, near the picnic site, and flags up different species of plants. Harlech Castle is a guaranteed child-pleaser, and a film at Theatr Harlech will occupy a wet afternoon.

CAMPING NEARBY

Nantcol Waterfalls (01341 241209, www.nantcol waterfalls.co.uk, open Mar-Oct, £8 adult, £4 child) is a lovely site in the hills, where you're lulled to sleep by the sound of tumbling water. There's swimming in the river and firewood to buy, and the shower and toilet blocks are pristine.

SNOWDONIA

Cae Gwyn Farm

Cae Gwyn Farm
Bronaber Farm, Trawsfynydd,
Gwynedd LL41 4YE
01766 540245, 07776 019336
enquiries@caegwynfarm.co.uk
www.caegwynfarm.co.uk
Map p28 ⑳
OS map SH714297

Number of pitches 90 people (tents),
2 campervans. No caravans/motorhomes.
B&B (4 doubles). Camping barn (sleeps 10).
Open All year.
Booking By phone. Advisable.
Typical cost Camping £8 adult.
B&B £24-£30. Barn £11-£13 adult.
Facilities Bike storage and wash; fridge
and freezer; microwave; showers (free);
toilets; washing-up area; Wi-Fi (patio).
Campfires Not allowed.
Dogs Allowed by arrangement.
Restrictions Children by arrangement.
No noise after 11pm.
Getting there By road From Dolgellau head
north on the A470. After 10 miles, you will
see a white arrow sign 'B&B Cae Gwyn Farm'
on the left, followed by a dark brown sign
'Cae Gwyn Farm B&B'. Turn left into the
drive just before the brown sign. Sat-nav
advice on the website. **By public transport**
Possible, but slow. Train to Barmouth,
then bus X94 to Dolgellau, then bus 35 to
Blaenau Ffestiniog (www.arrivabus.co.uk).
Buses stop at Cae Gwyn on request every
1-2 hrs, depending on the season, time of
the day and weather conditions.

The preponderance of muddy young men and their
even muddier mountain bikes at Cae Gwyn Farm
is no accident. Two miles down the A470 is Coed
y Brenin, a Forestry Commission-run parcel of
land that just happens to be the best mountain
biking centre in Wales. The campsite caters for
them well, with a lockable storage shed, a jet-
hose for cleaning off the dirt, a basic bunk barn
and a series of small camping fields. The fridge,
freezer and microwave in the washing-up room
near the farmhouse are handy too. There's also
B&B accommodation for softies.

A working sheep farm, Cae Gwyn is set in a
slight valley, sheltered by trees. The ground is
soft but boggy, which can be tricky when it rains
(which it does frequently in these parts) – the

driest fields are Rhinog View and Meadow. On
calm summer evenings the midges can approach
plague proportions, but with a bit of a breeze and
some sunshine the place is transformed. In any
case, all is forgiven come the morning, when the
sight of the mist rising from the valley is magical.
There's the added attraction of stunning views to
Rhinog Fawr and Rhinog Fach ('Big' and 'Little',
respectively), part of the little-visited mountain
range between here and the sea.

Less attractive are the numerous white notices
listing various dos and don'ts – a legacy of the
previous owners. The friendly current incumbents,
Sue and Dave Hill (and affable sheepdog Del),
are much more laid-back and always ready for
a chat or to offer information on local points of
interest. They're also planning some changes,
most notably to the number of loos and showers;
currently there are only three of each, which is
nowhere near enough when the campsite is full.
They're also in a rather rundown and unappealing
condition – not that the bikers care. The Hills are
more relaxed about noise too, and are happy to
take campers on spec. Children aren't banned,
but it's not really a family site.

If you need to stock up on food, the historic
market town of Dolgellau is ten miles away down
the A470, across a little stone bridge. Once a
prosperous wool centre, it's full of doughty-
looking buildings made of dolerite, the local grey
stone, and has an irritating one-way system. It's
worth taking a stroll around – pick up a map from
the tourist information centre (01341 422888,
closed Tue, Wed Nov-Easter) in the main square.

EATING & DRINKING

Head north up the A470 and turn right at the holiday
village sign to reach the Rhiw Goch Inn (01766
540374), a huge pub and restaurant perched on the
hill above the village's log cabins. It's a bit dark and
gloomy, but the staff are very friendly and the food
(spag bol, Welsh lamb, steaks) is heart-warming if
unremarkable. Trawsfynydd village – a couple of
miles further on, and not far from the defunct nuclear
power station – has a newsagent, butcher, general
store, post office, off-licence and also a couple of
reasonable pubs.

About five miles south is the Tyn-y-Groes (01341
440275, www.tynygroes.com), once a coaching inn and
now a convivial spot for a pint of Snowdonia Ale and
large platefuls of standard pub food. The miniscule
back garden, full of bird feeders, is a delight.

There's a Somerfield supermarket, a couple of
greengrocers and assorted coffee shops, pubs and
eateries in busy Dolgellau. Dylanwad Da (01341

Cae Gwyn

Coed y Brenin

ATTRACTIONS & ACTIVITIES

The forests and hills around Cae Gwyn are ideal terrain for walkers and cyclists. There's also good fly-fishing to be had, especially at the massive Llyn Trawsfynydd, for native brown trout, rainbow trout, perch, rudd and grass carp; you can buy fishing permits in Trawsfynydd village. Hiking and camping gear is available from Cader Idris (01341 422195, www.cader-idris.co.uk, closed Sun) in Dolgellau.

The rugged Rhinogs – much less visited than Snowdon's peaks further north – are usually approached from the west, via the two valleys of Cwm Nantcol and Cwm Bychan, leading to the so-called Roman Steps (actually a medieval packhorse trail), but you can come from the other direction. In fact, you can walk straight from the campsite on to a path that leads through meadow and forest, skirting around the northern flank of Rhinog Fawr, to join the Steps.

Hardcore bikers fling themselves around the rocky, rollercoaster trails at Coed y Brenin (01341 440747, www.mbwales.com). There's one easy route for families, but most tracks are aimed at experienced technical riders. There are walking and running paths too, plus a visitor centre, bike shop and café in a stylish circular wooden building with outdoor seating. It's midge hell in damp weather.

For a more mellow time, head south to the Mawddach Trail (www.mawddachtrail.co.uk), which runs from Dolgellau to Barmouth along a disused railway line on the edge of the Mawddach estuary. Mounts can be hired at Dolgellau Cycles (01341 423332, www.dolgellaucycles.co.uk, closed Mon mid Oct-Easter).

The well preserved and strikingly located Harlech Castle (01766 780552, www.cadw.wales.gov.uk) was one of the 'iron ring' of fortresses built by Edward I to control the unruly Welsh, and the inspiration for the stirring tune 'Men of Harlech'. It's about 17 miles away on the coast.

CAMPING NEARBY

Halfway between Dolgellau and Barmouth on the north side of the estuary, Tyddyn Du campsite (01341 430644, www.freewebs.com/tyddyndu, open end Mar- Oct) has been in operation since the 1940s. Modest facilities match the modest prices (£7 adult, £3.00 child), and campfires are permitted.

On the opposite side of the estuary is Graig Wen (see p251) and further south, perched on a clifftop by the sea, is Cae Du (see p247).

> ## Site specific
>
> ✔ The area is fantastic for mountain bikers and walkers, and much less crowded than Snowdon. The site's owners are lovely too.
>
> ✘ The camping fields can get soggy, and the facilities need an upgrade.

422870, www.dylanwad.co.uk, closed Mon-Wed, Sun) is a modern-looking café and wine shop that turns into a bistro in the evening. But the best cooking in the area is just outside the town, near Llanelltyd, at award-winning Mawddach (see p252), set in a stunning converted barn with a glass front.

Hafod y Llan

**Hafod y Llan
Nant Gwynant, Beddgelert,
Gwynedd LL55 4NL**
01766 510129
alison.ellis@nationaltrust.org.uk
www.craflwyn.org
Map p28 ㉑
OS map SH627507

Number of pitches Approx 30 tents.
No caravans/motorhomes.
Open 1 week before Easter-Oct.
Booking No booking.
Typical cost £6.50 adult, £3 under-16s.
Facilities Showers (50p); toilets;
washing-up area.
Campfires Allowed, in fire rings.
Firewood available (£6.50 unlimited).
Dogs Allowed, on lead.
Restrictions Large single-sex groups
by arrangement. No noise after 10pm.
Getting there By road The campsite is
off the A498 (Beddgelert to Capel Curig
road), about 3 miles north of Beddgelert.
Just past Caffi Gwynant, turn left – clearly
signposted to the campsite   and continue
for half a mile through the farm to the
car park. **By public transport** Train to
Porthmadog. Snowdon Sherpa Express
bus S97 runs approx every 2 hrs and stops
at the foot of the Watkin Path, which is
also the turn-off to the campsite. Journey
takes 25 mins. More information on
www.snowdoniagreenkey.co.uk.

Hafod y Llan means 'summer dwelling' and
this absolute gem of a campsite, situated at
the foot of Snowdon, is a lovely spot in which
to dwell for a few days, in summer or otherwise.
There's been camping here for generations;
the current incarnation, run with low-key efficiency
and some style by the National Trust, is a
model of simplicity.

The single field is sheltered by trees and
drystone walls, with a mountain stream bubbling
along one side, and dark cliffs rearing behind.
At the bottom is the car park (vehicles aren't
allowed on the field), the buildings of Hafod Farm
(not accessible to campers) and the neat shower
and toilet block. Beyond that lies a gorgeous
view across sun-kissed meadows to tree-covered
slopes. The power lines that run across the site
are the only unsightly element.

Watkin Path

SNOWDONIA

You can't book, so just turn up and hope there's room. An extra field is opened at the height of the summer, but it's the car park that determines numbers: when that's full, the campsite is full. Complete the self-service envelope at the information shack (the friendly wardens are only around in the morning and evening, except at weekends and bank holidays), then choose where to set up your tent. Avoid the boulders and bumpy sections, and make sure you're 20 feet away from any other tent and near one of the big metal fire rings, with their hefty log seating. For £6.50 you can help yourself to as much firewood as you please from the woodpile in the car park. It's bone-dry, barkless and cut into manageable chunks; there's no way you won't have a roaring blaze within minutes.

The facilities might be a bit basic for some. Water comes from the stream and should be boiled before drinking, and the two washing-up sinks – outside, at the rear of the toilet block – only have cold water. But the showers are immaculate: brightly painted in white and green, with not a speck of dirt.

Compact, quiet, surrounded by stunning scenery and close to one of the main footpaths up Snowdon: Hafod y Llan is the stuff of campers' dreams. Hardcore walkers camp here, of course, but it's also favoured by families and has a loyal band of regulars. Although only half a mile from the main road (and a commendable café), the site feels wonderfully isolated and secret. If it rains – not an uncommon occurrence in these parts – repair to the nearest town, Beddgelert, three miles away, for a pint and some food in the warmth.

EATING & DRINKING

Back on the main road, next to the turn-off to the campsite, is daytime-only Caffi Gwynant (01766 890855, www.cafesnowdon.co.uk, closed Tue all year, Mon Sept-June, all Jan). Housed in a converted 19th-century chapel, it's a corker of a café, serving sturdy, satisfying breakfasts (full Welsh, porridge, muesli) and tasty sandwiches, wraps, jacket potatoes and hot dishes for lunch. Vegetarians have plenty of choice. Maps, souvenirs, packed lunches and internet access are also available.

Otherwise, Beddgelert – a picturesque place with its old stone bridge, if veering on the twee – has

Site specific

✔ The location at the foot of Snowdon is gorgeous. Campfire fans will love the limitless supply of firewood.

✘ You can't book, so it's a gamble that you'll find a pitch in high summer.

Beddgelert

assorted cafés, pubs and a popular pizzeria/ice-cream parlour. Beddgelert Bistro (*see p266*) is a favourite too. For faded grandeur, visit the enormous Royal Goat Hotel (01766 890224, www.royalgoathotel.co.uk, closed Jan-mid Feb), which provides the usual pub grub and afternoon teas as well good-value, slap-up dinners in its more formal dining room. For local salmon and trout or Welsh lamb steaks with seasonal vegetables, try the Tanronen Inn (01766 890347, www.tanronnen.co.uk).

There's a small general store in Beddgelert, but the nearest supermarket is 11 miles away in Porthmadog.

ATTRACTIONS & ACTIVITIES

You're in the middle of some of the best hiking country in Britain, so pull on your boots and get going. If you need any walking or camping equipment, Y Warws (01766 890416, www.y-warws.co.uk) on the Caernarfon road in Beddgelert should be able to help.

Cut through the top of the campsite, past a series of waterfalls and clear pools (popular bathing and sunning spots on summer weekends) to join the Watkin Path. It's one of the toughest routes up Snowdon, involving an ascent of 3,000 feet, with the topmost section via a steep and unstable scree slope. Just an hour's walk, though, past the disused tramway and derelict buildings of the old slate quarry and a strange graveyard of slate shards, will bring you within the embrace of Snowdon's horseshoe.

Alternatively, mountain bikes are for hire from Beddgelert Bike Hire (*see p266*) in the centre of Beddgelert Forest. And there's a steam train round every bend in North Wales, it seems. The closest –

passing through Beddgelert – is the Welsh Highland Railway (*see p266*), which runs from Caernarfon to Porthmadog. There you can join the Ffestiniog Railway (01766 516000, www.festrail.co.uk) for its 13-mile journey via tunnels and horseshoe bends, and across some spectacular mountainscapes to the slate-quarrying town of Blaenau Ffestiniog.

AMUSING THE KIDS

If Snowdon is a step too far, try the two-mile trail around the farm and campsite (pick up a leaflet at the information point in the car park).

The nearest all-weather attraction is Beddgelert's Sygun Copper Mine (01766 890595, www.sygun coppermine.co.uk, closed Oct-Mar except new year and Feb half-term), where you tour echoing mine workings and caverns frequented by wild-bearded miner dummies, then potter around a museum of antiquities. Panning for gold, adventure playgrounds and archery games are tagged on for child-pleasing purposes.

CAMPING NEARBY

Llyn Gwynant (*see p264*) is just up the road. In the other direction, just before Beddgelert, Cae Du Campsite (01766 890345, www.caeducampsite.co.uk, open Apr-Oct, £16-£18 for two people) has room for 85 tents and 25 caravans next to the River Glaslyn. It's a peaceful spot – no groups, no music – and security-conscious, with barriers that are locked at 10pm.

A mile north of Beddgelert, in Beddgelert Forest, is Forest Holidays' only campsite in Wales (01766 890288, www.forestholidays.co.uk, open all year, £8-£14 for two people).

Llyn Gwynant

Llyn Gwynant
Hafod Lwyfog, Nantgwynant,
Gwynedd LL55 4NW
enquiries@gwynant.com
www.gwynant.com
Map p28 ㉒
OS map SH648525

Number of pitches 440 tents, 10 caravans/
motorhomes. 3 barns (sleeping 20-30).
1 static caravan (sleeps 4).
Open Mar-Nov.
Booking Only taken for groups of
more than 20, by email.
Typical cost £7-£9 adult, £4 5-15s.
Barn £10-£12 adult, £8 5-15s.
Static caravan £200-£225 per week.
Facilities Disabled facilities (toilet and
shower); shop (from summer 2010);
showers (free); toilets; washing-up facilities.
Campfires Allowed. Firewood available (£4).
Dogs Allowed, on lead (£1).
Restrictions No radios/stereos.
No noise after 11.30pm.
Getting there By road The campsite is on
the A498 (Beddgelert to Capel Curig road),
about 5 miles north of Beddgelert at the
northern end of Llyn Gwynant lake. You
can only access it by taking a left turn
while travelling north; if you're heading
south you'll have to turn round in the layby
beside the lake. **By public transport**
The Snowdon Sherpa S97 bus runs daily
from Porthmadog train station, and takes
about half an hour to Nantgwynant. From
other directions you may need to change
bus; check timetables for the service at
www.snowdoniagreenkey.co.uk.

Below Snowdonia's famous horseshoe, the
drama of the peaks gives way to softer, springy
green slopes and wooded river valleys beloved
of walkers, cyclists and watersports enthusiasts.
There's plenty of room for them all to convene in
the Nantgwynant valley, along with their children,
dogs and kayaks, at this popular tent settlement
on the wide shores of Llyn Gwynant lake.

Room for 440 pitches there may be, but you
can't see many tents from the road, and the
scale of the site isn't immediately apparent –
thanks, in part, to the restrictions on the number
of caravans allowed. Only the bevy of efficient,
often Antipodean, young wardens sporting dark
green company T-shirts gives a clue to Llyn
Gwynant's businesslike nature.

Sir Clough Williams-Ellis, Welsh architect of
Portmeirion village fame, bought the site in the
1930s to save it from developers. The land has
stayed in the family ever since, although much of
the countryside around it was gifted to the nation
and became part of Snowdonia National Park.

Some of the fields have coveted lakeside
pitches; on hot days you can crawl from tent to
wake-up dip in the glacial waters of Llyn Gwynant.
Others are in the shadow of the rocky foothills
of the Snowdon horseshoe (plucky early risers
can make straight for the Watkin Path up to Yr
Wyddfa, Snowdon's summit – the warden can
tell you how). Another field is car-free, with grassy
slopes that children love rolling down. Even in
high season it's relatively easy to find a quiet
pitch, with just you, your tent and your firepit.
There's also a secluded static caravan, Nutshell,
and a simple but solid camping barn complex,
which can be booked by larger groups.

Down a path from the reception cabin and
small shop stands the attractive stone shower
block, with washing-up facilities to one side.
Standpipes are dotted about the campground;

Site specific

✔ The lakeside location means that the wholesale pleasures of swimming, boating and walking are just a quick step from your tent flap. There's also easy access to Snowdon's peaks.

✘ Wardens, rules and the quantity of other campers (and families) may deter child-free travellers and hardened outdoor enthusiasts seeking wilderness and freedom. The site can be heaving in August, if the weather is good.

the water comes from a mountain stream, passed through an ultra-violet purification process.

This is a green site, in every sense. Recycling is expected, and a lengthy explanation as to why only wood bought here can be used in the firepits is pinned up in the shower block. Radios are banned, so in the evening all you can hear is snatches of conversation and laughter, the strum of guitars and the odd expletive as another marshmallow is lost to the flames. As we tortured jelly babies around our firepit, someone in a faraway field was launching paper lanterns into the night sky – just like in *Danny the Champion of the World*. The children were in heaven.

Llyn Gwynant from the north-east; the campsite is just visible next to the water.

EATING & DRINKING

The nearest pub, the Pen y Gwryd Hotel (01286 870211, www.pyg.co.uk, closed Nov, Dec), is two miles north of the campsite at the junction of the A498 and A4086. A long-time mountaineering pub (it was used by the 1953 Everest expedition) it has become something of a national treasure; call in for a pint and some bar food.

Set at the start of Snowdon's Watkin Path, lovely Caffi Gwynant (*see p262*) is accessible via a pretty two-mile walk around Llyn Gwynant, with a path through Hafod y Llan Farm.

Groceries, pubs, restaurants, ice-creams and pizza can all be found about four miles away in Beddgelert village, one of Snowdonia's pin-ups. The antique-filled Beddgelert Bistro (01766 890543, www.beddgelert-bistro.co.uk, opening days vary off-season) is a fine place for local lamb, Anglesey seafood or homely cream teas. Families may prefer pizza and ice-cream, courtesy of Glaslyn Ices & Glandwr Café (01766 890339, www.glaslynices.co.uk, closed Nov-Feb).

ATTRACTIONS & ACTIVITES

Swimming in the lake is free and fun; if you haven't brought your own canoe or kayak, these can be hired from £5 per hour. In high season, with advance warning, the campsite can arrange instruction in boat-based activities, as well as orienteering, coasteering, climbing and abseiling.

Reception can provide details of nearby walks and scrambles, and there are several bike trails within an easy ride of the campsite. Beddgelert Bike Hire (01766 890434, www.beddgelertbikes.co.uk) is based in the middle of Forestry Commission-run Beddgelert Forest (the entrance is off the A4085, just north of

the village) – hire a bike and then head straight on to one of the routes through the woods.

For a heady dose of myth, legend and history (white dragon vs red dragon, Saxon vs Welsh), take the A498 to the remains of the ancient hill fort of Dinas Emrys, dating from the fifth century.

Some 13 miles away, occupying its own private peninsula on Snowdonia's southern shores, idiosyncratic Portmeirion Village (01766 772311, www.portmeirion-village.com) was created by Clough Williams-Ellis and is best known for its starring role in the 1960s TV series *The Prisoner*.

AMUSING THE KIDS

Given a fair wind and a bit of encouragement, children make friends and have fun messing about by the lake and riding their bikes around the site.

For many youngsters with a Thomas fixation, it's the steam trains of the Welsh Highland Railway (01766 516000, www.festrail.co.uk), based at Caernarfon, 20 minutes' away, that save the day. Another option is the Snowdon Mountain Railway (0844 493 8120, www.snowdonrailway.co.uk, closed mid Nov-early Mar). Britain's only rack and pinion railway, it allows an effort-free ascent to Snowdon's summit, there to enjoy the handsome new visitor centre and café.

CAMPSITES NEARBY

Many campsites in the Beddgelert area are caravan-heavy and quite expensive, but there are more agreeable options. Two miles away, Hafod y Llan (*see p261*) is a lovely National Trust site that costs a fiver a night, is for tents only and allows campfires. For other suggestions, *see p263*.

Gwern Gof Uchaf

**Gwern Gof Uchaf
Capel Curig, Betws-y-Coed,
Conwy LL24 0EU**
01690 720294
www.tryfanwales.co.uk
Map p28 ㉓
OS map SH673604

Number of pitches 50 tents/motorhomes.
No caravans. Bunkhouse (sleeps 14).
Open All year.
Booking Camping no bookings.
Bunkhouse by phone.
Typical cost Camping £5 adult, £4 child.
Bunkhouse £10 per person.
Facilities Showers (free); toilets;
washing-up area.
Campfires Allowed, in designated areas.
Dogs Not allowed.
Getting there By road The campsite is on
the A5, about 3 miles west of Capel Curig. If
heading west, it's on the left-hand side, just
before the Llyn Ogwen lake. It is signposted,
though can be confused with nearby Gwern
Gof Isaf. **By public transport** Train to
Bangor, from where the Snowdon Sherpa
bus S6 (www.gwynedd.gov.uk) runs daily
along the A5 to Betws-y-Coed – though there
are more buses starting from Bethesda. It
takes 25 mins and stops by the lake, within
walking distance of the campsite.

The preponderance of husky individuals sporting ropes, helmets and carabiners, heading purposefully up the rocky ridges surrounding Gwern Gof Uchaf, establishes this place as a climbers' favourite. The campsite's position, cowering under Tryfan's distinctive, bristling crags and looking out across the blue waters of Llyn Ogwen, is splendidly wild and woolly. It's a small and simple set-up, with few rules and regulations, although the no-dogs stricture is important – the campsite is on a working farm run by Sue and Bryn Williams, whose sheep amble across the forbidding slopes of the mountain.

Uchaf Gwern Gof ('uchaf' means higher) sits between Bethesda and Capel Curig, and is not to be confused with the equally enchanting Gwern Gof Isaf campsite ('isaf' means lower) just down the road. Most campers make use of Capel Curig, where, among the many outdoor pursuits shops, there are a couple of tea rooms, a grocer and two decent pubs. The main draw of Bethesdais

the butcher's shop, where you can buy beef and lamb raised on the Williams farm.

Tents can be pitched on the field in front of the farmhouse, which runs marshily down to the A5, or higher up on a little mezzanine field, strewn with mossy boulders and reached via a short, rocky path. You can just turn up, pitch camp and wait for a Williams to ask for your fee. (Being farmers, they tend to leave the campers to it during the latter part of the day, but are around early in the morning.)

There's a shower block with two unisex showers and a washing area, kept clean and orderly through the morning rush. An up-to-date weather forecast for the area is pinned up here. Attractive little stone outbuildings once used for livestock house two loos each for men and women, and a variety of dribbly outdoor taps with sinks are used for pot washing. The bunkhouse is spartan but comfortable, with bunk beds, central heating and a proper kitchen.

Most visitors head out early, with the most serious hikers donning their walking boots and striding off into the sunrise as soon as they've rinsed their tea mugs and finished their cereal bars. They return with the dusk to heat up dinner over a gas ring – several picnic tables are provided for mealtimes – and flop on to their camping mats to discuss the next day's climb. This is a resting place for tired bodies, so there are few frills; Tryfan's challenging flanks are your main entertainment.

EATING & DRINKING

It's strictly bring-your-own at the campsite, with provisions available in Bethesda and Capel Curig. Around three miles away, at the western end of Llyn Ogwen, the Ogwen Falls Snack Bar (01248 600683) is run by a friendly couple, who refuel calorie-craving Tryfan scalers with cold drinks, bacon sandwiches, cakes, ice lollies, hot chocolate and, in winter, Welsh beefburgers. It's open from about 8.30am until dusk daily in high season, and on most weekends in winter.

In Capel Curig, the Bryn-Glo Café (01690 720215, closed Mon, Tue all year, Wed, Thur in off-season) serves scones for tea and steak pies and comfort food for dinner. If you've had a hard day's hiking, the Bryn Tyrch Inn (01690 720223, www.bryntyrchinn.co.uk) does a welcome line in warming dishes such as lamb and rosemary sausages, goulash and shepherdess pie with lentils and goat's cheese. Booking advised.

Tyn-y-Coed (01690 720331, www.tyn-y-coed.co.uk) is a splendid roadside inn on the A5 just outside Capel Curig, with a wide range of local ales, malt whiskies and good-value bar meals. The Pinnacle Pursuits General Stores (01690 720201), one of many outdoor equipment specialists in the area, also has a café.

ATTRACTIONS & ACTIVITIES

Of the Gyderau range's peaks, Tryfan is the star attraction. Although it is only the 14th highest mountain in Wales, its rugged spine is an irresistible challenge, and has often proved too much for inexperienced walkers in harsh weather.

Just beyond the Ogwen Falls Snack Bar and Idwal Cottage Youth Hostel, the Lyn Idwal path runs around a glaciated valley and Tryfan's Bristly Ridge, leading to the Devil's Kitchen – a dramatic, deep cleft in the rock, so named because it looks like a dark, satanic chimney. There's gentler walking, and beauty spots for picnicking, in the Gwydyr Forest around Betws-y-Coed, eight miles away.

Lyn Ogwen, a shallow, trout-filled lake, is the source of the Ogwen river (which flows down to Bangor and the sea), so this is angling country too.

If you need to polish your outward-bounder skills the Plas y Brenin Centre (01690 720214, www.pyb. co.uk) in Capel Curig offers a ski slope, canoeing, and climbing instruction on an indoor wall.

You're never far from a stately pile in North Wales, and the closest duo are ruined Dolwyddelan Castle (01443 336000, www.cadw.wales.gov.uk, open Apr-Sept) in Dolwyddelan, and Gwydir Castle (01492 641687, www.gwydircastle.co.uk) in Llanrwst, supposedly one of Wales's most haunted houses. It's a private dwelling, but is open to the public Mar-Oct (closed Mon except bank holidays, Sat).

AMUSING THE KIDS

Youngsters who have had a bellyful of rocky scree might like to visit one of Snowdonia's many old-fashioned railways. Adjacent to Betws-y-Coed train station, the Conwy Valley Railway & Museum (01690 710568, www.conwyrailwaymuseum.co.uk) offers plenty of railway memorabilia and working models, plus a ten-minute ride on a miniature steam train. The Llanberis Lake Railway (01286 870549,

www.lake-railway.co.uk), a 20-minute drive away, is an ex-quarry steam engine that tootles along the shores of Lake Padarn, fitting in a children's play area and picnic place en route.

Alternatively, children can swing through the trees on a high ropes course at Tree Top Adventure (01690 710914, www.ttadventure.co.uk), just outside Betws-y-Coed. More vertiginous fun is on offer at Ropes & Ladders (01286 872310, www.ropesand ladders.co.uk) in Padarn Country Park, Llanberis. Booking is advisable for both.

CAMPING NEARBY

Gwern Gof Isaf Farm (01690 720276, www.gwern gofisaf.co.uk, open all year) is also run by a pair of farmers called Williams – David and Elizabeth this time – and is a similarly appealing set-up, with slightly more in the way of home comforts, including some hook-ups for caravans and two smart bunkhouses. It can claim seniority over Uchaf as it opened in 1906. Sir John Hunt stayed here when he was training on Tryfan prior to leading the 1953 Everest expedition. A tent pitch costs £5 per person.

Other similar-priced options open all year include Bryn Tyrch Farm (01690 720414), next to the pub of the same name at the foot of the Clogwyn Mawr; and Dol-Gam (01690 720228, www.dolgam-snowdonia.co.uk), part of a family farm on the banks of the River Llugwy, under Moel Siabod.

Site specific

✔ Rocks and ridges are all around, and you can set out on some of the most dramatic walks and scrambles in the country.

✘ The fields become muddy in wet weather – and there's no shortage of rain in Snowdonia. Facilities are basic, so it's hard to get away from the mud.

Tan-y-Bryn Farm

Tan-y-Bryn Farm
Bryn Pydew, Llandudno Junction,
Conwy LL31 9JZ
01492 549296
Map p28 24
OS map SH815796

Number of pitches 10 tents, 5 caravans/
motorhomes. B&B (1 room).
Open All year.
Booking By phone. Essential.
Typical cost Tent £10 2 people,
£18 6 people. Caravan/motorhome
£13 2 people. B&B £40-£50.
Facilities Disabled facilities (toilet
and shower); electric hook-ups (6);
shower (£1); toilets; washing-up area.
Campfires Not allowed.
Dogs Allowed, on lead (£1).
Certain breeds not allowed.
Restrictions No noise after 11pm.
Getting there By road At junction 19 of the
A55, follow signs for the A470 to Llandudno.
At the next roundabout take the third exit.
Turn right on to Esgyryn Road, next right on
to Pydew Road, and right again in the centre
of Bryn Pydew village on to Bryn Pydew
Road. The campsite is half a mile on the
left. (Caravans must come from the opposite
direction, via junction 20 and Mochdre.)
By public transport Llandudno Junction is
the nearest train station, but no buses go
nearby. A taxi costs about £5.50 (Roger's
Taxis, 01492 572224), or it's a 3-mile walk.

Tan-y-Bryn Farm is located on the **Creuddyn**
peninsula, at the very top of Wales. Its lofty
position on what seems like an endless hill
(especially if you're on a tent-laden bike)
furnishes the site with distant sea views, even
if the beaches are about five miles away. You
can see the limestone headland known as
Great Orme sticking out from Conwy Bay, the
resorts of Llandudno and Penrhyn Bay, and,
at night, the twinkly lights of seaside towns
spread along the north coast.

Every bit as sustaining as the views is the
warm welcome extended by Karen and David
Jones, who run the site – and a little B&B
business – from their working farm. It's a small,
sweet, bucolic site, with a chicken coop beyond
the farm cottage reception area, and sheep
grazing the field below. If all this doesn't sound

like the pristine, tarmacked holiday camp of
statics you've just driven into on your climb up
the hill, you've gone awry and entered the other
Tan-y-Bryn Farm, which is nothing to do with the
Joneses and doesn't take tents. Beat a hasty
retreat and carry on a couple of hundred yards.

The site is made up of three gently sloping
camping fields; the main field is the flattest. The
farmyard, a couple of minutes' walk down the
drive from the fields, offers shower and washing
facilities, a toilet and a neat washing-up and
information room, with a clean fridge-freezer
and a noticeboard listing local businesses.

Karen and David could not be more hospitable,
providing complimentary hot drinks for weatherbeaten campers travelling without a stove and
free-range eggs (for a small remuneration).

Some of the regulars have been coming to the
site for more than 30 years, and are as friendly
as its owners. Their devotion means it's best to
book well ahead during high season, and for the
May Day bank holiday, when everyone pitches up
for Llandudno's Victorian Extravaganza.

EATING & DRINKING

For a fee, Karen and David can furnish you with
the ingredients for a cooked breakfast, and there
are several supermarkets in Llandudno Junction.

According to locals, the Queen's Head (01492
546570, www.queensheadglanwydden.co.uk) in
Glanwydden is the best eating place nearby. As well
as a good pint, it offers a smart lunch and dinner
menu (Conwy fish soup, Anglesey scallops, Welsh
lamb and mint sausages), daily specials and
a sterling line in Sunday roasts.

Llandudno Junction has one café and a couple of
pubs, but you're better off heading to Conwy, just
across the estuary. On the High Street, the Castle
Hotel (01492 582800, www.castlewales.co.uk) is
a handsome former coaching inn, now home to
Dawsons Restaurant. You can eat less formally in
the bar, but the restaurant menu, with its emphasis
on wholesome Welsh ingredients (lamb, beef, locally
smoked haddock, goat's cheeses and cheddar) is a
triumph of imaginative, hearty local cuisine.

Conwy also has what many claim to be the best
chippy in Wales: Galleons (01492 544638), on the
corner of Berry Street. Tuck into a princely plate
of haddock and chips in the restaurant, or pick up
a takeaway to eat on the quay.

ATTRACTIONS & ACTIVITIES

Ten minutes' drive away on the edge of the Conwy
estuary, next to Llandudno Junction, the RSPB
Conwy reserve (01492 584091, www.rspb.org.uk)

provides a refuge for all kinds of dippers and waders, along with autumn starling flocks.

From the Junction, you can drive across the estuary to the lovely walled town of Conwy. Frowning down on the town from its rocky outcrop, Conwy Castle (01492 592358, www.cadw.wales.gov.uk) was once part of Edward I's iron ring of fortresses, built to contain the Welsh. It's now maintained by them – or, more accurately, Cadw, which protects Wales' historic monuments. Cadw also looks after Plas Mawr (01492 580167, www.conwy.com/plasmawr, closed Mon, all Nov-Mar), a wonderfully preserved Elizabethan townhouse with lavish plasterwork and friezes. Overlooking the quay is Britain's smallest house (01492 593484), a one-up, one-down just six feet wide.

Bodnant Garden (01492 650460, www.nationaltrust. org.uk, closed mid Nov-mid Feb), a few miles south of the Junction at Tal y Cafn, is undeniably impressive, with views to Snowdonia, Italianate terraces and dramatic woodlands running down to a river valley. Star of the show is the laburnum arch, which in May attracts visitors from all over the world.

The Victorian seaside town of Llandudno has numerous attractions, including a tiny cable car (01492 877205, closed Nov-Easter) that ascends to the summit of the limestone headland of Great Orme, and the lovingly restored Great Orme Tramway (01492 879306, www.greatormetramway.co.uk, closed Nov-Mar). There's also a pier and donkey rides on the wide sandy Blue Flag beach. Visit in early May to catch Llandudno's Victorian Extravaganza (www.victorian-extravaganza.co.uk) in full, crinoline-clad swing.

It's a half-hour drive to Betws-y-Coed and the mountainscapes of Snowdonia.

AMUSING THE KIDS

For children who feel there's more to fresh air and exercise than yomping up the Welsh hills, there's a useful playground a few minutes' walk from the site.

A couple of miles away, in Colwyn Bay, the Welsh Mountain Zoo (01492 532938, www.welshmountain zoo.org) has views over the bay, landscaped gardens and a captive breeding programme for endangered species, such as resident snow leopards Otilia and Szechuan, born in 2009.

Llandudno's many attractions are also designed for family consumption, and children go a bundle on the cable cars, tramway and Ski & Snowboard Centre (01492 874707, www.llandudnoskislope.co.uk).

CAMPSITES NEARBY

Maes y Bryn (01492 640730, www.maesybryn campsite.co.uk, open Easter-Oct, £12 for two people), near Llanwrst, is a small campsite on a farm. It's ideal if you can't decide whether to go for mountains or coast, because it's handy for both Betws-y-Coed and the Snowdonia peaks, and the Vale of Conwy running to the northern coastal resorts.

Trwyn yr Wylfa Farm (01492 622357, open Apr-Sept, £5 adult, £2-£3 child) is on a working farm near Penmaenmawr. It's clean, basic and quiet, with fantastic views over Puffin Island.

Site specific

✔ The relaxed and friendly atmosphere that you only really find when you pitch up at a campsite as tiny as this one.

✘ It's pretty basic, with just one shower. And the nearest town, Llandudno Junction, isn't up to much, although the unattractive leisure complex with multiplex cinema might be useful on rainy days.

SNOWDONIA

Nant-y-Big

Nant-y-Big
Cilan, Abersoch, Pwllheli,
Gwynedd LL53 7DB
01758 712686
www.nantybig.co.uk
Map p28 ㉕
OS map SH310249

Number of pitches 38 tents,
42 caravans/motorhomes.
Open Apr-Oct.
Booking By phone, online. Essential.
Typical cost Tent £8 adult, £3 3-16s.
Caravan/motorhome from £16.
Facilities Electric hook-ups (42);
showers; toilets; washing-up area.
Campfires Not allowed.
Dogs Allowed, on lead (£1.50).
Restrictions No noise after 11pm.
Getting there By road Follow the A497
to Pwllheli, then the A499 to Abersoch.
Drive through the town heading towards
Cilan Uchaf. About 600 yards after Sarn
Bach, you'll see a green metal shed on
your left. The turning for Nant-y-Big is
30 yds further on, marked by a 'No-through
Road' sign (easy to miss). **By public
transport** Train to Pwllheli, from where the
18 bus (Nefyn Coaches, 01758 720904)
goes to Abersoch daily. The campsite is
a couple of miles from here, though twice
a day the service goes to Sarn Bach, less
than a mile away.

In August, Abersoch, a jolly seaside town
on the southern tip of the Llyn Peninsula,
does a pretty good impression of Rock in
Cornwall. The narrow pavements can scarcely
hold the groups of mooching teenagers in
Abercrombie & Fitch and Dulwich daddies in
ill-advised shorts. They drive around in hefty
Range Rovers, dismayed by the yellow lines
outside the more popular restaurants. They
come for the beach – for sailing, surfing,
wakeboarding and more.

On the hills above the town, serried ranks
of caravans, towed and static, tell the story of
Abersoch's success, and those who want to pitch
a tent out of sight of them will be disappointed.
Nant-y-Big, a couple of miles further south, is a
reasonable choice for tent owners, although it's
also got its fair share of statics, tucked away in
a small field by the reception caravan.

Three separate camping areas radiate out
from an old barn, where swallows swoop in
and out in summer. A whitewashed outbuilding
houses toilets and washing facilities. Those
who want to be near the ugly modern shower
blocks (young saplings have been planted in
front of them, promising some camouflage in
years to come) can either share a field with
caravans and tourers, or choose a tent-only field
further up the lane. Campers who set more store
by beauty than cleanliness plump for the very
top field, with its stunning views over the area's
most revered surfing beach, Porth Ceiriad.

It's just a short stroll down a bracken-lined
path to this glorious sandy strand, where
legendary rollers smash over the heads of
whooping bodyboarders. Be prepared to tighten
guy ropes: the wind whipping up the cliffs from
the sea makes a mockery of flimsy tents.
Weatherbeaten surfer/campers who spend
their day in wetsuits pitch by slopes that are
even closer to the beach, where there's a little
green shack with loos and basins. Off-season,
when the holidaying hordes have gone, the
campsite becomes an eyrie for bird watchers,
sea fishers and coastal walkers.

Mr Jones Sr and Jr, who run the site, are on
hand most of the time to answer queries, take
pitch fees and freeze ice packs.

EATING & DRINKING

Refreshments of all sorts can be found in Abersoch,
along with various shops including a Spar. When
it rains, the popular cafés with decent coffee and
ice-cream, such as Abersoch Café (01758 713456)
and Blades Cafe (01758 713158), fill up quickly, but
most hotels offer morning coffee and breakfast.

Top choice for a congenial evening out is Angelina's
Italian restaurant (01758 712353, www.angelinas.
co.uk, closed lunch and Sun), which shows a
praiseworthy preoccupation with locally sourced
produce (the likes of sea bass, Welsh lamb and beef)
and seasonal vegetables. The most lavish feed is
available at the highly regarded, family-friendly
Porth Tocyn Hotel (01758 713303, www.porthtocyn
hotel.co.uk, closed Nov-Easter), which sits aloof
on the hills above the town. Booking is essential for
the popular Sunday buffet lunch. The oft-praised
restaurant in the Venetia Hotel (01758 713354,
www.venetiawales.com, closed lunch, all Jan,
reduced opening in winter) is another upmarket
choice, with an appealing Italian menu.

Pwllheli, about seven miles from Abersoch, is
considered Llyn's capital, so is better for shopping,
pubs and cafés.

ATTRACTIONS & ACTIVITIES

The 84-mile Llyn Coastal Path, which circumnavigates the whole peninsula, runs through the campsite; head east to reach Abersoch, or west around the Mynydd Cilan headland for views of the magnificent four-mile crescent that is Porth Neigwl (Hell's Mouth) beach, where you can watch surfers part company with their boards.

Surfers can hire or buy equipment from the West Coast Surf Shop (01758 713067, www.west coastsurf.co.uk); tuition may be available too. The Abersoch Sailing School (01758 712963, www. abersochsailingschool.com) teaches all ages, and the Abersoch Regatta in early August is a real family crowd-pleaser with its crab-catching and best-dressed beach hut competitions.

Site specific

✔ Ideal for surfers, thanks to the proximity to the beaches of Porth Ceiriad and Porth Neigwl, acknowledged as the best in the area by the surfing fraternity.

✘ Finding the campsite is tricky. There is no signpost whatsoever on the winding road above Abersoch; it is, in fact, down a nameless lane marked by a T-junction sign. Also, the static caravans are a bit dispiriting.

Away from the seaside, Llyn Adventures (07751 826714, www.llynadventures.com) runs orienteering, mountaineering, river canoeing and bushcraft courses at a variety of venues around the peninsula.

En route to Pwllheli, at Llanbedrog, a Victorian-gothic building – supposedly haunted – houses Wales' oldest art gallery, Oriel Plas Glyn-y-Weddw (01758 740763, www.oriel.org.uk, closed Tue). It attracts a big crowd with its changing exhibitions and workshops. The tea room, with its own-made cakes, garden tables and lovely views, is a bonus.

AMUSING THE KIDS

Outdoorsy children aged four and up can enjoy pony trekking at Cilan Riding Centre (01758 713276, www.abersochholidays.net), not far from the campsite at Cilan Fawr. Or they can try their hand at pot-throwing and plate-painting at Myntho Pottery (01758 740023, closed mid Sept-Easter except Oct half-term), about a mile from Llanbedrog.

CAMPING NEARBY

Trehelli, a farm at Rhiw (01758 780281, open Mar-Nov, tents £15) has astounding views of Hell's Mouth and is gratifyingly close to the beach, although facilities are basic for the price.

Otherwise, Sarn Farm (01758 713583, open Apr-Oct, £16 for two adults and two children) is a caravan and tent site with a laundrette and hook-ups. A families-only site, it's within walking distance of the beach.

Mynydd Mawr

Mynydd Mawr
Llanllawen Fawr, Aberdaron, Pwllheli,
Gwynedd LL53 8BY
01758 760223
info@llanllawen.co.uk
www.aberdaroncaravanand
campingsite.co.uk
Map p28 ㉖
OS map SH144259

Number of pitches 40 tents/caravans/
motorhomes.
Open Mar-Oct.
Booking By phone, email. Advisable.
Typical cost Tent from £8 1 person, £10
2 people. Caravan/motorhome from £10.
Facilities Electric hook-ups (18); showers
(50p); toilets; washing-up facilities.
Campfires Allowed, off ground.
Firewood available on request.
Dogs Allowed.
Restrictions Groups by arrangement.
Getting there By road Head for the end
of the Llyn Peninsula on either the B4417
or the B4413, which meet near Bryncroes.
From there, continue on the B4413 towards
Aberdaron; just before the village, turn
right to Uwchmynydd. Go past the (closed)
restaurant and Ty Newydd Farm campsite
on the left, until you reach a white cottage.
Mynydd Mawr is another 200 yards, on the
left. **By public transport** The nearest train
station is at Pwllheli. From there, the 8B
bus to Uwchmynydd (01758 720904,
www.gwynedd.gov.uk) stops at the end
of the lane leading to the campsite; check
with the driver).

It runs Mon-Sat and takes an hour.This is the
last camping spot on the Llyn Peninsula before
you fall into Bardsey Sound. 'We're the Land's
End of Wales!' says owner and farmer Robert
Jones, with quiet pride. He has turned three
of his grazing fields into a delightful campsite,
and manages to find time between his more
pressing agricultural duties to check his campers
are happy ones and that his shower block
and recycling bins are all in order. It helps that
one of his six children, Ewan, is an able farmer
himself (he's a former winner of the Welsh
Young Shepherd of the Year award). Ewan and
Robert come out with their border collies Siân
and Tess to move sheep and advise on walks

along the tricky Llyn Peninsula Coastal Path,
which runs along the cliffs to the seaside
village of Aberdaron and beyond.

This is a small, quiet, family site, which people
return to year after year (booking is advised).
Pitches are allocated in advance, so ask if you
can have one in the field with the shower block;
hedges provide some shelter. There are three
scrupulously clean toilets and a shower each
for men and women. Barbecues and campfires
are allowed, as long as they're raised off the
grass (bring your own firepit/container). Bring
a kite too. The Joneses sometimes bring out
their tea van, selling own-made cakes, ice-cream
and drinks, and a new café should be ready for
the 2012 season.

People come for the walking, the views and
the call of the seabirds. The coastal heathland
is precious and under threat; it's a rich habitat
for rare beauties, such as golden-hair lichen
and the spotted rock-rose (which flowers for
only one day), yellowhammers and unusual
butterflies. Twitchers are chuffed to see
choughs wheeling and calling over the cliff
paths. A clamber up the steep path to the west
lead to the old coastguard station, which now
houses a National Trust information point.

As you take the rocky descent to the sea,
keeping Bardsey Island (Ynys Enlli) – a point of
pilgrimage for centuries and 'the island of 20,000
saints' – in front of you, you can see the ruins
of St Mary's Chapel, where pilgrims prayed for
safe passage acoss the treacherous sea to
the island. A standing stone marks the pilgrims'
launching point. Ffynnon Fair (St Mary's Well)
is a freshwater spring covered twice daily by
the sea, but miraculously containing clear,
apparently fresh water as the tide goes out.

EATING & DRINKING

Lovely, simple, undeveloped Aberdaron, about two
miles away, is your nearest source of refreshment.
It has a Spar-cum-butcher's-cum-post office and a
newsagent that also sells alcohol.

The most historically significant place to eat is
undoubtedly Y Gegin Fawr (01758 760359, closed
dinner and Nov-Easter). This squat, whitewashed
stone building was once a communal kitchen
where 13th-century pilgrims lined their stomachs
before boarding a boat for Bardsey. Today, it serves
cakes and cream teas, assorted hot dishes and
locally caught crab and lobster. On fine evenings
there's nothing nicer than a portion of fish and
chips from the takeaway near the stone bridge
(open until 9pm).

LYNN PENINSULA

The campsite (top and centre); St Hywyn's Church (bottom left); the chip shop (bottom right).

Site specific

✔ The campsite is quiet and isolated, with fabulous scenery all around. Some gorgeous sandy beaches are close at hand.

✘ There are only two showers, so you may have to queue in the morning, or rise at the crack of dawn.

More refined dishes, making use of local lamb, beef and seafood, can be sampled at the two village pubs, the Ship (01758 760204, www.theshiphotel aberdaron.co.uk) and Gwesty Ty Newydd (01758 760207, www.gwesty-tynewydd.co.uk). The first has won awards for its food, the second is on the beach and commands enticing views.

There's a wider choice of shops and eateries, and weekly markets, at Pwllheli, about 18 miles away.

ATTRACTIONS & ACTIVITIES

The coast is rocky, so it's nigh on impossible to get into the sea, though some local swimmers dive in from the rocks. The nearest beach for bathing and bucket-and-spade fun is at Aberdaron. Adjacent to the beach, St Hywyn's Church may be the most delightfully located place of worship in the world. One of Wales's most famous sons, the poet RS Thomas, was vicar here until his retirement in 1978.

Beautiful, unspoilt Whistling Sands beach (Porth Oer), about four miles away on the north coast, is also good for swimming. Its café, Mrs Fish

(01758 760321, closed end Oct-Easter), serves big breakfasts and hot food all day, alongside Welsh-made ice-cream, cakes and hot chocolate.

Bardsey Island, with its wildlife reserve, lighthouse and ruined 13th-century abbey, is a mysterious, magical place. Several boats make the two-mile crossing in decent weather, but Colin Evans' Bardsey Boat Trips (07971 769895, www.bardsey boattrips.com) is the only really local one, leaving from Porth Meudwy in Aberdaron. Visitors get about three hours to explore the 1.5-mile long island.

Plas yn Rhiw (01758 780219, www.national trust.org.uk, closed Nov-Mar; check website for opening times rest of the year), six miles away near Rhiw, is the former home of the three Keating sisters, who brought it in 1938. The gardens, with views over Hell's Mouth, are very fine, and there's a woodland walk and a picnic area.

AMUSING THE KIDS

The beaches provide day-long amusement on sunny days, while Pwllheli, with its cinema and gift shops, holds the key to keeping children entertained in inclement weather.

CAMPSITES NEARBY

Up the lane from Mynydd Mawr, Ty Newydd Farm Campsite (01758 760581,www.tynewyddfarm-site. co.uk, open Easter-Oct, from £7) is a more developed, but not over-large option with its own café and landscaped garden. It's very family-friendly, with guinea pigs in hutches and plants for sale. Also beautifully located and well equipped is Tir Glyn (01758 760248, www.tirglyn.com, open Easter-Oct, £12-£15 for two to four people).

Walk up the hill behind the tent field for the best sunset views.

Scotland

.Cashel, Loch Lomond, p287.

Solway View

Solway View Holidays
Balmangan Farm, Borgue, Kirkcudbright,
Dumfries & Galloway DG6 4TR
01557 870206
n.picken@btconnect.com
www.solwayviewholidays.com
Map p29 ❶
OS map NX650457

SOUTHERN SCOTLAND

Number of pitches 20 tents/caravans/
motorhomes. 3 wigwams (sleeping 5).
Open All year.
Booking By phone, email. Advisable.
Typical cost Camping from £10 2 people.
Wigwam from £30 2 people.
Facilities Disabled facilities (toilet
and shower); electric hook-ups (11);
laundry facilities; showers (free); toilets;
washing-up area; play area.
Campfires Allowed. Firewood available (£5).
Dogs Allowed (free-£2).
Restrictions Groups by arrangement.
No noise after 11pm.
Getting there By road From the A75,
turn south (there are various options)
to Kirkcudbright and then join the B727;
after about 4 miles take the turn-off for
Brighouse. Follow the road up the hill,
then take the left-hand fork for Ross Bay.
After a mile, you'll see the farmhouse
on the right. **By public transport** Train
to Dumfries, from where Stagecoach bus
502 (0871 200 2233, www.stagecoach
bus.com, Mon-Sat) or 501 (Sun) takes
an hour to Kirdcudbright. From there you
can get another bus, the 517 (Mon, Wed,
Thur only), but it will take 30 mins; it's
better to catch a cab (Kirkcudbright Taxis,
01557 331177, £8) or arrange for the
campsite to pick you up.

When Patricia and Neil Picken, the owners of
Solway View, spent their honeymoon camping
in Canada, they were immensely impressed to
find that the pitches at each site they visited
were thoughtfully provided with not just a
barbecue, but a proper picnic bench. The pair
resolved to set up their own site offering just
that, and Solway View has been going from
strength to strength. It attracts a flow of repeat
visitors, who book for the following year on the
way out – and urge the owners not to tell too
many other people about it.

Most campers visiting Scotland instantly beat the well-trodden path north to the Highlands, bypassing the south-west in favour of the drama of the mountains and glens. They're missing a trick. Dumfries & Galloway is gorgeous in its own right, and visitors will be rewarded by a spectacular coastline and rolling countryside. Warm currents from the Gulf Stream temper the climate, and the area is famous for its gardens, where incongruously exotic species flourish.

Solway View sits on the edge of a 330-acre farm, overlooking the estuary of the River Dee and with wide-open views across the fields to the Solway Firth. A trail cuts through the farm, leading into woodland (carpeted with bluebells in spring) and past small secluded bays.

It's an intimate site with just 20 generously sized pitches and newly installed, squeaky-clean facilities. If the allure of cooking over an open fire pales, there's a communal camper's kitchen with two gas hobs, a large table and a sink. Three wooden 'wigwams' offer a cosy alternative to a night under canvas, with electricity, basic catering facilities and raised bed platforms; mattresses are provided, but you need to bring your own pillows and bedding.

Just under six miles away is Kirkcudbright (pronounced 'kur-coo-bree'), a bustling harbour town with assorted restaurants and shops, pastel-painted houses, predictably fine chippies and several art galleries. In the early 20th century, the town was the epicentre of a thriving artists' colony, thanks to its picturesque appearance and buccolic setting; 'If one lives in Galloway, one either fishes or paints,' declared novelist Dorothy L Sayers, in 1921.

EATING & DRINKING

Eggs are available from the farm, and the holiday park just up the road at Brighouse Bay has a well-stocked shop for everyday essentials.

Kirkcudbright has supermarkets, two butchers and two bakers, and plenty of options for eating out. An upmarket but fuss-free option for great quality (and family-friendly) food is the Castle Restaurant (5 Castle Street, 01557 330569, www.thecastle restaurant.net). Note that it's sometimes closed for lunch, so ring first.

Around half an hour's drive from Solway View, the market town of Castle Douglas – still home to

a weekly livestock market – was recently designated a Food Town (www.cd-foodtown.org). Over 50 local businesses produce quality food and drink, and King Street is lined with enticing restaurants, delis, bakers and butchers, along with an old-fashioned sweet shop.

Slightly further afield in Newton Stewart, relaxed Café Cree (48 Victoria Street, 01671 404203, www.cafecree.co.uk) offers everything from chunky beef enchiladas to stem ginger and chocolate scones, sourcing ingredients from within a 20-mile radius and serving vegan and gluten-free options too.

ATTRACTIONS & ACTIVITIES

Take short scenic walks along the farm trails, or venture further by bike; Sustrans cycle route 7 runs past the site. You can hire cycles from William Law (01557 330579, www.lawskirkcudbright.co.uk, closed Sun winter on St Cuthbert Street in Kirkcudbright. Alternatively, zip around taking in the scenery on a Vespa, rented at £30 a day from Scooters by the Beach (01776 840276).

For foodies, Castle Douglas makes for a perfect day out. The Galloway Craft Guild Shop (01556 506822, www.gallowaycraftguild.co.uk, closed Sun) on King Street is also worth a browse, stocking work by 60 local craftspeople. Just outside the town, Threave Castle (07711 223101, www.historic-scotland.gov.uk, closed Nov-Mar) is a one-off: a formidable 14th-century tower built by the wonderfully named Archibald the Grim. It's on an island in the River Dee and only accessible by rowing boat.

Meanwhile, Kirkcudbright's artistic leanings live on, with plenty of local artists and various galleries; the Tolbooth Art Centre (01557 331556, closed Sun Nov-Apr) recounts the town's artistic history, while the upper studios house a changing roster of contemporary exhibitions. Set on the High Street, Broughton House (0844 493 2246, www.nts.org.uk, closed Nov-Mar) is a delightful 18th-century townhouse with an exquisite riverside garden.

AMUSING THE KIDS

Close to home, there's a rope swing for children to play on, and the option of a picnic and a paddle in the nearby bays; just don't get caught out by the tide.

The Cream o' Galloway Organic Farm (01557 815222, www.creamogalloway.co.uk, closed Nov-mid Mar), a 20-minute drive away, has a woodland adventure playground with a zip-wire, lookout tower and maze, and an indoor play area for rainy days. Scoff a sundae in the ice-cream parlour.

From May to August, the Kirkcudbright Summer Festivities bring all manner of events and entertainment, including a children's festival, a fancy-dress competition and a grand parade.

CAMPING NEARBY

Brighouse Bay (01557 870267, www.gillespie-leisure. co.uk, open Apr-Oct, from £12.55 for two people) is an all-singing, all-dancing holiday park, with a brilliant shop and an indoor swimming pool.

Site specific

✔ Picnic benches and barbecues or firepits come as standard on every pitch.

✗ The local public transport is erratic, to say the least. You really need a car to make the most of the surrounding area.

SOUTHERN SCOTLAND

Seal Shore

**Seal Shore Camping & Touring Park
Kildonan, Isle of Arran KA27 8SE**
01770 820320
enquiries@campingarran.com
www.campingarran.com
Map p29 ❷
OS map NS030207

ARGYLL & THE ISLANDS

Number of pitches 43 tents/caravans/
motorhomes.
Open Mar-Nov.
Booking By post (phone or email first).
Essential.
Typical cost Camping £1-£4 tent,
£2-£3 caravan/motorhome, plus £6 adult,
£3 child.
Facilities Disabled facilities (toilet and
shower); fridge-freezers; games room;
laundry facilities; shop; showers (free);
toilets; washing-up area.
Campfires Not allowed on site.
Allowed on beach.
Dogs Allowed (£1).
Restrictions No noise after 10pm.
Getting there By road From Ardrossan
on the mainland, take the ferry (08000
665000, www.calmac.co.uk, 55 mins)
to Brodick. From there head south for
12 miles on the A841, then turn left at
Kildonan. The campsite is about half a
mile further on. **By public transport** Bus
323 connects with every ferry that lands
at Brodick, and stops just outside the
campsite; journey takes 35 mins.

Don't be surprised if you're greeted at Seal
Shore's reception by an affable six-year-old boy,
who will book you in, outline the site rules and
show you around – although he may draw the
line at actually pitching your tent for you. This
is Freddie, grandson of the owner, Maurice;
a charming emissary of this sociable, family-
friendly site.

Located in the village of Kildonan, on the
southern tip of the Isle of Arran, Seal Shore
is deservedly popular. The front camping field
is bordered by a sandy private beach, and views
from the tents take in Pladda island and its
white-painted 19th-century lighthouse; in the
distance is Ailsa Craig island. Wildlife-watching
is a breeze, as seals bask on the sands, with
blissful disregard for gawping campers, and
gannets skim the waves in search of unwary
fish. The sharp-eyed might also spot otters
at dusk, or see lazily cruising porpoises.

Two well-kept, slightly sloping fields house
an informal medley of caravans, tents and
motorhomes, around a cluster of purpose-built
facilities. All the essentials are covered: a
double-glazed shower and toilet block, a basic
TV and games room (which also has books and
ancient magazines), covered washing-up areas
and a roofed cooking area with two barbecues.
The latest feature is a campers' kitchen, which
houses a fridge-freezer, kettle and microwave.
You can light a campfire on the beach provided
you clean up afterwards.

With its flowering palms and pots of colourful,
lovingly tended annuals, Seal Shore has stayed
true to its original remit: to create a campsite
'that looks and feels a bit like a garden centre'.
The on-site shop stocks milk, bread and tins,
as well as all the useful bits and pieces you
invariably forget to pack, such as batteries.
It also does a good line in buckets and spades,
pocket-money treats and ice pops – a mere
15p a throw.

The location, though, is what keeps campers
coming back. If you nab one of the front-row
pitches you may face some stiff sea breezes,
but the views are sublime. Staying here is all
about appreciating simple pleasures and tuning
into a slower pace of life. Children can play in
the rock pools on the beach, and a five-minute
walk will bring you to the sheltered Silversands
beach, which is perfect for swimming.

For even more bracing bathing, just outside the
village of Lagg (around five miles away), a narrow
track leads down to Cleat's Shore. Scotland's
only official naturist beach, it's not a busy spot.

EATING & DRINKING

Campers can store provisions in a couple of large
communal fridge-freezers; any alcohol stowed here,
the owners warn, is liable to go astray. Fresh fish,
crab and lobster is often available in the shop; the
site's owner, Maurice, is a keen fisherman.

Kildonan village shop, a mile away, offers a
decent selection of general groceries; alternatively,
there is a Co-op supermarket in Lamlash, about
eight miles away, and two others in Brodick. For
convenience, it's hard to beat Kildonan Hotel (01770
820207, www.kildonanhotel.com), next door to the
campsite. The seating area on the beach is a superb
spot for enjoying a pint when the sun's out, and it
also serves food.

Less than five miles away, in Kilmory, the Lagg
Hotel (01770 870255, www.lagghotel.com, closed

Nov-Mar) is an attractive 18th-century coaching inn, set amid lovely gardens and woodland. The food is smart but unpretentious, with a menu that ranges from upmarket pub classics (burger with beetroot chutney, beer-battered fish and chips) to proper mains, such as roast pigeon or bream with saffron mash.

At Kilmory's Torrylinn Creamery (01770 870240, closed Sat, Sun), you can watch the cheese being made; visit at the end of your holiday and go home with a block of the creamy, mature cheddar cheese.

ATTRACTIONS & ACTIVITIES

Known as 'Scotland in miniature', thanks to its geographical diversity (beaches, mountains, valleys, lochs, islands), Arran also offers a tremendous range of sights (castles, prehistoric ruins, wildlife, a distillery) and outdoor activities (hiking, fishing, cycling, horse riding, climbing, kayaking). It's only 19 miles long by ten miles wide, with just one road around the perimeter and the 'string road' across the centre – it's easy to get about by car or bus.

A good start is to visit the tourist information centre (01770 303774) at Brodick Pier. Here, you can pick up a map and guidebook for the Arran Coastal Way (www.coastalway.co.uk), a footpath around the perimeter of the island. Arran Bike Club (www.arranbikeclub.com) has information

on assorted on- and off-road cycling routes; bikes can be hired from Arran Adventure (01770 302244, www.arranadventure.com) in Brodick – which also gives lessons in kayaking, climbing, sailing, archery and other sports.

Seal Shore itself has a tennis/volleyball area, and campers can also fish for trout in a nearby loch. Cairnhouse Riding Centre (01770 860466), at Blackwaterfoot on the west coast, 12 miles away, offers treks and lessons. For those in need of an adrenalin shot, Ocean Breeze Rib Tours (01770 820275, www.obrt.co.uk, no trips Oct-Mar), based in Lamlash, runs adventure boat tours around the coast, taking in the various islands.

AMUSING THE KIDS

What with keeping an eye on the seals, playing a set or two of tennis and poking around the rock pools, children can easily spend a couple of days on and around the campsite before they get bored.

It's an easy half-hour walk – manageable with a buggy or wheelchair – to the 103-foot high Eas Mor waterfall. The log cabin that stands in a clearing at the top of the fall has a library and interpretation centre; you can leave an unwanted book and take a replacement. For older kids, there's also the popular but slightly more challenging walk to Glenashdale Falls near Whiting Bay.

In Kildonan, Clan Horse Arran (01770 820361, closed Nov-Mar) is a rare-breeds farm housing charming Shetland and Highland ponies, as well as assorted sheep, donkeys, pot-bellied pigs and geese; bring a picnic and make a day of it.

CAMPING NEARBY

Middleton's Caravan & Camping Park (01770 600251 Mar-Sept, 01770 600634 Oct-Feb, www.middleton scamping.com) is in Lamlash. Manicured to the point of feeling slightly municipal, it lacks the magic of Seal Shore, but is comfortable enough, with disabled access and decent showers. It's open Mar-Oct; tents start at £2.50, plus £5 adult, £2.50 5-15s.

Site specific

✔ The blissful beachside location, and its accessibility. Even without a car, getting to Seal Shore is a doddle: the ferry connections are short and painless, and the bus from Brodick ferry terminal stops at the entrance.

✗ The covered cooking area is tiny: if the heavens open, you may have a long wait for your supper.

ARGYLL & THE ISLANDS

Machrihanish

**Machrihanish Camping & Caravan Park
East Trodigal, Campbeltown,
Argyll PA28 6PT**
01586 810366/07999 806959
mail@campkintyre.co.uk
www.campkintyre.co.uk
Map p29 ❸
OS map NR648206

Number of pitches 90 tents/caravans/
motorhomes. 5 wigwams (sleeping 2, 4).
Open Jan, Mar-Oct, Dec.
Booking By phone, email. Advisable;
essential July, Aug and bank holidays.
Typical cost Camping £5.50 adult,
£2.50 child. Wigwam £24.50-£40
2-4 people.
Facilities Disabled facilities (toilet and
shower); electric hook-ups (27); laundry
facilities; shop; showers (free); toilets;
washing-up area.
Campfires Not allowed.
Dogs Allowed (free-£1).
Getting there By road Take the A83
to Campbeltown, then the B842 to
Stewarton. After half a mile, turn right
to Machrihanish; it's about 3.5 miles
to the campsite, which is clearly signed.
By public transport There are 2 flights
a day Mon-Fri from Glasgow International
to Campbeltown (www.flybe.com, journey
40 mins). From there, local buses to
Machrihanish stop just outside the
campsite, or you can get a taxi (01586
551122). Buses run from Glasgow to
Campbeltown (www.citylink.co.uk) but,
at about 4.5 hrs, it's a very long journey.

Machrihanish, situated at the tip of the Kintyre
peninsula on the west coast, has an inevitable
end-of-the-road feel – but in a good way. The
long trek down the sliver of coastline takes in
soul-stirring ocean views, with hair-raising bends
in the road heightening the sense of adventure
as you slowly wend your way south.

After driving past endless fields of placid
dairy cows to the end of the A83, and then
through Campbeltown, it's a relief to reach the
entrance to this lovely, eight-acre site. Adorned
with hand-carved wooden beasties and an
old boat that is now enjoying a second life as
a flowerbed, it's all slightly ramshackle, but
wonderfully welcoming nonetheless.

The policy here is to pitch like with like (families,
couples, singles). It works a treat, as evident
from the number of repeat visitors, the throngs
of kids playing hide-and-seek around the site, and
the availability of seasonal pitches and summer
storage on request. The five wooden wigwams
add to the friendly, village-like feel, while the
sheltered banks stave off the fiercest of the
blustery sea breezes. All mod-cons are provided
in the wigwams, including heating, lighting, a
microwave, crockery and cutlery and a small
fridge. Foam mattresses cover wooden sleeping
platforms. Aside from other campers, your only
immediate neighbours are the cows.

The three mile-long sandy beach is a 700-yard
stroll along the main road. Nearby is the village
of Machrinanish, which comprises a pub, a few
houses and the various buildings connected to
the golf course that adjoins the quiet beach.

The campground may be off the beaten track,
but its facilities are a sight for sore eyes.
Seasoned campers will appreciate the splendid
showers, with a wide shelf for toiletries, and the
comprehensive disabled and parent-and-child
facilities. You can hire hair-straighteners,
hairdryers and even an iron and ironing board.

Try to get the pitch to the left as you enter
the site, just beyond the static caravans, with
its proximity to the cosy, inviting 'campers'
caravan'. Equipped with a microwave, sink,
crockery, TV and music player, this is just the
place to pass the time with your fellow campers
in inclement weather.

EATING & DRINKING

The campsite's shop has bread, milk and eggs,
along with a selection of tins, sweets and crisps,
but for proper groceries you'll need to stock up in
Campbeltown, five miles away.

For quality pub fare, try the Old Club House
(01586 810099, www.thewaygolfbegan.com) in
Machrinanish, where the menu includes steamed Loch
Etive mussels, own-made soup, and steak and ale pie.
It's often fully booked for dinner, so call ahead.

Glenbarr Nursery (01583 421200, www.glenbarr-
nursery.co.uk) near Tarbert, some 12 miles north of
Campbeltown, offers delicious home-baking, light
lunches, and pickles and chutneys to take away.

ATTRACTIONS & ACTIVITIES

The beach's golden sands are on your doorstep,
for sandcastle-building, swimming and picnics; it's
also good for surfing. Once you've exhausted its
charms, you could tackle a stretch of the Kintyre
Way (www.kintyreway.com), a long-distance walking

Site specific

✔ The campers' caravan is a huge plus. The thrilling convenience of an electric kettle, after several nights under canvas with a temperamental single-burner gas stove, is impossible to convey.

✘ Once the self-proclaimed 'whisky capital of the world' and the centre of a thriving herring industry, nearby Campbeltown is now rather down on its luck.

route that starts at Tarbert harbour and ends at Dunaverty Bay, at the south end of the peninsula.

Golf aficionados will be in heaven here. Established in 1876, the Machrihanish Golf Club (01586 810213, www.machgolf.com) has inspiring views across to the islands of Jura and Islay. Its first hole is considered one of the finest opening holes in the world and, as one 19th-century golfer remarked, the undulating setting seems 'specifically designed by the Almighty for playing golf'.

For rainy days, the delightful Picture House (01586 533899, www.weepictures.co.uk) in Campbeltown is a community-owned art deco cinema. Dating from 1913, it's the oldest purpose-built cinema in Scotland.

In August, the acclaimed Mull of Kintyre Music Festival (01586 552056, www.mokfest.com) features pipe bands, brass bands, modern and Highland dancers, Gaelic choirs and more, with performances in venues around Campbeltown.

AMUSING THE KIDS

Mull of Kintyre Seatours (01586 552056, 07785 542811, www.mull-of-kintyre.co.uk), based in Campbeltown, offers all manner of wildlife-watching trips. Sanda Island is home to seals and (in breeding season) puffins, while Ailsa Craig is famed for its gannet colony. Calm summer days bring sightings of basking sharks, porpoises and bottlenose dolphins in Kilbrannan Sound; if you're lucky, you might spot a minke or pilot whale. Thrill-seekers can opt for a 'fast blast' – 30 minutes of skimming over the waves around Davaar Island and Campbeltown Loch.

In the village of Peniver, five miles north of Campbeltown, there's pony trekking at the Crosshill Trekking & Training Centre at High Peninver Farm (closed Mon, Wed, contact Claire Peters on 01586 551791). Best are the one-hour rides along the beach, which are suitable for riders of all ages and abilities.

CAMPING NEARBY

A dozen miles north of Campbeltown, the grassy, level pitches at Killegruer Caravan Site (01583 421241, open Apr-mid Oct, pitch £14) are set by a sandy bay, with glorious views at sunset. The toilets and showers are immaculate, and there's a children's play area.

Around nine miles north of Killegruer, Point Sands Holiday Park (01583 441263, www.pointsandsholidaypark.co.uk, open Apr-end Oct, pitch £7 per night, £5 adult) has a beachside site for caravans and tents, holiday homes set back among the pines, a playground and a small shop. From nearby Tayinloan, you can catch a ferry to the wonderfully unspoilt Isle of Gigha.

Cove Park

Cove Park
Peaton Hill, Cove,
Argyll & Bute G84 0PE
01436 850123
information@covepark.org
www.covepark.org
Map p29 ❹
OS map NS217860

Number of pitches 6 cubes (sleeping 2;
1 single with wheelchair access). 2 pods
(sleeping 4, 5).
Open Late Nov-mid Apr; call for exact dates.
Booking By phone. Essential.
Minimum stay 2 nights.
Typical cost Cube £40 per night.
Pod £100 per night.
Facilities Bathrooms; disabled facilities
(1 cube); kitchens; laundry facilities
(main building, Mon-Fri); toilets.
Campfires Not allowed.
Dogs Not allowed.
Getting there By road Take the A814 to
Garelochhead, then the B833 that heads
south on the other side of Gare Loch.
After about 3 miles, turn right on to Peaton
Road across the Rosneath peninsula
towards Ardpeaton; it's about 1.5 miles
to Cove Park. **By public transport** A couple
of options. Train to Helensburgh (45 mins),
then bus 316 (01436 820300, www.wilsons
ofrhu.co.uk/local_services.html), which
takes 40 mins to Ardpeaton, half a mile
from Cove Park. Or get a taxi from
Helensburgh for £16 (Garelochhead Taxis,
01436 810810). Alternatively, train to
Gourock (60 mins), then connecting ferry
to Kilcreggan (12 mins), then taxi (£5,
Kilcreggan Taxis, 01436 842428).

There are places to stay in the Scottish
countryside that offer the spirit of camping,
if not an actual night under canvas – or, more
accurately these days, nylon. But if you can
wake up in the morning, be outdoors in two
shakes and enjoy a stunning view, then maybe
a tent isn't strictly necessary after all.

So it goes at Cove Park on the Rosneath
peninsula in Argyll. This part of Scotland might
not be far from central Glasgow (just under 25
miles, as the crow flies), but given the Firth of
Clyde and the confusion of sea lochs hereabouts,
you feel very far away indeed. The peninsula is

joined to the mainland at Garelochhead by a
narrow strip of land – but for a quirk of geology,
it could easily have been an island. Otherwise
it is splendidly isolated, cut off to the east by
Gare Loch and to the west by the lower reaches
of Loch Long. (Though the nuclear weapons
stored at Coulport and Faslane mean the public
transport is better than you might expect.)

Set on a wooded hillside on the western
side of the peninsula, in a 50-acre site that
was once a conservation park, Cove Park looks
directly across the water to Cowal. It opened
in its present guise in 1999, as an artists'
retreat. From around April to November, it is
occupied solely by painters, sculptors, writers
and musicians who come here as part of an
official creative residency programme. In
the winter months, however, the accommodation
is open to anyone.

Instead of tents and caravans, there are
six cubes and two pods, whose turfed roofs
lend a feel of ethical hi-tech hits Middle Earth.
The accommodation is exemplary, the views
incomparable, and the peace passeth all
understanding; with no radios or televisions, this
is an ideal spot for a quiet, reflective getaway.

Constructed around sturdy oak frames,
the pods, named Oak and Taransay, have a
distinctive, arched shape and sit companionably
side by side. Both have two ensuite bedrooms
(with double beds in Oak, and bunks and a
single pull-out bed in Taransay) and fully-equipped
kitchens (Taransay has two). In the living room,
a wooden ladder leads up to a little mezzanine
alcove, where you can curl up with a book and
take in the beautiful views.

Originally built for the TV series *Castaway*,
filmed on the Hebridean island of Taransay, the
pods were designed to withstand biting winds
and driving rain. Even on the coldest of days, they

Site specific

✔ The sense of solitude and the views –
across the waters of Loch Long and the hills
of Cowal – make this a supremely peaceful
spot. While you stay cosy indoors, even
winter squalls start to look interesting.

✘ No shop, no bar, no café, no nothing.
The accommodation is like a home from
home, but you really need to be self-
sufficient. Also, it's only open in winter.

provide a snug retreat, thanks to solid insulation and underfloor heating. A stay here certainly isn't about roughing it; think freestanding baths, custom-made kitchens and pristine white walls.

The cubes, meanwhile, are ingeniously-revamped shipping containers, five with double beds, and the sixth with a single bed and facilities for a disabled guest. With a bed in the corner, an open-plan lounge area, a basic kitchen and a partitioned-off shower room, this is the essence of pared-down chic. A sliding glass door opens on to the balcony, overlooking landscaped ponds and the loch beyond. In such stripped-down surrounds, it is the view that is the focus – and you don't have to be an artist to feel inspired.

EATING & DRINKING

There is no shop nearby, so you'll need to head to the villages at the north and south of the peninsula – Garelochhead and Kilcreggan, respectively. Both are within a 15-minute drive of Cove Park, and also have an assortment of pubs and cafés. The best is Café Craft (01436 811344, www.cafecraft.org), on Main Road in Garelochhead. This is where to come for breakfast fry-ups with all the trimmings, sandwiches, burgers and cream teas.

The closest and most obvious venue for eats and drinks, though, is Knockderry House Hotel (01436 842283, www.knockderryhouse.co.uk), by the village of Cove. It aims for a country house style, and dinner is seasonal and fairly upmarket: pan-seared mackerel with Scottish girolles, say, or braised Perthshire lamb. The light bites menu has simpler dishes (fish and chips, own-made burgers, seasonal salads) and cheaper prices.

If you can bear the drive, swanky Cameron House Hotel (01389 755565, www.devere.co.uk) on the west shore of Loch Lomond has an acclaimed whisky bar and no less than four restaurants, including Martin Wishart at Loch Lomond (01389 722504, www.martin-wishart.co.uk, closed Mon, Tue, closed lunch Wed-Fri).

Expect elevated Franco-Scottish cuisine, courtesy of the Edinburgh-based, Michelin-starred chef.

ATTRACTIONS & ACTIVITIES

Cove Park is a decent base for hill walking, given that the mountains above Arrochar at the head of Loch Long are close by. The Cobbler (2,900 feet) is the most craggy, dramatic and engaging, although its immediate neighbours – Beinn Narnain, Beinn Ime, Ben Vane and Ben Vorlich – are all bigger. It almost goes without saying that winter walking in the Scottish hills is not for the inexperienced. You need proper equipment, a certain level of fitness and the sense to turn back when the weather gets too bad.

The other nearby mountain of note is Ben Lomond (3,195 feet), on the east side of Loch Lomond – though it's a circuitous hour-long drive to Rowardennan, where you start the ascent. Loch Lomond itself is an iconic beauty spot and a couple of firms offer boat trips, even in winter. Cruise Loch Lomond (01301 702356, www.cruiselochlomondltd.com) operates from Tarbet, 15 miles away; Sweeney's Cruises (01389 752376, www.sweeney.uk.com) from Balloch, 20 miles away. At Balloch you'll also find Loch Lomond Shores (01389 751035, www.lochlomondshores.com), a shopping complex with restaurants, cafés and an information centre, along with an aquarium.

AMUSING THE KIDS

At Loch Lomond Shores, the Loch Lomond Aquarium (01389 721500, www.sealifeeurope.com) is open year-round. There are rock pools, a ray bay, otter feeding sessions and an underwater shark tunnel.

CAMPING NEARBY

Open all year, though not for the faint-hearted in winter, Ardgartan Caravan Park & Campsite (01301 702293, www.forestholidays.co.uk) is set at the top of Loch Long, under the craggy Arrochar Alps. As well as camping and caravan pitches (£11.50-£25.50 for two people), it has 14 brand-new log cabins.

Cashel

Cashel Caravan Park & Campsite
Rowardennan, Loch Lomond,
Lanarkshire G63 0AW
01360 870234 campsite
0845 130 8224 booking
cashel.site@forestholidays.co.uk
www.forestholidays.co.uk
Map p29 ❺
OS map NS395939

Number of pitches 20 tents,
140 caravans/motorhomes.
Open Apr-Oct.
Booking By phone, online. Advisable.
Minimum stay 2-3 nights if booking.
Typical cost £11-£25 2 people, £5-£6.50
extra adult, £3-£4 extra child. Non-CCC/FEC
members additional £3.50.
Facilities Disabled facilities (toilet and
shower); laundry facilities; play area; showers
(free); shop; toilets; washing-up area.
Campfires Not allowed.
Dogs Allowed, on lead.
Restrictions No single-sex groups. No
noise after 10pm, gates locked 10.30pm.
Getting there By road Take the A811
or A809 to Drymen, then the B837 to
Balmaha. Continue through Balmaha
(beware of the road surface and sharp
right up a steep hill after the harbour);
Cashel is on the left, after about 4 miles.
By public transport From the nearest train
station at Balloch, bus 309 (McColl's
Coaches, 01389 754321) runs daily and
takes 40 mins to Balmaha. From there, a
taxi to the campsite is £10 (Drymen Taxi
Services, 01360 660077). A taxi from
Balloch will set you back about £27.

If there's such a thing as a one-stop campsite, this is it. Cashel's location in the Queen Elizabeth Forest Park, on the bonnie eastern bank of Loch Lomond, with the peak of Ben Lomond looming behind, means it's perfect for walking, boating, canoeing and generally revelling in the Scottish countryside. Remote, yet accessible by public transport or car (it's just an hour or so from Glasgow), this is a first-class option for outdoor enthusiasts of all kinds, and brilliant for families.

People come here because the campsite basically is the forest: the site runs down to the loch, and is backed by a thick fringe of trees.

Separate pitches for tents and caravans face the water, with a tiny pebble beach just yards away. Campers enjoy relative freedom to choose where to pitch, as long as they leave a minimum of six metres between tents. At busy times you may end up feeling too close to the public path for comfort, but the ground is level and the whole site intelligently laid out, with all amenities a comfortable stroll away. A few pre-erected tents are usually available through Eurocamp (0844 406 0402, www.eurocamp.co.uk).

Run by Forest Holidays, Cashel is well managed and achieves the standard to which all campsites should aspire: proper showers, clean toilets, a

sheltered washing-up area and views to die for. The well-tended window boxes outside reception and regularly checked facilities show a reassuring attention to detail. Access is 24/7 on foot; if you arrive when reception is shut, simply park, pitch and report to the office by 10am next day. The only drawback is the midges: all those trees, coupled with the no-campfires rule, is a gilt-edged invitation to the dreaded beasties.

Cashel's location on the West Highland Way (www.west-highland-way.co.uk) – which runs 95 miles from near Glasgow to Fort William – means there are visitors year round, though numbers drop noticeably at the end of the high season. The main problem in summer is trying to fit everything in As well as hiking, exploring the forest and taking boat trips on the loch, the Native Forest Centre across the road (closed Mon) has information, exhibitions and ranger-led events. A mile south is Millarochy Bay, which on a fine day is absolute heaven.

A couple of miles north is the tiny hamlet of Rowardennan, with its beautifully located youth hostel, while Balmaha, four miles south, is the place for boat trips around the loch.

EATING & DRINKING

Load up at the Co-op supermarket in Balloch, 17 miles south, before you arrive – the campsite shop stocks just milk, bread and basic groceries. The shop's kettle is useful for emergency cups of tea when you're too wet/exhausted/lazy to make your own.

It's a few minutes by car to the Rowardennan Hotel (01360 870273, www.rowardennanhotel.co.uk), which offers well-priced sandwiches and jacket potatoes (including a haggis version), as well as more ambitious locally sourced options. It has two bars and a dining room.

Balmaha's relaxed and friendly Oak Tree Inn (01360 870 357, www.oak-tree-inn.co.uk) serves generous platefuls of decent pub food (cullen skink, steak and mushroom pie), with pleasant seating outside in the shade of a 500-year-old oak.

If you fancy more traditional British fare, there's always the Golden Star Tandoori (01389 721077), half an hour away in Balloch.

Site specific

✔ The location, on the shore of Loch Lomond, is stunning, and the range of outdoor options at your fingertips immense.

✘ Midges, predictably, are a menace. Apply liberal quantities of repellent, swallow your pride and wear a head net, or eat a kilo of garlic – whatever it takes to keep them at bay.

ATTRACTIONS & ACTIVITIES

The youth hostel (01360 870259, www.syha.org.uk, open Mar-end Oct) in Rowardennan village doubles as an activity centre, offering windsurfing, canoeing, archery and orienteering.

Walkers have trails aplenty through the forest and along the West Highland Way, which runs adjacent to Loch Lomond, with superb views to compensate for the sometimes tortuous route. If you want to bag a Munro, Ben Lomond (3,195 feet) is the most southerly one in Scotland. The easiest 'tourist' path up – allow five hours for the round-trip – starts at the car park just north of Rowardennan Hostel.

Many visitors bring their own boats to Cashel (it has its own slipway). Don't worry if you forgot yours: trips around Loch Lomond leave from the campsite. Or head to pretty Balmaha, where sailing boats bob offshore and the busy boatyard runs daily cruises, including trips to nearby Inchcailloch Island, one of many on the loch. It takes about 90 minutes to walk the island's nature trail, which takes in the ruins of an ancient chapel and graveyard.

The Loch Lomond Highland Games (www.llhgb. com) are held in Balloch in July; they're wonderfully traditional, so expect Highland dancing, pipe bands and caber-tossing.

AMUSING THE KIDS

There's a family room, baby room and small play area on site, although most children, in the spirit of the surroundings, seem to prefer tearing around on bikes. For some, the best thing about the forest is 'weeing on the trees'. On site rangers run a host of activities for youngsters, covering everything from den building to bat watching and forest safaris. Buy some bacon from the shop and try crabbing from the pier: a child-friendly activity whose rewards far outweigh the level of effort and skill involved.

Loch Lomond Shores – an upmarket shopping and dining centre just north of Balloch, and something of a tourist hub – is home to the Loch Lomond Aquarium (see p286) and a cinema.

CAMPING NEARBY

The Camping & Caravanning Club has a picturesque site a couple of miles south next to Milarrochy Bay (01360 870236, www.campingandcaravanning club.co.uk/milarrochybay, open Apr-Oct), with room for 150 tents, caravans and motorhomes. A pitch costs £5.90-£9.05, plus £7.10 for non-members.

Forest Holidays' other campsite in the Queen Elizabeth Forest Park is a 30-minute drive away at Cobleland (01877 382392, open late Mar-Oct), on the banks of the River Forth. A standard pitch for two people costs £11-£14, plus £3.50 for non-members.

Or there's the National Trust Scotland's camping area just north of Rowardennan Hostel, which is as basic as it gets – a grassy pitch, a burn and a beach. That's it. You can only stay one night and must disappear without trace by 10am next morning. Good practice if you're working up to wild camping.

Mains Farm

Mains Farm Wigwams
Thornhill, Stirlingshire FK8 3QR
01786 850735
info@mainsfarmwigwams.com
www.mainsfarmwigwams.com
Map p29 ⑥
OS map NS664997

Number of pitches 60 tents/caravans/
motorhomes. 14 wigwams (sleeping 5).
Enquire about tipis.
Open Camping Easter-Oct. Wigwams
Feb-Oct.
Booking By phone (before 9pm), email.
Essential.
Typical cost £6 tent, £9 caravan/
motorhome, £2 extra adult, £1.50
extra child. Wigwam £15 adult, £5 child
(minimum £30).
Facilities Disabled facilities (1 wigwam
adapted); electric hook-ups (20, reserve
on 01786 850605); laundry facilities;
showers (20p); toilets; washing-up area.
Campfires Allowed. Firewood available (£5).
Dogs Allowed, on lead.
Getting there By road Exit the M9 motorway
at Stirling at junction 10. Follow the A84
for about 4 miles, then turn left on to the
A873 towards Thornhill and Aberfoyle. It's
another 4 miles to Thornhill village; the
campsite is located off Main Street and is
signposted. **By public transport** Train to
Stirling, then bus 11 (www.firstgroup.com,
0871 200 2233, 4 times a day, no service
Sun) to Thornhill; journey takes 30 mins.
On Sun, there's a Harlequin Coach service
from Stirling bus station to Thornhill at 9am.
Mains Farm is a short walk from the centre
of the village.

Thornhill, in the old county of Stirlingshire, is
somewhat overshadowed by the prettiness of
the Trossachs to the west, where lochs and
mountains are ten a penny, and by the history-
steeped town of Stirling and its dramatic castle
to the east. Mind you, the village is handy for
both. In the immediate vicinity, the main
geographical feature is the flood plain of the
River Forth, encompassing the almost spookily
flat Blair Drummond Moss and Flanders Moss.
It is this strange landscape that Thornhill calls
home, with views south to the Gargunnock
and Fintry Hills.

In the centre of the village, behind the school,
you'll find Mains Farm. The owners grow barley
and raise sheep, but some years ago diversified
into other activities to keep the farm going –
hence the wigwams and camping and caravan
site. Everything tends to cluster around the
farmhouse, including all the facilities, although
the field where campers pitch their tents is
on the other side of the B-road – a bit of a trek
for the basic but functional shower and toilet
block. There's also a washing-up area, washing
machine and drying area.

The camping field itself is a large, open
expanse, with no marked pitches; camp by
the hedges for shelter from the wind. Fires
are allowed, though you need to check with the
warden first. All in all, it's a nice enough spot to
set up camp – though the wigwams across the
road are the site's main draw. These are rather
like small, wooden garden sheds; triangular in
elevation, and with bench seating that doubles
as sleeping space. Mattresses are provided,
but you'll need to bring your own pillows and
duvets. The wigwams also have electric lights,
sockets and a kettle, along with heating and
a fridge (the last two run on metered electricity
– buy a card at reception).

The wigwams have outdoor firepits – and should
the weather put a damper on your plans, you can
always retreat to the well-equipped kitchen and
dining area. It has proper cookers, microwaves,
toasters and kettles, plus plenty of crockery and
pans, and walls daubed with cartoon cowboys;
note that it's only open to wigwam residents.

This is not a distant Highland wilderness;
you're within sight of some fairly suburban-looking
houses, and you could walk round the corner to

Site specific

✔ Wigwams and tipis are usually
associated with playful five-year-olds
who either have toy versions or a rich
fantasy life. At Mains Farm they're real,
and grown-ups are allowed inside – without
embarrassment or injury to adult dignity.

✘ A damp canvas tipi is not the most
fragrant type of accommodation, so consider
a wigwam in wet weather. The school
playground adjacent to the site gets noisy
at break-time, although it's quiet during the
Scottish school holidays in July and August.

CENTRAL SCOTLAND

Lake of Menteith

the pub if you wanted. But why not suspend your disbelief and give in to your inner cowboy? Whistle an Ennio Morricone tune, lose the self-consciousness and just get to lollygaggin' around.

EATING & DRINKING

If you're a hardcore self-caterer, there are shops in the village. Every Wednesday from March to December, Thornhill Community Hall near Mains Farm hosts a market and coffee shop (10am-1pm). In season, you can buy produce that locals grow in their gardens.

The village inn, the Lion & Unicorn (01786 850204, www.lion-unicorn.co.uk), does straightforward food (steaks, scampi, Arbroath smoked fish cakes). Around four miles west, the Lake of Menteith Hotel (01877 385258, www.lake-hotel.com) is more upmarket. The tranquil, cream-painted restaurant offers understated but elegant cooking; organic brown trout to start, say, followed by pan-seared wild stone bass with pink fir apple potatoes, celeriac and fennel. Alternatively, just have a burger or a pot of mussels in the bar.

The tourist village of Aberfoyle, around eight miles west, has more options – and if you head uphill just behind Aberfoyle, you come to the Queen Elizabeth Forest Park, with its Bluebell Café (01877 382900, closed Jan-mid Feb). There are bacon rolls at breakfast, then lunchtime soups, salads and paninis. In decent weather, grab a terrace table for excellent views over the forest.

A 20-minute drive from Thornhill, Stirling has all you could want in terms of pubs and restaurants. The pick of the bunch is the Austro-Caledonian crossover Hermann's (01786 450632, www.hermanns.co.uk), on Broad Street – the chef-proprietor is from the Tirol, and does a mean schnitzel.

ATTRACTIONS & ACTIVITIES

Aberfoyle is on the doorstep of the Trossachs, an area of rugged, Highland-style comeliness. The David Marshall Lodge visitor centre is a focus for the wider Queen Elizabeth Forest Park (01877 382258, www.forestry.gov.uk/qefp, closed mid Dec-Feb), which gives you a taste of this environment. Aside from a decent café, the park has all kinds of trails and ranger-led events. Its biggest wow-factor attraction is Go Ape! (0845 6439215, www.goape.co.uk, closed Tue term-time, Mon-Fri Nov, all Dec-mid Mar), with a zip-wire ride (a scary 430 yards) and adventure course.

For a more placid couple of hours, stop short of Aberfoyle, taking a left off the B8034 at the Lake of Menteith. Near the Lake of Menteith Hotel, there is a car park, a jetty and a boatman, who will take you over to a tiny island in the lake. Here, you can explore the ruins of 13th-century Inchmahome Priory (01877 385294, www.historic-scotland.gov.uk).

Otherwise, the most obvious day out from Mains Farm is Stirling, with its prominent castle (01786 450000, www.historic-scotland.gov.uk).

AMUSING THE KIDS

Try Blair Drummond Safari Park (01786 841456, www.blairdrummond.com), between Thornhill and Stirling. Residents range from tigers to meercats.

CAMPING NEARBY

Around two and a half miles south of Aberfoyle, Trossachs Holiday Park (01877 382614, www.trossachsholidays.co.uk, open Mar-Oct, £14-£20 for two people) is an extensive and manicured set-up with holiday lodges as well as space for tents and caravans. It offers mountain bike hire, woodland walks, a children's play area and more.

Comrie Croft

Number of pitches 34 tents. 5 Swedish kåtas (sleeping 4). Farmhouse (sleeps 14). Lodge (sleeps 56). No caravans/motorhomes.
Open All year.
Booking By phone, email. Essential high season.
Typical cost Tent £7-£9 adult, £3.50-£4.50 5-16s. Kåta £36-£72 per night; £168-£308 per week. Farmhouse & Lodge: dorm beds £16-£18, private rooms from £19 adult, half-price 5-16s.
Facilities Bike hire (from £16 adult half-day); disabled facilities (toilet and shower); laundry facilities (in hostel, restricted use); shop; shower (free); toilets; washing-up area.
Campfires Allowed, in firepits. Firewood available (£5).
Dogs Allowed, on lead.
Restrictions No vehicle access after 10pm, no noise after 11pm.
Getting there By road From Perth, take the A85. Comrie Croft is about 4.5 miles after Crieff, before Comrie itself, and is well signposted. **By public transport** Train to Perth. From there, Stagecoach bus 15/15A (www.stagecoachbus.com) runs every hour to Comrie, going past the campsite; the journey takes about 1 hr.

Comrie Croft
Braincroft, Comrie,
Perthshire PH7 4JZ
01764 670140
info@comriecroft.com
www.comriecroft.com
Map p29 **❼**
OS map NN803231

By night, the glow of campfires at Comrie Croft silhouettes a backdrop of trees rising in the hills beyond. Offering semi-wild camping, with delightful added extras, this relatively new venture in the heart of the Perthshire countryside, just outside the pretty village of Comrie, is a runaway success. And rightly so.

There is space for a dozen tents on the field beside the main building, which is close to the washing facilities, shop and car park. A brood of chickens lives just by the reception area, providing campers with fresh eggs, and sheep dot the neighbouring fields. Campfires are allowed in the firepits; in case of wet weather, there's a communal area with benches and a firepit, with a vast awning made from a parachute.

More pioneering spirits can head up to the birch glade pitches, and either hire one of the cosy kåtas – Swedish tipis, which are just the thing for the Highland climate – or set up camp beneath the trees. You may well startle a wandering roe deer on the way to bed, and budding Dr Dolittles will love it.

The kåtas are kitted out with a wood-burning stove for heating and cooking, kitchen equipment and a big sleeping platform, insulated with sheep's wool. You'll need to bring your own bedding. Outside, there's a hammock, and a brazier made from a recycled wheel. You're provided with a wind-up lantern and head torches (useful for midnight toilet trips).

Extras include a farmhouse and a lodge, converted from an old farm building, for self-catering accomodation in dorms and private rooms. There's also a shop and a 'conference room' which is as far removed from the corporate image those words conjure up as it's possible to get.

It's the perfect place for a family holiday, especially for younger children. Campsite manager George Sloan is just as likely to be found hosting impromptu wood-whittling sessions, surrounded by a throng of fascinated kids, as he is to be constructing boardwalks through the woodlands. We defy you to leave without booking again for the following year.

EATING & DRINKING

The eco-store stocks a well-considered range of provisions, including bread, croissants, yoghurt and local sausages, along with souvenirs and biking and camping gear.

Otherwise, head to Comrie, a couple of miles away. It's a picturesque and beautifully kept village with a butcher's, bakery and two supermarkets. On Dundas Street, you'll find the Comrie Fish & Chip Shop and BYO restaurant; there's no phone, but it's open 5-9pm daily. Set in an 18th-century cottage, the Deil's Cauldron (01764 670352, www.deilscauldron.co.uk, closed Mon, dinner Sun) is a friendly restaurant and wine bar, with a garden patio. Its traditional menu might include own-made soup or cottage pie for lunch, and Highland venison or lamb haggis with neeps and tatties for dinner.

For fine dining, reserve a table at the Royal Hotel (01764 679200, www.royalhotel.co.uk) – a name conferred by Queen Victoria, no less. It's a swish hotel with a smart restaurant, where the menu tends to stick to the classics: pan-fried venison steak glazed with stilton, perhaps, or fillet of hake wrapped in parma ham and some handmade chocolates for afters.

Site specific

✔ Ideal for first-time campers, and a godsend for the modern parent yearning to take their offspring on a more authentic family holiday.

✘ It's difficult to find any drawbacks. Families with small children may find getting to the woodland pitches a bit of a climb.

ATTRACTIONS & ACTIVITIES

Perthshire is marvellous biking country, with a vast network of trails, many starting behind the campsite. Comrie Croft rents mountain bikes (www.comriecroftbikes.co.uk), with reduced rates for guests. Alternatively, the Rafting Company (01887 829292, www.theraftingcompany.co.uk) offers everything from introductory sessions to fast and furious white-water adventures.

Walkers fare well too. From Comrie, the Glen Lednock circular walk is an enjoyable two-hour trek through the woods, taking in a set of rapids and the 'De'ils Cauldron' waterfall. Setting off from Crieff, about five miles to the east, Lady Mary's Walk runs along the banks of the River Earn through an avenue of oaks, beeches and sweet chestnuts – at their resplendent best in autumn. For more ideas, visit Crieff's tourist information centre (01764 652578, www.crieff.co.uk), which sells maps and illustrated walking guides.

It's also just a few miles to the village of St Fillans and Loch Earn, which marks the north-eastern edge of the huge Loch Lomond & the Trossachs

National Park (www.lochlomond-trossachs.org) for yet more prime walking and cycling.

For history rather than hills, the imposing towers of medieval Huntingtower Castle (01738 627231, www.historic-scotland.gov.uk, closed Thur, Fri Nov-Mar) are 20 miles away, on the outskirts of Perth.

The Comrie Fortnight in late July/early August brings pipes and drums, a pram derby, storytelling, pet shows and other time-honoured delights, culminating in a float parade on the final Sunday.

AMUSING THE KIDS

The inhabitants of the Auchingarrich Wildlife Centre (01764 679469, www.auchingarrich.co.uk), just outside Comrie, include prairie dogs, porcupines, skunks, bush babies and meercats. There's also a coffee shop, an indoor play barn and a hatchery, where baby rabbits, chicks and guinea pigs hold children

entranced. For those that prefer their nature wild and sharp of talon, next door is Raptor World (07976 227699, www.raptorworld.co.uk, closed end Oct-Apr),with its owls, hawks and falcons.

A day out in Perth, some 40 minutes' drive away, is another option. Perth Theatre (01738 621031, www. perththeatre.co.uk, usually closed Sun) has a family-friendly vibe, a charming Edwardian auditorium and a café-bar/restaurant. For wet days, Perth Leisure Pool (01738 492431, www.liveactive.co.uk) has flumes, whirlpools, bubble beds and a lagoon.

CAMPING NEARBY

West Lodge Caravan Park (01764 670354, www. westlodgecaravanpark.co.uk, open Apr-Oct) is a small, well-equipped park a mile east of Comrie – though the fleet of static caravans aren't to everyone's taste. Prices from £12 per pitch, plus £1 per person.

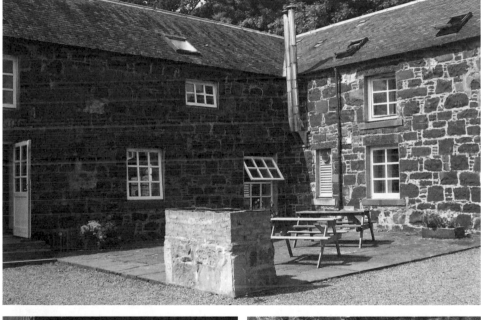

CENTRAL SCOTLAND

Red Squirrel

Red Squirrel
Glencoe, Argyll PH49 4HX
01855 811256
squirrels@amserves.net
www.redsquirrelcampsite.com
Map p29 ❽
OS map NN119573

Number of pitches 250 tents,
5 caravans/motorhomes.
Open All year.
Booking By phone.
Typical cost £9 adult, £7.50 per extra
adult, 50p under-12.
Facilities Showers (free); toilets;
washing-up area.
Campfires Allowed, on fire areas until 11pm.
Dogs Allowed.
Restrictions No noise or campfires after
11pm. Hen and stag nights by arrangement.
Getting there By road The A82 from
Glasgow to Fort William goes through
Glencoe. The minor road to both the
Clachaig Inn and the campsite is
signposted. If heading north, the turn-off
is on the right, about 3.5 miles before Glen
Coe village. If you come through Glen Coe
village, Red Squirrel is less than 2 miles
along the minor road on the north side
of the River Coe. **By public transport**
The nearest train station is at Fort William,
20 miles away. From there, the main bus
service to Glasgow takes 30 mins to Glen
Coe, stopping at the crossroads where
the A82 passes the village; it's then about
1.5 miles on foot to the campsite. If you're
coming from Glasgow, the bus takes 2.5 hrs
to Glen Coe.

To understand the Red Squirrel campsite, you
need to understand Glen Coe: unforgiving, ornery
and stunning mountain country. Its topological
drama of swirling high peaks and ridges would
be more than enough to guarantee its status as
a Scottish must-see, but the glen also enjoys a
terrible notoriety. The background to the Glen Coe
massacre is a complicated tale, but the headline
facts are that one night in February 1692, the
Maclains of Glen Coe were turned out of their
houses and hunted down by British army troops,
who had been billeted on them for a few weeks.
It was a heinous breach of trust: 38 locals were
killed, while dozens fled and died of exposure in
the bleak winter weather. More than 300 years
later, Glen Coe attracts people who know of its
dark past, but are also interested in its robust
physical challenges.

Consequently, Red Squirrel has few frills but
few real proscriptions either. Tucked into the
woodland under the hills to the east side of
the River Coe, it accommodates everyone from
hard-bitten solo climbers to sociable groups.
Choose whichever corner of the 22-acre site
appeals – hidden away on the wooded island,
perhaps, or in the family area by the wardens'
office. Unless it's high season, you can usually
find a secluded spot. Campfires are allowed,
although not past 11pm; after that, staff have
been known to make the rounds, armed with
watering cans and buckets.

At times, it can feel like a cross between a
medieval siege camp and a modern shanty town;
you can't miss the colourful hand-painted signs,
inscribed with bright red capital letters ('WE SELL
REPELLENT', accompanied by a midge-bitten,
anguished-looking youth, is particularly striking).
Facilities are basic but clean, with green-painted
Portakabins and a wooden shelter with two
enormous sinks for washing-up.

People come here to get away: away from
the ubiquitous pettifogging that goes with
contemporary urban life. If you're singing sea
shanties at 1am, someone will tell you to shut
up; if your fire looks as if it's getting out of hand,
someone will have a word. Otherwise, you're
left to your own devices and your own sense
of responsibility, which is why Red Squirrel is
so popular with a certain kind of camper. Dainty
toilet facilities, souvenir tea towels and green,
pleasant landscapes? Sorry, but no. A moment
or two of liberty, somewhere handy nearby for
a decent pint, and a location that's a stepping
stone to the convolutions far above? Hell, yes.
Be careful though: as recently as January 2009,
three men were killed in an avalanche on
Buachaille Etive Mor. These hills are not to
be taken lightly.

EATING & DRINKING

There is really only one show in town when it comes
to food and drink – the legendary Clachaig Inn (01855
811252, www.clachaig.com). It's around a mile down
the road; go out of the campsite entrance, then turn
right. Everyone from hairy hardcore climbers to
random tourists turns up here in the evening for a
conveyor belt of decent pub grub: boar sausages,
venison casserole or spinach and chickpea pie, for
example. The main bar – the Boots Bar – has a stone

THE HIGHLANDS

floor, wooden tables, an open stove and good cask ales from breweries such as Atlas, Houston Brewing Company and Williams Brothers; musicians play too. With the hubbub of conversation, bar staff shouting food orders and everyone from Black Sabbath to the White Stripes on the sound system, it can get pretty lively; the Bidean Lounge provides a more placid and child-friendly alternative.

Otherwise, the Glen Coe Visitor Centre (08444 932222, www.glencoe-nts.org.uk, closed Jan, Feb) is

---

Site specific

✔ You can sit around the fire, looking up at mountains you're going to climb the next day, with the smell of wood smoke in your nostrils and a can of beer in your hand.

✘ After chucking-out time at the nearby Clachaig Inn, the sound of well-refreshed campers trying to find their tents in the dark can get a little irritating. Groups of middle-aged gentlemen, having a lads' weekend like they did 20 years before, are often the worst offenders.

---

a mile east of Glencoe village on the A82, and has a basic café serving soup, sandwiches and cakes. There are tables outside. For dishes such as local langoustine with garlic butter, or chargrilled venison with port and redcurrant sauce, head for the Holly Tree Hotel (01631 740292, www.hollytreehotel.co.uk) at Kentallen. Head west on the A82 to Ballachulish, then take the A828 – about 20 minutes.

ATTRACTIONS & ACTIVITIES

These could be summed up in three words: climbing and walking. On its north side, Glen Coe has the celebrated ridge known as the Aonach Eagach, incorporating mountains such as Meall Dearg and Sgorr nam Fiannaidh. To the south is Bidean nam Bian, with its assorted tops and ridges, peaking out at 3,773 feet; the eastern entrance to the glen is watched over by the iconic Buachaille Etive Mor massif, with its main top of Stob Dearg (3,352 feet). If you haven't brought your boots, then your only option is to gawp at the scenery. If you don't want to gawp at the scenery, you really are in the wrong place.

The nearest town of any heft is Fort William, 20 miles north up the A82, although it is a Highland tourist centre of around 10,000 people, not a heaving metropolis. Just north of Fort William, off the A82,

is the Nevis Range (01397 705825, www.nevis range.co.uk, closed mid Nov-mid Dec). This has a world-class mountain bike downhill track, snowboarding and skiing facilities and a cable car that takes you some way up the peak of Aonach Mor. Although it stops well short of the top, the views are tremendous.

AMUSING THE KIDS

Leave the PSPs and iPods in the boot of the car. If the kids don't enjoy the River Coe burbling alongside the site, the dancing flames of the campfire and other bucolic delights, put them up for adoption. Alternatively, ask for suggestions at the Glen Coe Visitor Centre, which runs children's Land Rover safaris, woodland walks and summer holiday pond-dipping and crafts sessions.

CAMPING NEARBY

Glencoe village is on Loch Leven, a sea loch that extends another five miles or so inland. Halfway up the south side of the loch is the civilised Caolasnacon Caravan & Camping Park (01855 831279, www. kinlochlevencaravans.com, open Easter-Oct, about £15 for two people). At the head of the loch, Kinlochleven has the Blackwater Hostel & Campsite (01855 831253, www.blackwaterhostel.co.uk, open all year, £7 camping, £15 hostel), popular with walkers following the West Highland Way.

Rothiemurchus

Rothiemurchus Camp & Caravan Park
Coylumbridge, near Aviemore,
Inverness-shire PH22 1QU
01479 812800
campandcaravan@rothie.net
www.rothiemurchus.com
Map p29 ⑨
OS map NH956113

Number of pitches 22 tents,
17 caravans/motorhomes.
Open Jan-Oct, Dec.
Booking By phone, email.
Typical cost Tent £16-£18 2 people,
£8-£9 extra adult, £2 extra child.
Caravan/motorhome £19.50-£22
2 people, £2-£2.50 extra person.
Facilities Disabled facilities (toilet
and shower); electric hook-ups (17);
laundry facilities; showers (free); toilets;
washing-up area.
Campfires Not allowed.
Dogs Allowed, in caravan/motorhome
only (£1).
Restrictions No groups. No noise
10.30pm-8am.
Getting there By road Take the A9 to
Aviemore and turn on to the B9152
towards Cairngorm and Glenmore. At the
roundabout, turn right on to the B970
towards Coylumbridge. The campsite is
about 1.5 miles further on, on the right,
and is clearly signed from the junction at
Aviemore. **By public transport** Train to
Aviemore, then bus 34 (10 mins, 0871
200 2233, www.stagecoachbus.com)
direct to the campsite – request that stop
when you board.

When tent-toting customers drive, walk or hobble
into Rothiemurchus, their first thought is often
'Am I in the wrong place?'. The reception lodge,
neat central green and wall-to-wall caravans
might suggest that the average camper is going
to look pretty anomalous here. Fortunately, initial
impressions are utterly wrong. The camping is
actually 'up the back' in the southern reaches
of the site, among the trees and beside the
waters of the Am Beanaidh.

Depending on tent size, choose your spot
from the higher pitches, surrounded by tall
Caledonian pines, or lower down by the river
and little stream. All the pitches are within easy

reach of the heated amenities block, where
five unisex bathrooms are equipped with a
shower, toilet and washbasin; there's also a
family room, with disabled-adapted facilities,
plus a dish-washing area and laundry room.

The smell of the pines, the reassuring
gurgle of the stream and the outdoors
playground of the Rothiemurchus Estate is
all around you – a privately owned expanse
that is managed with wildlife and visitors very
much in mind. It's a ten-minute walk to the
Rothiemurchus Centre in Inverdruie, the main
information point for the estate, and another
mile or so further on to the shops, pubs and
restaurants of Aviemore.

The well-trodden footpath from Coylumbridge
that climbs slowly towards the legendary hill
pass known as the Lairig Ghru is immediately
adjacent to the tents; whether you follow it into
the ancient woodland for just 20 minutes or go
the whole way through to Deeside is up to you.
The campsite is also a great base for exploring
the sub-arctic plateau of the Cairngorm
mountains, or enjoying a stroll around nearby
Loch an Eilein. East of Rothiemurchus is
Glenmore Forest, with Loch Morlich in its centre;
to the north, via the manageable Ryvoan Pass,
a hill track takes you from Glenmore towards
Abernethy Forest.

A remnant of the ancient Wood of Caledon,
the forests of Rothiemurchus, Abernethy and
Glenmore are home to red and roe deer, red
squirrels, capercaillie, occasional otters,
golden eagles and, in the summer, ospreys.
People come here to walk, to glory in the
environment, or to take advantage of the

THE HIGHLANDS

organised activities on offer from the estate: everything from archery to white-water rafting.

EATING & DRINKING

The daytime Druie Café Restaurant at the Rothiemurchus Centre serves breakfast, lunch, cakes and coffee, with a focus on beef, vension and fish from the estate and seasonal produce. There's also a fabulous farm shop, specialising in local and Scottish produce, honey, cheeses, and bottled beers from the nearby Cairngorm Brewery.

Aviemore is the obvious choice for eating out; you can get everything from cheese nachos to curry. The Old Bridge Inn (01479 811137, www.oldbridge inn.co.uk) is a good spot for beer and pub grub, while the Mountain Café (01479 812473, www.mountain cafe-aviemore.co.uk), above an outdoors shop, offers breakfasts, soups and sandwiches, along with coffee and exemplary cakes. The Cairngorm Hotel (01479 810233, www.cairngorm.com) is Scottish through and through. It has a traditional bar, with the occasional accordionist, while its restaurant menu includes mince and tatties, and haggis on a soda scone with mustard sauce. What it lacks in finesse, it makes up for in soul.

If you want to venture further afield – and upmarket – it's a half-hour drive to the hotel dining room at the Cross at Kingussie (01540 661166, www.thecross.co.uk, closed dinner Mon, Sun). Or there's the highly civilised Boat Hotel (01479 831258, www.boat hotel.co.uk), seven miles away at Boat of Garten.

ATTRACTIONS & ACTIVITIES

First, visit the Rothiemurchus Centre (01479 812345). Whether you want to canoe across a loch, go mountain biking, pony trekking or off-road driving, catch some fish or even try deer-stalking, the centre's staff can guide you. There are also miles of forest footpaths around the estate, and several of the tallest hills in Britain are nearby.

Off the estate, just east of Loch Morlich, Glenmore Lodge (01479 861256, www.glenmorelodge.org.uk) is Scotland's national training centre for outdoors activities. This is the ideal place to learn about mountain craft, navigation, scrambling and first aid – all the things you should know if you want to tackle the big country

To see some dramatic birds of prey, visit the RSPB Loch Garten Visitor Centre (01479 831476, www.rspb.org.uk, closed Sept-Mar), a couple of miles from Boat of Garten village, where ospreys nest every summer. And for a lazy way to experience the high Cairngorms plateau, travel on the funicular railway (01479 861261, www.cairngormmountain. co.uk) up Cairngorm mountain itself.

AMUSING THE KIDS

Aside from the myriad activities on offer at the Rothiemurchus Centre, the 50-strong reindeer herd that roams around Cairngorm is a surefire winner. Staff at Reindeer House (01479 861228, www.cairngormreindeer.co.uk, closed three weeks Jan), just east of Loch Morlich, organise a daily visit to the mountain, weather permitting. Once native, reindeer were hunted into extinction and only reintroduced in 1952.

CAMPING NEARBY

Forest Holidays' site at Glenmore (0845 130 8224, 01479 861271, www.forestholidays.co.uk, open all year, £11-£20.50 for two people plus £3.50 supplement for non-members) sits cheek by jowl with Loch Morlich. It also offers some sense of camping in the pines, but is further from Aviemore than Rothiemurchus.

Site specific

✔ Sitting by the Am Beanaidh under a canopy of pines, after a day spent in the millennia-old wildwood, you wouldn't want to be anywhere else. Also, local Speyside whiskies seem to taste better outdoors.

✘ The walk back from Aviemore isn't too appealing in the evening. The first section to Inverdruie is fine, but the final half mile or so is on an unlit B-road with cars whizzing past. Bring a torch.

Lazy Duck

Lazy Duck Hostel & Camping
Nethy Bridge, Inverness-shire PH25 3ED
01479 821642
lazyduckhostel@googlemail.com
www.lazyduck.co.uk
Map p29 ⑩
OS map NJ016204

Number of pitches 4 tents, plus 1 pitch reserved for hikers/cyclists. No caravans/motorhomes. Woodman's hut (sleeps 2). Hostel (sleeps 8).
Open Apr-Oct; by arrangement other times.
Booking By phone, email. Essential. Woodman's hut minimum stay 2 nights.
Typical cost Tent £10 1 person, £5 extra person. Woodman's hut £60. Hostel £15 per person.
Facilities Bush shower (free); sauna (£3); toilet; washing-up area.
Campfires Chimenea and firewood supplied (free).
Dogs Not allowed.
Restrictions No large tents (over 3-person).
Getting there By road From the A95 (between Aviemore and Keith), turn on to the B970 at Speybridge. After 4 miles, turn left just before the bridge at Nethy Bridge, continue for another mile or so and then take a right for the campsite. **By public transport** Take the train to Inverness. From there, catch bus 15X and get off at the Nethy Bridge Causer stop, about a mile from the campsite (Mon-Fri, journey 1 hr). At weekends you can change at Aviemore, then catch bus 504 (0871 200 2233, www.stagecoachbus.com). Or get a taxi from Aviemore rail station for about £15 (Geordie's Taxis, 01479 810118).

The ducks here aren't so much lazy as the most pampered creatures ever to have waddled the earth, but you can hardly begrudge them when they share their charming home so generously. The Lazy Duck is a picture-perfect idyll, set in a forest clearing on the edge of the village of Nethy Bridge in the heart of the Cairngorms. The ducks' ranks are swelled by a clutch of hens, an extremely cocky rooster and a couple of enormous Skane geese, who beadily watch their human guests' every move.

With space for just four or five small tents, it's the details that make this quirky site special.

Owners David and Valery Dean have put as much thought into the needs of their temporary campers as their avian residents, and simple pleasures rule. In short, it's the most charming, homespun camping experience the Highlands has to offer.

The campground occupies a grassy, three-acre forest clearing, sheltered by eight soaring Caledonian pine trees. A hammock, strung between the trees, is perfect for lazy summer afternoons, and there's a rope swing for the children. To the south, rare-breed Soay sheep munch the grass; to the east are the duck ponds. Red squirrels are frequent visitors to the feeding station. For camping refuseniks, there's a snug little hostel, with eight beds; if you reserve in advance, it can be booked in its entirety.

A sign in the washing area advises that 'You are following in the footsteps of the Locaber MacDonalds, who from the 1890s tethered their horses among these ancient Caledonian pine trees next to the Caochan Fuaran burn.' The authenticity of the pioneer vibe becomes apparent when you see the basic bush shower: a bucket suspended from a tree.

Still, the site also has a covered cooking and eating area with a wicker sofa, table, stools and plenty of cushions, along with comprehensive recycling facilities – as befits the back-to-nature ethos. Best of all is the chimenea (freestanding fireplace) and seating area, where stacks of firewood are essential accessories on chilly evenings. If you're still feeling the cold, hop into the two-person woodshed sauna.

Completed in autumn 2011 is the woodman's hut, ideal for couples. Built of local pine and larch and modelled on traditional woodcutters' accommodation, it's the cosiest retreat imaginable, wood-panelled throughout, with a kingsize box bed by the window, a wood-burning stove and a Victorian copper urn for hot water. There's a tiny stove (but no fridge) and, outside, a compost loo and a shower open to the sky – for hardy souls only.

EATING & DRINKING

Eggs are available on site, as is salad – picked from the garden on request. In Nethy Bridge, the Spar-cum-post office (01479 821217) stocks a respectable range of groceries, and is open daily from 8am to 6pm. The sausages at SG Mustard's the Butcher (01479 821245) are legendary, and fresh fish is available from George, who visits the campsite every Wednesday 8-9am. Monday is fish and chip night, with a van setting up shop outside the post office from 6pm.

Site specific

✔ For a charming, back-to-nature experience, Lazy Duck is in a league of its own. For families or first-time campers, it doesn't get much better than this.

✘ The site is quite tricky to find; keep a close lookout for the sign. The washbasin in the single toilet is teeny-tiny.

Just over 12 miles away, Aviemore's outdoor gear shops and restaurants serve more ambitious needs. Try not to succumb to the lure of the supermarket as you approach the high street; there's a comprehensive array of independent food shops, which are much more fun. Just outside the centre, the Old Bridge Inn (01479 811137, www.oldbridgeinn.co.uk) serves hearty local food in convivial surroundings.

The menu at the Cairn Hotel (01479 841212, www.cairnhotel.co.uk) in Carrbridge, seven miles north of Aviemore, includes poached Scottish salmon and venison sausage casserole, along with baked potatoes and toasties. A 20-minute drive south of the campsite, at Rothiemurchus, is the Druie Café Restaurant (see p301).

In Nethy Bridge itself, gorgeous mountain views and slap-up Sunday lunches are offered in grand, country-house style at the Mountview Hotel (01479 821248, www.mountviewhotel.co.uk, closed lunch). Booking is recommended for all places.

ATTRACTIONS & ACTIVITIES

The Lazy Duck is set in the magnificent surroundings of the Cairngorms National Park (01479 873535, www.cairngorms.co.uk), whose ancient granite hills, heather moorlands, pine forests, marshes and lochs cover almost 1,500 square miles and are home to 25 per cent of all Britain's endangered species. Discover the park at your own pace on the mountain trails, or take a guided walk with a ranger.

Another option is a ramble along part of the Speyside Way (www.speysideway.org), a 60-mile path that runs from the Moray coast to the edge of the Cairngorms. It passes through Grantown-on-Spey, Nethy Bridge before reaching Aviemore; Nethy Bridge to Boat of Garten is a pleasant five-mile walk, passing through the ancient pinewoods of Abernethy Forest.

If you'd rather see the landscape on four wheels, take a quad trek at Alvie Estate (01479 810330, www.alvie-estate.co.uk), four miles south of Aviemore.

The off-road trails head across open moorland and through the forest to the banks of the River Spey. Alternatively, opt for a spot of horse riding (07831 495397) or go fishing in one of the estate's lochs.

The glossily-painted steam engines of the Strathspey Steam Railway (01479 810725, www.strathspeyrailway.co.uk) run from nearby Broomhill Station to Boat of Garten and Aviemore, past grazing sheep and the spectacular backdrop of the mountains; services are most frequent between April and October.

If you're visiting in August, this is when Nethy Bridge hosts the Abernethy Highland Games (www.nethybridge.com/highlandgames). Pipe bands play, kilted dancers perform, and competitors' mettle is tested with track and field events – and a hotly contested tug of war.

AMUSING THE KIDS

Heaven for children is just a 30-minute drive away, at the Landmark Forest Adventure Park (0800 731 3446, www.landmarkpark.co.uk) in Carrbridge. Highlights include a treetop trail, waterfall raft-ride, high-wire adventure course, climbing wall and 50-foot Skydive – not for the faint-hearted.

On wet days, make for the MacDonald Aviemore Highland Resort (01479 815275, www.macdonald hotels.co.uk/aviemore), whose giant 'leisure arena' includes an indoor pool with a snaking yellow waterslide and a wave machine, along with a Jacuzzi, sauna and steam room for the grown-ups.

CAMPING NEARBY

Despite its name, the Grantown-on-Spey Caravan Park (01479 872474, www.caravanscotland.com, open Jan-Nov, last two weeks Dec) also offers a separate camping area for tents, along with two cosy wigwams (which are more like little wooden huts). A tent pitch for two people costs £10-£22 per night, a wigwam £32-£42.

Glenbrittle

Glenbrittle Campsite
Carbost, Isle of Skye IV47 8TA
01478 640404
www.dunvegancastle.com
Map p29 ⑪
OS map NG409214

Number of pitches 200 tents/motorhomes.
No caravans.
Open Apr-Sept.
Booking No booking.
Typical cost £6.40 adult, £4.20 child.
Facilities Electric hook-ups (9); shop;
showers (free); toilets; washing-up area.
Campfires Allowed on beach.
Dogs Allowed.
Getting there By road From the A87
(the main road on Skye), take a left on to
the A863 to Dunvegan. Just before Drynoch,
turn left on to the B8009 towards Carbost.
The road to Glenbrittle is the first on the
left; the campsite is 8 miles away, at the
end of the road. **By public transport** Tricky
but possible! Train to Kyle of Lochalsh (one
of the most scenic rail journeys in Britain).
From Kyle, a bus runs 11 times a day to
Portree, from where there's a bus 3 times
a day to Carbost. You'll then have to catch
a taxi to Glenbrittle. More information
from Portree Visitor Information Centre
(01478 612137).

There can't be many campsites in Britain
where the setting is quite so dramatic – and
the nightlife quite so quiet. Wedged on a gently
sloping shelf where the mountains meet the sea
midway down the west coast of Skye, Glenbrittle
offers campers a simple choice of scenery:
one way for the massive bulk of the Black
Cuillins and the most famous mountain ridge in
Scotland; the other for a fine sandy beach and
the Hebridean Sea. There's nothing to block
either view. And the reason for the nighttime
peace? Everybody is about to get up very early
in the morning to have a helluva lot of fresh air,
because this is a climber's paradise.

The weather is crucial to Glenbrittle. A good
forecast, and it will fill; a bad one, and it won't
(you can't begin). If the mountain tops are in
cloud, as they are much of the time, there's
little point in setting off uphill, and there's no
wet weather entertainment anywhere in the
vicinity. But even on bad days this is still a
tremendously powerful and visually spectacular
amphitheatre of mountains, and there's lots
of great walking along the shoreline to Rubh'
an Dùnain, four miles away. The type of visitors
who make it down the winding, single-track road
(larger vehicles should proceed with caution)
into Glenbrittle come prepared for anything.
They are motivated by the beauty of the place,
whatever the weather.

The site is on land owned by Hugh Macleod of
Macleod, 30th clan chief, whose main residence
is Dunvegan Castle in the north of Skye, but
you're unlikely to see him wandering around
checking the tightness of your guy ropes. The
mountains are Macleod's too, but this is open-
access land, and every year thousands of hardy
souls make it up the scree-covered slopes to
clamber along the length of the Cuillin ridge.
It's possible to do the whole thing in a day, just,
but you do have to start early.

The site is big (120 pitches, mainly for tent
campers, although it's rarely even half full) and
glossy-grassed, and you can park next to your
tent, provided the ground is dry enough. It's
on a gentle slope in a treeless area, so can
be exposed to westerly winds. A little rise just
before the beach begins provides some shelter
for smaller tents.

Facilities are simple and clean, the site
wardens, brothers Alex and Kenny McGregor,
are friendly, and there are plans afoot to have –
oh, luxury of luxuries – some washing machines.
But until then there's the basic shower block
(four showers and three toilets each for men
and women) and a shop selling essential
groceries – and even more essential outdoors
equipment. Fires aren't allowed on the site,
but you can make one on the beach (collect
driftwood or forage in the woods behind the
campsite) – hopefully the smoke will keep the
pesky midges at bay too.

You do need to have the right kit before you
set out, for climbing or for walking, or you could
be putting your life in danger; there have been
fatalities here. It's reassuring to know that
there's a Skye Mountain Rescue base in
Glenbrittle, although the first call in case of
emergency should always be to the police.

EATING & DRINKING

There's no café or restaurant on site, nor in
Glenbrittle as a whole, and the nearest warm, dry
eaterie is eight miles away at Carbost, where the
Old Inn (01478 640205, www.carbost.f9.co.uk,
closed Nov-Mar) serves hearty, inexpensive meals,

ISLE OF SKYE

and provides basic bunkhouse accommodation, mainly for the climbing community.

The other popular venue for campers, climbers and walkers is the Sligachan Hotel (01478 650204, www.sligachan.co.uk), 14 miles away en route to Portree, which is Skye's main town and the nearest shopping centre of any size. The Sligachan has a big barn of a bar popular with young travellers, and serves typically budget-priced burgers, baked potatoes, its own-brewed Cuillin ales and more than 200 whiskies. It's a cheerful, noisy place, with an international clientele.

Should you want something really posh, then head south 33 miles to Kinloch Lodge (01471 833333, www.kinloch-lodge.co.uk) on the Sleat peninsula. It's owned and run by Claire and Godfrey Macdonald; he's the lord and erstwhile landowner of much of the southern part of Skye, and she's the famous cookery writer. You can be sure of eating well, but you will have to look presentable.

ATTRACTIONS & ACTIVITIES

The main attraction is the big outdoors: walking, climbing, fishing. If the mountains are not for you, then several rocky burns run off the slopes on the path to Rubh' an Dùnain, and on sunny days the pools can be great playgrounds for kids. The beach has a broad swathe of sand at low tide, but the sea is pretty chilly and only the brave venture in.

Carbost is the home of the Talisker distillery (01478 614308, www.discovering-distilleries.com/talisker) producer of the Isle of Skye's distinctive malt whisky, and it hosts daily guided tours and tastings from £6 a head. It's closed Sat Nov-Mar and Sun Sept-June.

From Sligachan, there's an excellent walk past the photogenic packhorse bridge and up the glen alongside the river. The path passes between the Cuillin ranges, with the main grouping of Black Cuillins to your right and the lower, round-shouldered Red Cuillins to your left. Eight miles later it emerges at Camasunary, a lovely sweep of a bay with views out to the islands of Soay and Rhum, and a popular bothy on the shore.

And then there's Portree itself (24 miles from Glenbrittle) a handsome little place with a variety of shops and cafés, and a picture-book harbour where you may well be able to accost a returning fisherman and make him an offer for a bag or two of prawns.

AMUSING THE KIDS

Although by no means beautiful or classic among Scottish fortresses, Dunvegan Castle (01470 521206, www.dunvegancastle.com, closed late Oct-Apr) offers a fair range of activities and interest, from boat trips

Isle of Skye: River Sligachan (top left); Old Man of Storr (top right); Blaven (bottom).

ISLE OF SKYE

to see the seals to the legend of the Fairy Flag, the most treasured possession of the Macleod clan. It's located on the north-west corner of the island, 28 miles from Glenbrittle.

CAMPING NEARBY

The Sligachan Hotel runs an 80-pitch site (open Apr-Sept, £5 per person) just across the road from the hotel. As at Glenbrittle, this is a scenically spectacular location, but it is next to one of Skye's busier roads, and the proximity of the hotel's Seumas bar means it is very much more sociable. In other words, you might not get such a quiet night's sleep.

Site specific

✔ This is organised wilderness camping for the physically active. And it's very peaceful: nobody makes the eight-mile trek down a twisting road to a place with no pub or bar for the sake of a wild night out.

✘ Midges will always be a problem at any Highland campsite. At least the proximity to the sea often brings an onshore breeze.

Morvich

Morvich Caravan Club Site
Shiel Bridge, Inverinate, Kyle,
Ross-shire IV40 8HQ
01599 511354
www.caravanclub.co.uk
Map p29 ⑫
OS map NG960210

Number of pitches 30 tents,
77 caravans/motorhomes.
Open End Mar-Nov.
Booking By phone, online (members
only) for caravans/motorhomes.
No booking for tents.
Typical cost Tent £4-£5.50 per pitch,
£4-£6 adult, £1.30-£2.10 child. Non-CC
members pay an additional £8 per group.
Membership £40 per year.
Facilities Disabled facilities (toilet and
shower); electric hook-ups (77); laundry
facilities; shop; showers (free); toilets;
washing-up area; Wi-Fi.
Campfires Not allowed.
Dogs Allowed, on lead.
Restrictions Groups by arrangement.
Getting there By road Take the A87 and
just over a mile after Shiel Bridge, at the
head of Loch Duich, turn right to Morvich.
After another mile turn right on to a single-
track road; the site entrance is 150 yds
on the left. **By public transport** Train
to Inverness. Bus 917 (08705 505050,
www.citylink.co.uk) runs three times a day
in summer to Skye, stopping at Allt-a-
Chruinn, half a mile from the campsite.
It's a long ride, though, nearly 2 hrs.

Soaring hills and craggy mountains provide
a breathtakingly lovely backdrop to Morvich,
which is set at the foot of a lush, wooded valley
near the southern end of Loch Duich. Sheltered
from the biting winds that blow off the sea, in
a designated National Scenic Area, it's an idyllic
spot in which to camp.

Don't let the fact that this is a Caravan Club
site conjure up images of enormous motorhomes
looming over your tent; caravans and tents are
in separate areas. One of the quietest spots is
the tent area with electric hook-ups, which has
room for a maximum of four tents. Other than
that, head for the far end of the main field, away
from the busy main entrance, with its stream
of cars, walkers and dog owners; it seems to
be an unspoken rule here that every caravan
must have a canine contingent. Tents, meanwhile,
tend to be tiny one- or two-person jobs.

Although a lesser campsite might rely on its
location to keep the punters rolling in, Morvich
isn't a place to rest on its laurels. The facilities
go above and beyond the call of duty: an
information room with leaflets on the area;
a lounge with a TV and board games; a drying
room for soggy cagoules and damp boots;
comprehensive laundry facilities and a covered
area for cooking. The toilet and shower block is
equally splendid, featuring individual dressing
cubicles with large sinks and copious hot
showers, facilities for disabled campers and a
parent and toddler room with a raised baby bath.

Much of the land that surrounds the site is
owned by the National Trust for Scotland, which
organises guided walks throughout the season,
along with sea kayaking lessons. The mountain
ridges of Kintail (including the famous Five
Sisters) and the surrounding West Affric nature
reserve are a wonderful place to get away from
it all; experienced climbers can scale the high
summits, and there are plenty of gentler paths
with panoramic views for more sedate excursions.
One of Scotland's most famous (and most
photographed) castles, Eilean Donan, is nearby
and the Isle of Skye is within striking range.

EATING & DRINKING

Basic groceries are available from the on-site shop,
which also stocks fresh milk, bread and rolls;
newspapers can also be delivered if you place your
order by 5pm the day before. The nearest town, Kyle
of Lochalsh, about 15 miles away, has a busy harbour
and a few shops, including a Co-op and a butcher's.

A couple of miles away, on the shores of Loch
Duich, the Kintail Lodge Hotel (01599 511275,
www.kintaillodgehotel.co.uk) serves morning coffee,
lunch and dinner in its conservatory, and evening
meals in the restaurant; local seafood and game often
make an appearance on the menu. The pub attached
to the hotel serves simple, sustaining grub – a bowl of
cullen skink (smoked haddock soup), say, or chicken,
ham and mushroom pie. Musicians play Thursday
evenings in summer, and once a month in winter.

ATTRACTIONS & ACTIVITIES

Set on an island where three great sea lochs converge,
Eilean Donan Castle (01599 555202, www.eilean
donancastle.com, closed Nov-Feb) is a wonderfully
wild and romantic spot – and instantly familiar,
thanks to its appearance on countless biscuit tins
and calendars. Reduced to ruins in the Jacobite
uprising of 1719, it was painstakingly rebuilt in

Site specific

✔ The glorious location, surrounded by mountains, and the princely facilities.

✘ This isn't really a 'destination' site in itself: you come, do some climbing, hiking or sightseeing, and move on.

the early 20th century – which explains why it's in such a pristine condition. There's a modern visitor centre with a decent café and souvenir shop (where you can buy your own calendar). The drive from the campsite, skirting Loch Duich, takes around 15 minutes.

From Eilean Donan, you could continue to Kyle of Lochalsh and drive across the massive steel and concrete bridge to Skye. Alternatively, head north to Plockton, a jaunty little lochside village in a wonderfully sheltered location on the edge of Loch Carron. A row of cottages curves around the harbour, interspered with the odd palm tree. Fishing and seal-spotting trips set off from the seafront, and there's a lively regatta in June; *Hamish Macbeth* was also filmed here. A sprinkling of shops and restaurants add to its appeal.

Accessible only on foot, the spectacular 370-foot Falls of Glomach are one of the highest waterfalls in Britain, tumbling down a narrow cleft in a sheer, rocky hillside. The round trip takes four or five hours, setting off from the National Trust for Scotland's Countryside Centre at Morvich (0844 493 2231, closed Oct-Mar); in summer, there are ranger-led walks.

From the sheltered sea lochs of Loch Duich to the coastline of Skye, the west coast is also a fantastic place to try sea kayaking. Courses are available for all abilities, and include activities for families with young children; for details, contact the National Trust for Scotland Ranger Service (0844 493 2231, www.nts.org.uk/seakayaking).

AMUSING THE KIDS

Aside from visiting Eilean Donan Castle, where children can gallop across the bridge on imaginary steeds and play at being valiant knights, there's not a great deal to do in these parts, aside from embracing the great outdoors. If it's too wet for kayaking, walking and picnics, you could consider a visit to the swimming pool at Lochalsh Leisure Centre (01599 534848, www.lochalshleisure.org.uk), which also has a sauna and steam room for knotty-muscled grown-ups.

CAMPING NEARBY

Some two and a half miles away in Shiel Bridge, just behind the petrol station and shop, is the Shiel Bridge Caravan Park (01599 511221, www.shielbridge caravanpark.co.uk, open Mar-Oct, tent £5.75 per person, caravan/motorhome £16.50 per night). Set at the foot of the Five Sisters of Kintail, it's perfect for hill walkers and climbers.

THE NORTH-WEST

Applecross

Applecross Campsite
Applecross, Strathcarron,
Ross-shire IV54 8ND
01520 744268
enquiries@applecross-campsite.co.uk
www.applecross.uk.com/campsite
Map p29 ⑬
OS map NG711444

Number of pitches 55 tents/caravans/
motorhomes. 10 camping huts (sleeping 4).
Open All year (reduced facilities winter).
Booking Online. Advisable.
Typical cost Camping £7 adult, £3 12-16s,
under 12s free. Camping hut £26-£34
2 people.
Facilities Café/restaurant (Apr-Sept);
electric hook-ups (10); laundry facilities;
shop; showers (free); toilets; washing-up
area.
Campfires Not allowed.
Dogs Allowed, on lead (£1-£5).
Restrictions No vehicle access after 10pm.
Getting there By road Take the A890 and
then the A896 to Tornapress. Here, turn on
to the Applecross road – it's about 11 miles
to the far side of the peninsula via the jaw-
dropping Bealach na Ba pass. The campsite
is on the left, just before the Applecross
Inn. Alternatively, there's the much longer
'coward's way'. Instead of turning left at
Tornapress, continue on the A896 towards
Loch Shieldag and take the coast road via
Arinacrinachd, Feammore and Kalnakill –
about 20 miles. **By public transport** Train
to Strathcarron or Achnasheen, then the
dial-a-bus service to Applecross (book ahead
on 01520 722205). No bus service on Sun.

They say it's better to travel than to arrive, but
they're wrong. The journey to Applecross is one
heck of a ride – along narrow, single-track roads,
punctuated by mercilessly tight hairpin bends.
The infamous Bealach na Ba (Gaelic for 'pass of
the cattle') ascends through towering mountain
passes, climbing 2,000 feet above sea level.
Long-abandoned crofts dot the moorland, and
sheep either block the road or eyeball you
territorially as you edge cautiously past. Then, on
the final stretch, just as you're about to abandon
all hope of ever arriving anywhere, you spot the
signs that warn – somewhat unnecessarily – that
the way is impassable in winter.

Remote? That's putting it mildly; this is a
landscape of epic vastness. Yet when you finally
pull up at Applecross, you'll find a convivial
home-from-home, with own-baked cakes for
sale at the reception. Not only does this place
get the essentials just right (a few minor quibbles
aside), but it also has a licensed café/restaurant
– set in a lushly planted polytunnel that would
look more at home in a plant nursery.

There are six acres of camping fields and
no restrictions on where to pitch. The furthest
field tends to be the quietest, and also has
the best views over the bay below, and the
strait that separates the peninsula from the
islands of Raasay, South Rona and Skye.

Once you've pitched camp, you might
appreciate a proper coffee from reception.
There's also one of those aggravating cash
machines that charges you to take your own
money out, along with a payphone (there's
no mobile phone reception). The site also
has a coin-operated washing machine and
tumble dryer. There are two showers apiece
in the male and female washrooms, by the
campsite entrance.

A five-minute walk from the campsite, the
village of Applecross (locally referred to as
'the Street') comprises a row of stone cottages,
looking out over the sea wall. Posters urge
visitors to support the local community by
'topping up a tenner' of petrol at the filling
station, which is run by volunteers, and there's
also a shop and a small heritage centre. The
crowning glory of the village, though, are its
two tremendous eating establishments: the
Applecross Inn and the Potting Shed.

Applecross Bay itself is a vast, sandy inlet,
with stunning views across the Inner Sound to
the islands. Its shallow waters are lovely for
swimming – though it may be a chilly dip. For
sheer drama, head to Sand, seven miles or so
north along the coast. Here, the beach is backed

Site specific

✔ Gorgeous views of the bay, the so-
laid-back-it's-horizontal vibe and Flower
Tunnel restaurant aside, it's got to be the
proximity to the legendary Applecross Inn,
five minutes' walk away.

✘ Did we mention there's no mobile
phone reception whatsoever?

by a mighty, 100-foot high dune. Kids race each other up, then slide joyfully down, while adults climb creakingly to the top, to gaze across to Skye – and attempt to catch their breath.

EATING & DRINKING

Groceries can be bought at the village shop, or from Alastair and Seonag's van; call 01520 744421 for details. From April to October, a produce market is held on the first Friday of every month, just past the hamlet of Milltown behind the fire station. Impromptu sales during the summer are also advertised on the village noticeboard, at the bottom of the hill on the way to the Applecross Inn.

The on-site Flower Tunnel (01520 744268, closed Nov-Mar) serves stone-baked pizzas and solid, sustaining bar food, such as venison burgers, soup and macaroni cheese; there's also a bar.

The village itself has two splendid options. Its walls groaning with accolades too numerous to mention, the Applecross Inn (01520 744262, www. applecross.uk.com) is invariably packed to the rafters. The peninsula's best produce finds its way on to the menu, from seafood to Applecross Estate venison and fabulous cheeses from the West Highland Dairy, along with local ales.

Local ingredients are also very much in evidence at the Potting Shed (01520 744440, www.applecross garden.co.uk), set in a formerly derelict walled garden, which now provides it with fruit, vegetables and herbs. The garden's yield is supplemented by venison, wild mushrooms and seafood fresh from the boats, including magnificent Applecross Bay prawns. Even if you're not eating here, you're welcome to look around the gardens; it's about a 20-minute walk from the campsite.

ATTRACTIONS & ACTIVITIES

There is an abundance of well-signed, scenic walks in the area, both along the coast and through the woodland. For details, visit www.applecrosswalks. org.uk, or pick up the walks leaflet on site. The Applecross Heritage Centre (www.applecross heritage.org.uk, closed Sun, all Nov-Easter), next to Clachan Church in the village, is worth a peek.

At Cuaig, nine miles north on the coast road, Croft Wool & Weavers (01520 755260, closed Mon, Sun, all Nov-Apr) sells jumpers, hats, gloves and handwoven cloth, rugs and shawls. It also runs weaving and spinning taster sessions and courses – with lessons often taking place outside, overlooking the sea.

For more dynamic pursuits, investigate Applecross Mountain & Sea Guides (01520 744394, www.apple cross.uk.com), which offers sea kayaking, hill walking and mountaineering trips. And if you're here in July, don't miss the Applecross Highland Games, held on one of the campsite's fields – booking is essential, as pitches are in great demand.

AMUSING THE KIDS

Take the youngsters on an educational adventure with a wild food walk with Gill Fairweather (01520 744375, Thur, June-Oct). If it rains, the covered play area in the Flower Tunnel has space, games and coloured chalks aplenty, and should keep the kids happy until they can head back to the beach.

CAMPING NEARBY

Follow the coast road north from Applecross, and you can't miss the Shieldaig Camping Area in Shieldaig. It's a basic, no-frills site, with a cold water tap and use of the public conveniences in the village. Just turn up and pay at the warden's house or honesty box.

Clachtoll Beach

Clachtoll Beach Campsite
134 Clachtoll, by Lochinver,
Sutherland IV27 4JD
01571 855377
mail@clachtollbeachcampsite.co.uk
www.clachtollbeachcampsite.co.uk
Map p29 ⑭
OS map NC043274

Number of pitches 40 tents/
caravans/motorhomes.
Open Easter-last weekend Sept.
Booking By phone, email (preferred).
Advisable; essential July, Aug.
Typical cost Tent £11-£15,
plus £1.50 adult, £1 child.
Facilities Disabled facilities (toilet
and shower); electric hook-ups (14);
laundry facilities; showers (free);
toilets; washing-up area.
Campfires Not allowed on site.
Allowed on beach.
Dogs Allowed, on lead.
Getting there By road Take the A837
towards Lochinver. Just before the village,
turn on to the B869 to Clachtoll. Follow the
single-track road for about 5 miles; as you
descend the hill towards the sea you will
see the bay and the campsite spread out
before you. **By public transport** Possible,
but very tortuous. Train to Inverness, then
Citylink bus 961 (journey 80 mins) to
Ullapool. From Ullapool, Stagecoach bus
67A takes 90 mins to Stoer, a mile north
of Clachtoll, but there's only one bus a day.
Contact Traveline Scotland (0871 200
2233, www.travelinescotland.com) for
more information and timetables.

Clachtoll is not a village in the idealised
Ambridge sense, although it's not an untypical
settlement for the north-west of Scotland: a
sparse cluster of houses, sheep wandering
around all over the place, and the Atlantic
Ocean on the doorstep. There is a bareness,
a minimalism, that feels the polar opposite of
the Home Counties in the remote south; you
can hardly believe you're on the same island.

The campsite has three fields and one
facilities block, and you can get from your tent
to Clachtoll's wild little stretch of white sands
in no time at all (camping isn't permitted on
the beach). There is no shop, no pub, no café –
although the facilities block does have a vending
machine dispensing hot drinks – and the nearest
village in any recognisable sense is Lochinver,
five miles south. Consequently, this is a site
where you pack everything you need into your car
boot or bicycle panniers and enjoy it for what it is:
remote and simple, with an all-pervasive taste of
the sea and the characteristic moonscape of the
Assynt countryside to the north, south and east.

Owner Jim Galway allows a maximum of about
40 tents and caravans, but it's only likely to get
that busy at the height of the season in July
and August during the school holidays.

Clachtoll has a certain old-fashioned feel
in that most parents are happy to let their
free-range children run around, play and explore
without any of the dark worries of modern towns
and cities. This is patently not a po-faced, rule-
bound establishment, but neither is it the kind
of site where you're going to have to complain
about someone making a noise when they roll
back from the pub at midnight; an easy-going
balance is struck.

And if you come without kids, maybe just
driving or cycling round the coast, looking for
somewhere to pitch a tent for the night, then
Clachtoll is ideal. If it's a clear summer's night,
before zipping up and wriggling into your sleeping
bag, you could take a beer or a cup of tea down
to the beach, sit and listen to the waves and
think – however briefly – that the world's not
such a bad place after all.

EATING & DRINKING

The busy fishing port of Lochinver, straddling
both sides of Loch Inver, should supply all your
provisions needs. There's a bank, post office, petrol
station, various shops including a small supermarket,
and a tourist information centre. It also has some
excellent places to eat.

The Albannach (01571 844407, www.thealbannach.
co.uk, closed lunch, closed Jan, Feb, closed Mon-Wed
Nov, Dec) is one of those far-flung Scottish hotels
with a Michelin star. Best to avoid hefty boots and
Gore-Tex chic if you you want to experience its
accomplished five-course loveliness: perhaps local
crab tartlet to start, then butternut squash soup,
roast venison as the main, artisan cheeses, and hot
chocolate soufflé for dessert.

The other Lochinver establishment aiming
upmarket is the Inver Lodge Hotel (01571 844496,
www.inverlodgehotel.co.uk, closed Nov-Easter),
which is better on the inside than the outside. More
economical alternatives include the Caberfeidh Bar &
Restaurant (01571 844321, www.thecaberfeidh.co.uk,

Site specific

✔ The space, the lovely beach, a patch of flat grass for the tent and the mad, distinctive geology of Assynt all around: it's the perfect antidote to urban living.

✘ Early in the season, and late, severe winds whip off the Atlantic, which makes camping less of a pleasure and more of an endurance sport. Also, this is the north-west coast of Scotland – always expect rain.

closed Mon, Tue, lunch Wed-Fri Nov-Mar), which serves decent pub grub; and the Lochinver Larder Riverside Bistro (01571 844356, closed dinner Nov-Mar), which operates as a café, shop and bistro. The same folk make renowned pies. In the opposite direction – around eight miles north along the B869 – is the hamlet of Drumbeg. The Drumbeg Hotel (01571 833236, www.drumbeghotel.co.uk, open dinner Tue-Sun, lunch Sun) is a friendly establishment with straightforward food and a bar.

If you're driving back to Clachtoll late at night, watch out for both sheep and deer on the road.

ATTRACTIONS & ACTIVITIES

The biggest single attraction is hill walking, both around Assynt and in Coigach immediately to the south. Peaks like Quinag, Suilven, Canisp and Stac Polly (which looks fearsome, but at just 2,000 feet is an accessible and popular climb) stand proud of the surrounding land, eroded into strange and fantastical shapes. The geology of the area is unique, and Scotland's far north-west has some of the most antique surface rocks on the planet: up to three billion years old. It has been a designated European

Geopark since 2004; see www.northwest-highlands-geopark.org.uk for more information.

The four-mile circular coastal walk from Stoer lighthouse to the Old Man of Stoer, a spectacular sea-stack, is great, if rough in places; start at Stoer lighthouse, six miles north of Clachtoll.

Norwest Sea Kayaking (01571 844281, www.norwestseakayaking.com, closed mid Oct-Apr), based at Lochinver, offers everything from introductory courses to expeditions along the coast and among the islands. Basking sharks, dolphins, minke whales and porpoises have all been seen just offshore in recent years.

There's a ranger's hut at Clachtoll beach, while the excellent visitor centre (01571 844330, open Easter-Oct) in Lochinver supplies fishing permits and is the area's main tourist information resource. If anyone can suggest activities for a rainy day, they can.

AMUSING THE KIDS

Bring balls, bats, boogie boards, wetsuits, Frisbees and other paraphernalia, point the kids at Clachtoll Beach after breakfast; rinse and repeat after lunch and supper. Vary the theme by sampling the drop-dead gorgeous beach at Achmelvich, about five miles away – head back along the B869 to the south, and it's signposted along a minor road to the right.

CAMPING NEARBY

The Shore Caravan Site (01571 844393, www.shorecaravansite.yolasite.com, open Apr-Oct) at Achmelvich is, like Clachtoll, right next to the beach, so offers a similarly breezy camping experience. A tent costs £6.50-£13.50 depending on size, plus £1 adult, 50p child. There are free hot showers, but dogs aren't allowed and you can't book. If the weather is looking too dodgy for a tent, Achmelvich also has a handy youth hostel (01571 844480, www.syha.org.uk, open mid Apr-mid Sept, £16 a night).

THE NORTH-WEST

Badrallach

Badrallach
Dundonnell, Ross-shire IV23 2QP
01854 633281
mail@badrallach.com
www.badrallach.com
Map p29 ⓯
OS map NH063917

Number of pitches 16 tents,
3 campervans/motorhomes.
B&B Airstream (sleeps 4). Cottage
(sleeps 4). Bothy (sleeps 9-12).
Open All year.
Booking By phone, online, post.
Advisable; essential July, Aug.
Typical cost Camping pitch £2.50,
plus £4 adult, £2.50 child. B&B Airstream
£40 adult, £20 child. Cottage 3 nights
weekend £200, week £260-£340.
Bothy £6 per person, £70 sole use.
Facilities Disabled facilities (toilet);
showers (free); toilets; washing-up area
Campfires Allowed, in designated areas.
Dogs Allowed.
Getting there By road Take the A835
north towards Ullapool. At Braemore
Junction turn left on to the A832. After
about 11 miles, turn right on to the single-
track road towards Badrallach. It's 7 miles
to the site. **By public transport** A couple
of options. Train to Inverness, then the
Westerbus (0871 2002233, one a day on
Mon, Wed, Sat) to the end of Badrallach
Road; or City Link bus Ullapool service
(08705 505050, www.citylink.co.uk, twice
daily) from Inverness to Braemore Junction.
Collection can be arranged from both drop-
off points with the campsite owners.

You have walked the ridges of the imposing
An Teallach massif, bagging the main tops of
Bidein a' Glas Thuill and Sgurr Fiona, both
pushing 3,500 feet. You've made your way back
down towards Little Loch Broom to collect the
car you left at Dundonnell, then driven across
the loch's old flood plain at Strath Beag. The
single track follows north, up the sparse hillside
underneath Beinn nam Ban, and finally goes
west again. Sheep and cattle wander at will
on the road, but finally you reach Badrallach:
no more than a few houses and the campsite.

Tonight there will be hot food, prepared on a
camping stove in the well-appointed bothy, fine

bottled beer from the local An Teallach Brewery
– Crofters' Pale Ale, perhaps – good company
and a self-mocking but half-serious declaration,
paraphrased from a far more accomplished
mountaineer. As you look back over Little Loch
Broom from your tent, towards An Teallach,
you raise your bottle of beer and say, with due
humility, 'We knocked the bastards off.'

Not everyone who comes here is a mountain
climber, however. Some just want to escape
the city and enjoy a sociable, faraway weekend
– north of Edinburgh and Glasgow, north of
Inverness, north of most things in the British
Isles. This is a far from ostentatious site,
but that's why it has proved so popular with
aficionados. Its social centre is the old stone
bothy – a converted barn, with a kitchen area
(it has a fridge and sink, but no cooking facilities)
and a lounge. If it's booked out by a group, other
campers only have access to the kitchen area.

The main camping meadow is in front: a grassy
expanse with marked pitches, a scattering
of wild orchids and beautiful views of the
surrounding hills; there's also an outlying field,
with firepits. Red deer, pine martins and foxes
occasionally stray on to the site, and golden
eagles have been spotted hereabouts.

The cottage is a more luxurious choice,
kitted out with peat stoves, feather duvets
and an unexpectedly modern upper level, with
an aluminium, barrel-vaulted ceiling. There's
a compact, well-equipped caravan on the main
field, as well as a lovely shiny Airstream – the
newest addition to the site – which combines
caravan cosiness with the added leg room of
a bigger mobile home. You can book it on a
B&B or self-catering basis.

Site specific

✔ If you got much further north, you would
fall off the edge. Badrallach is untrammelled
and unfussy, with friendly, approachable
owners. As long as you bring a sense of self-
sufficiency, it can be a transcendent spot.

✘ On a bad weather day – hardly uncommon
in the north-west of Scotland – activity
options are limited to sitting around chatting,
reading or playing games. If the bothy is
booked by a group you're confined to
your tent, or will have to jump in the car and
seek entertainment elsewhere.

Little Loch Broom

Bothy

Visitors
Please
report to
Croft office

A few minutes' walk from the camping area is the north shore of Little Loch Broom – one of the main recreational options in the area, hills notwithstanding. Some people fish, or mess about in boats (Badrallach's owners, the Stotts, hire out various watercraft), while others simply enjoy the peace.

This is the Scoraig peninsula after all, idling between Loch Broom and Little Loch Broom, with no major roads and no through routes – unless you count the track to the hamlet of Scoraig itself, another five miles along the loch shore. Do something, do nothing, or just watch the light playing on the slopes of An Teallach.

EATING & DRINKING

For groceries, Dundonnell Stores and post office (01854 633208) is 14 miles away. Otherwise it's Ullapool (an hour's drive), where there is a chemist, supermarket and doctor.

There are no pubs or restaurants on the sparsely populated peninsula. Drive the seven miles or so back along the minor road to the A832, then turn right; just under two miles along you'll find the Dundonnell Hotel (01854 633204, www.dundonnell hotel.com, closed Nov-Mar). Slightly frilly in places, it offers a restaurant menu in summer and bar food all year round.

Around two miles further on at Camusnagaul is Maggie's Tea Room (01854 633326, www. camusnagaul.com, closed Sun, all Oct-Mar), which serves tea and coffee, cakes and light meals, including local smoked salmon sandwiches and Orkney pickled herring salads.

ATTRACTIONS & ACTIVITIES

At the risk of repetition, much that happens here is weather-dependent. On site, the owners have all kinds of outdoors equipment for rent that will keep most people happy for days on end. This includes kayaks, Zodiac inflatables, an 18-foot clinker-built boat called *Shetland Willy* and fishing rods. If you know what you're doing, and the weather obliges, then they're yours for a fee; see the website for details. The hydrophobic can hire mountain bikes (call ahead, as the site only has three or four) to explore the Scoraig peninsula, fly a power-kite or even ride a blokart (a land-sailing buggy); basic instruction is provided, along with helmets and protective clothing.

Alternatively, you could go for a walk along the loch shore or try a more ambitious climb, using Badrallach as a base to reach the likes of An Teallach, Sgurr Mor in the Fannaichs to the south, or Beinn Dearg to the east – for experienced and properly equipped hill walkers only, of course.

For an outdoors thrill that takes next to no effort, head for the Corrieshalloch Gorge and the Falls of Measach (0844 4932224, www.nts.org.uk) – a plunging, mile-long box canyon with 150-foot high falls. The views from the Victorian suspension bridge, while not for the vertiginous, are spectacular. The site is about 19 miles away, close to where the A832 meets the main A835 to Ullapool, and the parking spot off the A835 is clearly signposted.

AMUSING THE KIDS

The site has two children's bikes for hire. Decent swimmers can paddle about in kayaks (under parental supervision), while intrepid over-14s can have a go at power-kiting. If you're expecting wet weather, the best advice is to bring games – and check whether you'll have access to the bothy.

CAMPING NEARBY

Diagonally across Little Loch Broom – a bracing and hypothermic two-and-a-half-mile swim from Badrallach, although quite a lot further by road – is the Northern Lights Campsite (01697 371379, open Apr-Sept) at Badcaul. Two people plus tent costs about £8.

Useful contacts

CAMPING
Camping & Caravanning Club
www.campingandcaravanning
club.co.uk
Scottish Camping
www.scottishcamping.com
UK Campsite
www.ukcampsite.co.uk

COUNTRYSIDE
Forestry Commission
www.forestry.gov.uk
National Parks
www.nationalparks.gov.uk

OUTDOOR ACTIVITIES
River & Lake Swimming Association
www.river-swimming.co.uk
Surfing GB
www.surfinggb.com
Sustrans
www.sustrans.org.uk

WALKING
Countryside Access
www.countrysideaccess.gov.uk
Includes maps of open access land.
National Trails
www.nationaltrail.co.uk
Take your pick from Britain's
15 long-distance paths.
Walk Highlands
www.walkhighlands.co.uk
Nearly 1,000 walks in Scotland.
Walking Britain
www.walkingbritain.co.uk
A splendid resource for walkers, with
walks classified from easy to severe.
Ordnance Survey
www.ordnancesurvey.co.uk
All the maps you could ever need.

CAMPING GEAR
GENERAL
Alpkit
www.alpkit.com
Derbyshire-based, online-only
operation, with fair prices and
a range that runs from sleeping
bags to tough rucksacks.
Cascade Designs
http://cascadedesigns.com
US company whose top-end brands
include MSR (cookware) and Therm-
a-Rest (self-inflating sleeping mats).
Coleman
www.coleman.com
The no-nonsense range features
a dependable two-burner stove.
Little Adventure Shop
www.littleadventureshop.co.uk
Camping kit for small fry.
Nordic Outdoor
www.nordicoutdoor.co.uk
Acclaimed specialist in high-quality
Scandinavian gear, including Exped

dry bags, Mora knives, Tentipi
tents and Nanok sleeping bags.
The North Face
www2.thenorthface.com
One of the best-known names in
camping, selling tents, sleeping
bags and other outdoor gear.
Outdoor Kit
www.outdoorkit.co.uk
Everything you could possibly
need, from mallets and Maglites
to boil-in-the-bag grub.
Outdoor Shop
www.theoutdoorshop.com
A comprehensive selection of
gear, from big-name brands.
Outdoor World
www.outdoorworld.co.uk
All the big-brand tents, plus stoves,
coolboxes and other accessories.
Rosker
www.rosker.com
Ridiculously handy products from
across the globe, from Light My Fire
firesteels to Heatmax handwarmers.
Summits
www.summits.co.uk
Scottish retailer selling camping,
climbing, walking and skiing gear.
Tiso
www.tiso.com
All encompassing Scottish outdoor
equipment specialist.

TENTS
Gelert
www.gelert.com
Covers all bases, starting with
foolproof 'Quick Pitch' tents. A good
range of general camping gear too.
Outwell
www.outwell.co.uk
The focus is on family tents:
handsome, sturdy constructions,
with impeccable attention to detail.
Robert Saunders
www.robertsaunders.co.uk
The lightweight tent pioneer.
Terra Nova
www.terra-nova.co.uk
Terra Nova, Wild Country and
Extremities brands, from tents
to socks and gloves.
Vango
www.vango.co.uk
A huge range of tents, from
pop-up cheapies and tipis to
super-lightweight trekking tents.
Vaude
www.vaude.co.uk
Serious mountaineering equipment,
along with reliable, classic tents.

STOVES
Primus
www.primus.se
Amundsen took a Swedish Primus

stove to the South Pole in 1911,
and Hillary and Tenzing Norgay
used one on Everest in 1953.
Trangia Stove
www.trangiastove.co.uk
Incredibly popular backpacking/
camping stove. Also Swedish.

BELL TENTS, YURTS & TIPIS
Bell Tent
www.belltent.co.uk
www.campingwithsoul.com
Beautifully made canvas bell tents,
plus classy accessories (enamel
tea pots, rugs, Moroccan lanterns)
from sister site Camping with Soul.
Canvas & Cast
www.canvasandcast.com
Heavy-duty bell tents and willow-
framed yurts.
The Contemporary Yurt Company
www.yurtco.co.uk
Four-to six-metre diameter yurts –
as seen at Yurtcamp (see p68).
Hummingbird Tipis
http://hummingbird-tipis.com
This family-run business also
supplies tipis to several big festivals.
Manataka Tipis
www.manatakatipis.co.uk
Everything from children's tipis
to 30-footers; note that poles
and groundsheets cost extra.
Round House Yurts
www.theroundhouse.uk.com
Hand-crafted yurts, with green ash
frames. Also available for hire.
Shelters Unlimited
www.tipis.co.uk
Made to-order tipis, with various
extras (coir matting, fire trivets).
Yurtworks
www.yurtworks.co.uk
Top-notch quality, from a company
with over 12 years' experience.

CAMPING-FRIENDLY FESTIVALS
Beautiful Days
www.beautifuldays.org
A chilled festival in Devon, organised
by festival stalwarts the Levellers.
Bestival
www.bestival.net
On the Isle of Wight, with lots of
well-known names and new music.
Green Man
www.greenman.net
Stunning Brecon Beacons setting.
Latitude
www.latitudefestival.com
Lots of space, and a relaxed vibe.
Shambala
www.shambalafestival.org
Small, quirky and sustainable.
Womad
www.womad.org
World music in Wiltshire.

A-Z index of campsites

A

Abbey Home Farm 105
Burford Road, Cirencester,
Gloucestershire GL7 5HF
(01285 640441, www.theorganic
farmshop.co.uk).

Applecross Campsite 310
Applecross, Strathcarron,
Ross-shire IV54 8ND (01520
744268, www.applecross.uk.com/
campsite).

B

Badrallach 314
Dundonnell, Ross-shire
IV23 2QP (01854 633281,
www.badrallach.com).

Batcombe Vale Campsite 87
Batcombe Vale, Shepton
Mallet, Somerset BA4 6BW
(01749 831207, www.batcombe
vale.co.uk).

Beacon Cottage Farm 47
Beacon Drive, St Agnes, Cornwall
TR5 0NU (01872 552347,
www.beaconcottagefarmholidays.
co.uk).

Blackberry Wood 132
Streat Lane, near Ditchling,
East Sussex BN6 8RS (01273
890035, www.blackberrywood.com).

**Britchcombe Countryside
Holidays** 114
Britchcombe Farm, Uffington,
Faringdon, Oxfordshire SN7 7QJ
(01367 821022).

Buckland Bell Campsite 90
Bell Inn, High Street, Buckland
Dinham, Somerset BA11 2QT
(01373 462956, www.bellat
buckland.co.uk).

Burnbake Campsite 99
Rempstone, Corfe Castle,
Wareham, Dorset BH20 5JH
(01929 480570,
www.burnbake.com).

C

Cae Du Campsite 247
Rhosllefain, Tywyn, Gwynedd
LL36 9ND (01654 711234).

Cae Gwyn Farm 258
Bronaber Farm, Trawsfynydd,
Gwynedd LL41 4YE (01766
540245, 07776 019336,
www.caegwynfarm.co.uk).

Caerfai Farm Campsite 213
St Davids, Pembrokeshire
SA62 6QT (01437 720548,
www.cawscaerfai.co.uk).

**Cashel Caravan Park
& Campsite** 287
Rowardennan, Loch Lomond,
Lanarkshire G63 0AW (01360
870234 campsite, 0845 130 8224
booking, www.forestholidays.co.uk).

Cherry Tree Farm Campsite 75
Cherry Tree Farm, Jones Hill,
Croyde, North Devon EX33 1NH
(01271 890495, www.cherrytree
croyde.co.uk).

Clachtoll Beach Campsite 312
134 Clachtoll, by Lochinver,
Sutherland IV27 4JD (01571
855377, www.clachtollbeach
campsite.co.uk).

**Clitheroe Camping
& Caravanning Club** 184
Edisford Road, Clitheroe, Lancashire
BB7 3LA (01200 425294, www.
campingandcaravanningclub.co.uk/
clitheroe).

Comrie Croft 293
Braincroft, Comrie, Perthshire
PH7 4JZ (01764 670140,
www.comriecroft.com).

Coombe View Farm 71
Branscombe, Seaton, South Devon
EX12 3BT (01297 680218,
www.branscombecamping.co.uk).

Cornish Tipi Holidays 59
Tregeare, Pendoggett, St Kew,
Cornwall PL30 3LW (01208 880781,
www.cornishtipiholidays.co.uk).

Cove Park 284
Peaton Hill, Cove, Argyll & Bute
G84 0PE (01436 850123,
www.covepark.org).

D

Debden House 138
Debden Green, Loughton, Essex
IG10 2NZ (020 8508 3008/6770,
www.debdenhouse.com).

**Deepdale Backpackers
& Camping** 154
Deepdale Farm, Burnham Deepdale,
Norfolk, PE31 8DD (01485 210256,
www.deepdalebackpackers.co.uk).

Deer's Glade 150
White Post Road, Hanworth,
Norwich, Norfolk NR11 7HN
(01263 768633, www.deersglade.
co.uk).

Doward Park 108
Great Doward, Symonds Yat,
Ross-on-Wye, Herefordshire
HR9 6BP (01600 890438,
www.dowardpark.co.uk).

E

**Eskdale Camping
& Caravanning Club** 192
Boot, Holmrook, Cumbria
CA19 1TH (01946 723253,
www.campingandcaravanningclub.
co.uk/eskdale).

Eweleaze Farm 93
Osmington Hill, Osmington,
Dorset DT3 6ED (01305 833690,
www.eweleaze.co.uk).

F

Fforest 220
Fforest Farm, Cilgerran,
Pembrokeshire SA43 2TB (01239
623633, www.coldatnight.co.uk).

**Fforest Fields Caravan
& Camping Park** 236
Fforest Fields, Hundred House,
Builth Wells, Powys LD1 5RT (01982
570406, www.fforestfields.co.uk).

G

Gibraltar Farm Campsite 186
Gibraltar Farm, Silverdale, Carnforth,
Lancashire LA5 0UA (01524 701736,
www.gibraltarfarm.co.uk).

Glenbrittle Campsite 305
Carbost, Isle of Skye IV47 8TA
(01478 640404, www.dunvegan
castle.com).

Gordale Scar Campsite 171
Gordale Farm, Malham, North
Yorkshire BD23 4DL (01729
830333, www.malhamdale.com/
camping.htm).

Graig Wen 251
Arthog, Dolgellau, Gwynedd
LL39 1BQ (01341 250482,
www.graigwen.co.uk).

Gwern Gof Uchaf 267
Capel Curig, Betws-y-Coed, Conwy
LL24 0EU (01690 720294,
www.tryfanwales.co.uk).

Gwerniago Farm 244
Pennal, Machynlleth, Powys
SY20 9JX (01654 791227,
www.gwerniago.co.uk).

Gwithian Farm Campsite 44
1 Church Town Road, Gwithian,
Hayle, Cornwall TR27 5BX
(01736 753127,
www.gwithianfarm.co.uk).

H

**Haddon Grove Caravan
& Campsite** 166
Haddon Grove Farm, Bakewell,
Derbyshire DE45 1JF
(01629 812343).

Hafod y Llan 261
Nant Gwynant, Beddgelert, Gwynedd
LL55 4NL (01766 510129,
www.craflwyn.org).

**Harbour Camping
& Caravan Park** 141
Ferry Road, Southwold, Suffolk
IP18 6ND (01502 722486 enquiries,
01502 588444 bookings,
www.waveney.gov.uk).

High Sand Creek Campsite 152
Greenway, Stiffkey, Norfolk
NR23 1QF (01328 830235).

Hightertown Farm Campsite 56
Lansallos, Looe, Cornwall
PL13 2PX (01208 265211,
www.nationaltrust.org.uk).

Hillend Camping Park 205
Llangennith, Gower, Swansea
SA3 1JD (01792 386204).

Hollybush Inn & Campsite 230
Old Brecon Road, Hay-on-Wye,
Herefordshire HR3 5PS (01497
847371, www.hollybushcamping.
co.uk).

Home Farm Radnage 111
City Road, Radnage, High Wycombe,
Buckinghamshire HP14 4DW
(01494 484136, www.homefarm
radnage.co.uk).

J

Jerusalem Farm 176
Jerusalem Lane, Booth, Halifax, West
Yorkshire HX2 6XB (01422 883246).

L

Lazy Duck Hostel & Camping 302
Nethy Bridge, Inverness-shire
PH25 3ED (01479 821642,
www.lazyduck.co.uk).

Little Meadow 81
Watermouth, Ilfracombe, North
Devon EX34 9SJ (01271 866862,
www.littlemeadow.co.uk).

Llanthony Priory 227
Court Farm, Llanthony,
Abergavenny, Monmouthshire
NP7 7NN (01873 890359,
www.llanthony.co.uk).

Llyn Gwynant 264
Hafod Lwyfog, Nantgwynant,
Gwynedd LL55 4NW (enquiries@
gwynant.com, www.gwynant.com).

Low Wray Campsite 189
Low Wray, near Ambleside,
Cumbria LA22 0JA (015394 63862,
www.nationaltrust.org.uk/
campsites/lakedistrict).

M

**Machrihanish Camping
& Caravan Park** 282
East Trodigal, Campbeltown, Argyll
PA28 6PT (01586 810366, 07999
806959, www.campkintyre.co.uk).

Mains Farm Wigwams 290
Thornhill, Stirlingshire FK8 3QR
(01786 850735, www.mainsfarm
wigwams.com).

Manor Farm 119
Blanket Street, West Worldham,
Alton, Hampshire GU34 3BD
(01420 80804, www.featherdown
farm.co.uk).

Masons Campsite 174
Appletreewick, Skipton,
North Yorkshire BD23 6DD
(01756 720275, www.masons
campsite.co.uk).

Middle Woodbatch Farm 157
Woodbatch Road, Bishop's
Castle, Shropshire SY9 5JT
(07989 496875, www.middle
woodbatchfarm.co.uk).

Morvich Caravan Club Site 308
Shiel Bridge, Inverinate, Kyle,
Ross-shire IV40 8HQ (01599
511354, www.caravanclub.co.uk).

Mynydd Mawr 274
Llanllawen Fawr, Aberdaron,
Pwllheli, Gwynedd LL53 8BY
(01758 760223, www.aberdaron
caravanandcampingsite.co.uk).

N

Namparra Campsite 41
Kuggar, Helston, Cornwall TR12 7LY
(01326 290040, www.namparra
campsite.co.uk).

Nant-y-Big 272
Cilan, Abersoch, Pwllheli, Gwynedd
LL53 7DB (01758 712686,
www.nantybig.co.uk).

New Hall Farm 160
New Hall Lane, Edingley,
Nottinghamshire NG22 8BS (01623
883041, www.newhallfarm.co.uk).

Newgale Camping Site 211
Wood Farm, Newgale, Pembrokeshire
SA62 6AR (01437 710253,
www.newgalecampingsite.co.uk).

North Lees Campsite 163
Birley Lane, Hathersage, Derbyshire
S32 1BR (01433 650838).

North Morte Farm 78
Mortehoe, Woolacombe, North Devon
EX34 7EG (01271 870381,
www.northmortefarm.co.uk).

O

The Orchard Campsite 145
28 Spring Lane, Wickham Market,
Woodbridge, Suffolk IP13 0SJ
(01728 746170, www.orchard
campsite.co.uk).

R

Red Squirrel 296
Glencoe, Argyll PH49 4HX
(01855 811256, www.redsquirrel
campsite.com).

Rhandirmwyn 233
Llandovery, Carmarthenshire
SA20 0NT (01550 760257,
www.campingandcaravanningclub.
co.uk/rhandirmwyn).

Rhydhowell Farm 218
Boncath, Pembrokeshire
SA37 0LA (01239 841267,
www.rhydhowellfarm.co.uk).

La Rosa 181
Murk Esk Cottage, Whitby, North
Yorkshire YO22 5AS (01947
606981,www.larosa.co.uk).

**Rothiemurchus Camp
& Caravan Park** 299
Coylumbridge, near Aviemore,
Inverness-shire PH22 1QU
(01479 812800,
www.rothiemurchus.com).

Roundhill 122
Beaulieu Road, Brockenhurst,
Hampshire SO42 7QH
(01590 624344 campsite,
0845 130 8224 booking,
www.forestholidays.co.uk).

Runnage Farm 65
Postbridge, Dartmoor,
South Devon PL20 6TN
(01822 880222, www.runnage
campingbarns.co.uk).

S

St Martin's Campsite 35
Oaklands Farm, Middletown,
St Martin's, Isles of Scilly
TR25 0QN (01720 422888,
www.stmartinscampsite.co.uk).

Seagull Campsite 32
Herm Island, Guernsey GY1 3HR
(01481 722377, www.herm-island.
com/camping).

**Seal Shore Camping
& Touring Park** 280
Kildonan, Isle of Arran
KA27 8SE (01770 820320,
www.campingarran.com).

Shell Island 255
Llanbedr, Gwynedd LL45 2PJ
(01341 241453, www.shell
island.co.uk).

Side Farm 198
Patterdale, Penrith, Cumbria
CA11 0NL (01768 482337,
www.lakedistrictcamping.co.uk/
campsites/northeast/
side_farm.htm).

Solway View Holidays 278
Balmangan Farm, Borgue,
Kirkcudbright, Dumfries & Galloway
DG6 4TR (01557 870206,
www.solwayviewholidays.com).

South Penquite Farm 62
Blisland, Bodmin, Cornwall
PL30 4LH (01208 850491,
www.southpenquite.co.uk).

INDEX

Spiers House 178
Cropton, Pickering, Yorkshire
YO18 8ES (01751 417591
campsite, 0845 130 8224 booking,
www.forestholidays.co.uk).

Stowford Manor Farm 102
Wingfield, Trowbridge, Wiltshire
BA14 9LH (01225 752253,
www.stowfordmanorfarm.co.uk).

Stubcroft Farm 124
Stubcroft Lane, East Wittering,
Chichester, West Sussex PO20 8PJ
(01243 671469, 07810 751665,
www.stubcroft.com).

T

Tan-y-Bryn Farm 270
Bryn Pydew, Llandudno Junction,
Conwy, Gwynedd LL31 9JZ
(01492 549296).

Three Cliffs Bay Holiday Park 202
North Hills Farm, Penmaen,
Gower, Swansea SA3 2HB
(01792 371218, www.threecliffs
bay.com).

Tom's Field Campsite & Shop 96
Tom's Field Road, Langton
Matravers, Swanage, Dorset
BH19 3HN (01929 427110,
www.tomsfieldcamping.co.uk).

Treen Farm Campsite 38
Treen Farm, St Levan,
Penzance, Cornwall TR19 6LF
(01736 810273, www.treenfarm
campsite.co.uk).

Trefalen Farm 208
Bosherston, near Pembroke,
Pembrokeshire SA71 5DR
(01646 661643).

Tregedna Farm Campsite 50
Tregedna Farm, Maenporth,
Falmouth, Cornwall TR11 5HL
(01326 250529, www.tregedna
farmholidays.co.uk).

Treloan Coastal Holidays 53
Treloan Lane, Gerrans, near
Portscatho, Roseland Peninsula,
Cornwall TR2 5EF (01872 580989,
www.coastalfarmholidays.co.uk).

Ty Parke 215
Llanreithan, Pembrokeshire
SA62 5LG (01348 837384,
www.typarke.co.uk).

Tyllwyd Farm 241
Cwmystwyth, Aberystwyth,
Ceredigon SY23 4AG (01974
282216 campsite, 01970
630281 cottage, www.welsh
accommodation.co.uk).

U

**Upper Booth Farm
& Campsite** 168
Edale, Hope Valley, Derbyshire
S33 7ZJ (01433 670250,
www.upperboothcamping.co.uk).

V

Vintage Vacations 116
Hazel Grove Farm, Ashey, near
Ryde, Isle of Wight PO33 4BD
(07802 758113, www.vintage
vacations.co.uk).

W

Wasdale Head Campsite 195
Wasdale Head, Seascale,
Cumbria CA20 1EX (01946
726220, www.nationaltrust.org.uk/
campsites/lakedistrict).

Welsummer 135
Chalk House, Lenham Road,
Harrietsham, Kent ME17 1NQ
(01622 844048, 07771
992355, www.welsummer
camping.com).

Westermill Farm 84
Exford, Exmoor, near Minehead,
Somerset TA24 7NJ (01643
831238, 07970 594808,
www.westermill.com).

Woodland Yurting 126
Keepers Barn, Tittlesfold,
The Haven, Billingshurst, West
Sussex RH14 9BG (01403 824057,
www.woodlandyurting.com).

Woodside Farm 148
Common Lane, Thurne, Great
Yarmouth, Norfolk NR29 3BX
(01692 670367, www.woodside-
farm.co.uk).

Wowo Campsite 129
Wapsbourne Manor Farm, Sheffield
Park, East Sussex TN22 3QT
(01825 723414, www.wowo.co.uk).

Y

Ynysfaen 224
Cwmwysg, Trecastle, Brecon,
Powys LD3 8YF (01874 636436,
www.campingatynysfaen.co.uk).

The Yurt Farm 238
Crynfryn, Penuwch, Tregaron,
Ceredigion SY25 6RE (01974
821594, www.theyurtfarm.co.uk).

Yurtcamp 68
Gorse Blossom Farm, Staplehill
Road, Liverton, Devon TQ12 6JD
(01626 824666, 07768 665544,
www.yurtcamp.co.uk).

INDEX